SELECTIONS FROM

GREEK AND ROMAN HISTORIANS

EDITED WITH AN INTRODUCTION BY

CHARLES ALEXANDER ROBINSON, JR.

Holt, Rinehart and Winston

NEW YORK

27516-0317

Sixth Printing, July, 1963

Introduction and Notes © 1957 by Charles Alexander Robinson, Jr.
Typography Design by Stefan Salter
All Rights Reserved
Printed in the United States of America
Library of Congress Catalog Card Number: 57-7740

MANIBVS · AMICI · PRAECLARISSIMI

IVORY LITTLEFIELD

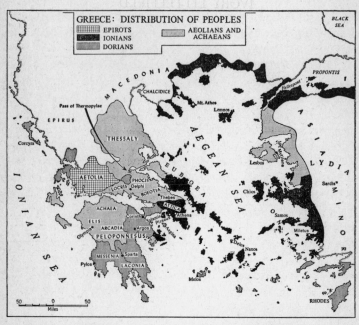

Within the map:

GREECE: DISTRIBUTION OF PEOPLES

- EPIROTS
- IONIANS
- DORIANS
- AEOLIANS AND ACHAEANS

BLACK SEA

MACEDONIA

CHALCIDICE

Mt. Athos

Lemnos

PROPONTIS

Hellespont

Pass of Thermopylae

EPIRUS

THESSALY

Corcyra

AEGEAN SEA

LYDIA

Lesbos

Mytilene

AETOLIA

LOCRIS

PHOCIS

Delphi

BOEOTIA

Thebes

ATTICA

Athens

EUBOEA

Chios

Sardis

ASIA MINOR

IONIAN SEA

ACHAEA

Corinth

Eleusis

Piraeus

Megara

Aegina

ELIS

Olympia

ARCADIA

PELOPONNESUS

Argos

Mycenae

Samos

Miletus

Delos

Naxos

MESSENIA

Sparta

Pylos

LACONIA

Melos

RHODES

50   0   50
Miles

From Stewart C. Easton, *The Heritage of the Past* (New York: Rinehart & Company, Inc., 1955). Drawn by Vincent Kotschar.

INTRODUCTION

The most distinguished ancient historians span a very significant period of time, roughly from Herodotus, a Greek who lived during the great fifth century B.C., to Tacitus, a Roman who published in the early second century A.D. an account of the world state in which he lived. In speaking of the Greek phase of man's long history, Arnold J. Toynbee remarked that the Greek or "Hellenic Civilization is perhaps the finest flower of the species that has ever yet come to bloom . . . [it] still outshines every other civilization that has ever come into existence up to the present." Edward Gibbon, on the other hand, had this to say concerning the Roman phase of history: "If a man were called to fix the period in the history of the world, during which the condition of the human race was most happy and prosperous, he would, without hesitation, name that which elapsed from the death of Domitian [A.D. 96] to the accession of Commodus [A.D. 180]. The vast extent of the Roman Empire was governed by absolute power, under the guidance of virtue and wisdom."

Taken all together, of course, ancient history is far longer than the subsequent periods of European history, the medieval and modern. But it is more germane to say that ancient history— particularly the half millennium from Herodotus to Tacitus— provides us with the opportunity to consider most of man's experiences at every level: one may study poor literature or good literature, realism in art or the primitive, despotism and democracy, high achievements of the mind and spirit, and decay. It is equally obvious that ancient history has long since ended: it has run its course; the passions which once fired men are dead; and now we can view the issues coolly. No other period of history is sufficiently long or complete, sufficiently complex and sophisticated, to provide quite this opportunity.

There is, moreover, one very special reason for concentrating on the Greek and Roman phases of ancient history. As Toynbee has put it, the decisive factor is that "the surviving materials for a study of Greco-Roman history are not only manageable in quantity and select in quality; they are also well balanced in their character." Another factor would be that Greek and Roman civilization lies at the basis of our own life. To grasp the classical world in its entirety, one must study philosophy and drama and other forms of literature, no less than the art and archaeology, such as sculpture and architecture, numismatics and inscriptions. It is obvious, however, that the ancient historians bring us directly to the subject and in so doing, not only give important narratives, but also ask eternal questions.

Rich and illuminating though the history of Greece and Rome is, the experiences of the two peoples were quite different. The history of Rome, superficially at least, can be readily understood and should be studied by everyone for its lesson. On balance, it is the story of a remarkable city-state which seemed to pile success upon monumental success; yet which in the end enmeshed itself and the civilized world in catastrophe. The history of Greece, on the other hand, is not for the man who must read as he runs, for it is subtler and in essence is a story of ideas, important ideas developing through the centuries and at every point hotly debated.

The great Greek and Roman historians, then, introduce us to very different experiences in the story of man. It would be a pity, however, to speak of their accounts as mere "documents" or "sources"—though that happens to be precise—for they also represent very great literature. Thus we are able, through distinguished translations, not only to immerse ourselves in significant moments of the past, but also to observe the literary style and shifting interests of brilliant thinkers from one generation to another. Needless to say, historical literature, like all else, grew from and was influenced by the forces and events of ancient civilization as it progressed.

To illustrate this, we need go no farther back than the

middle of the sixth century before Christ, when an extraordinary people embarked on their imperial career. These were the Persians, who, though themselves Indo-Europeans, had long lived in the Semitic Near East, the ancient Orient as it is often called. Under their remarkable king, Cyrus the Great, they overthrew their kinsmen the Medes, and then in a series of battles defeated Croesus, the fabulously wealthy king of Lydia, and burned Sardis, his capital, to the ground. The Lydians, in the course of extending their own empire within Asia Minor, had conquered most of the Greek city-states along the coast and had adopted Greek culture to a large degree. Now that the Lydian Empire had fallen to the Persians, many Greeks found themselves incorporated in a state which rapidly expanded as far east as the borders of India. When finally, in 539 B.C., Cyrus captured Babylon, the capital of the Chaldean Empire, he was the absolute, though wise and tolerant, master of the largest empire the world had ever seen.

This year, 539 B.C., is a cardinal date in the history of the ancient Near East. For more than two millenniums Semitic power and influences had dominated Mesopotamia and the adjoining lands. Now there was a new Indo-European force, a mighty world state, which was to solidify Asia and Egypt in a comparatively real peace. Stretching at its greatest extent from European Thrace to India, the Achaemenid dynasty of the Persians was to endure for more than two centuries, until the coming of Alexander the Great. Inevitably, perhaps, Cyrus and his immediate successors longed to conquer the Greeks of the mainland —the peninsula across the Aegean Sea from Ionia, as the western littoral of Asia Minor was called. The stage of history, that is to say, now contained both East and West. Eventually the decisive issue of Europeanism versus Orientalism was decided by the immortal battles which constituted the chief interest of the "Father of History," as Cicero called Herodotus.

The Persian conquest of Asia Minor meant that the center of Greek resistance shifted to the city-states of the mainland, particularly to Athens, Sparta, and Corinth. These and other states now set the pace in the developing Greek culture. The brilliant days of Ionia were over, at least for the moment. This was a double tragedy, for the Greek renaissance had occurred in Asia Minor. During the amazing sixth century B.C. Ionia had witnessed not only a rapid economic growth, but also the flowering of a beautiful art, the refinement of lyric poetry, and high achievement in philosophy and science.

The keen, rational mind of the Greek, which in time produced the scientific point of view toward all things connected with the world and man, and especially an eagerness to know the past of the human race, led to the birth of historical thought. This had begun with a pseudo history, which traced Greek descent from Prometheus, the benefactor of mankind, or dealt with the problem of creation. Other writers, known as logographers, interested themselves in the present and in human affairs. The greatest of them, Hecataeus of Miletus in Asia Minor (*ca.* 500 B.C.), may be regarded as the founder of the science of history. Against pseudo history he applied in his *Genealogies* a free, inquiring mind, unwilling to give any greater weight to Greek tradition, simply because he was a Greek, than to that of another race. An awakening consciousness of the distinction between myth and fact is shown by his own words: "I write what I believe to be true, for the various stories of the Greeks are, in my opinion, ridiculous."

This spirit of scientific inquiry received a tremendous impetus after the Greek repulse of the Persians in the opening decades of the fifth century B.C. Now Athens built her empire and under the leadership of Pericles quickly became "the teacher of Greece." The intellectual movement of the Periclean Age embraced and nurtured the desire for serviceable knowledge, an interest in mankind, and an absorption in the present; inevitably this movement found notable expression in history.

The first historian whose works have been preserved was Herodotus (*ca.* 484–425 B.C.). We are unable, therefore, to say definitely how great an advance he made beyond Hecataeus, his most distinguished predecessor, although we know that he borrowed extensively from him. Born in the period of the wars with Persia, Herodotus lived through the earlier years of the terrible conflict between Athens and Sparta, known as the Peloponnesian War. His native place was Halicarnassus, in Asia Minor. He spent much of his life at Athens, during its most vibrant days, and traveled to Egypt, into Asia as far as Susa, the administrative capital of the Persian Empire, to the countries about the Black Sea, to Italy—in brief, to most of the known world. Everywhere he gathered material which found its way into his work. His sources, accordingly, are of uneven value, but where he relied on his own observations Herodotus is, on the whole, thoroughly reliable.

Just as some of his predecessors were the literary descendants of Hesiod, the Boeotian poet who sang of creation, Herodotus was a son of Homer. His work might well be described as a great prose epic, with an admixture of influences from Sophocles and contemporary drama. A brief preface explains the object of his work: "This is a presentation of the *Inquiry—Historia—of Herodotus of Halicarnassus* to the end that time may not obliterate the great and marvelous deeds of Hellenes and barbarians,[1] and especially that they may not forget the causes for which they waged war with one another." In his search for causes Herodotus narrates from earliest times the notable achievements of all the peoples who were involved in the Persian Wars, and thus his production may be described as a universal history. He used the Persian Wars as the unifying element of his work, and though he was fairly ignorant of strategy and tactics, *The Persian Wars*, in nine books, remains our chief source for the conflict. A fairminded historian and a friend of Pericles, Herodotus described the glorious deeds of Athens, for it was Athens that had saved Greece from Oriental conquest.

---

[1] This was the customary Greek word for foreigners; the Greeks called themselves Hellenes (we use the Latin word for them), and the lands wherever they were settled, Hellas—hence their civilization is known as Hellenism. The Greeks generally referred to the Persians as Medes and to their ruler as the Great King. To "Medize" was to sympathize with the Persians. We may add that writers at Athens usually dated events in the year of the city's chief official (*archon*), though eventually it became the general custom to date from the foundation of the Olympic Games (776 B.C.).

As far as we know, Herodotus was the first to apply the word "history," in its original sense of inquiry, to this field of literature. It aptly describes his method of gathering information by personal inquiry of those who were supposed to know. Often unsatisfied with an individual source, he pursued his investigation among various authorities and thus introduced the comparative method of research. We find him, accordingly, often expressing doubt as to what he hears, comparing the more with the less credible, or reasoning about the reliability of his source. Although his work abounds in myths and fictions, for no one loved a good story more than Herodotus, and although he was often at the mercy of untrustworthy informants, he was far from credulous. Even the fictitious tales are of value for illustrating the thought and life of the age.

Another great quality of Herodotus is his broad-mindedness, to which his cosmopolitan birthplace, on the borderland between Hellas and the Persian Empire, and his extensive travels contributed. He could understand that many foreign customs were at least as good as the Hellenic, that there were great and admirable characters among the barbarians, and that monarchy as well as democracy had its good features. A comparison of Egyptian with Hellenic tradition taught him the emptiness of the claim of certain Greeks to near descent from a god. His comparative study of religion convinced him that his countrymen entertained many false notions as to their own gods and the beginnings of the human race. Regarding the existence of the gods, however, and their providential dealings with men, the historian betrays no skepticism. With other enlightened men of his age he believes in a Divine Providence, who rules the world and in a kindly spirit watches over men, revealing his will through omens, dreams, and oracles. Like the Athenian dramatist Aeschylus, he seems to believe that the downfall of the great—for example, of Xerxes— is in punishment for insolence (*hybris*), which unusual prosperity often induces. The divine working of Nemesis (Retribution) and the transitory nature of human fortunes lie at the bottom of his philosophy of history.

In religion, though casting off much that is extraneous,

Herodotus holds firmly to the enlightened orthodoxy of the time, while in moral character and purpose he stands on a level with the best men of his century. From the point of view of strict historical science, he doubtless advances beyond Hecataeus and yet is still crude and imperfect. On the other hand, his broad sympathy and kindly interest in everything human, his high religious and moral principles, his inexhaustible fund of anecdotes illustrative of customs and character, his charming style and genial personality have given his literary production a universal and eternal interest.

The victories over the Persians filled the Greeks, and especially the Athenians, who had taken the initiative in resistance, with tremendous enthusiasm and confidence. Fear of Persia, nevertheless, remained. Consequently Athens was able to persuade the states most vulnerable to another Persian attack—those along the Asia Minor and northern Aegean coasts, and the islands—to join in a defensive league. Its capital was the sacred island of Delos. Although it soon became evident that Persia was no longer a danger, the Athenians nonetheless transformed the Delian League into an empire, with its capital at Athens, in Attica. Henceforth, too, the imperial tribute was to be used as the Athenians saw fit. Beautiful buildings now rose on their Acropolis; intellectual creativity, trade, and democratic institutions developed and flourished as never before.

The person chiefly responsible for this achievement was Pericles, an aristocrat who led the democratic forces of his city-state. He has, of course, given his name to one of the greatest ages in the history of man. Nevertheless, his ambitious policies eventually roused the fears of Sparta, the head of an empire to the south, in the Peloponnesus. Though Sparta won the ensuing Peloponnesian War, she gained little from it. The war had continued so long (431–404 B.C.), and had produced such cruelty and suffering, that Greece was never again the same. An epoch in Greek history came to an end.

General George C. Marshall, speaking at Princeton University in his capacity as Secretary of State, remarked, "I doubt seriously whether a man can think with full wisdom and with deep convictions regarding certain of the basic international issues to day who has not at least reviewed in his mind the period of the Peloponnesian War and the fall of Athens." It would be enlightening to know the conclusions General Marshall had in mind, but unfortunately he did not say. On the other hand, a review of the evidence makes it difficult to avoid the observation that imperialism leads but to the grave.

Of course, many causes contributed to the Peloponnesian War. Rivalry in trade was one. Difference in outlook was another, for the Athenians were Ionian in blood and outlook, democratic and progressive, the possessors of a far-flung maritime empire; whereas the Dorian Spartans of Laconia (Lacedaemonians, as they were often called) were reactionary and narrow-minded, and in their splendid isolation headed a powerful land empire. There is no doubt, however, that because Athens was an innovator and the policies she pursued were so new and radical, other Greeks feared being engulfed by her expansion.

The historian of this war was an Athenian who took part in it, Thucydides (*ca.* 471–399 B.C.), the son of Olorus. Because he was able to raise the events of the war to a universal plane, showing its eternal patterns and exposing the forces that move political man, he is generally regarded as the greatest historian produced by antiquity. In his power and eloquence, moreover, he can stand at ease beside Winston Churchill.

Thucydides resembled other men of the Periclean Age, not only in intensity of thought and style, but also in the fact that he was a man of action, as well as words.[2] Having been a general in the Peloponnesian War, he could season his writings with practical experience. His slowness in coming to the protection of Amphipolis, however, led to his exile in 424 B.C. At the outbreak of the war he had foreseen that it would be memorable and had begun to collect material for his account of it. Now, during twenty years of exile, he traveled about, visited the scenes of military operations, and ascertained facts from eyewitnesses.

---

[2] The Athenian dramatist Sophocles was another outstanding example of the Greek ideal. In 443 B.C. he was chief treasurer of the Athenian Empire; the next year he produced his *Antigone;* two years later he was a general before Samos.

Doubtless he kept a record of events, which he corrected and expanded with the acquisition of new and more precise information. At the close of the war he undertook a final recomposition of his work. The first book contains a valuable sketch of the earlier years of Greece; the others describe the momentous conflict between Athens and Sparta. Unfortunately, however, death prevented Thucydides from concluding his work, and it comes to an end in the course of his treatment of the year 411 B.C.

Thucydides' chief claim to fame lies in his critical attitude to his sources. He knew the value of his evidence and was completely impartial. Though he loved Athens, he did not hesitate to criticize her. Like Pericles, he admired magnificence and display, and like Pericles he was an imperialist. He believed that it was natural for a state to expand, since the state represented power; and war, he felt, was but an expression of the state's growth. Thucydides' desire for exact knowledge, which characterizes his method in writing history, can be found in this statement from the first book: "Of the events of the war I have not ventured to speak from any information, nor according to any notion of my own; I have described nothing but what I either saw myself or learned from others of whom I made the most careful and particular inquiry. The task was a laborious one, because eyewitnesses of the same occurrences gave different accounts of them, as they remembered or were interested in the actions of one side or the other."

The Peloponnesian War, Thucydides believed, was the most important event in the entire history of Greece; indeed, he was convinced that, as compared with the present, the past was insignificant. In studying the war, he was interested in the causes underlying the political actions of states. With Thucydides the forces that make history are first the statesmen, who consciously operate to effect a given purpose; secondarily the people in their assembly, moved by capricious feeling to a wise or foolish resolution. The ideal republic, therefore, is one like Athens in the Age of Pericles, in which the best and wisest citizen is able to control the rest. Unlike the modern historian, then, Thucydides did not examine searchingly the general economic and social conditions which tended to bring Athenians and Peloponnesians into conflict.

The Peloponnesian War, in eight books, is a literary masterpiece, influenced in part by the Sophists.[3] The speeches, which occupy a large part of the work, are, so to speak, its soul. Usually they are given in pairs, representing the opposing views of a situation or a question for decision before an assembly. The language of the speeches is Thucydides'; the ideas, so far as they could be ascertained, are the orators', though even here, as the actual speeches were unwritten, the historian exercised large discretion in including what he considered appropriate to the occasion. Generally, therefore, the speeches embody Thucydides' conception of the situation which they present, and express most adequately his keen analytical intelligence.

Notwithstanding certain differences between ancient and modern conceptions of history, we may still look to Thucydides as a master, in important respects unrivaled. In his own personal reserve, in the determination with which he pursues his single aim, rejecting every extraneous matter, in the relentless analysis, which lays bare the souls of individuals, factions, and communities, in the fairness and mental placidity with which he treats personal enemies and opposing parties, in intellectual depth, keenness, and grasp, he may safely be said to have thus far no equal.

Because of Thucydides' untimely death, we are dependent upon a fourth-century historian, Xenophon of Athens (*ca.* 434–354 B.C.), for a description of the concluding years of the Peloponnesian War. Xenophon was a member of a well-to-do conservative family. From his social environment he absorbed the sentiments that distinguished his rank, including a punctilious regard for the externals of religion, the habit of ethical reflection, refinement of feeling and speech, an interest in military training

---

[3] This was a class of men who professed to teach all knowledge essential to the statesman. Traveling from city to city, they imparted instruction to all who desired it and were able to pay the fee. The most eminent Sophist, Protagoras of Abdera (*ca.* 485–410 B.C.), boldly stated, "Man is the measure of all things." This declaration directed attention to the mind and its relation to the outside world, and, by shifting the center of attention from the world to man, promoted the growth of individualism.

and in out-of-door sports, courage, a dislike of the multitude, and fidelity to his class—in a word, Hellenic chivalry. Xenophon's interest in personal traits, which is largely lacking in Thucydides, marks him as a true child of his individualistic age. He had traveled much and acquired a wide knowledge of the world; and in his breadth of mind, his liberal education, and his ethical and religious principles he represents the best features of the educated class of his generation.

Xenophon was banished from his native Athens for treason and wrote under Spartan patronage. To his inborn shallowness, accordingly, he has added a partisanship for Sparta and an undue admiration for its king, Agesilaus. His *Agesilaus* and his *Cyropaedeia* (a historical romance on the model education of the Persian prince, Cyrus) reveal his superficial interest in individuals, whereas his genuine attachment to Socrates brought out the best in him. In his *Memorabilia* of Socrates, Xenophon faithfully photographs the exterior of the great philosopher and his teachings, but, as always, he is unable to penetrate to the depths.

Xenophon is probably best known for his *Anabasis*, which tells how ten thousand and more Greeks marched with Cyrus against his brother, the Great King, and, though defeated at the gates of Babylon, returned alive—a lesson, incidentally, that was not lost on a greater military man, Alexander of Macedon. The *Anabasis* is especially valuable for the insight it affords us into the composition and psychology of a mercenary army, drawn from many parts of Hellas and passing through various phases of success and peril.

On the other hand, Xenophon's chief historical work is *The Hellenica*, a narrative description of events in Greece, in seven books, from 411 to 362 B.C. Thus Xenophon not only picks up where Thucydides breaks off and continues through the fall of Athens, but goes on to tell how Sparta created an empire and failed, and then how Thebes did likewise. Such was the aftermath of the Peloponnesian War.

Though Greece in the fourth century before Christ did indeed witness well-nigh constant warfare between the various city-states and the empires they created—all accompanied by an economic depression and the meddling of the Persian king in Greek politics—the time was also one of great achievement. This was, of course, the period of Plato, Aristotle, and Praxiteles. Nevertheless, despite much thought given to the matter, the Greeks failed to resolve their chief dilemma, the apparent incompatibility of autonomy and federation. It remained for an outside power—the Macedonian monarchy to the north was so regarded by the citizens of the ancient city-states—to resolve the dilemma. First Philip, the remarkable king of Macedon, united the Greeks in a confederacy, and then his even more extraordinary son, Alexander the Great, conquered the Persian Empire (334–323 B.C.).

It is quite true that on Alexander's death his empire was divided into large kingdoms: the Antigonid in Macedonia, the Seleucid in Asia (out of which was carved, still later, the Kingdom of Pergamum in Asia Minor), and the Ptolemaic in Egypt. But the rulers were Macedonians and Greeks—the slight distinction between the two peoples was soon lost—and Greek culture, Hellenism, was adopted in varying degree by the vast new world. That is why the three centuries between Alexander's death (323 B.C.) and Rome's final rounding off of her dominion at the battle of Actium (31 B.C.) are known as the Hellenistic Age.

Many states of Old Greece found it advisable, in this period of large monarchies, to band together in federal unions. One of these was the Aetolian League, limited largely to central and western Greece, and another was the Achaean League, in the Peloponnesus. The day of the large state, however, had irrevocably arrived, and it was only a matter of time before Rome, the rising giant of the West, should conquer all. Indeed, not long after the conclusion of her titanic struggle with Hannibal, Rome became involved in the affairs of the eastern Mediterranean. Her gradual encroachment in Greece must have pleased many Romans, who admired and adopted much of Greek culture, though probably the Augustan poet Horace summed up the final result best in his famous line, "Captive Greece took her barbarian conqueror captive."

At any rate, more than a century before her complete conquest of Greece, Rome took a thousand hostages from the Achaean League (167 B.C.). Among them was Polybius, a citizen of Arcadian Megalopolis in the Peloponnesus. Polybius (*ca.* 205–123 B.C.) ranks second only to Thucydides among Greek historians. He was born into a prominent family and played an active military and diplomatic role in the affairs of the Achaean League. As a hostage in Rome, he became the friend of Scipio Aemilianus and other important Romans; as such, he was present at the fall of Numantia and Carthage. This was a moment at Rome of tremendous interest in things Greek, and the Scipios, who enjoyed great prestige because of their victory over Hannibal and the subsequent glorious expansion of Rome's frontiers, were the leaders of the new movement. The Scipionic Circle, as it was called, claimed Polybius as one of its ornaments. Under his influence, and that of other Greeks, a vigorous impetus was given the development of Latin literature.

Polybius quickly grew to admire Rome and was inspired with the ambition to tell the moving story of the new world power. *The Histories,* which he composed, covered the period from 264 B.C. (the First Punic War) to the destruction of Corinth and Carthage (146 B.C.). Of the thirty-nine books, the first five survive entire, together with many other extracts.

Polybius believed that contemporary politicians could learn much from the past, and he therefore addressed himself to them and not to the general public. The result is that his work, though written in the common Greek of his day, does not make exciting reading in the popular sense. Moreover, he is digressive and verbose; he is unfair to Carthage and allots too much space to the Achaean League. Nevertheless, Polybius was a scientific historian of broad vision—deeply interested in causes and principles—who diligently studied his sources and often traveled to various sites to verify his data. Though he lacked detachment, he was industrious and, with his own experience in political affairs, succeeded to a large degree in writing an immensely valuable account of the Mediterranean world. From our point of view, it is most fortunate that this philosophic historian, at this particular time, should have chosen to reflect upon and include a critical discus-

From C. A. Robinson, Jr., *Ancient History*

sion of the constitutions and political institutions of Rome and of his homeland; here, at least, he was the master of Thucydides. The days of Greece's freedom were fast drawing to a close, and a long perspective opened up to Polybius. The future, however, belonged to Rome, as he himself foresaw.

In 814 B.C., as the best historical tradition has it, the ancient Phoenician[4] city of Tyre founded Carthage on the northern coast

---

[4] "Punic" in Latin. Excavated material, it may be added, points to *ca.* 725 B.C. as the date of Carthage's foundation.

THE ROMAN EMPIRE
AT THE DEATH OF AUGUSTUS, 14 A.D.

Scale of Miles

Areas added by Augustus are underlined
Later annexations are dated

A.P. Alpes Penninae
A.C. Alpes Cottiae
A.M. Alpes Maritimae

(New York: The Macmillan Company, 1951). Drawn by Erwin Raisz.

of Africa. Thence arose a wealthy and powerful state, with an empire, chiefly commercial in nature, that controlled parts of southern Spain, all Sardinia, and about a third of Sicily. Most of the rest of Sicily was in the hands of Syracuse and other Greek states. It was the quarreling of Greeks and Carthaginians in Sicily that involved Rome—now, after long growth,[5] the head of a united Italian federation—in her first trans-Italian venture.

---

[5] The Augustan poet Vergil has given us the familiar and thrilling picture of Rome's founding: "Such toil it cost to found the Roman race." Excavations prove that Rome was founded many centuries before the traditional date of 753 B.C. Livy dates events "from the foundation of the

As one result of the ensuing conflict between Rome and Carthage—the First Punic War (264–241 B.C.)—victorious Rome was immediately confronted with a multitude of problems. There was, for example, the necessity of organizing the provincial administration of newly conquered lands; there was also the fact of strange foreign influences pouring in from Greek Sicily. Another result was the desire of Carthage—and particularly of its leading general, Hamilcar Barca—to make up in Spain for the losses in Sicily and elsewhere.

The activity of Hamilcar Barca in Spain threatened the interests of Massilia (Marseilles), a Greek city not far from the mouth of the River Rhone in southern Gaul. Massilia, as it happened, was an ally of Rome, and in the charged atmosphere of the day the Second Punic War (218–201 B.C.) broke out. Hamilcar Barca's gifted son Hannibal, one of the greatest generals in antiquity, then led a force of 40,000 infantry, 9,000 cavalry, and a number of elephants across the Alps, amid suffering and losses, into Italy. Against him stood Rome's military federation of 700,-000 infantry and 70,000 cavalry. Hannibal won victory after immense victory, despite little support from home and despite his failure to construct siege machinery, which seems strange, since he had arrived in a land of fortified cities. He devastated southern Italy, and yet, though he never lost a battle until the last one, at Zama in Africa, he did lose the war. The proud victor, Publius Cornelius Scipio, acclaimed as Africanus, returned to his capital to celebrate a splendid triumph; and Rome, as the mistress of the western Mediterranean, now became increasingly involved in the Greek East.

Polybius, it will be recalled, included an account of this war, the most terrible of ancient conflicts, in his *Histories*; it also constituted a major interest of Livy, Rome's great historian. Livy (Titus Livius, 59 B.C.–A.D. 17) came from Padua in northern Italy. His life spanned one of the truly momentous eras in

---

city," and therefore one subtracts the year he gives from 754 B.C. in order to obtain the date in our calendar. Modern studies show that Livy's figures for the sizes of armies, for example, need revision (generally downward); this also holds for Herodotus and others.

history, although we know almost nothing about him personally. Born in the year of the consulship of Caesar and Bibulus, he spent his youth amid the civil wars of the dying Roman Republic. When Caesar's grandnephew, Octavian—Augustus, as he was soon called—defeated Antony and Cleopatra off the west coast of Greece (the battle of Actium, 31 B.C.), the entire civilized world—that is to say, the Latin West and the Greek or Hellenistic East, which was in large part Semitic—was united under one political administration, that of the new Roman Empire. Mankind now settled down to enjoy the famous Augustan Age and the boundless majesty of the Roman Peace, which was destined to last until A.D. 235. We speak of this quarter millennium of Roman imperial history as the Principate, for, though government was shared by the princeps (first citizen, or emperor as we should say) and Senate, it was the princeps who gave it its peculiar character.[6]

Although he outlived Rome's first emperor by three years and died in the reign of Tiberius, Livy's active life lay within the Augustan Age. As the most eminent author of prose at this time, he was, with Vergil and Horace, one of the shining lights of the period. Like the artists and architects, the writers of prose and poetry made their own particular contributions to the new spirit, stirring appeals to the populace to lay aside the recent bitterness of party strife for the blessings of peace. With the encouragement of Augustus and Maecenas, the emperor's friend and patron of the arts, the Golden Age of Roman literature aimed to purify and ennoble the present by bringing it the life of the good and great past, but the conscious archaism seems to raise its own doubts.

Livy's *History of Rome* was an eloquent history of Rome from the earliest days to 9 B.C., to the death in Germany of Drusus, the stepson of Augustus and brother of Tiberius. Of the one hundred and forty-two books, only thirty-five survive. These

---

[6] The Principate came to an end when the Senate no longer chose the emperor or helped him to rule. This happened some time after A.D. 235, during the fifty years of military anarchy (see note 12, below). The later Roman Empire was an autocracy.

tell the story of Rome up to 167 B.C., when Macedonia was organized as a Roman province and Polybius and the other hostages of the Achaean League were carried off to Italy. A few fragments survive from other books, but the recovery of them all—which must have described in detail the fall of the Roman Republic and the establishment of the Empire—would be the greatest possible addition to our knowledge of ancient history.

The surviving books are, of course, our chief source for the earlier periods of Roman history and notably for an account of Rome's struggle with Hannibal. Livy's style is vivid and absorbing, for he wrote, not for the educated few, as Polybius did, but to interest the general public. He was referred to in antiquity as truthful, and certainly he appears to us as generally impartial. He was independent enough to speak of the vices of his own day, even though Augustus, attempting to restore morality, must have wished otherwise. On the other hand, Livy was occasionally inaccurate, even sloppy, in his researches. If he had been more of a critical historian, he would have carefully examined the wealth of records available to him—inscriptions, learned specialized works, and the like. As it was, he drew for the first years chiefly from the early poet Ennius and from Fabius Pictor, a distinguished Roman annalist of the third century B.C.

Livy's response—if he were charged with failure to check his sources industriously and critically—would probably be that he was bringing the great past to the present for its elevating effect. Indeed, he says quite frankly that the purpose of history is to teach moral lessons by examples. Not an antiquarian, he nevertheless tells about prodigies, for he reasoned that his public would insist on their inclusion as representative of early times. Livy's particular greatness lies in his sound judgment and general fairness, in his graphic admiration for what he supposed to be the truth and the right.

Despite their friendship for one another, Augustus spoke of Livy as a "Pompeian," as one who would have preferred to see Pompey and republicanism triumph over Julius Caesar and (as it was in effect) monarchy. For there is no doubt that Livy's sympathies were republican. With his fine rhetorical training he would have been an influential orator had he lived a few years earlier. He loved Rome's greatness and felt—without sufficient warrant, we may add—that Rome owed her position as mistress of the world to the discipline, character, and innate merits of the old aristocracy. Nevertheless, he did his share to celebrate the imperial government because he admired its law and order as much as he hated the violence and vulgarity of his youth. The vast compass and the stately style of his history, which remind one of the noble Pantheon of Agrippa and the splendid residences on the Palatine, glorified the deeds of old in the hope that they might inspire men of his and later days to do likewise.

As we have already remarked, Livy's account of the war with Hannibal brings out not only the glorious nature of Rome's victory but also some of the attendant problems. For one thing, the Senate had guided Rome so well, both during and after the crisis, that there was an increasing disposition on the part of ordinary citizens not to insist on their ancient political rights. For another, the ruin of farms during the war drove many small farmers into the city to join the ever-growing landless populace.[7] This was the beginning of the idle city mob, which by imperial times insisted on "bread and circuses." But even in the second century B.C. there was a real question whether or not the Roman people, as represented in Rome itself, were fit to govern a growing empire. The spoils of empire had an increasingly deleterious effect on the body politic.

Rome's new crisis, that is to say, was a domestic one, and not the threat of another foreign invasion. As the second century B.C. wore on, Tiberius and Gaius Gracchus, two brothers, addressed themselves to some of these problems, but they were thwarted by the reactionary Senate. Thus began the Roman Revolution which, after a century of civil wars, brought the Republic to an end.

These terrible years saw the rise of personal commanders, such as Marius and Sulla; the conspiracy of Catiline to overthrow

---

[7] The abandoned farms were bought up by the rich, thus leading to the ugly development of large estates (*latifundia*) with their slaves and tenant farmers (*coloni*). This was accompanied by a decrease in the number of men eligible to serve in the legions.

the state, and his defeat by Cicero, Rome's greatest orator and staunch defender of republicanism; and the establishment, in 59 B.C., of an informal working arrangement among the three most powerful Romans of the day. This unofficial union is called the First Triumvirate. It consisted of Pompey the Great, vain, pompous, and honorable, the most famous military man alive; Crassus, a member of the equestrian (business) class and one of the richest men in the world; and Gaius Julius Caesar (100–44 B.C.), a patrician of the ancient Julian gens, but politically active in the popular party. Each man had something to gain from the other, but the death of Crassus sharpened the rivalry between Pompey and Caesar. Finally, after his conquest of Gaul—which for the first time opened up northwestern and central Europe to Roman civilization and, of immediate consequence, gave him a personal army of veterans—Caesar turned on Pompey and over-whelmed him at Pharsalus in Greece (48 B.C.).

This last generation of the Roman Republic, intellectually speaking, is often referred to as the Ciceronian Age, because the famous orator and philosopher Cicero deeply influenced the thought and politics of his day. There is no doubt that he had his weaknesses and sometimes wavered in politics, but in the last analysis, when great issues were involved, he was always found on the side he believed to be right. This was also, very clearly, an age of action, and in such a time historical writing was bound to rank with oratory in importance, particularly since it gave the author the opportunity to press his own personal bias. Noble families recorded the deeds of illustrious ancestors, and to give their narratives a brilliant coloring they filled them with lively stories and startling incidents, however exaggerated and false.

One of these romancers was Valerius Antias, who early in the first century B.C. composed his *Annals* of Rome from a strongly aristocratic point of view. Sallust (86–36 B.C.), on the other hand, wrote with a frankly democratic bias, and yet his *History,* most of which is unfortunately lost, gave a valuable description of the events following Sulla's death. His *Jugurthine War* and *Conspiracy of Catiline* analyze the character of society and the motives of conduct. When the great men of Rome began to attract all eyes, a widespread interest developed in biography, but the most famous of the biographers cannot be acquitted of inferior and untrustworthy work. This was Cornelius Nepos (*ca.* 100–25 B.C.), a Gaul from the Po Valley, whose *Eminent Men* treated distinguished Romans and foreigners in parallel biographies; most of his *Lives* which we still possess are of Greek generals.[8]

A striking contrast with the diffuse rhetoric of Valerius Antias, and indeed in a class by itself, is the historical narrative of Caesar, a model of its kind, plain and direct, with a mastery of expression but no pretension to ornament. His *Commentaries* on the Gallic War and on the Civil War tell the story of his campaigns, and were written, in part at least, to explain, justify, and further his cause among the Roman people. Factually accurate, Caesar speaks with modesty of his own achievements and generously excuses the mistakes or praises the merits of others.

Caesar's *Commentaries* are a monument to his skill as a historian and reveal one facet of his many-sided nature. He was a complex man. With the possible exceptions of Alexander the Great and Hannibal, Julius Caesar was the most brilliant military genius the world had thus far produced. He was also an orator of clarity and force, no less than a master of simple prose. His capacity was boundless, his personality so warm that it won the passionate devotion of his followers. He was mild to the conquered; and when political enemies laid down their arms, they found him a friend and benefactor. Beginning as an unscrupulous politician, Caesar grew into a great statesman.

When one considers the multitude and variety of Caesar's reforms, it is difficult to believe that he was in Rome only sixteen

---

[8] The greatest of ancient biographers, and one of the most attractive writers of all time, was Plutarch, a Greek who lived in the early imperial period. Born about A.D. 50 at Chaeronea in Boeotia, he composed *Parallel Lives* of famous Greeks and Romans which celebrated the glorious past; his fascinating biography of Alexander the Great is of prime importance. Plutarch's *Lives,* as well as the writings of the Apostle Paul and the *Meditations* of the emperor Marcus Aurelius, reminds us that the Roman Empire continued to have a Greek, no less than a Latin, literature.

months between the crossing of the Rubicon[9] against Pompey and his assassination. He planned, for example, a codification of the laws, a general tax revision, and a census; the construction of Forums, libraries, and temples at Rome; the dredging of the Tiber and the enlargement of Ostia, Rome's port; the drainage of the Pomptine (Pontine) marshes to the south; the building of roads; a canal at Corinth; colonization; a calendar, which the civilized world used until Pope Gregory XIII (1582) made the slight changes we now have. He admitted many provincials, especially Spaniards and Gauls, to Roman citizenship and even to the Senate, which he probably wished in time to become representative of the whole Roman Empire. These are some of the chief things which Caesar planned or accomplished as dictator. His reforms were imaginative and far-reaching and helped to bind the Greco-Roman world more closely together and to promote its stability and prosperity.

Were it not for the fact that Caesar sounded the death knell of the Roman Republic and made the Empire inevitable, we might applaud him with few reservations. It can be argued, however, that if Caesar had not done this, someone else would have and that in any case it was all to the good. To judge this extraordinary man, his many-sided character, and his life work is not easy. One person who made a notable attempt was Suetonius (ca. A.D. 75–160). Suetonius was secretary to the emperor Hadrian, whose reign is often regarded as the very apex of ancient civilization. In his official capacity, Suetonius had access to valuable documents no less than to important people, their conversations and opinions. Unfortunately, he had a weakness for racy stories, and accordingly his *Lives of the Twelve Caesars* from Julius Caesar to Domitian is often a chaotic mixture of useful facts and foolish gossip. His life of the Divine Julius,

---

[9] This small river, on the east coast of northern Italy, marked the southern limit of Caesar's provincial command. To cross it into Italy proper, at the head of armed forces, was treason against the state. Little wonder that Caesar should exclaim, as he took the step, *Alea jacta est!* This was the regular phrase in Latin games when the dice were thrown. It was too late then to change one's mind; as we might express it, "The die is cast."

nevertheless, is at once a fair sample of literary taste popular in the second century A.D. and, within its limitations, a mine of information concerning the genius who brought civilization from one epoch into another.

Caesar's murder on the Ides of March (March 15, 44 B.C.) was a world tragedy, for it plunged mankind again into desolating war. In the new struggle, however, the question at issue was not the form of government to be adopted, but the identity of the general who would succeed to Caesar's power. This, as we have seen, was Caesar's grandnephew, Octavian or Augustus. The Augustan Age brought the blessings of peace and prosperity to a mighty empire that was soon to stretch from Scotland to Iran, and it is easy to understand the enthusiasm of Livy and Vergil for it. As Horace expressed it, "Now Faith and Peace and Honor and Antique Modesty and neglected Virtue dare return, and Plenty appears in view, rich with her overflowing horn." The provinces, grateful for a fair and skillful administration at last, acclaimed Augustus a benefactor of the human race. The only important thing lacking in the new world was the opportunity of political democracy. Men had often striven for this in the past, though never with complete success. If few seemed to care for it now, considering the other advantages, the future was to pass judgment on the wisdom of their decision.

Augustus ruled so long (27 B.C.–A.D. 14) that it was impossible for men to contemplate a return to the days of the Roman Republic. So far as there was any opposition to the imperial regime, it lay within the Senate, but on Augustus' death the Senate elected Tiberius as his successor (A.D. 14–37). Tiberius was the son-in-law and adopted son of Augustus, and the son of Augustus' third wife, Livia, who had previously married Tiberius Claudius Nero. These two aristocratic families, now joined together—the Julian and Claudian—gave Rome her emperors for the next half century.[10] The suicide A.D. 68 of Nero, the last of the Julio-

---

[10] The other emperors of the Julio-Claudian dynasty were Gaius (popularly called Caligula, A.D. 37–41), Claudius (A.D. 41–54), and Nero (A.D. 54–68). Emperors commonly adopted their designated successor. (See the chart on p. xxxviii.)

Claudian dynasty, wrote its own sad commentary on the decisions forced by the battle of Actium ninety-nine years earlier. In that dim past, the military basis of the princeps' authority had been carefully concealed, but now it was all too obvious. After a brief struggle, known as the Year of the Four Emperors,[11] the imperial mantle fell on Vespasian (A.D. 69–79), the choice of the army besieging Jerusalem. Vespasian hurried to Rome to accept from the Senate the powers already conferred by the army and to found a new dynasty, the Flavian. As Tacitus remarks, "The fatal secret of the empire had been discovered, that emperors could be chosen elsewhere than in Rome."

Vespasian was succeeded by his sons, Titus (A.D. 79–81)— "the delight and darling of mankind," as Suetonius describes him —and Domitian (A.D. 81–96), a scholar turned autocrat in Rome itself. Tacitus considered all these earlier emperors usurpers and tyrants, and since he had to wait for Domitian to die before he felt safe to write, he has left in his resentment a one-sided picture that has colored the judgment of posterity.

Since the welfare of the entire Roman Empire depended in large part on the ability and personality of the princeps, the ancient historians wrote their accounts chiefly in terms of the reigning emperor, his relations with the Senate, and his defense of the frontiers. Spicy gossip about life in the capital interested most of them, too. This preoccupation is to be regretted, for we know (thanks chiefly to excavations and modern scholarship, in general) that there was another side to the picture: a powerful, peaceful, prosperous world composed of Roman, Greek, and Oriental cultures. The provinces, moreover, would insist that the emperors be given full credit for this; and we ourselves, on our part, must remember that as a rule the crimes and caprices of certain emperors usually touched only the capital, and only the upper crust of its society, at that.

At any rate, the literary pulse, after the death of Augustus,

---

[11] Galba (A.D. 68–69, the Spanish legate, upon whom Tacitus passed the verdict that he would have been judged fit to rule, had he not ruled); Otho (A.D. 69, choice of the imperial praetorian guard stationed in Rome); Vitellius (A.D. 69, legate, or governor, of Lower Germany); and Vespasian.

never again beat so high, and consequently the period of the early Roman Empire is spoken of as the Silver Age of Latin literature. Certain emperors—notably Tiberius and Domitian—refused to patronize literature. Nevertheless, an army officer in the reign of Tiberius, Velleius Paterculus by name, wrote a short *History of Rome* to A.D. 30. Wordy and pompous, he achieves some accuracy in his statements of fact, but he overflows with eulogy of Tiberius, like a partisan rather than a calm-tempered historian. The same criticism applies to his contemporary, Valerius Maximus. The object of his untrustworthy *Memorable Acts and Sayings* seems to have been to supply the youth of the day with material for declamations.

On the other hand, as we have already intimated, Publius Cornelius Tacitus (*ca.* A.D. 55–117)—Rome's greatest historian and the last great writer of classic Latin—had his own, senatorial bias; this is the principal charge that can be laid against him. Since the Senate was the only continuing center of republican opposition to the emperor, Tacitus had to bide his time till the death of Domitian and wait till the reigns of Nerva and Trajan to write. Nerva's reign opened the rule of the so-called "Five Good Emperors," [12] when the emperors were chosen on the basis of merit rather than birth. Tacitus declared that Nerva united two things that had hitherto been considered incompatible, monarchy and liberty.

Tacitus probably came from an aristocratic, wealthy family in northern Italy. He tells us that, although he hopes for good emperors, he can endure any kind whatsoever. And this was true,

---

[12] Nerva (A.D. 96–98), Trajan (A.D. 98–117), Hadrian (A.D. 117–138), Antoninus Pius (A.D. 138–161), and Marcus Aurelius (A.D. 161–180). This period corresponded with the widest and most prosperous development in the history of Rome and became famous as the Golden Age of the Empire. The last Antonine emperor, Commodus (A.D. 180–192), was a monster, an illuminating comment on the dynastic principle, for his father had lacked the resolution to pass him by. The world held together, however, during the succeeding Severan dynasty, but the murder A.D. 235 of the last of its number, Severus Alexander, brought both the Principate and the Roman Peace to an end. This introduced fifty years of military anarchy, until the ancient world was riveted together again by the Oriental despotism of Diocletian and Constantine, Rome's first Christian emperor.

for, despite his loathing for Domitian, he held the praetorship under him and went on to be the governor of a province, probably Belgium. Later, under Trajan, he was consul and A.D. 112 the governor of Asia Minor. He was the friend of the Younger Pliny and pleaded many legal cases with him. Not much more is known about him personally, except that A.D. 78 he married the daughter of Cnaeus Julius Agricola, the future governor of Britain.

The writings of Tacitus, however, shed a strong light on his standards and prejudices. An aristocrat, he admired the Roman Republic, which had built a great empire; he accepted the imperial regime, nevertheless, though not its tyrannical emperors, corrupt nobility, and vulgar masses. As a historian, he was not primarily interested in research and the careful accuracy that went with it, but rather in writing great literature, in portraying individuals and their motives vividly, and in describing events dramatically. He had a moral purpose in writing. As he put it: "My purpose is not to relate at length every motion, but only such as were conspicuous for excellence or notorious for infamy. This I regard as history's highest function, to let no worthy action be uncommemorated, and to hold out the reprobation of posterity as a terror to evil words and deeds." Tacitus' method resulted in a one-sided, rather than a deliberately misrepresented, picture of the past. Quite rightly, for example, he paints the last years of Tiberius' reign as a tyranny—but it was a tyranny affecting chiefly Rome, and where is Tacitus' account of the masses of the world? It is Tacitus' omissions that we deplore, his lack of Thucydidean impartiality and objectivity.

Tacitus began his literary career early in life. By A.D. 81 he had finished his *Dialogue on Oratory,* which outlines the type of ideal education suitable for his own day, a quite different time from that of Cicero and the fiery end of the Republic. Soon after the murder of Domitian, Tacitus published his *Life of Agricola,* a sensitive and moving, if eulogistic, biography of his father-in-law, with a valuable account of Britain and Roman provincial administration. Agricola conquered Wales and extended the boundary of his province to the Highlands of Scotland (Caledonia); as a protection against raiding tribes, he built a road and forts from Newcastle on the Tyne to the Solway Firth, a general scheme of defense that was to be followed by Hadrian and Antoninus Pius. In spite of his demonstrated military ability, Agricola was refused permission to attack Ireland, on the ground that it would cost too much, but he did succeed in sailing round the northern tip of Britain, thus establishing what had long been forgotten, that it was in fact an island. Eventually recalled by the jealous Domitian, Agricola proved by his life, as Tacitus remarks, that "great men can exist under evil rulers."

Tacitus published his *Germania* in the same year as the *Agricola* (A.D. 98). The *Germania* is the only extant Roman description of the tribes of Central Europe, their organization, religion, and customs. Tacitus next composed his *Histories,* an account of Rome from the Year of the Four Emperors to Domitian's death (A.D. 69–96). Of its twelve books—for that was the original number, probably—only the first four and a part of the fifth survive (covering A.D. 69 and 70). Tacitus' last and greatest work, the *Annals,* was finished shortly before his death; it treated the history of Rome from Augustus' death to that of Nero (A.D. 14–68). The *Annals* consisted originally, probably, of eighteen books, but only the first four, parts of the fifth and sixth, and almost all of Books XI to XVI, survive. This material gives us the reign of Tiberius (A.D. 14–37), much of Claudius' (from A.D. 47 to 54), and almost all of Nero's (from A.D. 54 to 66).[13]

If the satirist in Tacitus is a little too prominent, and thus leaves something to be desired as far as sound judgment is sometimes concerned, there can be no doubt whatever of his literary artistry. His grand style is typical of the Silver Age, in that the long Ciceronian periods are abandoned in favor of short, concentrated sentences. So, too, commonplace words are avoided, and in their place we find poetic expressions; this was due to the influence of rhetoric, which sought to break down the boundary between poetry and prose. Tacitus' brevity of expression is as famous as his sententious phrases, which have been quoted ever

---

[13] Tacitus did not live to realize his hope of describing, in other works, the reigns of Augustus, Nerva, and Trajan—those preceding and following, that is to say, the "tyrannical" period covered by the *Annals* and *Histories.*

since. Of Roman conquest he said, "They make a solitude and call it peace." Rome itself, he declared, had become a place "where all things hideous and shameful from every part of the world find their center and are popular." Of the transience of political systems he said: "Princes die but society is eternal"; on the psychology of power: "The cause of hatred is all the stronger if it is unjust"; "In a community of might concord seldom rules"; "Among the powerful and those greedy of power, serenity is deceptive." He called the Christians "haters of mankind."

In one important respect Tacitus' psychological vision is one-sided, for it is permeated with pessimism. He says, moreover, that history must be written without preconceived antipathies or sympathies, and yet this member of the senatorial aristocracy ignored the blessings the imperial government brought the provinces. Is it possible, however, that, had Domitian been a different sort of man, had the Empire treated his youth differently, Tacitus might not have hated the emperors as "tyrants"? Or should we ourselves stop and examine our own preconceived picture of the "glorious" Roman Peace, inherited as it has been from generations of writers, and ask whether Tacitus did not, in fact, come pretty near the truth, so far as essentials are concerned? After all, did not the battle of Actium, which gave the Roman throne to Augustus and eventually crushed a complex world in a despotic state socialism, prevent ancient man forever afterward from solving his problems on his own initiative?

As we said at the outset, the most distinguished Greek and Roman historians provide us with great literature. They also tell us about momentous events and forces, men and life, sophisticated civilizations of sustained length, and clashing cultures. But they do even more than that, because as profound and brilliant thinkers they penetrate to the depths and thus speak directly and helpfully to us and the crises of our day. No other period in history can so stimulate our own thinking.

CHARLES ALEXANDER ROBINSON, JR.

Providence, Rhode Island
January, 1957

BIBLIOGRAPHICAL NOTE

Translations of all the extant Greek and Roman histories may be found in the *Loeb Classical Library*, Cambridge, Mass., various dates; and of Herodotus, Thucydides, Xenophon, and Arrian in F. R. B. Godolphin (editor), *The Greek Historians*, 2 vols., New York, 1942. Interesting excerpts may be found in W. C. McDermott and W. E. Caldwell (editors), *Readings in the History of the Ancient World*, New York, 1951. There are good studies of the ancient historians in J. B. Bury, *The Ancient Greek Historians*, New York, 1919; J. H. Finley, Jr., *Thucydides*, Cambridge, Mass., 1942; T. R. Glover, *Herodotus*, Berkeley, 1924; A. W. Gomme, *Essays in Greek Literature and History*, Oxford, 1937, and *A Historical Commentary on Thucydides*, Oxford, in progress; M. L. W. Laistner, *The Greater Roman Historians*, Berkeley, 1947; J. L. Myres, *Herodotus*, Oxford, 1953.

Various aspects of Greek and Roman history are treated by F. E. Adcock, *The Roman Art of War under the Republic*, Cambridge, Mass., 1940; G. P. Baker, *Hannibal*, London, 1930; J. Buchan, *Julius Caesar*, London, 1936, and *Augustus*, Boston, 1937; B. W. Henderson, *The Great War between Athens and Sparta*, London, 1927; B. H. Liddell-Hart, *A Greater than Napoleon, Scipio Africanus*, London, 1927; F. B. Marsh, *The Founding of the Roman Empire*, 2nd ed., Oxford, 1927, and *The Reign of Tiberius*, Oxford, 1931; C. A. Robinson, Jr., *Alexander the Great*, New York, 1947; R. S. Rogers, *Studies in the Reign of Tiberius*, Baltimore, 1943; M. I. Rostovtzeff, *The Social and Economic History of the Roman Empire*, Oxford, 1926, and *The Social and Economic History of the Hellenistic World*, 3 vols., Oxford, 1941; A. N. Sherwin-White, *The Roman Citizenship*, Oxford

1939; R. Syme, *The Roman Revolution*, Oxford, 1939; F. W. Walbank, *The Decline of the Roman Empire in the West*, London, 1946; A. E. Zimmern, *The Greek Commonwealth: Politics and Economics in Fifth-century Athens*, 5th ed., Oxford, 1931.

For reference or general study may be recommended J. B. Bury and Others (editors), *Cambridge Ancient History*, 12 vols., 5 vols. of plates, New York, 1923–1939 (2nd eds. of this monumental work are in progress); M. Cary, *The Geographic Background of Greek and Roman History*, Oxford, 1949; M. Cary and Others, *Oxford Classical Dictionary*, Oxford, 1949; E. Gibbon, *The History of the Decline and Fall of the Roman Empire*, ed. by J. B. Bury, 7 vols., London, 1909–1914 (the *Portable Gibbon* in one vol., ed. by D. A. Saunders, New York, 1952); A. J. Toynbee, *A Study of History*, abridgment by D. C. Somervell, 2 vols., London, 1947 and 1957, and *Civilization on Trial*, London, 1948; F. W. Walbank, *A Historical Commentary on Polybius*, Oxford, in progress.

ACKNOWLEDGMENTS

It is a pleasure and duty to express my hearty thanks to various friends who have kindly helped me with the planning of this book and with the difficult choice of the selections. Especially am I indebted to Professors Walter Allen, Jr., University of North Carolina, G. F. Else, University of Iowa, J. P. Harland, University of North Carolina, R. M. Haywood, New York University, E. A. Robinson, Fordham University, R. S. Rogers, Duke University. The book owes more than I can ever say to the criticisms of my wife, Celia Robinson. I also acknowledge a general debt to the works of others, especially, perhaps, to those mentioned in the Bibliographical Note. I am indebted to The Macmillan Company for permission to base certain of my remarks in the Introduction on passages in G. W. Botsford and C. A. Robinson, Jr., *Hellenic History*, 4th ed., New York, 1956, and in my *Ancient History*, New York, 1951; the map of the Roman Empire was first published in the latter book and was drawn by Dr. Erwin Raisz of the Institute of Geographical Exploration, Harvard University. The map of Greece, by Vincent Kotschar, was first published in Stewart C. Easton's *The Heritage of the Past*, New York, 1955, and is reproduced by permission of Rinehart & Company, Inc. H. G. Dakyns' translation of Xenophon is reprinted with the kind permission of Macmillan & Co., Ltd., London; T. Forester's revision of Alexander Thomson's translation of Suetonius has been used through the courtesy of G. Bell & Sons, Ltd., London.

C. A. R., JR.

THE JULIO-CLAUDIAN LINE OF EMPERORS

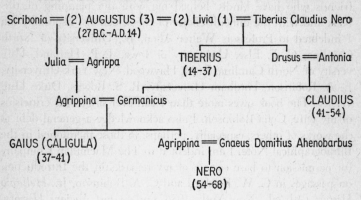

Scribonia ══ (2) AUGUSTUS (3) ══ (2) Livia (1) ══ Tiberius Claudius Nero
       (27 B.C.–A.D. 14)

Julia ══ Agrippa   TIBERIUS   Drusus ══ Antonia
                      (14–37)

Agrippina ══ Germanicus   CLAUDIUS
                           (41–54)

GAIUS (CALIGULA)   Agrippina ══ Gnaeus Domitius Ahenobarbus
    (37–41)

                         NERO
                        (54–68)

CONTENTS

Introduction   vii

Map of Greece (Drawn by V. Kotschar)   vi

Map of the Roman Empire, A.D. 14 (Drawn by E. Raisz)   xx-xxi

HERODOTUS
    From THE PERSIAN WARS (*Translated by George Raw-
    linson*)   2

THUCYDIDES
    From THE PELOPONNESIAN WAR (*Translated by Ben-
    jamin Jowett*)   56

XENOPHON
    From THE HELLENICA (*Translated by H. G. Dakyns*)   130

POLYBIUS
    From THE HISTORIES (*Translated by Evelyn S. Shuck-
    burgh*)   136

LIVY
    From THE HISTORY OF ROME (*Translated by D. Spillan
    and Cyrus Edmonds*)   162

SALLUST
    From THE JUGURTHINE WAR (*Translated by John
    Selby Watson*)   208

SUETONIUS
    From THE LIVES OF THE TWELVE CAESARS: JULIUS
    CAESAR (*Translated by Alexander Thomson, revised by
    T. Forester*)   222

TACITUS

From THE ANNALS (*Translated by Alfred John Church and William Jackson Brodribb*)   242

From THE HISTORIES (*Translated by Alfred John Church and William Jackson Brodribb*)   311

From THE LIFE OF AGRICOLA (*Translated by Alfred John Church and William Jackson Brodribb*)   321

From THE GERMANIA (*Translated by Alfred John Church and William Jackson Brodribb*)   328

HERODOTUS

Translated by George Rawlinson

THE PERSIAN WARS

Solon and Croesus. The Persians. The Egyptians. Persian forms of government. The Ionian Revolt. The Battle of Marathon. Eulogy of Athens. The Battle of Thermopylae. The Battle of Salamis.

[A fabulous meeting between Solon, the famous Athenian reformer of 594 B.C., and Croesus, the Hellenized Lydian king, though cast as an exponent of non-Greek ways. Herodotus is trying here to emphasize the fundamental difference of ideals between East and West, so that the reader may understand the nature of the contestants in the forthcoming Persian Wars.]

When all these conquests had been added to the Lydian empire, and the prosperity of Sardis was now at its height, there came thither, one after another, all the sages of Greece living at the time, and among them Solon, the Athenian. He was on his travels, having left Athens to be absent ten years, under the pretense of wishing to see the world, but really to avoid being forced to repeal any of the laws which, at the request of the Athenians, he had made for them. Without his sanction the Athenians could not repeal them, as they had bound themselves under a heavy curse to be governed for ten years by the laws which should be imposed on them by Solon.

On this account, as well as to see the world, Solon set out upon his travels, in the course of which he went to Egypt to the court of Amasis, and also came on a visit to Croesus at Sardis. Croesus received him as his guest, and lodged him in the royal palace. On the third or fourth day after, he bade his servants conduct Solon over his treasuries, and show him all their greatness and magnificence. When he had seen them all, and, so far as time allowed, inspected them, Croesus addressed this question to him. "Stranger of Athens, we have heard much of thy wisdom and of thy travels through many lands, from love of knowledge and a wish to see the world. I am curious therefore to inquire of thee, whom, of all the men that thou hast seen, thou deemest the most happy?" This he asked because he thought himself the happiest of mortals: but Solon answered him without flattery, according to his true sentiments, "Tellus of Athens, sire." Full of astonishment at what he heard, Croesus demanded sharply, "And wherefore dost thou deem Tellus happiest?" To which the other replied, "First, because his country was flourishing in his days, and he himself had sons both beautiful and good, and he lived to see children born to each of them, and these children all grew up; and further because, after a life spent in what our people look upon as comfort, his end was surpassingly glorious. In a battle between the Athenians and their neighbors near Eleusis, he came to the assistance of his countrymen, routed the foe, and died upon the field most gallantly. The Athenians gave him a public funeral on the spot where he fell, and paid him the highest honors."

Thus did Solon admonish Croesus by the example of Tellus, enumerating the manifold particulars of his happiness. When he had ended, Croesus inquired a second time, who after Tellus seemed to him the happiest, expecting that at any rate, he would be given the second place. "Cleobis and Bito," Solon answered; "they were of Argive race; their fortune was enough for their wants, and they were besides endowed with so much bodily strength that they had both gained prizes at the Games. Also this tale is told of them:—There was a great festival in honor of the goddess Hera at Argos, to which their mother must needs be taken in a car. Now the oxen did not come home from the field in time: so the youths, fearful of being too late, put the yoke on their own necks, and themselves drew the car in which their mother rode. Five and forty furlongs did they draw her, and stopped before the temple. This deed of theirs was witnessed by the whole assembly of worshipers, and then their life closed in the best possible way. Herein, too, God showed forth most evidently, how much better a thing for man death is than life. For the Argive men, who stood around the car, extolled the vast strength of the youths; and the Argive women extolled the mother who was blessed with such a pair of sons; and the mother herself, overjoyed at the deed and at the praises it had won, standing straight before the image, besought the goddess to bestow on Cleobis and Bito, the sons who had so mightily honored her, the highest blessing to which mortals can attain. Her prayer ended, they offered sacrifice and partook of the holy banquet, after which the two youths fell asleep in the temple. They never woke more, but so passed from the earth. The Argives, looking on them as among the best of men, caused statues of them to be made, which they gave to the shrine at Delphi."

When Solon had thus assigned these youths the second place, Croesus broke in angrily, "What, stranger of Athens, is my happiness, then, so utterly set at nought by thee, that thou dost not even put me on a level with private men?"

"Oh! Croesus," replied the other, "thou askedst a question concerning the condition of man, of one who knows that the power above us is full of jealousy, and fond of troubling our lot. A long life gives one to witness much, and experience much oneself, that one would not choose. Seventy years I regard as the limit of the life of man. In these seventy years are contained, without reckoning intercalary months, twenty-five thousand and two hundred days. Add an intercalary month to every other year, that the seasons may come round at the right time, and there will be, besides the seventy years, thirty-five such months, making an addition of one thousand and fifty days. The whole number of the days contained in the seventy years will thus be twenty-six thousand two hundred and fifty, whereof not one but will produce events unlike the rest. Hence man is wholly accident. For thyself, oh! Croesus, I see that thou art wonderfully rich, and art the lord of many nations; but with respect to that whereon thou questionest me, I have no answer to give, until I hear that thou hast closed thy life happily. For assuredly he who possesses great store of riches is no nearer happiness than he who has what suffices for his daily needs, unless it so hap that luck attend upon him, and so he continue in the enjoyment of all his good things to the end of life. For many of the wealthiest men have been unfavored of fortune, and many whose means were moderate have had excellent luck. Men of the former class excel those of the latter but in two respects; these last excel the former in many. The wealthy man is better able to content his desires, and to bear up against a sudden buffet of calamity. The other has less ability to withstand these evils (from which, however, his good luck keeps him clear), but he enjoys all these following blessings: he is whole of limb, a stranger to disease, free from misfortune, happy in his children, and comely to look upon. If, in addition to all this, he end his life well, he is of a truth the man of whom thou art in search, the man who may rightly be termed happy. Call him, however, until he die, not happy but fortunate. Scarcely, indeed, can any man unite all these advantages: as there is no country which contains within it all that it needs, but each, while it possesses some things, lacks others, and the best country is that which contains the most; so no single human being is complete in every respect—something is always lacking. He who unites the greatest number of advantages, and retaining them to the day of his death, then dies peaceably, that man alone, sire, is, in my judgment, entitled to bear the name of 'happy.' But in every matter it behoves us to mark well the end: for oftentimes God gives men a gleam of happiness, and then plunges them into ruin."

Such was the speech which Solon addressed to Croesus, a speech which brought him neither largess nor honor. The king saw him depart with much indifference, since he thought that a man must be an arrant fool who made no account of present good, but bade men always wait and mark the end. (*I*, 29-33)

[*The customs of the Persians.*]

The customs which I know the Persians to observe are the following. They have no images of the gods, no temples nor altars, and consider the use of them a sign of folly. This comes, I think, from their not believing the gods to have the same nature with men, as the Greeks imagine. Their wont, however, is to ascend the summits of the loftiest mountains, and there to offer sacrifice to Zeus, which is the name they give to the whole circuit of the firmament. They likewise offer to the sun and moon, to the earth, to fire, to water, and to the winds. These are the only gods whose worship has come down to them from ancient times. At a later period they began the worship of Urania, which they borrowed from the Arabians and Assyrians. Mylitta is the name by which the Assyrians know this goddess, whom the Arabians call Alitta, and the Persians Mitra.

To these gods the Persians offer sacrifice in the following manner: they raise no altar, light no fire, pour no libations; there is no sound of the flute, no putting on of chaplets, no consecrated barley-cake; but the man who wishes to sacrifice brings his victim to a spot of ground which is pure from pollution, and there calls upon the name of the god to whom he intends to offer. It is usual to have the turban encircled with a wreath, most commonly of myrtle. The sacrificer is not allowed to pray for blessings on himself alone, but he prays for the welfare of the king, and of the whole Persian people, among whom he is of necessity included. He cuts the victim in pieces, and having boiled the flesh, he lays it out upon the tenderest herbage that he can find, trefoil especially. When all is ready, one of the Magi comes forward and chants a hymn, which they say recounts the origin of the gods. It is not lawful to offer sacrifice unless there is a Magus present. After waiting a short time the sacrificer carries the flesh of the victim away with him, and makes whatever use of it he may please.

Of all the days in the year, the one which they celebrate most is their birthday. It is customary to have the board furnished on that day with an ampler supply than common. The richer Persians cause an ox, a horse, a camel, and an ass to be baked whole and so served up to them: the poorer classes use instead the smaller kinds of cattle. They eat little solid food but abundance of dessert, which is set on table a few dishes at a time; this it is which makes them say that "the Greeks, when they eat, leave off hungry, having nothing worth mention served up to them after the meats; whereas, if they had more put before them, they would not stop eating." They are very fond of wine, and drink it in large quantities. To vomit or obey natural calls in the presence of another, is forbidden among them. Such are their customs in these matters.

It is also their general practice to deliberate upon affairs of weight when they are drunk; and then on the morrow, when they are sober, the decision to which they came the night before is put before them by the master of the house in which it was made; and if it is then approved of, they act on it; if not, they set it aside. Sometimes, however, they are sober at their first deliberation, but in this case they always reconsider the matter under the influence of wine.

When they meet each other in the streets, you may know if the persons meeting are of equal rank by the following token; if they are, instead of speaking, they kiss each other on the lips. In the case where one is a little inferior to the other, the kiss is given on the cheek; where the difference of rank is great, the inferior prostrates himself upon the ground. Of nations, they honor most their nearest neighbors, whom they esteem next to themselves; those who live beyond these they honor in the second degree; and so with the remainder, the further they are removed, the less the esteem in which they hold them. The reason is, that they look upon themselves as very greatly superior in all respects to the rest of mankind, regarding others as approaching to excellence in proportion as they dwell nearer to them; whence it comes to pass that those who are the farthest off must be the most degraded of mankind. Under the dominion of the Medes, the several nations of the empire exercised authority over each other in this order. The Medes were lords over all, and governed the nations upon their borders, who in their turn governed the States beyond, who likewise bore rule over the nations which adjoined on them. And this is the order which the Persians also follow in their distribution of honor; for that people, like the Medes, has a progressive scale of administration and government.

There is no nation which so readily adopts foreign customs as the Persians. Thus, they have taken the dress of the Medes, considering it superior to their own; and in war they wear the Egyptian breastplate. As soon as they hear of any luxury, they instantly make it their own: and hence, among other novelties, they have learnt unnatural lust from the Greeks. Each of them has several wives, and a still larger number of concubines.

Next to prowess in arms, it is regarded as the greatest proof of manly excellence, to be the father of many sons. Every year the king sends rich gifts to the man who can show the largest number: for they hold that number is strength. Their sons are carefully instructed from their fifth to their twentieth year, in three things alone,—to ride, to draw the bow, and to speak the truth. Until their fifth year they are not allowed to come into the sight of their father, but pass their lives with the women. This is done that, if the child die young, the father may not be afflicted by its loss.

To my mind it is a wise rule, as also is the following—that the king shall not put any one to death for a single fault, and that none of the Persians shall visit a single fault in a slave with any extreme penalty; but in every case the services of the offender shall be set against his misdoings; and, if the latter be found to outweigh the former, the aggrieved party shall then proceed to punishment.

The Persians maintain that never yet did any one kill his own father or mother; but in all such cases they are quite sure that, if matters were sifted to the bottom, it would be found that the child was either a changeling or else the fruit of adultery; for it is not likely, they say, that the real father should perish by the hands of his child.

They hold it unlawful to talk of anything which it is unlawful to do. The most disgraceful thing in the world, they think, is to tell a lie; the next worst, to owe a debt: because, among other reasons, the debtor is obliged to tell lies. If a Persian has the leprosy he is not allowed to enter into a city, or to have any dealings with the other Persians; he must, they say, have sinned against the sun. Foreigners attacked by this disorder are forced to leave the country: even white pigeons are often driven away, as guilty of the same offense. They never defile a river with the secretions of their bodies, nor even wash their hands in one; nor will they allow others to do so, as they have a great reverence for rivers. There is another peculiarity, which the Persians themselves have never noticed, but which has not escaped my observation. Their names, which are expressive of some bodily or mental excellence, all end with the same letter—the letter which is called San by the Dorians, and Sigma by the Ionians. Any one who examines will find that the Persian names, one and all without exception, end with this letter.

Thus much I can declare of the Persians with entire certainty, from my own actual knowledge. There is another custom which is spoken of with reserve, and not openly, concerning their dead. It is said that the body of a male Persian is never buried, until it has been torn either by a dog or a bird of prey. That the Magi have this custom is beyond a doubt, for they practice it without any concealment. The dead bodies are covered with wax, and then buried in the ground.

The Magi are a very peculiar race, differing entirely from the Egyptian priests, and indeed from all other men whatsoever. The Egyptian priests make it a point of religion not to kill any live animals except those which they offer in sacrifice. The Magi, on the contrary, kill animals of all kinds with their own hands, excepting dogs and men. They even seem to take a delight in the employment, and kill, as readily as they do other animals, ants and snakes, and such like flying or creeping things. However, since this has always been their custom, let them keep to it. (I, 131-140)

[The Egyptians.]

Concerning Egypt itself I shall extend my remarks to a great length, because there is no country that possesses so many wonders, nor any that has such a number of works which defy description. Not only is the climate different from that of the rest of the world, and the rivers unlike any other rivers, but the people also, in most of their manners and customs, exactly reverse the common practice of mankind. The women attend the markets and trade, while the men sit at home at the loom; and here, while

the rest of the world works the woof up the warp, the Egyptians
work it down; the women likewise carry burthens upon their
shoulders, while the men carry them upon their heads. They eat
their food out of doors in the streets, but retire for private purposes
to their houses, giving as a reason that what is unseemly, but
necessary, ought to be done in secret, but what has nothing unseemly about it, should be done openly. A woman cannot serve
the priestly office, either for god or goddess, but men are priests to
both; sons need not support their parents unless they choose, but
daughters must, whether they choose or no.

In other countries the priests have long hair, in Egypt their
heads are shaven; elsewhere it is customary, in mourning, for near
relations to cut their hair close; the Egyptians, who wear no hair
at any other time, when they lose a relative, let their beards and
the hair of their heads grow long. All other men pass their lives
separate from animals, the Egyptians have animals always living
with them; others make barley and wheat their food; it is a disgrace to do so in Egypt, where the grain they live on is spelt, which
some call *zea*. Dough they knead with their feet; but they mix
mud, and even take up dirt, with their hands. They are the only
people in the world—they at least, and such as have learnt the
practice from them—who use circumcision. Their men wear two
garments apiece, their women but one. They put on the rings
and fasten the ropes to sails inside; others put them outside. When
they write or calculate, instead of going, like the Greeks, from left
to right, they move their hand from right to left; and they insist,
notwithstanding, that it is they who go to the right, and the Greeks
who go to the left. They have two quite different kinds of writing,
one of which is called sacred, the other common.

They are religious to excess, far beyond any other race of
men, and use the following ceremonies:—They drink out of
brazen cups, which they scour every day: there is no exception
to this practice. They wear linen garments, which they are specially careful to have always fresh washed. They practice circumcision for the sake of cleanliness, considering it better to be cleanly
than comely. The priests shave their whole body every other day,
that no lice or other impure thing may adhere to them when they

are engaged in the service of the gods. Their dress is entirely of linen, and their shoes of the papyrus plant: it is not lawful for them to wear either dress or shoes of any other material. They bathe twice every day in cold water, and twice each night; besides which they observe, so to speak, thousands of ceremonies. They enjoy, however, not a few advantages. They consume none of their own property, and are at no expense for anything; but every day bread is baked for them of the sacred grain, and a plentiful supply of beef and of goose's flesh is assigned to each, and also a portion of wine made from the grape. Fish they are not allowed to eat; and beans,—which none of the Egyptians ever sow, or eat, if they come up of their own accord, either raw or boiled—the priests will not even endure to look on, since they consider it an unclean kind of pulse. Instead of a single priest, each god has the attendance of a college, at the head of which is a chief priest; when one of these dies, his son is appointed in his room.

Male kine are reckoned to belong to Epaphus, and are therefore tested in the following manner:—One of the priests appointed for the purpose searches to see if there is a single black hair on the whole body, since in that case the beast is unclean. He examines him all over, standing on his legs, and again laid upon his back; after which he takes the tongue out of his mouth, to see if it be clean in respect of the prescribed marks (what they are I will mention elsewhere); he also inspects the hairs of the tail, to observe if they grow naturally. If the animal is pronounced clean in all these various points, the priest marks him by twisting a piece of papyrus round his horns, and attaching thereto some sealing-clay, which he then stamps with his own signet-ring. After this the beast is led away; and it is forbidden, under the penalty of death, to sacrifice an animal which has not been marked in this way.

The following is their manner of sacrifice:—They lead the victim, marked with their signet, to the altar where they are about to offer it, and setting the wood alight, pour a libation of wine upon the altar in front of the victim, and at the same time invoke the god. Then they slay the animal, and cutting off his head, proceed to flay the body. Next they take the head, and

heaping imprecations on it, if there is a market-place and a body
of Greek traders in the city, they carry it there and sell it instantly;
if, however, there are no Greeks among them, they throw the
head into the river. The imprecation is to this effect:—They pray
that if any evil is impending either over those who sacrifice, or
over universal Egypt, it may be made to fall upon that head.
These practices, the imprecations upon the heads, and the libations of wine, prevail all over Egypt, and extend to victims of all
sorts; and hence the Egyptians will never eat the head of any
animal. (II, 35-39)

With respect to the Egyptians themselves, it is to be remarked that those who live in the grain country, devoting themselves, as they do, far more than any other people in the world,
to the preservation of the memory of past actions, are the best
skilled in history of any men that I have ever met. The following
is the mode of life habitual to them:—For three successive days
in each month they purge the body by means of emetics and
clysters, which is done out of a regard for their health, since they
have a persuasion that every disease to which men are liable is
occasioned by the substances whereon they feed. Apart from any
such precautions, they are, I believe, next to the Libyans, the
healthiest people in the world—an effect of their climate, in my
opinion, which has no sudden changes. Diseases almost always
attack men when they are exposed to a change, and never more
than during changes of the weather. They live on bread made of
spelt, which they form into loaves called in their own tongue
cyllestis. Their drink is a wine which they obtain from barley, as
they have no vines in their country. Many kinds of fish they eat
raw, either salted or dried in the sun. Quails also, and ducks and
small birds, they eat uncooked, merely first salting them. All other
birds and fishes, excepting those which are set apart as sacred, are
eaten either roasted or boiled.

In social meetings among the rich, when the banquet is ended,
a servant carries round to the several guests a coffin, in which
there is a wooden image of a corpse, carved and painted to resemble nature as nearly as possible, about a cubit or two cubits
in length. As he shows it to each guest in turn, the servant says,

"Gaze here, and drink and be merry; for when you die, such will you be." (*II, 77-78*)

There is another custom in which the Egyptians resemble a particular Greek people, namely the Lacedaemonians. Their young men, when they meet their elders in the streets, give way to them and step aside; and if an elder come in where young are present, these latter rise from their seats. In a third point they differ entirely from all the nations of Greece. Instead of speaking to each other when they meet in the streets, they make an obeisance, sinking the hand to the knee.

They wear a linen tunic fringed about the legs, and called *calasiris;* over this they have a white woolen garment thrown on afterward. Nothing of woolen, however, is taken to their temples or buried with them, as their religion forbids it. Here their practice resembles the rites called Orphic and Bacchic, but which are in reality Egyptian and Pythagorean; for no one initiated in these mysteries can be buried in a woolen shroud, a religious reason being assigned for the observance.

The Egyptians likewise discovered to which of the gods each month and day is sacred; and found out from the day of a man's birth, what he will meet with in the course of his life, and how he will end his days, and what sort of man he will be—discoveries whereof the Greeks engaged in poetry have made a use. The Egyptians have also discovered more prognostics than all the rest of mankind besides. Whenever a prodigy takes place, they watch and record the result; then, if anything similar ever happens again, they expect the same consequences.

With respect to divination, they hold that it is a gift which no mortal possesses, but only certain of the gods: thus they have an oracle of Heracles, one of Apollo, of Athena, of Artemis, of Ares, and of Zeus. Besides these, there is the oracle of Latona at Buto, which is held in much higher repute than any of the rest. The mode of delivering the oracles is not uniform, but varies at the different shrines.

Medicine is practiced among them on a plan of separation; each physician treats a single disorder, and no more: thus the country swarms with medical practitioners, some undertaking to cure diseases of the eye, others of the head, others again of the teeth, others of the intestines, and some those which are not local.

The following is the way in which they conduct their mournings and their funerals:—On the death in any house of a man of consequence, forthwith the women of the family beplaster their heads, and sometimes even their faces, with mud; and then, leaving the body indoors, sally forth and wander through the city, with their dress fastened by a band, and their bosoms bare, beating themselves as they walk. All the female relations join them and do the same. The men too, similarly begirt, beat their breasts separately. When these ceremonies are over, the body is carried away to be embalmed.

There are a set of men in Egypt who practice the art of embalming, and make it their proper business. These persons, when a body is brought to them, show the bearers various models of corpses, made in wood, and painted so as to resemble nature. The most perfect is said to be after the manner of him whom I do not think it religious to name in connection with such a matter; the second sort is inferior to the first, and less costly; the third is the cheapest of all. All this the embalmers explain, and then ask in which way it is wished that the corpse should be prepared. The bearers tell them, and having concluded their bargain, take their departure, while the embalmers, left to themselves, proceed to their task. The mode of embalming, according to the most perfect process, is the following:—They take first a crooked piece of iron, and with it draw out the brain through the nostrils, thus getting rid of a portion, while the skull is cleared of the rest by rinsing with drugs; next they make a cut along the flank with a sharp Ethiopian stone, and take out the whole contents of the abdomen, which they then cleanse, washing it thoroughly with palm wine, and again frequently with an infusion of pounded aromatics. After this they fill the cavity with the purest bruised myrrh, with cassia, and every sort of spicery except frankincense, and sew up the opening. Then the body is placed in natrum for seventy days, and covered entirely over. After the expiration of that space of time, which must not be exceeded, the body is washed, and wrapped round, from head to foot, with bandages of fine linen cloth, smeared over with gum, which is used generally by the Egyptians in the place of glue, and in this state it is given back to the relations, who enclose it in a wooden case which they have had made for the purpose, shaped into the figure of a man. Then fastening the case, they place it in a sepulchral chamber, upright against the wall. Such is the most costly way of embalming the dead. (II, 80-86)

Till the death of Rhampsinitus, the priests said, Egypt was excellently governed, and flourished greatly; but after him Cheops succeeded to the throne, and plunged into all manner of wickedness. He closed the temples, and forbade the Egyptians to offer sacrifice, compelling them instead to labor, one and all, in his service. Some were required to drag blocks of stone down to the Nile from the quarries in the Arabian range of hills; others received the blocks after they had been conveyed in boats across the river, and drew them to the range of hills called the Libyan. A hundred thousand men labored constantly, and were relieved every three months by a fresh lot. It took ten years' oppression of the people to make the causeway for the conveyance of the stones, a work not much inferior, in my judgment, to the pyramid itself. This causeway is five furlongs in length, ten fathoms wide, and in height, at the highest part, eight fathoms. It is built of polished stone, and is covered with carvings of animals. To make it took ten years, as I said—or rather to make the causeway, the works on the mound where the pyramid stands, and the underground chambers, which Cheops intended as vaults for his own use: these last were built on a sort of island, surrounded by water introduced from the Nile by a canal. The pyramid itself was twenty years in building. It is a square, eight hundred feet each way, and the height the same, built entirely of polished stone, fitted together with the utmost care. The stones of which it is composed are none of them less than thirty feet in length.

The pyramid was built in steps, battlement-wise, as it is called, or, according to others, altar-wise. After laying the stones for the base, they raised the remaining stones to their places by means of machines formed of short wooden planks. The first machine raised them from the ground to the top of the first step.

On this there was another machine, which received the stone upon its arrival, and conveyed it to the second step, whence a third machine advanced it still higher. Either they had as many machines as there were steps in the pyramid, or possibly they had but a single machine, which, being easily moved, was transferred from tier to tier as the stone rose—both accounts are given, and therefore I mention both. The upper portion of the pyramid was finished first, then the middle, and finally the part which was lowest and nearest the ground. There is an inscription in Egyptian characters on the pyramid which records the quantity of radishes, onions, and garlic consumed by the laborers who constructed it; and I perfectly well remember that the interpreter who read the writing to me said that the money expended in this way was 1600 talents of silver. If this then is a true record, what a vast sum must have been spent on the iron tools used in the work, and on the feeding and clothing of the laborers, considering the length of time the work lasted, which has already been stated, and the additional time—no small space, I imagine—which must have been occupied by the quarrying of the stones, their conveyance, and the formation of the underground apartments. (*II, 124-125*)

[*Persian forms of government.*]

. . . Otanes recommended that the management of public affairs should be entrusted to the whole nation. "To me," he said, "it seems advisable that we should no longer have a single man to rule over us—the rule of one is neither good nor pleasant. Ye cannot have forgotten to what lengths Cambyses went in his haughty tyranny; and the haughtiness of the Magi ye yourselves have experienced. How indeed is it possible that monarchy should be a well-adjusted thing, when it allows a man to do as he likes without being answerable? Such license is enough to stir strange and unwonted thoughts in the heart of the worthiest of men. Give a person this power, and straightway his manifold good things puff him up with pride, while envy is so natural to human kind that it cannot but arise in him. But pride and envy together include all wickedness—both of them leading on to deeds of savage violence. True it is that kings, possessing as they do all that heart can desire, ought to be void of envy; but the contrary is seen in their conduct toward the citizens. They are jealous of the most virtuous among their subjects, and wish their death; while they take delight in the meanest and basest, being ever ready to listen to the tales of slanderers. A king, besides, is beyond all other men inconsistent with himself. Pay him court in moderation, and he is angry because you do not show him more profound respect— show him profound respect, and he is offended again, because (as he says) you fawn on him. But the worst of all is, that he sets aside the laws of the land, puts men to death without trial, and subjects women to violence. The rule of the many, on the other hand, has, in the first place, the fairest of names, to wit, *isonomy*; and further, it is free from all those outrages which a king is wont to commit. There, places are given by lot, the magistrate is answerable for what he does, and measures rest with the commonalty. I vote, therefore, that we do away with monarchy, and raise the people to power. For the people are all in all."

Such were the sentiments of Otanes. Megabyzus spoke next, and advised the setting up of an oligarchy:—"In all that Otanes has said to persuade you to put down monarchy," he observed, "I fully concur; but his recommendation that we should call the people to power seems to me not the best advice. For there is nothing so void of understanding, nothing so full of wantonness as the unwieldy rabble. It were folly not to be borne, for men, while seeking to escape the wantonness of a tyrant, to give themselves up to the wantonness of a rude unbridled mob. The tyrant, in all his doings, at least knows what he is about, but a mob is altogether devoid of knowledge; for how should there be any knowledge in a rabble, untaught, and with no natural sense of what is right and fit? It rushes wildly into state affairs with all the fury of a stream swollen in the winter, and confuses everything. Let the enemies of the Persians be ruled by democracies; but let us choose out from the citizens a certain number of the worthiest, and put the government into their hands. For thus both we ourselves shall be among the governors, and power being entrusted to the best men, it is likely that the best counsels will prevail in the state."

This was the advice which Megabyzus gave, and after him Darius came forward, and spoke as follows:—"All that Megabyzus said against democracy was well said, I think; but about oligarchy he did not speak advisedly; for take these three forms of government—democracy, oligarchy, and monarchy—and let them each be at their best, I maintain that monarchy far surpasses the other two. What government can possibly be better than that of the very best man in the whole state? The counsels of such a man are like himself, and so he governs the mass of the people to their heart's content; while at the same time his measures against evildoers are kept more secret than in other states. Contrariwise, in oligarchies, where men vie with each other in the service of the commonwealth, fierce enmities are apt to arise between man and man, each wishing to be leader, and to carry his own measures; whence violent quarrels come, which lead to open strife, often ending in bloodshed. Then monarchy is sure to follow; and this too shows how far that rule surpasses all others. Again, in a democracy, it is impossible but that there will be malpractices. These malpractices, however, do not lead to enmities, but to close friendships, which are formed among those engaged in them, who must hold well together to carry on their villanies. And so things go on until a man stands forth as champion of the commonalty, and puts down the evil-doers. Straightway the author of so great a service is admired by all, and from being admired soon comes to be appointed king; so that here too it is plain that monarchy is the best government. Lastly, to sum up all in a word, whence, I ask, was it that we got the freedom which we enjoy?—did democracy give it us, or oligarchy, or a monarch? As a single man recovered our freedom for us, my sentence is that we keep to the rule of one. Even apart from this, we ought not to change the laws of our forefathers when they work fairly; for to do so is not well."

Such were the three opinions brought forward at this meeting: the four other Persians voted in favor of the last. Otanes, who wished to give his countrymen a democracy, when he found the decision against him, arose a second time, and spoke thus before the assembly:—"Brother conspirators, it is plain that the king who is to be chosen will be one of ourselves, whether we make the choice by casting lots for the prize, or by letting the people decide which of us they will have to rule over them, or in any other way. Now, as I have neither a mind to rule nor to be ruled, I shall not enter the lists with you in this matter. I withdraw, however, on one condition—none of you shall claim to exercise rule over me or my seed for ever." The six agreed to these terms, and Otanes withdrew and stood aloof from the contest. And still to this day the family of Otanes continues to be the only free family in Persia; those who belong to it submit to the rule of the king only so far as they themselves choose; they are bound, however, to observe the laws of the land like the other Persians.

After this the six took council together, as to the fairest way of setting up a king: and first, with respect to Otanes, they resolved, that if any of their own number got the kingdom, Otanes and his seed after him should receive year by year, as a mark of special honor, a Median robe, and all such other gifts as are accounted the most honorable in Persia. And these they resolved to give him, because he was the man who first planned the outbreak, and who brought the seven together. These privileges, therefore, were assigned specially to Otanes. The following were made common to them all:—It was to be free to each, whenever he pleased, to enter the palace unannounced, unless the king were in the company of one of his wives; and the king was to be bound to marry into no family excepting those of the conspirators. Concerning the appointment of a king, the resolve to which they came was the following:—They would ride out together next morning into the skirts of the city, and he whose steed first neighed after the sun was up should have the kingdom. (III, 80-84)

And now, when the morning broke, the six Persians, according to agreement, met together on horseback, and rode out to the suburb. As they went along they neared the spot where the mare was tethered the night before, whereupon the horse of Darius sprang forward and neighed. Just at the same time, though the sky was clear and bright, there was a flash of lightning, followed by a thunder-clap. It seemed as if the heavens conspired with Darius, and hereby inaugurated him king: so the five other nobles leaped with one accord from their steeds, and bowed down before him and owned him for their king. (*III, 86*)

[*The unsuccessful Revolt of Ionia from Persia, 499–494 B.C.*]

On the return of Hippias to Asia from Lacedaemon, he moved heaven and earth to set Artaphernes against the Athenians, and did all that lay in his power to bring Athens into subjection to himself and Darius. So when the Athenians learnt what he was about, they sent envoys to Sardis, and exhorted the Persians not to lend an ear to the Athenian exiles. Artaphernes told them in reply, "that if they wished to remain safe, they must receive back Hippias." The Athenians, when this answer was reported to them, determined not to consent, and therefore made up their minds to be at open enmity with the Persians.

The Athenians had come to this decision, and were already in bad odor with the Persians, when Aristagoras the Milesian, dismissed from Sparta by Cleomenes the Lacedaemonian, arrived at Athens. He knew that, after Sparta, Athens was the most powerful of the Grecian states. Accordingly he appeared before the people, and, as he had done at Sparta, spoke to them of the good things which there were in Asia, and of the Persian mode of fight—how they used neither shield nor spear, and were very easy to conquer. All this he urged, and reminded them also, that Miletus was a colony from Athens, and therefore ought to receive their succor, since they were so powerful—and in the earnestness of his entreaties he cared little what he promised—till, at the last, he prevailed and won them over. It seems indeed to be easier to deceive a multitude than one man—for Aristagoras, though he failed to impose on Cleomenes the Lacedaemonian, succeeded with the Athenians, who were thirty thousand. Won by his persuasions, they voted that twenty ships should be sent to the aid of the Ionians, under the command of Melanthius, one of the citizens, a man of mark in every way. These ships were the beginning of mischief both to the Greeks and to the barbarians. (V, 96-97)

The Athenians now arrived with a fleet of twenty sail, and brought also in their company five triremes of the Eretrians; which had joined the expedition, not so much out of goodwill toward Athens, as to pay a debt which they already owed to the people of Miletus. For in the old war between the Chalcideans and Eretrians, the Milesians fought on the Eretrian side throughout, while the Chalcideans had the help of the Samian people. Aristagoras, on their arrival, assembled the rest of his allies, and proceeded to attack Sardis, not however leading the army in person, but appointing to the command his own brother Charopinus, and Hermophantus, one of the citizens, while he himself remained behind in Miletus.

The Ionians sailed with this fleet to Ephesus, and, leaving their ships at Coressus in the Ephesian territory, took guides from the city, and went up the country, with a great host. They marched along the course of the river Cayster, and, crossing over the ridge of Tmolus, came down upon Sardis and took it, no man opposing them;—the whole city fell into their hands, except only the citadel, which Artaphernes defended in person, having with him no contemptible force.

Though, however, they took the city, they did not succeed in plundering it; for, as the houses in Sardis were most of them built of reeds, and even the few which were of brick had a reed thatching for their roof, one of them was no sooner fired by a soldier than the flames ran speedily from house to house, and spread over the whole place. As the fire raged, the Lydians, and such Persians as were in the city, enclosed on every side by the flames, which had seized all the skirts of the town, and finding themselves unable to get out, came in crowds into the market-place, and gathered themselves upon the banks of the Pactolus. This stream, which comes down from Mount Tmolus, and brings the Sardians a quantity of gold-dust, runs directly through the market-place of Sardis, and joins the Hermus, before that river reaches the sea. So the Lydians and Persians, brought together in this way in the market-place and about the Pactolus, were forced to stand on their defense; and the Ionians, when they saw the enemy in part resisting, in part pouring toward them in dense crowds, took fright, and drawing off to the ridge which is called Tmolus, when night came, went back to their ships.

Sardis however was burnt, and, among other buildings, a temple of the native goddess Cybele was destroyed; which was the reason afterward alleged by the Persians for setting on fire the temples of the Greeks. As soon as what had happened was known, all the Persians who were stationed on this side the Halys drew together, and brought help to the Lydians. Finding however, when they arrived, that the Ionians had already withdrawn from Sardis, they set off, and, following close upon their track, came up with them at Ephesus. The Ionians drew out against them in battle array; and a fight ensued, wherein the Greeks had very greatly the worse. Vast numbers were slain by the Persians: among other men of note, they killed the captain of the Eretrians, a certain Evalcidas, a man who had gained crowns at the games, and received much praise from Simonides the Cean. Such as made their escape from the battle dispersed among the several cities. (V, 99-102)

. . . King Darius received tidings of the taking and burning of Sardis by the Athenians and Ionians; and at the same time he learnt that the author of the league, the man by whom the whole matter had been planned and contrived, was Aristagoras the Milesian. It is said that he no sooner understood what had happened, than, laying aside all thought concerning the Ionians, who would, he was sure, pay dear for their rebellion, he asked, "Who the Athenians were?" and, being informed, called for his bow, and placing an arrow on the string, shot upward into the sky, saying, as he let fly the shaft—"Grant me, Zeus, to revenge myself on the Athenians!" After this speech, he bade one of his servants every day, when his dinner was spread, three times repeat these words to him—"Master, remember the Athenians." (V, 105)

[To punish Eretria, a city-state of Euboea, and Athens for interfering in the Ionian Revolt, a Persian fleet sets off, guided by Hippias, son of the deceased Athenian tyrant, Pisistratus. The Battle of Marathon, 490 B.C.]

. . . Meantime the Persian pursued his own design, from day to day exhorted by his servant to "remember the Athenians," and likewise urged continually by the Pisistratidae, who were ever accusing their countrymen. Moreover it pleased him well to have a pretext for carrying war into Greece, that so he might reduce all those who had refused to give him earth and water. As for Mardonius, since his expedition had succeeded so ill, Darius took the command of the troops from him, and appointed other generals in his stead, who were to lead the host against Eretria and Athens; to wit, Datis, who was by descent a Mede, and Artaphernes, the son of Artaphernes, his own nephew. These men received orders to carry Athens and Eretria away captive, and to bring the prisoners into his presence. (VI, 94)

The Persian fleet now drew near and anchored at Tamynae, Choereae, and Aegilia, three places in the territory of Eretria. Once masters of these posts, they proceeded forthwith to disembark their horses, and made ready to attack the enemy. But the Eretrians were not minded to sally forth and offer battle; their only care, after it had been resolved not to quit the city, was, if possible, to defend their walls. And now the fortress was assaulted in good earnest, and for six days there fell on both sides vast numbers, but on the seventh day Euphorbus, the son of Alcimachus, and Philagrus, the son of Cyneas, who were both citizens of good repute, betrayed the place to the Persians. These were no sooner entered within the walls than they plundered and burnt all the temples that there were in the town, in revenge for the burning of their own temples at Sardis; moreover, they did according to the orders of Darius, and carried away captive all the inhabitants.

The Persians, having thus brought Eretria into subjection after waiting a few days, made sail for Attica, greatly straitening the Athenians as they approached, and thinking to deal with them as they had dealt with the people of Eretria. And, because there was no place in all Attica so convenient for their horse as Marathon, and it lay moreover quite close to Eretria, therefore Hippias, the son of Pisistratus, conducted them thither.

When intelligence of this reached the Athenians, they likewise marched their troops to Marathon, and there stood on the defensive, having at their head ten generals, of whom one was Miltiades. (*VI, 101-103*)

And first, before they left the city, the generals sent off to Sparta a herald, one Pheidippides, who was by birth an Athenian, and by profession and practice a trained runner. This man, according to the account which he gave to the Athenians on his return, when he was near Mount Parthenium, above Tegea, fell in with the god Pan, who called him by his name, and bade him ask the Athenians "wherefore they neglected him so entirely, when he was kindly disposed toward them, and had often helped them in times past, and would do so again in time to come?" The Athenians, entirely believing in the truth of this report, as soon as their affairs were once more in good order, set up a temple to Pan under the Acropolis, and, in return for the message which I have recorded, established in his honor yearly sacrifices and a torch-race.

On the occasion of which we speak, when Pheidippides was sent by the Athenian generals, and, according to his own account, saw Pan on his journey, he reached Sparta on the very next day after quitting the city of Athens. Upon his arrival he went before the rulers, and said to them—

"Men of Lacedaemon, the Athenians beseech you to hasten to their aid, and not allow that state, which is the most ancient in all Greece, to be enslaved by the barbarians. Eretria, look you, is already carried away captive; and Greece weakened by the loss of no mean city."

Thus did Pheidippides deliver the message committed to him. And the Spartans wished to help the Athenians, but were unable to give them any present succor, as they did not like to break their established law. It was then the ninth day of the first decade; and they could not march out of Sparta on the ninth, when the moon had not reached the full. So they waited for the full of the moon.

The barbarians were conducted to Marathon by Hippias, the son of Pisistratus, who the night before had seen a strange vision in his sleep. He dreamt of lying in his mother's arms, and conjectured the dream to mean that he would be restored to Athens, recover the power which he had lost, and afterward live to a good old age in his native country. Such was the sense in which he interpreted the vision. He now proceeded to act as guide to the Persians; and, in the first place, he landed the prisoners taken from Eretria upon the island that is called Aegileia, a tract belonging to the Styreans, after which he brought the fleet to anchor off Marathon, and marshaled the bands of the barbarians as they disembarked. As he was thus employed it chanced that he sneezed and at the same time coughed with more violence than was his wont. Now, as he was a man advanced in years, and the greater number of his teeth were loose, it so happened that one of them was driven out with the force of the cough, and fell down into the sand. Hippias took all the pains he could to find it; but the tooth was nowhere to be seen: whereupon he fetched a deep sigh, and said to the bystanders:

"After all, the land is not ours; and we shall never be able to bring it under. All my share in it is the portion of which my tooth has possession."

So Hippias believed that in this way his dream was out.

The Athenians were drawn up in order of battle in a sacred close belonging to Heracles, when they were joined by the Plataeans, who came in full force to their aid. Some time before, the Plataeans had put themselves under the rule of the Athenians; and these last had already undertaken many labors on their behalf. . . .

The Athenian generals were divided in their opinions; and some advised not to risk a battle, because they were too few to engage such a host as that of the Medes, while others were for fighting at once; and among these last was Miltiades. He therefore, seeing that opinions were thus divided, and that the less worthy counsel appeared likely to prevail, resolved to go to the polemarch, and have a conference with him. For the man on whom the lot fell to be polemarch at Athens was entitled to give his vote with the ten generals, since anciently the Athenians allowed him an equal right of voting with them. The polemarch at this juncture was Callimachus of Aphidnae; to him therefore Miltiades went, and said:—

"With thee it rests, Callimachus, either to bring Athens to

slavery, or, by securing her freedom, to leave behind thee to all future generations a memory beyond even Harmodius and Aristogeiton. For never since the time that the Athenians became a people were they in so great a danger as now. If they bow their necks beneath the yoke of the Medes, the woes which they will have to suffer when given into the power of Hippias are already determined on; if, on the other hand, they fight and overcome, Athens may rise to be the very first city in Greece. How it comes to pass that these things are likely to happen, and how the determining of them in some sort rests with thee, I will now proceed to make clear. We generals are ten in number, and our votes are divided; half of us wish to engage, half to avoid a combat. Now, if we do not fight, I look to see a great disturbance at Athens which will shake men's resolutions, and then I fear they will submit themselves; but if we fight the battle before any unsoundness show itself among our citizens, let the gods but give us fair play, and we are well able to overcome the enemy. On thee therefore we depend in this matter, which lies wholly in thine own power. Thou hast only to add thy vote to my side and thy country will be free, and not free only, but the first state in Greece. Or, if thou preferrest to give thy vote to them who would decline the combat, then the reverse will follow."

Miltiades by these words gained Callimachus; and the addition of the polemarch's vote caused the decision to be in favor of fighting. Hereupon all those generals who had been desirous of hazarding a battle, when their turn came to command the army, gave up their right to Miltiades. He, however, though he accepted their offers, nevertheless waited, and would not fight, until his own day of command arrived in due course.

Then at length, when his own turn was come, the Athenian battle was set in array, and this was the order of it. Callimachus the polemarch led the right wing; for it was at that time a rule with the Athenians to give the right wing to the polemarch. After this followed the tribes, according as they were numbered, in an unbroken line; while last of all came the Plataeans, forming the left wing. And ever since that day it has been a custom with the Athenians, in the sacrifices and assemblies held each fifth year at Athens, for the Athenian herald to implore the blessing of the gods on the Plataeans conjointly with the Athenians. Now, as they marshaled the host upon the field of Marathon, in order that the Athenian front might be of equal length with the Median, the ranks of the center were diminished, and it became the weakest part of the line, while the wings were both made strong with a depth of many ranks.

So when the battle was set in array, and the victims showed themselves favorable, instantly the Athenians, so soon as they were let go, charged the barbarians at a run. Now the distance between the two armies was little short of eight furlongs. The Persians, therefore, when they saw the Greeks coming on at speed, made ready to receive them, although it seemed to them that the Athenians were bereft of their senses, and bent upon their own destruction; for they saw a mere handful of men coming on at a run without either horsemen or archers. Such was the opinion of the barbarians; but the Athenians in close array fell upon them, and fought in a manner worthy of being recorded. They were the first of the Greeks, so far as I know, who introduced the custom of charging the enemy at a run, and they were likewise the first who dared to look upon the Median garb, and to face men clad in that fashion. Until this time the very name of the Medes had been a terror to the Greeks to hear.

The two armies fought together on the plain of Marathon for a length of time; and in the mid battle, where the Persians themselves and the Sacae had their place, the barbarians were victorious, and broke and pursued the Greeks into the inner country; but on the two wings the Athenians and the Plataeans defeated the enemy. Having so done, they suffered the routed barbarians to fly at their ease, and joining the two wings in one, fell upon those who had broken their own center, and fought and conquered them. These likewise fled, and now the Athenians hung upon the runaways and cut them down, chasing them all the way to the shore, on reaching which they laid hold of the ships and called aloud for fire.

It was in the struggle here that Callimachus the polemarch, after greatly distinguishing himself, lost his life; Stesilaus too, the son of Thrasilaus, one of the generals, was slain; and Cynaegirus, the son of Euphorion, having seized on a vessel of the enemy's by the ornament at the stern, had his hand cut off by the blow of an axe, and so perished; as likewise did many other Athenians of note and name.

Nevertheless the Athenians secured in this way seven of the vessels; while with the remainder the barbarians pushed off, and taking aboard their Eretrian prisoners from the island where they had left them, doubled Cape Sunium, hoping to reach Athens before the return of the Athenians. The Alcmaeonidae were accused by their countrymen of suggesting this course to them; they had, it was said, an understanding with the Persians, and made a signal to them, by raising a shield, after they were embarked in their ships.

The Persians accordingly sailed round Sunium. But the Athenians with all possible speed marched away to the defense of their city, and succeeded in reaching Athens before the appearance of the barbarians: and as their camp at Marathon had been pitched in a precinct of Heracles, so now they encamped in another precinct of the same god at Cynosarges. The barbarian fleet arrived, and lay to off Phalerum, which was at that time the haven of Athens; but after resting awhile upon their oars, they departed and sailed away to Asia.

There fell in this battle of Marathon, on the side of the barbarians, about six thousand and four hundred men; on that of the Athenians, one hundred and ninety-two. Such was the number of the slain on the one side and the other. A strange prodigy likewise happened at this fight. Epizelus, the son of Cuphagoras, an Athenian, was in the thick of the fray, and behaving himself as a brave man should, when suddenly he was stricken with blindness, without blow of sword or dart; and this blindness continued thenceforth during the whole of his after life. The following is the account which he himself, as I have heard, gave of the matter: he said that a gigantic warrior, with a huge beard, which shaded all his shield, stood over against him; but the ghostly semblance passed him by, and slew the man at his side. Such, as I understand, was the tale which Epizelus told. (*VI, 105-117*)

After the full of the moon two thousand Lacedaemonians came to Athens. So eager had they been to arrive in time, that they took but three days to reach Attica from Sparta. They came, however, too late for the battle; yet, as they had a longing to behold the Medes, they continued their march to Marathon, and there viewed the slain. Then, after giving the Athenians all praise for their achievement, they departed and returned home. (VI, 120)

[Eulogy of Athens. The Battle of Thermopylae, 480 B.C. The purpose of Leonidas, the Spartan king, was to hold the Pass of Thermopylae until the Greek fleet, under the Athenian general Themistocles, had engaged the Persian fleet at Artemisium, off northern Euboea.]

And here I feel constrained to deliver an opinion which most men, I know, will mislike, but which, as it seems to me to be true, I am determined not to withhold. Had the Athenians, from fear of the approaching danger, quitted their country, or had they without quitting it submitted to the power of Xerxes, there would certainly have been no attempt to resist the Persians by sea; in which case, the course of events by land would have been the following. Though the Peloponnesians might have carried ever so many breastworks across the Isthmus, yet their allies would have fallen off from the Lacedaemonians, not by voluntary desertion, but because town after town must have been taken by the fleet of the barbarians; and so the Lacedaemonians would at last have stood alone, and, standing alone, would have displayed prodigies of valor, and died nobly. Either they would have done thus, or else, before it came to that extremity, seeing one Greek state after another embrace the cause of the Medes, they would have come to terms with King Xerxes; and thus, either way Greece would have been brought under Persia. For I cannot understand of what possible use the walls across the Isthmus could have been, if the King had had the mastery of the sea. If then a man should now say that the Athenians were the saviors of Greece, he would not exceed the truth. For they truly held the scales; and whichever side they espoused must have carried the day. They too it was who, when they had determined to maintain the freedom of Greece, roused up that portion of the Greek nation which had not gone over to the Medes; and so, next to the gods, *they* repulsed the invader. Even the terrible oracles which reached them from Delphi, and struck fear into their hearts, failed to persuade them to fly from Greece. They had the courage to remain faithful to their land, and await the coming of the foe. (*VII, 139*)

King Xerxes pitched his camp in the region of Malis called Trachinia, while on their side the Greeks occupied the straits. These straits the Greeks in general call Thermopylae (the Hot Gates); but the natives, and those who dwell in the neighborhood, call them Pylae (the Gates). Here then the two armies took their stand; the one master of all the region lying north of Trachis, the other of the country extending southward of that place to the verge of the continent.

The Greeks who at this spot awaited the coming of Xerxes were the following:—From Sparta, three hundred men-at-arms: from Arcadia, a thousand Tegeans and Mantineans, five hundred of each people; a hundred and twenty Orchomenians, from the Arcadian Orchomenus; and a thousand from other cities: from Corinth, four hundred men: from Phlius, two hundred: and from Mycenae eighty. Such was the number from the Peloponnese. There were also present, from Boeotia, seven hundred Thespians and four hundred Thebans.

Besides these troops, the Locrians of Opus and the Phocians had obeyed the call of their countrymen, and sent, the former all the force they had, the latter a thousand men. For envoys had gone from the Greeks at Thermopylae among the Locrians and Phocians, to call on them for assistance, and to say—"They were themselves but the vanguard of the host, sent to precede the main body, which might every day be expected to follow them. The sea was in good keeping, watched by the Athenians, the Eginetans, and the rest of the fleet. There was no cause why they should fear; for after all the invader was not a god but a man; and there never had been, and never would be, a man who was not liable to misfortunes from the very day of his birth, and those misfortunes greater in proportion to his own greatness. The assailant therefore, being only a mortal, must needs fall from his glory." Thus urged, the Locrians and the Phocians had come with their troops to Trachis.

The various nations had each captains of their own under whom they served; but the one to whom all especially looked up, and who had the command of the entire force, was the Lacedaemonian, Leonidas. . . .

. . . He had now come to Thermopylae, accompanied by the three hundred men which the law assigned him, whom he had himself chosen from among the citizens, and who were all of them fathers with sons living. On his way he had taken the troops from Thebes, whose number I have already mentioned, and who were under the command of Leontiades, the son of Eurymachus. The reason why he made a point of taking troops from Thebes, and Thebes only, was, that the Thebans were strongly suspected of being well inclined to the Medes. Leonidas therefore called on them to come with him to the war, wishing to see whether they would comply with his demand, or openly refuse, and disclaim the Greek alliance. They, however, though their wishes leant the other way, nevertheless sent the men.

The force with Leonidas was sent forward by the Spartans in advance of their main body, that the sight of them might encourage the allies to fight, and hinder them from going over to the Medes, as it was likely they might have done had they seen that Sparta was backward. They intended presently, when they had celebrated the Carneian festival, which was what now kept them at home, to leave a garrison in Sparta, and hasten in full force to join the army. The rest of the allies also intended to act similarly; for it happened that the Olympic festival fell exactly at this same period. None of them looked to see the contest at Thermopylae decided so speedily; wherefore they were content to send forward a mere advance guard. Such accordingly were the intentions of the allies.

The Greek forces at Thermopylae, when the Persian army drew near to the entrance of the pass, were seized with fear; and a council was held to consider about a retreat. It was the wish of the Peloponnesians generally that the army should fall back upon the Peloponnese, and there guard the Isthmus. But Leonidas, who saw with what indignation the Phocians and Locrians heard of this plan, gave his voice for remaining where they were, while they sent envoys to the several cities to ask for help, since they were too few to make a stand against an army like that of the Medes.

While this debate was going on, Xerxes sent a mounted spy to observe the Greeks, and note how many they were, and see what they were doing. He had heard, before he came out of Thessaly, that a few men were assembled at this place, and that at their head were certain Lacedaemonians, under Leonidas, a descendant of Heracles. The horseman rode up to the camp, and looked about him, but did not see the whole army; for such as were on the further side of the wall (which had been rebuilt and was now carefully guarded) it was not possible for him to behold; but he observed those on the outside, who were encamped in front of the rampart. It chanced that at this time the Lacedaemonians held the outer guard, and were seen by the spy, some of them engaged in gymnastic exercises, others combing their long hair. At this the spy greatly marveled, but he counted their number, and when he had taken accurate note of everything, he rode back quietly; for no one pursued after him, nor paid any heed to his visit. So he returned, and told Xerxes all that he had seen.

Upon this, Xerxes, who had no means of surmising the truth —namely, that the Spartans were preparing to do or die manfully —but thought it laughable that they should be engaged in such employments, sent and called to his presence Demaratus the son of Ariston, who still remained with the army. When he appeared, Xerxes told him all that he had heard, and questioned him concerning the news, since he was anxious to understand the meaning of such behavior on the part of the Spartans. Then Demaratus said:—

"I spake to thee, O King! concerning these men long since, when we had but just begun our march upon Greece; thou, however, didst only laugh at my words, when I told thee of all this, which I saw would come to pass. Earnestly do I struggle at all times to speak truth to thee, sire; and now listen to it once more.

These men have come to dispute the pass with us; and it is for this that they are now making ready. 'Tis their custom, when they are about to hazard their lives, to adorn their heads with care. Be assured, however, that if thou canst subdue the men who are here and the Lacedaemonians who remain in Sparta, there is no other nation in all the world which will venture to lift a hand in their defense. Thou hast now to deal with the first kingdom and town in Greece, and with the bravest men."

Then Xerxes, to whom what Demaratus said seemed altogether to surpass belief, asked further, "how it was possible for so small an army to contend with his?"

"O King!" Demaratus answered, "let me be treated as a liar, if matters fall not out as I say."

But Xerxes was not persuaded any the more. Four whole days he suffered to go by, expecting that the Greeks would run away. When, however, he found on the fifth that they were not gone, thinking that their firm stand was mere impudence and recklessness, he grew wroth, and sent against them the Medes and Cissians, with orders to take them alive and bring them into his presence. Then the Medes rushed forward and charged the Greeks, but fell in vast numbers: others however took the places of the slain, and would not be beaten off, though they suffered terrible losses. In this way it became clear to all, and especially to the King, that though he had plenty of combatants, he had but very few warriors. The struggle, however, continued during the whole day.

Then the Medes, having met so rough a reception, withdrew from the fight; and their place was taken by the band of Persians under Hydarnes, whom the King called his "Immortals": they, it was thought, would soon finish the business. But when they joined battle with the Greeks, 'twas with no better success than the Median detachment—things went much as before—the two armies fighting in a narrow space, and the barbarians using shorter spears than the Greeks, and having no advantage from their numbers. The Lacedaemonians fought in a way worthy of note, and showed themselves far more skillful in fight than their adversaries, often turning their backs, and making as though they

were all flying away, on which the barbarians would rush after
them with much noise and shouting, when the Spartans at their
approach would wheel round and face their pursuers, in this
way destroying vast numbers of the enemy. Some Spartans likewise fell in these encounters, but only a very few. At last the
Persians, finding that all their efforts to gain the pass availed
nothing, and that, whether they attacked by divisions or in any
other way, it was to no purpose, withdrew to their own quarters.

During these assaults, it is said that Xerxes, who was watching
the battle, thrice leaped from the throne on which he sat, in
terror for his army.

Next day the combat was renewed, but with no better success on the part of the barbarians. The Greeks were so few that
the barbarians hoped to find them disabled, by reason of their
wounds, from offering any further resistance; and so they once
more attacked them. But the Greeks were drawn up in detachments according to their cities, and bore the brunt of the battle
in turns,—all except the Phocians, who had been stationed on
the mountain to guard the pathway. So, when the Persians found
no difference between that day and the preceding, they again
retired to their quarters.

Now, as the King was in a great strait, and knew not how he
should deal with the emergency, Ephialtes, the son of Eurydemus,
a man of Malis, came to him and was admitted to a conference.
Stirred by the hope of receiving a rich reward at the King's hands,
he had come to tell him of the pathway which led across the
mountain to Thermopylae; by which disclosure he brought destruction on the band of Greeks who had there withstood the
barbarians. (VII, 201-213)

Great was the joy of Xerxes on this occasion; and as he approved highly of the enterprise which Ephialtes undertook to
accomplish, he forthwith sent upon the errand Hydarnes, and the
Persians under him. The troops left the camp about the time of
the lighting of the lamps. The pathway along which they went
was first discovered by the Malians of these parts, who soon afterward led the Thessalians by it to attack the Phocians, at the time
when the Phocians fortified the pass with a wall, and so put

themselves under covert from danger. And ever since, the path has always been put to an ill use by the Malians. (*VII, 215*)

The Persians took this path, and, crossing the Asopus, continued their march through the whole of the night, having the mountains of Oeta on their right hand, and on their left those of Trachis. At dawn of day they found themselves close to the summit. Now the hill was guarded, as I have already said, by a thousand Phocian men-at-arms, who were placed there to defend the pathway, and at the same time to secure their own country. They had been given the guard of the mountain path, while the other Greeks defended the pass below, because they had volunteered for the service, and had pledged themselves to Leonidas to maintain the post.

The ascent of the Persians became known to the Phocians in the following manner:—During all the time that they were making their way up, the Greeks remained unconscious of it, inasmuch as the whole mountain was covered with groves of oak; but it happened that the air was very still, and the leaves which the Persians stirred with their feet made, as it was likely they would, a loud rustling, whereupon the Phocians jumped up and flew to seize their arms. In a moment the barbarians came in sight, and, perceiving men arming themselves, were greatly amazed; for they had fallen in with an enemy when they expected no opposition. Hydarnes, alarmed at the sight, and fearing lest the Phocians might be Lacedaemonians, inquired of Ephialtes to what nation those troops belonged. Ephialtes told him the exact truth, whereupon he arrayed his Persians for battle. The Phocians, galled by the showers of arrows to which they were exposed, and imagining themselves the special object of the Persian attack, fled hastily to the crest of the mountain, and there made ready to meet death; but while their mistake continued, the Persians, with Ephialtes and Hydarnes, not thinking it worth their while to delay on account of Phocians, passed on and descended the mountain with all possible speed.

The Greeks at Thermopylae received the first warning of the destruction which the dawn would bring on them from the seer Megistias, who read their fate in the victims as he was sacrificing. After this deserters came in, and brought the news that the Persians were marching round by the hills: it was still night when these men arrived. Last of all, the scouts came running down from the heights, and brought in the same accounts, when the day was just beginning to break. Then the Greeks held a council to consider what they should do, and here opinions were divided: some were strong against quitting their post, while others contended to the contrary. So when the council had broken up, part of the troops departed and went their ways homeward to their several states; part however resolved to remain, and to stand by Leonidas to the last.

It is said that Leonidas himself sent away the troops who departed, because he tendered their safety, but thought it unseemly that either he or his Spartans should quit the post which they had been especially sent to guard. For my own part, I incline to think that Leonidas gave the order, because he perceived the allies to be out of heart and unwilling to encounter the danger to which his own mind was made up. He therefore commanded them to retreat, but said that he himself could not draw back with honor; knowing that, if he stayed, glory awaited him, and that Sparta in that case would not lose her prosperity. For when the Spartans, at the very beginning of the war, sent to consult the oracle concerning it, the answer which they received from the Pythoness was, "that either Sparta must be overthrown by the barbarians, or one of her kings must perish." The prophecy was delivered in hexameter verse, and ran thus:—

"O ye men who dwell in the streets of broad Lacedaemon!
 Either your glorious town shall be sacked by the children of Perseus
 Or, in exchange, must all through the whole Laconian country
 Mourn for the loss of a king, descendant of great Heracles.
 HE cannot be withstood by the courage of bulls nor of lions,
 Strive as they may; he is mighty as Zeus; there is nought that shall
    stay him,
 Till he have got for his prey your king, or your glorious city."

The remembrance of this answer, I think, and the wish to secure the whole glory for the Spartans, caused Leonidas to send the allies away. This is more likely than that they quarreled with him, and took their departure in such unruly fashion.

To me it seems no small argument in favor of this view, that the seer also accompanied the army, Megistias, the Acarnanian,— said to have been of the blood of Melampus, and the same who was led by the appearance of the victims to warn the Greeks of the danger which threatened them,—received orders to retire (as it is certain he did) from Leonidas, that he might escape the coming destruction. Megistias, however, though bidden to depart, refused, and stayed with the army; but he had an only son present with the expedition, whom he now sent away.

So the allies, when Leonidas ordered them to retire, obeyed him and forthwith departed. Only the Thespians and the Thebans remained with the Spartans; and of these the Thebans were kept back by Leonidas as hostages, very much against their will. The Thespians, on the contrary, stayed entirely of their own accord, refusing to retreat, and declaring that they would not forsake Leonidas and his followers. So they abode with the Spartans, and died with them. Their leader was Demophilus, the son of Diadromes.

At sunrise Xerxes made libations, after which he waited until the time when the forum is wont to fill, and then began his advance. Ephialtes had instructed him thus, as the descent of the mountain is much quicker, and the distance much shorter, than the way round the hills, and the ascent. So the barbarians under Xerxes began to draw nigh; and the Greeks under Leonidas, as they now went forth determined to die, advanced much further than on previous days, until they reached the more open portion of the pass. Hitherto they had held their station within the wall, and from this had gone forth to fight at the point where the pass was the narrowest. Now they joined battle beyond the defile, and carried slaughter among the barbarians, who fell in heaps. Behind them the captains of the squadrons, armed with whips, urged their men forward with continual blows. Many were thrust into the sea, and there perished; a still greater number were trampled to death by their own soldiers; no one heeded the dying. For the Greeks, reckless of their own safety and desperate, since they knew that, as the mountain had been crossed, their destruction was nigh at hand, exerted themselves with the most furious valor against the barbarians.

By this time the spears of the greater number were all shivered, and with their swords they hewed down the ranks of the Persians; and here, as they strove, Leonidas fell fighting bravely, together with many other famous Spartans, whose names I have taken care to learn on account of their great worthiness, as indeed I have those of all the three hundred. There fell too at the same time very many famous Persians: among them, two sons of Darius, Abrocomes and Hyperanthes, his children by Phratagune, the daughter of Artanes. Artanes was brother of King Darius, being a son of Hystaspes, the son of Arsames; and when he gave his daughter to the King, he made him heir likewise of all his substance; for she was his only child.

Thus two brothers of Xerxes here fought and fell. And now there arose a fierce struggle between the Persians and the Lacedaemonians over the body of Leonidas, in which the Greeks four times drove back the enemy, and at last by their great bravery succeeded in bearing off the body. This combat was scarcely ended when the Persians with Ephialtes approached; and the Greeks, informed that they drew nigh, made a change in the manner of their fighting. Drawing back into the narrowest part of the pass, and retreating even behind the cross wall, they posted themselves upon a hillock, where they stood all drawn up together in one close body, except only the Thebans. The hillock whereof I speak is at the entrance of the straits, where the stone lion stands which was set up in honor of Leonidas. Here they defended themselves to the last, such as still had swords using them, and the others resisting with their hands and teeth; till the barbarians, who in part had pulled down the wall and attacked them in front, in part had gone round and now encircled them upon every side, overwhelmed and buried the remnant which was left beneath showers of missile weapons.

Thus nobly did the whole body of Lacedaemonians and Thespians behave; but nevertheless one man is said to have distinguished himself above all the rest, to wit, Dieneces the Spartan.

A speech which he made before the Greeks engaged the Medes, remains on record. One of the Trachinians told him, "Such was the number of the barbarians, that when they shot forth their arrows the sun would be darkened by their multitude." Dieneces, not at all frightened at these words, but making light of the Median numbers, answered, "Our Trachinian friend brings us excellent tidings. If the Medes darken the sun, we shall have our fight in the shade." Other sayings too of a like nature are reported to have been left on record by this same person.

Next to him two brothers, Lacedaemonians, are reputed to have made themselves conspicuous: they were named Alpheus and Maro, and were the sons of Orsiphantus. There was also a Thespian who gained greater glory than any of his countrymen: he was a man called Dithyrambus, the son of Harmatidas.

The slain were buried where they fell; and in their honor, nor less in honor of those who died before Leonidas sent the allies away, an inscription was set up, which said,—

> "Here did four thousand men from Pelops' land
> Against three hundred myriads bravely stand."

This was in honor of all. Another was for the Spartans alone:—

> "Go, stranger, and to Lacedaemon tell
> That here, obeying her behests, we fell."

This was for the Lacedaemonians. The seer had the following:—

> "The great Megistias' tomb you here may view,
>   Whom slew the Medes, fresh from Spercheius' fords.
> Well the wise seer the coming death foreknew,
>   Yet scorned he to forsake his Spartan lords."

These inscriptions, and the pillars likewise, were all set up by the Amphictyons, except that in honor of Megistias, which was inscribed to him (on account of their sworn friendship) by Simonides, the son of Leoprepes. (*VII, 217-228*)

[*A storm prevented the fleets from coming into decisive action at Artemisium, and Themistocles withdrew toward Athens. The Battle of Salamis, 480 B.C.*]

Meanwhile, the Grecian fleet, which had left Artemisium, proceeded to Salamis, at the request of the Athenians, and there cast anchor. The Athenians had begged them to take up this position, in order that they might convey their women and children out of Attica, and further might deliberate upon the course which it now behoved them to follow. Disappointed in the hopes which they had previously entertained, they were about to hold a council concerning the present posture of their affairs. For they had looked to see the Peloponnesians drawn up in full force to resist the enemy in Boeotia, but found nothing of what they had expected; nay, they learnt that the Greeks of those parts, only concerning themselves about their own safety, were building a wall across the Isthmus, and intended to guard the Peloponnese, and let the rest of Greece take its chance. These tidings caused them to make the request whereof I spoke, that the combined fleet should anchor at Salamis.

So while the rest of the fleet lay to off this island, the Athenians cast anchor along their own coast. Immediately upon their arrival, proclamation was made, that every Athenian should save his children and household as he best could; whereupon some sent their families to Egina, some to Salamis, but the greater number to Troezen. This removal was made with all possible haste, partly from a desire to obey the advice of the oracle, but still more for another reason. The Athenians say that they have in their Acropolis a huge serpent, which lives in the temple, and is the guardian of the whole place. Nor do they only say this, but, as if the serpent really dwelt there, every month they lay out its food, which consists of a honey-cake. Up to this time the honey-cake had always been consumed; but now it remained untouched. So the priestess told the people what had happened; whereupon they left Athens the more readily, since they believed that the goddess had already abandoned the citadel. As soon as all was removed, the Athenians sailed back to their station.

And now, the remainder of the Grecian sea-force, hearing that the fleet which had been at Artemisium was come to Salamis, joined it at that island from Troezen—orders having been issued previously that the ships should muster at Pogon, the port of the

Troezenians. The vessels collected were many more in number than those which had fought at Artemisium, and were furnished by more cities. The admiral was the same who had commanded before, to wit, Eurybiades, the son of Eurycleides, who was a Spartan, but not of the family of the kings: the city, however, which sent by far the greatest number of ships, and the best sailers, was Athens. (*VIII, 40-42*)

Since the passage of the Hellespont and the commencement of the march upon Greece, a space of four months had gone by; one, while the army made the crossing, and delayed about the region of the Hellespont; and three while they proceeded thence to Attica, which they entered in the archonship of Calliades. They found the city forsaken; a few people only remained in the temple, either keepers of the treasures, or men of the poorer sort. These persons, having fortified the citadel with planks and boards, held out against the enemy. It was in some measure their poverty which had prevented them from seeking shelter in Salamis; but there was likewise another reason which in part induced them to remain. They imagined themselves to have discovered the true meaning of the oracle uttered by the Pythoness, which promised that "the wooden wall" should never be taken—the wooden wall, they thought, did not mean the ships, but the place where they had taken refuge.

The Persians encamped upon the hill over against the citadel, which is called Ares' Hill by the Athenians, and began the siege of the place, attacking the Greeks with arrows whereto pieces of lighted tow were attached, which they shot at the barricade. And now those who were within the citadel found themselves in a most woeful case; for their wooden rampart betrayed them; still, however, they continued to resist. It was in vain that the Pisistratidae came to them and offered terms of surrender—they stoutly refused all parley, and among their other modes of defense, rolled down huge masses of stone upon the barbarians as they were mounting up to the gates: so that Xerxes was for a long time very greatly perplexed, and could not contrive any way to take them.

At last, however, in the midst of these many difficulties, the barbarians made discovery of an access. For verily the oracle had spoken truth; and it was fated that the whole mainland of Attica should fall beneath the sway of the Persians. Right in front of the citadel, but behind the gates and the common ascent—where no watch was kept, and no one would have thought it possible that any foot of man could climb—a few soldiers mounted from the sanctuary of Aglaurus, Cecrops' daughter, notwithstanding the steepness of the precipice. As soon as the Athenians saw them upon the summit, some threw themselves headlong from the wall, and so perished; while others fled for refuge to the inner part of the temple. The Persians rushed to the gates and opened them, after which they massacred the suppliants. When all were slain, they plundered the temple, and fired every part of the citadel.

Xerxes, thus completely master of Athens, despatched a horseman to Susa, with a message to Artabanus, informing him of his success hitherto. The day after, he collected together all the Athenian exiles who had come into Greece in his train, and bade them go up into the citadel, and there offer sacrifice after their own fashion. I know not whether he had had a dream which made him give this order, or whether he felt some remorse on account of having set the temple on fire. However this may have been, the exiles were not slow to obey the command given them.

I will now explain why I have made mention of this circumstance: there is a temple of Erechtheus the Earthborn, as he is called, in this citadel, containing within it an olive-tree and a sea. The tale goes among the Athenians that they were placed there as witnesses by Poseidon and Athena, when they had their contention about the country. Now this olive-tree had been burnt with the rest of the temple when the barbarians took the place. But when the Athenians, whom the King had commanded to offer sacrifice, went up into the temple for the purpose, they found a fresh shoot, as much as a cubit in length, thrown out from the old trunk. Such at least was the account which these persons gave.

Meanwhile, at Salamis, the Greeks no sooner heard what had befallen the Athenian citadel, than they fell into such alarm that some of the captains did not even wait for the council to come to a vote, but embarked hastily on board their vessels, and hoisted sail as though they would take to flight immediately. The rest, who stayed at the council board, came to a vote that the fleet should give battle at the Isthmus. . . . (*VIII, 51-56*)

The men belonging to the fleet of Xerxes, after they had seen the Spartan dead at Thermopylae, and crossed the channel from Trachis to Histiaea, waited there by the space of three days, and then sailing down through the Euripus, in three more came to Phalerum. In my judgment, the Persian forces both by land and sea, when they invaded Attica, were not less numerous than they had been on their arrival at Sepias and Thermopylae. For against the Persian loss in the storm and at Thermopylae, and again in the sea-fights off Artemisium, I set the various nations which had since joined the King—as the Malians, the Dorians, the Locrians, and the Boeotians—each serving in full force in his army except the last, who did not number in their ranks either the Thespians or the Plataeans; and together with these, the Carystians, the Andrians, the Tenians, and the other people of the islands, who all fought on this side except the five states already mentioned. For as the Persians penetrated further into Greece, they were joined continually by fresh nations. (*VIII, 66*)

The Greeks at the Isthmus toiled unceasingly, as though in the greatest peril; since they never imagined that any great success would be gained by the fleet. The Greeks at Salamis, on the other hand, when they heard what the rest were about, felt greatly alarmed; but their fear was not so much for themselves as for the Peloponnese. At first they conversed together in low tones, each man with his fellow, secretly, and marveled at the folly shown by Eurybiades; but presently the smothered feeling broke out, and another assembly was held; whereat the old subjects provoked much talk from the speakers, one side maintaining that it was best to sail to the Peloponnese and risk battle for that, instead of abiding at Salamis and fighting for a land already taken by the enemy; while the other, which consisted of the Athenians, Eginetans, and Megarians, was urgent to remain and have the battle fought where they were.

Then Themistocles, when he saw that the Peloponnesians would carry the vote against him, went out secretly from the council, and, instructing a certain man what he should say, sent him on board a merchant ship to the fleet of the Medes. The man's name was Sicinnus; he was one of Themistocles' household slaves, and acted as tutor to his sons; in after times, when the Thespians were admitting persons to citizenship, Themistocles made him a Thespian, and a rich man to boot. The ship brought Sicinnus to the Persian fleet, and there he delivered his message to the leaders in these words:—

"The Athenian commander has sent me to you privily, without the knowledge of the other Greeks. He is a well-wisher to the King's cause, and would rather success should attend on you than on his countrymen; wherefore he bids me tell you that fear has seized the Greeks and they are meditating a hasty flight. Now then it is open to you to achieve the best work that ever ye wrought, if only ye will hinder their escaping. They no longer agree among themselves, so that they will not now make any resistance—nay, 'tis likely ye may see a fight already begun between such as favor and such as oppose your cause." The messenger, when he had thus expressed himself, departed and was seen no more.

Then the captains, believing all that the messenger had said, proceeded to land a large body of Persian troops on the islet of Psyttaleia, which lies between Salamis and the mainland; after which, about the hour of midnight, they advanced their western wing toward Salamis, so as to enclose the Greeks. At the same time the force stationed about Ceos and Cynosura moved forward, and filled the whole strait as far as Munychia with their ships. This advance was made to prevent the Greeks from escaping by flight, and to block them up in Salamis, where it was thought that vengeance might be taken upon them for the battles fought near Artemisium. The Persian troops were landed on the islet of Psyttaleia, because, as soon as the battle began, the men and wrecks were likely to be drifted thither, as the isle lay in the very path of the coming fight,—and they would thus be able to save their own men and destroy those of the enemy. All these movements were made in silence, that the Greeks might have no knowledge of them; and they occupied the whole night, so that the men had no time to get their sleep.

I cannot say that there is no truth in prophecies, or feel inclined to call in question those which speak with clearness, when I think of the following—

"When they shall bridge with their ships to the sacred strand of
    Artemis
 Girt with the golden falchion, and eke to marine Cynosura,
 Mad hope swelling their hearts at the downfall of beautiful Athens—
 Then shall godlike Right extinguish haughty Presumption,
 Insult's furious offspring, who thinketh to overthrow all things.
 Brass with brass shall mingle, and Ares with blood shall empurple
 Ocean's waves. Then—then shall the day of Grecia's freedom
 Come from Victory fair, and Cronus' son all-seeing."

When I look to this, and perceive how clearly Bacis spoke, I neither venture myself to say anything against prophecies, nor do I approve of others impugning them.

Meanwhile, among the captains at Salamis, the strife of words grew fierce. As yet they did not know that they were encompassed, but imagined that the barbarians remained in the same places where they had seen them the day before.

In the midst of their contention, Aristides, the son of Lysimachus, who had crossed from Egina, arrived in Salamis. He was an Athenian, and had been ostracized by the commonalty; yet I believe, from what I have heard concerning his character, that there was not in all Athens a man so worthy or so just as he. He now came to the council, and, standing outside, called for Themistocles. Now Themistocles was not his friend, but his most determined enemy. However, under the pressure of the great dangers impending, Aristides forgot their feud, and called Themistocles out of the council, since he wished to confer with him. He had heard before his arrival of the impatience of the Peloponnesians to withdraw the fleet to the Isthmus. As soon therefore as Themistocles came forth, Aristides addressed him in these words:—

"Our rivalry at all times, and especially at the present season, ought to be a struggle, which of us shall most advantage our country. Let me then say to thee, that so far as regards the departure of the Peloponnesians from this place, much talk and little will be found precisely alike. I have seen with my own eyes that which I now report: that, however much the Corinthians or Eurybiades himself may wish it, they cannot now retreat; for we are enclosed on every side by the enemy. Go in to them, and make this known."

"Thy advice is excellent," answered the other; "and thy tidings are also good. That which I earnestly desire to happen, thine eyes have beheld accomplished. Know that what the Medes have now done was at my instance; for it was necessary, as our men would not fight here of their own free will, to make them fight whether they would or no. But come now, as thou hast brought the good news, go in and tell it. For if I speak to them, they will think it a feigned tale, and will not believe that the barbarians have enclosed us around. Therefore do thou go to them, and inform them how matters stand. If they believe thee, 'twill be for the best; but if otherwise, it will not harm. For it is impossible that they should now flee away, if we are indeed shut in on all sides, as thou sayest."

Then Aristides entered the assembly, and spoke to the captains: he had come, he told them, from Egina, and had but barely escaped the blockading vessels—the Greek fleet was entirely enclosed by the ships of Xerxes—and he advised them to get themselves in readiness to resist the foe. Having said so much, he withdrew. And now another contest arose; for the greater part of the captains would not believe the tidings.

But while they still doubted, a Tenian trireme, commanded by Panaetius the son of Sosimenes, deserted from the Persians and joined the Greeks, bringing full intelligence. For this reason the Tenians were inscribed upon the tripod at Delphi among those who overthrew the barbarians. With this ship, which deserted to their side at Salamis, and the Lemnian vessel which came over before at Artemisium, the Greek fleet was brought to the full number of 380 ships; otherwise it fell short by two of that amount.

The Greeks now, not doubting what the Tenians told them, made ready for the coming fight. At the dawn of day, all the men-at-arms were assembled together, and speeches were made to them, of which the best was that of Themistocles; who throughout contrasted what was noble with what was base, and bade them, in all that came within the range of man's nature and constitution, *always* to make choice of the nobler part. Having thus wound up his discourse, he told them to go at once on board their ships, which they accordingly did; and about this time the trireme, that had been sent to Egina for the Aeacidae, returned; whereupon the Greeks put to sea with all their fleet.

The fleet had scarce left the land when they were attacked by the barbarians. At once most of the Greeks began to back water, and were about touching the shore, when Ameinias of Pallene, one of the Athenian captains, darted forth in front of the line, and charged a ship of the enemy. The two vessels became entangled, and could not separate, whereupon the rest of the fleet came up to help Ameinias, and engaged with the Persians. Such is the account which the Athenians give of the way in which the battle began; but the Eginetans maintain that the vessel which had been to Egina for the Aeacidae, was the one that brought on the fight. It is also reported, that a phantom in the form of a woman appeared to the Greeks, and, in a voice that was heard from end to end of the fleet, cheered them on to the fight; first, however, rebuking them, and saying—"Strange men, how long are ye going to back water?"

Against the Athenians, who held the western extremity of the line toward Eleusis, were placed the Phoenicians; against the Lacedaemonians, whose station was eastward toward the Piraeus, the Ionians. Of these last a few only followed the advice of Themistocles, to fight backwardly; the greater number did far otherwise. I could mention here the names of many trierarchs who took vessels from the Greeks, but I shall pass over all excepting Theomestor, the son of Androdamas, and Phylacus, the son of Histiaeus, both Samians. I show this preference to them, inasmuch as for this service Theomestor was made tyrant of Samos by the Persians, while Phylacus was enrolled among the King's bene-factors, and presented with a large estate in land. In the Persian tongue the King's benefactors are called *Orosangs*.

Far the greater number of the Persian ships engaged in this battle were disabled—either by the Athenians or by the Eginetans. For as the Greeks fought in order and kept their line, while the barbarians were in confusion and had no plan in anything that they did, the issue of the battle could scarce be other than it was. Yet the Persians fought far more bravely here than at Euboea, and indeed surpassed themselves; each did his utmost through fear of Xerxes, for each thought that the King's eye was upon himself.

What part the several nations, whether Greek or barbarian, took in the combat, I am not able to say for certain; Artemisia, however, I know, distinguished herself in such a way as raised her even higher than she stood before in the esteem of the King. For after confusion had spread throughout the whole of the King's fleet, and her ship was closely pursued by an Athenian trireme, she, having no way to fly, since in front of her were a number of friendly vessels, and she was nearest of all the Persians to the enemy, resolved on a measure which in fact proved her safety. Pressed by the Athenian pursuer, she bore straight against one of the ships of her own party, a Calyndian, which had Damasithy-mus, the Calyndian king, himself on board. I cannot say whether she had had any quarrel with the man while the fleet was at the Hellespont, or no—neither can I decide whether she of set purpose attacked his vessel, or whether it merely chanced that the Ca-lyndian ship came in her way—but certain it is, that she bore down upon his vessel and sank it, and that thereby she had the good fortune to procure herself a double advantage. For the com-mander of the Athenian trireme, when he saw her bear down on one of the enemy's fleet, thought immediately that her vessel was a Greek, or else had deserted from the Persians, and was now fighting on the Greek side; he therefore gave up the chase, and turned away to attack others.

Thus in the first place she saved her life by the action, and was enabled to get clear off from the battle; while further, it fell out that in the very act of doing the King an injury she raised herself to a greater height than ever in his esteem. For as Xerxes beheld the fight, he remarked (it is said) the destruction of the vessel, whereupon the bystanders observed to him—"Seest thou, master, how well Artemisia fights, and how she has just sunk a ship of the enemy?" Then Xerxes asked if it were really Artemisia's doing; and they answered, "Certainly; for they knew her ensign": while all made sure that the sunken vessel belonged to the opposite side. Everything, it is said, conspired to prosper the queen—it was especially fortunate for her that not one of those on board the Calyndian ship survived to become her accuser. Xerxes, they say, in reply to the remarks made to him, observed—"My men have behaved like women, my women like men!"

There fell in this combat Ariabignes, one of the chief commanders of the fleet, who was son of Darius and brother of Xerxes; and with him perished a vast number of men of high repute, Persians, Medes, and allies. Of the Greeks there died only a few; for, as they were able to swim, all those that were not slain outright by the enemy escaped from the sinking vessels and swam across to Salamis. But on the side of the barbarians more perished by drowning than in any other way, since they did not know how to swim. The great destruction took place when the ships which had been first engaged began to fly; for they who were stationed in the rear, anxious to display their valor before the eyes of the King, made every effort to force their way to the front, and thus became entangled with such of their own vessels as were retreating.

In this confusion the following event occurred: Certain Phoenicians belonging to the ships which had thus perished made their appearance before the King, and laid the blame of their loss on the Ionians, declaring that they were traitors, and had willfully destroyed the vessels. But the upshot of this complaint was that the Ionian captains escaped the death which threatened them, while their Phoenician accusers received death as their reward. For it happened that, exactly as they spoke, a Samothracian vessel bore down on an Athenian and sank it, but was attacked and crippled immediately by one of the Eginetan squadron. Now the

Samothracians were expert with the javelin, and aimed their weapons so well, that they cleared the deck of the vessel which had disabled their own, after which they sprang on board, and took it. This saved the Ionians. Xerxes, when he saw the exploit, turned fiercely on the Phoenicians—(he was ready, in his extreme vexation, to find fault with any one)—and ordered their heads to be cut off, to prevent them, he said, from casting the blame of their own misconduct upon braver men. During the whole time of the battle Xerxes sat at the base of the hill called Aegaleos, over against Salamis; and whenever he saw any of his own captains perform any worthy exploit he inquired concerning him; and the man's name was taken down by his scribes, together with the names of his father and his city. Ariaramnes too, a Persian, who was a friend of the Ionians, and present at the time whereof I speak, had a share in bringing about the punishment of the Phoenicians.

When the rout of the barbarians began, and they sought to make their escape to Phalerum, the Eginetans, awaiting them in the channel, performed exploits worthy to be recorded. Through the whole of the confused struggle the Athenians employed themselves in destroying such ships as either made resistance or fled to shore, while the Eginetans dealt with those which endeavored to escape down the strait; so that the Persian vessels were no sooner clear of the Athenians than forthwith they fell into the hands of the Eginetan squadron.

It chanced here that there was a meeting between the ship of Themistocles, which was hasting in pursuit of the enemy, and that of Polycritus, son of Crius the Eginetan, which had just charged a Sidonian trireme. The Sidonian vessel was the same that captured the Eginetan guard-ship off Sciathus, which had Pytheas, the son of Ischenous, on board—that Pytheas, I mean, who fell covered with wounds, and whom the Sidonians kept on board their ship, from admiration of his gallantry. This man afterward returned in safety to Egina; for when the Sidonian vessel with its Persian crew fell into the hands of the Greeks, he was still found on board. Polycritus no sooner saw the Athenian trireme than, knowing at once whose vessel it was, as he observed that it bore the ensign of the admiral, he shouted to Themistocles jeeringly, and asked him, in a tone of reproach, if the Eginetans did not show themselves rare friends to the Medes. At the same time, while he thus reproached Themistocles, Polycritus bore straight down on the Sidonian. Such of the barbarian vessels as escaped from the battle fled to Phalerum, and there sheltered themselves under the protection of the land army.

The Greeks who gained the greatest glory of all in the sea-fight of Salamis were the Eginetans, and after them the Athenians. The individuals of most distinction were Polycritus the Eginetan, and two Athenians, Eumenes of Anagyrus, and Ameinias of Pallene; the latter of whom had pressed Artemisia so hard. And assuredly, if he had known that the vessel carried Artemisia on board, he would never have given over the chase till he had either succeeded in taking her, or else been taken himself. For the Athenian captains had received special orders touching the queen; and moreover, a reward of ten thousand drachmas had been proclaimed for anyone who should make her prisoner, since there was great indignation felt that a woman should appear in arms against Athens. However, as I said before, she escaped; and so did some others whose ships survived the engagement; and these were all now assembled at the port of Phalerum.

The Athenians say that Adeimantus, the Corinthian commander, at the moment when the two fleets joined battle, was seized with fear, and being beyond measure alarmed, spread his sails, and hasted to fly away; on which the other Corinthians, seeing their leader's ship in full flight, sailed off likewise. They had reached in their flight that part of the coast of Salamis where stands the temple of Athena Sciras, when they met a light bark, a very strange apparition: it was never discovered that any one had sent it to them; and till it appeared they were altogether ignorant how the battle was going. That there was something beyond nature in the matter they judged from this—that when the men in the bark drew near to their ships, they addressed them, saying—"Adeimantus, while thou playest the traitor's part, by withdrawing all these ships, and flying away from the fight, the Greeks whom thou hast deserted are defeating their foes as completely as they ever wished in their prayers." Adeimantus, however, would not believe what the men said; whereupon they told him, "he might take them with him as hostages, and put them to death if he did not find the Greeks winning." Then Adeimantus put about, both he and those who were with him; and they rejoined the fleet when the victory was already gained. Such is the tale which the Athenians tell concerning them of Corinth; these latter, however, do not allow its truth. On the contrary, they declare that they were among those who distinguished themselves most in the fight. And the rest of Greece bears witness in their favor.

In the midst of the confusion Aristides, the son of Lysimachus, the Athenian, of whom I lately spoke as a man of the greatest excellence, performed the following service. He took a number of the Athenian heavy-armed troops, who had previously been stationed along the shore of Salamis, and, landing with them on the islet of Psyttaleia, slew all the Persians by whom it was occupied.

As soon as the sea-fight was ended, the Greeks drew together to Salamis all the wrecks that were to be found in that quarter, and prepared themselves for another engagement, supposing that the King would renew the fight with the vessels which still remained to him. Many of the wrecks had been carried away by a westerly wind to the coast of Attica, where they were thrown upon the strip of shore called Colias. Thus not only were the prophecies of Bacis and Musaeus concerning this battle fulfilled completely, but likewise, by the place to which the wrecks were drifted, the prediction of Lysistratus, an Athenian soothsayer, uttered many years before these events, and quite forgotten at the time by all the Greeks, was fully accomplished. The words were—

"Then shall the sight of the oars fill Colian dames with amazement."

Now this must have happened as soon as the King was departed.

Xerxes, when he saw the extent of his loss, began to be afraid lest the Greeks might be counseled by the Ionians, or without their advice might determine, to sail straight to the Hellespont and break down the bridges there; in which case he would be blocked up in Europe, and run great risk of perishing. He therefore made up his mind to fly; but as he wished to hide his purpose alike from the Greeks and from his own people, he set to work to carry a mound across the channel to Salamis, and at the same time began fastening a number of Phoenician merchant ships together, to serve at once for a bridge and a wall. He likewise made many warlike preparations, as if he were about to engage the Greeks once more at sea. Now, when these things were seen, all grew fully persuaded that the King was bent on remaining, and intended to push the war in good earnest. Mardonius, however, was in no respect deceived; for long acquaintance enabled him to read all the King's thoughts. Meanwhile, Xerxes, though engaged in this way, sent off a messenger to carry intelligence of his misfortune to Persia.

Nothing mortal travels so fast as these Persian messengers. The entire plan is a Persian invention; and this is the method of it. Along the whole line of road there are men (they say) stationed with horses, in number equal to the number of days which the journey takes, allowing a man and horse to each day; and these men will not be hindered from accomplishing at their best speed the distance which they have to go, either by snow, or rain, or heat, or by the darkness of night. The first rider delivers his dispatch to the second, and the second passes it to the third; and so it is borne from hand to hand along the whole line, like the light in the torch-race, which the Greeks celebrate to Hephaestus. The Persians give the riding post in this manner, the name of "Angarum."

At Susa, on the arrival of the first message, which said that Xerxes was master of Athens, such was the delight of the Persians who had remained behind that they forthwith strewed all the streets with myrtle boughs, and burnt incense, and fell to feasting and merriment. In like manner, when the second message reached them, so sore was their dismay that they all with one accord rent their garments, and cried aloud, and wept and wailed without

stint. They laid the blame of the disaster on Mardonius; and
their grief on the occasion was less on account of the damage
done to their ships than owing to the alarm which they felt about
the safety of the King. Hence their trouble did not cease till
Xerxes himself, by his arrival, put an end to their fears. (*VIII,*
74-99)

THUCYDIDES

Translated by Benjamin Jowett

THE PELOPONNESIAN WAR

Introduction. The early history of Greece. The background of the Peloponnesian War. The congress at Sparta. The resources and strategy of the combatants. Pericles' Funeral Oration. Plague at Athens. An estimate of Pericles. The debate on Mytilene. Revolution at Corcyra. The Melian Dialogue. The Sicilian Expedition. The sea battle at Syracuse, retreat by land, and end of the Expedition.

[*Introduction. The early history of Greece.*]

Thucydides, an Athenian, wrote the history of the war in which the Peloponnesians and the Athenians fought against one another. He began to write when they first took up arms, believing that it would be great and memorable above any previous war. For he argued that both states were then at the full height of their military power, and he saw the rest of the Hellenes either siding or intending to side with one or other of them. No movement ever stirred Hellas more deeply than this; it was shared by many of the Barbarians, and might be said even to affect the world at large. The character of the events which preceded, whether immediately or in more remote antiquity, owing to the lapse of time cannot be made out with certainty. But, judging from the evidence which I am able to trust after most careful inquiry, I should imagine that former ages were not great either in their wars or in anything else.

The country which is now called Hellas was not regularly settled in ancient times. The people were migratory, and readily left their homes whenever they were overpowered by numbers.

There was no commerce, and they could not safely hold intercourse with one another either by land or sea. The several tribes cultivated their own soil just enough to obtain a maintenance from it. But they had no accumulations of wealth, and did not plant the ground; for, being without walls, they were never sure that an invader might not come and despoil them. Living in this manner and knowing that they could anywhere obtain a bare subsistence, they were always ready to migrate; so that they had neither great cities nor any considerable resources. The richest districts were most constantly changing their inhabitants; for example, the countries which are now called Thessaly and Boeotia, the greater part of the Peloponnesus with the exception of Arcadia, and all the best parts of Hellas. For the productiveness of the land increased the power of individuals; this in turn was a source of quarrels by which communities were ruined, while at the same time they were more exposed to attacks from without. Certainly Attica, of which the soil was poor and thin, enjoyed a long freedom from civil strife, and therefore retained its original inhabitants. And a striking confirmation of my argument is afforded by the fact that Attica through immigration increased in population more than any other region. For the leading men of Hellas, when driven out of their own country by war or revolution, sought an asylum at Athens; and from the very earliest times, being admitted to rights of citizenship, so greatly increased the number of inhabitants that Attica became incapable of containing them, and was at last obliged to send out colonies to Ionia.

The feebleness of antiquity is further proved to me by the circumstance that there appears to have been no common action in Hellas before the Trojan War. And I am inclined to think that the very name was not as yet given to the whole country, and in fact did not exist at all before the time of Hellen, the son of Deucalion; the different tribes, of which the Pelasgian was the most widely spread, gave their own names to different districts. But when Hellen and his sons became powerful in Phthiotis, their aid was invoked by other cities, and those who associated with them gradually began to be called Hellenes, though a long time elapsed before the name prevailed over the whole country.

Of this Homer affords the best evidence; for he, although he lived long after the Trojan War, nowhere uses this name collectively, but confines it to the followers of Achilles from Phthiotis, who were the original Hellenes; when speaking of the entire host he calls them Danaäns, or Argives, or Achaeans. Neither is there any mention of Barbarians in his poems, clearly because there were as yet no Hellenes opposed to them by a common distinctive name. Thus the several Hellenic tribes (and I mean by the term Hellenes those who, while forming separate communities, had a common language, and were afterward called by a common name), owing to their weakness and isolation, were never united in any great enterprise before the Trojan War. And they only made the expedition against Troy after they had gained considerable experience of the sea.

Minos is the first to whom tradition ascribes the possession of a navy. He made himself master of a great part of what is now termed the Hellenic sea; he conquered the Cyclades, and was the first colonizer of most of them, expelling the Carians and appointing his own sons to govern in them. Lastly, it was he who, from a natural desire to protect his growing revenues, sought, as far as he was able, to clear the sea of pirates.

For in ancient times both the Hellenes, and those Barbarians, whose homes were on the coast of the mainland or in islands, when they began to find their way to one another by sea had recourse to piracy. They were commanded by powerful chiefs, who took this means of increasing their wealth and providing for their poorer followers. They would fall upon the unwalled and straggling towns, or rather villages, which they plundered, and maintained themselves chiefly by the plunder of them; for, as yet, such an occupation was held to be honorable and not disgraceful. This is proved by the practice of certain tribes on the mainland who, to the present day, glory in piratical exploits, and by the witness of the ancient poets, in whose verses the question is invariably asked of newly-arrived voyagers, whether they are pirates; which implies that neither those who are questioned disclaim, nor those who are interested in knowing censure the occupation. On land also neighboring communities plundered each other; and there are many parts of Hellas in which the old practices still continue, as for example among the Ozolian Locrians, Aetolians, Acarnanians, and the adjacent regions of the continent. The fashion of wearing arms among these continental tribes is a relic of their old predatory habits. For in ancient times all Hellenes carried weapons because their homes were undefended and intercourse was unsafe; like the Barbarians they went armed in their every-day life. And the continuance of the custom in certain parts of the country indicates that it once prevailed everywhere.

The Athenians were the first who laid aside arms and adopted an easier and more luxurious way of life. Quite recently the old-fashioned refinement of dress still lingered among the elder men of their richer class, who wore under-garments of linen, and bound back their hair in a knot with golden clasps in the form of grass-hoppers; and the same customs long survived among the elders of Ionia, having been derived from their Athenian ancestors. On the other hand, the simple dress which is now common was first worn at Sparta; and there, more than anywhere else, the life of the rich was assimilated to that of the people. The Lacedaemonians too were the first who in their athletic exercises stripped naked and rubbed themselves over with oil. But this was not the ancient custom; athletes formerly, even when they were contending at Olympia, wore girdles about their loins, a practice which lasted until quite lately, and still prevails among Barbarians, especially those of Asia, where the combatants in boxing and wrestling matches wear girdles. And many other customs which are now confined to the Barbarians might be shown to have existed formerly in Hellas.

In later times, when navigation had become general and wealth was beginning to accumulate, cities were built upon the sea-shore and fortified; peninsulas too were occupied and walled-off with a view to commerce and defense against the neighboring tribes. But the older towns both in the islands and on the con-tinent, in order to protect themselves against the piracy which so long prevailed, were built inland; and there they remain to this day. For the piratical tribes plundered, not only one another, but all those who, without being seamen, lived on the sea-coast. (*I, 1-7*)

As Hellas grew more powerful and the acquisition of wealth became more and more rapid, the revenues of her cities increased, and in most of them tyrannies were established; they had hitherto been ruled by hereditary kings, having fixed prerogatives. The Hellenes likewise began to build navies and to make the sea their element. The Corinthians are said to have first adopted something like the modern style of marine, and the oldest Hellenic triremes to have been constructed at Corinth. A Corinthian ship-builder, Ameinocles, appears to have built four ships for the Samians; he went to Samos about three hundred years before the end of the Peloponnesian War. And the earliest naval engagement on record is that between the Corinthians and Corcyraeans which occurred about forty years later. Corinth, being seated on an isthmus, was naturally from the first a center of commerce; for the Hellenes within and without the Peloponnese in the old days, when they communicated chiefly by land, had to pass through her territory in order to reach one another. Her wealth too was a source of power, as the ancient poets testify, who speak of "Corinth the rich." When navigation grew more common, the Corinthians, having already acquired a fleet, were able to put down piracy; they offered a market both by sea and land, and with the increase of riches the power of their city increased yet more. Later, in the time of Cyrus, the first Persian king, and of Cambyses his son, the Ionians had a large navy; they fought with Cyrus, and were for a time masters of the sea around their own coasts. Polycrates, too, who was a tyrant of Samos in the reign of Cambyses, had a powerful navy and subdued several of the islands, among them Rhenea, which he dedicated to the Delian Apollo. And the Phocaeans, when they were colonizing Massalia, defeated the Carthaginians on the sea.

These were the most powerful navies, and even these, which came into existence many generations after the Trojan War, appear to have consisted chiefly of fifty-oared vessels and galleys of war, as in the days of Troy; as yet triremes were not common. But a little before the Persian War and the death of Darius, who succeeded Cambyses, the Sicilian tyrants and the Corcyraeans had them in considerable numbers. No other maritime powers of any consequence arose in Hellas before the expedition of Xerxes. The Aeginetans, Athenians, and a few more had small fleets, and these mostly consisted of fifty-oared vessels. Even the ships which the Athenians built quite recently at the instigation of Themistocles, when they were at war with the Aeginetans and in expectation of the Barbarian, even these ships with which they fought at Salamis were not completely decked.

So inconsiderable were the Hellenic navies in recent as well as in more ancient times. And yet those who applied their energies to the sea obtained a great accession of strength by the increase of their revenues and the extension of their dominion. For they attacked and subjugated the islands, especially when the pressure of population was felt by them. Whereas by land, no conflict of any kind which brought increase of power ever occurred; what wars they had were mere border feuds. Foreign and distant expeditions of conquest the Hellenes never undertook; for they were not as yet ranged under the command of the great states, nor did they form voluntary leagues or make expeditions on an equal footing. Their wars were only the wars of the several neighboring tribes with one another. The conflict in which the rest of Hellas was most divided, allying itself with one side or the other, was the ancient war between the Chalcidians and Eretrians.

There were different impediments to the progress of the different states. The Ionians had attained great prosperity when Cyrus and the Persians, having overthrown Croesus and subdued the countries between the river Halys and the sea, made war against them and enslaved the cities on the mainland. Some time afterward, Darius, strong in the possession of the Phoenician fleet, conquered the islands also.

Nor again did the tyrants of the Hellenic cities extend their thoughts beyond their own interest, that is, the security of their persons, and the aggrandizement of themselves and their families. They were extremely cautious in the administration of their government, and nothing considerable was ever effected by them; except in wars with their neighbors, as in Sicily, where their power attained its greatest height. Thus for a long time everything conspired to prevent Hellas from uniting in any great action and to paralyze enterprise in the individual states.

At length the tyrants both at Athens and in the rest of Hellas (which had been under their dominion long before Athens), at least the greater number of them, and with the exception of the Sicilian the last who ever ruled, were put down by the Lacedaemonians. For although Lacedaemon, after the conquest of the country by the Dorians who now inhabit it, remained long unsettled, and indeed longer than any country which we know, nevertheless she obtained good laws at an earlier period than any other, and has never been subject to tyrants; she has preserved the same form of government for rather more than four hundred years, reckoning to the end of the Peloponnesian War. It was the excellence of her constitution which gave her power, and thus enabled her to regulate the affairs of other states. Not long after the overthrow of the tyrants by the Lacedaemonians, the battle of Marathon was fought between the Athenians and the Persians; ten years later, the Barbarian returned with the vast armament which was to enslave Hellas. In the greatness of the impending danger, the Lacedaemonians, who were the most powerful state in Hellas, assumed the lead of the confederates, while the Athenians, as the Persian host advanced, resolved to forsake their city, broke up their homes, and, taking to their ships, became seamen. The Barbarian was repelled by a common effort; but soon the Hellenes, as well those who had revolted from the King as those who formed the original confederacy, took different sides and became the allies either of the Athenians or of the Lacedaemonians; for these were now the two leading powers, the one strong by land and the other by sea. The league between them was of short duration; they speedily quarreled and, with their respective allies, went to war. Any of the other Hellenes who had differences of their own now resorted to one or other of them. So that from the Persian to the Peloponnesian War, the Lacedaemonians and the Athenians were perpetually fighting or making peace, either with one another or with their own revolted allies; thus they attained military efficiency, and learned experience in the school of danger.

The Lacedaemonians did not make tributaries of those who acknowledged their leadership, but took care that they should be governed by oligarchies in the exclusive interest of Sparta. The Athenians, on the other hand, after a time deprived the subject cities of their ships and made all of them pay a fixed tribute, except Chios and Lesbos. And the single power of Athens at the beginning of this war was greater than that of Athens and Sparta together at their greatest, while the confederacy remained intact.

Such are the results of my inquiries, though the early history of Hellas is of a kind which forbids implicit reliance on every particular of the evidence. Men do not discriminate, and are too ready to receive ancient traditions about their own as well as about other countries. . . . There are many other matters, not obscured by time, but contemporary, about which the other Hellenes are equally mistaken. . . . So little trouble do men take in the search after truth; so readily do they accept whatever comes first to hand.

Yet any one who upon the grounds which I have given arrives at some such conclusion as my own about those ancient times, would not be far wrong. He must not be misled by the exaggerated fancies of the poets, or by the tales of chroniclers who seek to please the ear rather than to speak the truth. Their accounts cannot be tested by him; and most of the facts in the lapse of ages have passed into the region of romance. At such a distance of time he must make up his mind to be satisfied with conclusions resting upon the clearest evidence which can be had. And, though men will always judge any war in which they are actually fighting to be the greatest at the time, but, after it is over, revert to their admiration of some other which has preceded, still the Peloponnesian, if estimated by the actual facts, will certainly prove to have been the greatest ever known.

As to the speeches which were made either before or during the war, it was hard for me, and for others who reported them to me, to recollect the exact words. I have therefore put into the mouth of each speaker the sentiments proper to the occasion, expressed as I thought he would be likely to express them, while at the same time I endeavored, as nearly as I could, to give the general purport of what was actually said. Of the events of the war I have not ventured to speak from any chance information, nor according to any notion of my own; I have described nothing but what I either saw myself, or learned from others of whom I made the most careful and particular inquiry. The task was a laborious one, because eye-witnesses of the same occurrences gave different accounts of them, as they remembered or were interested in the actions of one side or the other. And very likely the strictly historical character of my narrative may be disappointing to the ear. But if he who desires to have before his eyes a true picture of the events which have happened, and of the like events which may be expected to happen hereafter in the order of human things, shall pronounce what I have written to be useful, then I shall be satisfied. My history is an everlasting possession, not a prize composition which is heard and forgotten.

The greatest achievement of former times was the Persian War; yet even this was speedily decided in two battles by sea and two by land. But the Peloponnesian War was a protracted struggle, and attended by calamities such as Hellas had never known within a like period of time. Never were so many cities captured and depopulated—some by Barbarians, others by Hellenes themselves fighting against one another; and several of them after their capture were repeopled by strangers. Never were exile and slaughter more frequent, whether in the war or brought about by civil strife. And traditions which had often been current before, but rarely verified by fact, were now no longer doubted. For there were earthquakes unparalleled in their extent and fury, and eclipses of the sun more numerous than are recorded to have happened in any former age; there were also in some places great droughts causing famines, and lastly the plague which did immense harm and destroyed numbers of the people. All these calamities fell upon Hellas simultaneously with the war, which began when the Athenians and Peloponnesians violated the thirty years' truce concluded by them after the recapture of Euboea. Why they broke it and what were the grounds of quarrel I will first set forth, that in time to come no man may be at a loss to know what was the origin of this great war. The real though unavowed cause I believe to have been the growth of the Athenian power, which terrified the Lacedaemonians and forced them into war; but the reasons publicly alleged on either side were as follows. (*I, 13-23*)

[*The background of the Peloponnesian War, 431–404* B.C. *The congress at Sparta.*]

Such were the causes of ill-feeling which at this time existed between the Athenians and Peloponnesians: the Corinthians complaining that the Athenians were blockading their colony of Potidaea, and a Corinthian and Peloponnesian garrison in it; the Athenians rejoining that a member of the Peloponnesian confederacy had excited to revolt a state which was an ally and tributary of theirs, and that they had now openly joined the Potidaeans, and were fighting on their side. The Peloponnesian war, however, had not yet broken out; the peace still continued; for thus far the Corinthians had acted alone.

But now, seeing Potidaea besieged, they bestirred themselves in earnest. Corinthian troops were shut up within the walls, and they were afraid of losing the town; so without delay they invited the allies to meet at Sparta. There they inveighed against the Athenians, whom they affirmed to have broken the treaty and to be wronging the Peloponnese. The Aeginetans did not venture to send envoys openly, but secretly they acted with the Corinthians, and were among the chief instigators of the war, declaring that they had been robbed of the independence which the treaty guaranteed them. The Lacedaemonians themselves then proceeded to summon any of the allies who had similar charges to bring against the Athenians, and calling their own ordinary assembly told them to speak. Several of them came forward and stated their wrongs. The Megarians alleged, among other grounds of complaint, that they were excluded from all harbors within the Athenian dominion and from the Athenian market, contrary to the treaty. The Corinthians waited until the other allies had stirred up the Lacedaemonians; at length they came forward, and, last of all, spoke as follows:—

"The spirit of trust, Lacedaemonians, which animates your own political and social life, makes you distrust others who, like ourselves, have something unpleasant to say, and this temper of mind, though favorable to moderation, too often leaves you in ignorance of what is going on outside your own country. Time after time we have warned you of the mischief which the Athenians would do to us, but instead of taking our words to heart, you chose to suspect that we only spoke from interested motives. And this is the reason why you have brought the allies to Sparta too late, not before but after the injury has been inflicted, and when they are smarting under the sense of it. Which of them all has a better right to speak than ourselves, who have the heaviest accusations to make, outraged as we are by the Athenians, and neglected by you? If the crimes which they are committing against Hellas were being done in a corner, then you might be ignorant, and we should have to inform you of them: but now, what need of many words? Some of us, as you see, have been already enslaved; they are at this moment intriguing against others, notably against allies of ours; and long ago they had made all their preparations in the prospect of war. Else why did they seduce from her allegiance Corcyra, which they still hold in defiance of us, and why are they blockading Potidaea, the latter a most advantageous post for the command of the Thracian peninsula, the former a great naval power which might have assisted the Peloponnesians?

"And the blame of all this rests on you; for you originally allowed them to fortify their city after the Persian War, and afterward to build their Long Walls; and to this hour you have gone on defrauding of liberty their unfortunate subjects, and are now beginning to take it away from your own allies. For the true enslaver of a people is he who can put an end to their slavery but has no care about it; and all the more, if he be reputed the champion of liberty in Hellas.—And so we have met at last, but with what difficulty! and even now we have no definite object. By this time we ought to have been considering, not whether we are wronged, but how we are to be revenged. The aggressor is not now threatening, but advancing; he has made up his mind, while we are resolved about nothing. And we know too well how by slow degrees

and with stealthy steps the Athenians encroach upon their neighbors. While they think that you are too dull to observe them, they
are more careful, but, when they know that you willfully overlook
their aggressions, they will strike and not spare. Of all Hellenes,
Lacedaemonians, you are the only people who never do anything:
on the approach of an enemy you are content to defend yourselves
against him, not by acts, but by intentions, and seek to overthrow
him, not in the infancy but in the fullness of his strength. How
came you to be considered safe? That reputation of yours was never
justified by facts. We all know that the Persian made his way
from the ends of the earth against Peloponnesus before you encountered him in a worthy manner; and now you are blind to the
doings of the Athenians, who are not at a distance as he was, but
close at hand. Instead of attacking your enemy, you wait to be
attacked, and take the chances of a struggle which has been deferred until his power is doubled. And you know that the Barbarian miscarried chiefly through his own errors; and that we
have oftener been delivered from these very Athenians by blunders
of their own, than by any aid from you. Some have already been
ruined by the hopes which you inspired in them; for so entirely did
they trust you that they took no precautions themselves. These
things we say in no accusing or hostile spirit—let that be understood—but by way of expostulation. For men expostulate with
erring friends, they bring accusation against enemies who have
done them a wrong.

"And surely we have a right to find fault with our neighbors,
if any one ever had. There are important interests at stake to
which, as far as we can see, you are insensible. And you have
never considered what manner of men are these Athenians with
whom you will have to fight, and how utterly unlike yourselves.
They are revolutionary, equally quick in the conception and in the
execution of every new plan; while you are conservative—careful
only to keep what you have, originating nothing, and not acting
even when action is most urgent. They are bold beyond their
strength; they run risks which prudence would condemn; and in
the midst of misfortune they are full of hope. Whereas it is your
nature, though strong, to act feebly; when your plans are most

prudent, to distrust them; and when calamities come upon you, to think that you will never be delivered from them. They are impetuous, and you are dilatory; they are always abroad, and you are always at home. For they hope to gain something by leaving their homes; but you are afraid that any new enterprise may imperil what you have already. When conquerors, they pursue their victory to the utmost; when defeated, they fall back the least. Their bodies they devote to their country as though they belonged to other men; their true self is their mind, which is most truly their own when employed in her service. When they do not carry out an intention which they have formed, they seem to themselves to have sustained a personal bereavement; when an enterprise succeeds, they have gained a mere installment of what is to come; but if they fail, they at once conceive new hopes and so fill up the void. With them alone to hope is to have, for they lose not a moment in the execution of an idea. This is the lifelong task, full of danger and toil, which they are always imposing upon themselves. None enjoy their good things less, because they are always seeking for more. To do their duty is their only holiday, and they deem the quiet of inaction to be as disagreeable as the most tiresome business. If a man should say of them, in a word, that they were born neither to have peace themselves nor to allow peace to other men, he would simply speak the truth.

"In the face of such an enemy, Lacedaemonians, you persist in doing nothing. You do not see that peace is best secured by those who use their strength justly, but whose attitude shows that they have no intention of submitting to wrong. Justice with you seems to consist in giving no annoyance to others and in defending yourselves only against positive injury. But this policy would hardly be successful, even if your neighbors were like yourselves; and in the present case, as we pointed out just now, your ways compared with theirs are old-fashioned. And, as in the arts, so also in politics, the new must always prevail over the old. In settled times the traditions of government should be observed: but when circumstances are changing and men are compelled to meet them, much originality is required. The Athenians have had a wider experience, and therefore the administration of their state unlike yours has been greatly reformed. But here let your procrastination end; send an army at once into Attica and assist your allies, especially the Potidaeans, to whom your word is pledged. Do not betray friends and kindred into the hands of their worst enemies; or drive us in despair to seek the alliance of others; in taking such a course we should be doing nothing wrong either before the Gods who are the witnesses of our oaths, or before men whose eyes are upon us. For the true breakers of treaties are not those who, when forsaken, turn to others, but those who forsake allies whom they have sworn to defend. We will remain your friends if you choose to bestir yourselves; for we should be guilty of an impiety if we deserted you without cause; and we shall not easily find allies equally congenial to us. Take heed then: you have inherited from your fathers the leadership of Peloponnesus; see that her greatness suffers no diminution at your hands."

Thus spoke the Corinthians. Now there happened to be staying at Lacedaemon an Athenian embassy which had come on other business, and when the envoys heard what the Corinthians had said, they felt bound to go before the Lacedaemonian assembly, not with the view of answering the accusations brought against them by the cities, but they wanted to put the whole question before the Lacedaemonians, and make them understand that they should take time to deliberate and not be rash. They also desired to set forth the greatness of their city, reminding the elder men of what they knew, and informing the younger of what lay beyond their experience. They thought that their words would sway the Lacedaemonians in the direction of peace. So they came and said that, if they might be allowed, they too would like to address the people. The Lacedaemonians invited them to come forward, and they spoke as follows:—

"We were not sent here to argue with your allies, but on a special mission; observing, however, that no small outcry has arisen against us, we have come forward, not to answer the accusations which they bring (for you are not judges before whom either we or they have to plead), but to prevent you from lending too ready an ear to their bad advice and so deciding wrongly about a very serious question. We propose also, in reply to the wider charges which are raised against us, to show that what we have acquired we hold rightfully and that our city is not to be despised.

"Of the ancient deeds handed down by tradition and which no eye of any one who hears us ever saw, why should we speak? But of the Persian War, and other events which you yourselves remember, speak we must, although we have brought them forward so often that the repetition of them is disagreeable to us. When we faced those perils we did so for the common benefit: in the solid good you shared, and of the glory, whatever good there may be in that, we would not be wholly deprived. Our words are not designed to deprecate hostility, but to set forth in evidence the character of the city with which, unless you are very careful, you will soon be involved in war. We tell you that we, first and alone, dared to engage with the Barbarian at Marathon, and that when he came again, being too weak to defend ourselves by land, we and our whole people embarked on shipboard and shared with the other Hellenes in the victory of Salamis. Thereby he was prevented from sailing to the Peloponnesus and ravaging city after city; for against so mighty a fleet how could you have helped one another? He himself is the best witness of our words; for when he was once defeated at sea, he felt that his power was gone and quickly retreated with the greater part of his army.

"The event proved undeniably that the fate of Hellas depended on her navy. And the three chief elements of success were contributed by us; namely, the greatest number of ships, the ablest general, the most devoted patriotism. The ships in all numbered four hundred, and of these, our own contingent amounted to nearly two-thirds. To the influence of Themistocles our general it was chiefly due that we fought in the strait, which was confessedly our salvation; and for this service you yourselves honored him above any stranger who ever visited you. Thirdly, we displayed the most extraordinary courage and devotion; there was no one to help us by land; for up to our frontier those who lay in the enemy's path were already slaves; so we determined to leave our city and sacrifice our homes. Even in that extremity we did not choose to desert the cause of the allies who still resisted, or by dispersing ourselves to become useless to them; but we embarked and fought, taking no offense at your failure to assist us sooner. We maintain then that we rendered you a service at least as great as you rendered us. The cities from which you came to help us were still inhabited and you might hope to return to them; your concern was for yourselves and not for us; at any rate you remained at a distance while we had anything to lose. But we went forth from a city which was no more, and fought for one of which there was small hope; and yet we saved ourselves, and bore our part in saving you. If, in order to preserve our land, like other states, we had gone over to the Persians at first, or afterward had not ventured to embark because our ruin was already complete, it would have been useless for you with your weak navy to fight at sea, but everything would have gone quietly just as the Persian desired.

"Considering, Lacedaemonians, the energy and sagacity which we then displayed, do we deserve to be so bitterly hated by the other Hellenes merely because we have an empire? That empire was not acquired by force; but you would not stay and make an end of the Barbarian, and the allies came of their own accord and asked us to be their leaders. The subsequent development of our power was originally forced upon us by circumstances; fear was our first motive; afterwards honor, and then interest stepped in. And when we had incurred the hatred of most of our allies; when some of them had already revolted and been subjugated, and you were no longer the friends to us which you once had been, but suspicious and ill-disposed, how could we without great risk relax our hold? For the cities as fast as they fell away from us would have gone over to you. And no man is to be reproached who seizes every possible advantage when the danger is so great.

"At all events, Lacedaemonians, we may retort that you, in the exercise of your supremacy, manage the cities of Peloponnesus to suit your own views; and that if you, and not we, had persevered in the command of the allies long enough to be hated, you would have been quite as intolerable to them as we are, and would have been compelled, for the sake of your own safety, to rule with a strong hand. An empire was offered to us: can you wonder that, acting as human nature always will, we accepted it and refused to give it up again, constrained by three all-powerful motives honor, fear, interest? We are not the first who have aspired to rule; the world has ever held that the weaker must be kept down by the stronger. And we think that we are worthy of power; and there was a time when you thought so too; but now, when you mean expediency you talk about justice. Did justice ever deter any one from taking by force whatever he could? Men who indulge the natural ambition of empire deserve credit if they are in any degree more careful of justice than they need be. How moderate we are would speedily appear if others took our place; indeed our very moderation, which should be our glory, has been unjustly converted into a reproach.

"For because in our suits with our allies, regulated by treaty, we do not even stand upon our rights, but have instituted the practice of deciding them at Athens and by Athenian law, we are supposed to be litigious. None of our opponents observe why others, who exercise dominion elsewhere and are less moderate than we are in their dealings with their subjects, escape this reproach. Why is it? Because men who practice violence have no longer any need of law. But we are in the habit of meeting our allies on terms of equality, and, therefore, if through some legal decision of ours, or exercise of our imperial power, contrary to their own ideas of right, they suffer ever so little, they are not grateful for our moderation in leaving them so much, but are far more offended at their trifling loss than if we had from the first plundered them in the face of day, laying aside all thought of law. For then they would themselves have admitted that the weaker must give way to the stronger. Mankind resent injustice more than violence, because the one seems to be an unfair advantage taken by an equal, the other is the irresistible force of a superior. They were patient under the yoke of the Persian, who inflicted on them far more grievous wrongs; but now our dominion is odious in their eyes. And no wonder: the ruler of the day is always detested by his subjects. And should your empire supplant ours, may not you lose the good-will which you owe to the fear of us? Lose it you certainly will, if you mean again to exhibit the temper of which you gave a specimen when, for a short time, you led the confederacy against the Persian. For the institutions under which you live are incompatible with those of foreign states; and further, when any of you goes abroad, he respects neither these nor any other Hellenic customs.

"Do not then be hasty in deciding a question which is serious; and do not, by listening to representations and complaints which concern others, bring trouble upon yourselves. Realize, while there is time, the inscrutable nature of war; and how when protracted it generally ends in becoming a mere matter of chance, over which neither of us can have any control, the event being equally unknown and equally hazardous to both. The misfortune is that in their hurry to go to war, men begin with blows, and when a reverse comes upon them, then have recourse to words. But neither you, nor we, have as yet committed this mistake; and therefore while both of us can still choose the prudent part, we tell you not to break the peace or violate your oaths. Let our differences be determined by arbitration, according to the treaty. If you refuse we call to witness the Gods, by whom your oaths were sworn, that you are the authors of the war; and we will do our best to strike in return."

When the Lacedaemonians had heard the charges brought by the allies against the Athenians, and their rejoinder, they ordered everybody but themselves to withdraw, and deliberated alone. The majority were agreed that there was now a clear case against the Athenians, and that they must fight at once. . . . (I, 66-79)

In arriving at this decision and resolving to go to war, the Lacedaemonians were influenced, not so much by the speeches of their allies, as by the fear of the Athenians and of their increasing power. For they saw the greater part of Hellas already subject to them. (I, 88)

[Both sides are ready for war. The strategy of Pericles, and the resources of Athens.]

On neither side were there any mean thoughts; they were both full of enthusiasm: and no wonder, for all men are energetic when they are making a beginning. At that time the youth of Peloponnesus and the youth of Athens were numerous; they had never seen war, and were therefore very willing to take up arms. All Hellas was excited by the coming conflict between her two chief cities. Many were the prophecies circulated and many the oracles chanted by diviners, not only in the cities about to engage in the struggle, but throughout Hellas. Quite recently the island of Delos had been shaken by an earthquake for the first time within the memory of the Hellenes; this was interpreted and generally believed to be a sign of coming events. And everything of the sort which occurred was curiously noted.

The feeling of mankind was strongly on the side of the Lacedaemonians; for they professed to be the liberators of Hellas. Cities and individuals were eager to assist them to the utmost, both by word and deed; and where a man could not hope to be present, there it seemed to him that all things were at a stand. For the general indignation against the Athenians was intense; some were longing to be delivered from them, others fearful of falling under their sway. (II, 8)

While the Peloponnesians were gathering at the Isthmus, and were still on their way, but before they entered Attica, Pericles the son of Xanthippus, who was one of the ten Athenian generals, knowing that the invasion was inevitable, and suspecting that Archidamus in wasting the country might very likely spare his lands, either out of courtesy and because he happened to be his friend, or by the order of the Lacedaemonian authorities (who had already attempted to raise a prejudice against him when they demanded the expulsion of the polluted family, and might take this further means of injuring him in the eyes of the Athenians), openly declared in the assembly that Archidamus was his friend, but was not so to the injury of the state, and that supposing the enemy did not destroy his lands and buildings like the rest, he would make a present of them to the public; and he desired that the Athenians would have no suspicion of him on that account. As to the general situation, he repeated his previous advice; they must prepare for war and bring their property from the country into the city; they must defend their walls but not go out to battle; they should also equip for service the fleet in which lay their strength. Their allies should be kept well in hand, for their power depended on the revenues which they derived from them; military successes were generally gained by a wise policy and command of money. The state of their finances was encouraging; they had on an average six hundred talents of tribute coming in annually from their allies, to say nothing of their other revenue; and there were still remaining in the Acropolis six thousand talents of coined silver. (The whole amount had once been as much as nine thousand seven hundred talents, but from this had to be deducted a sum of three thousand seven hundred expended on various buildings, such as the Propylaea of the Acropolis, and also on the siege of Potidaea.) Moreover there was uncoined gold and silver in the form of private and public offerings, sacred vessels used in processions and games, the Persian spoil and other things of the like nature, worth at least five hundred talents more. There were also at their disposal, besides what they had in the Acropolis, considerable treasures in various temples. If they were reduced to the last extremity they could even take off the plates of gold with which the image of the goddess was overlaid; these, as he pointed out, weighed forty talents, and were of refined gold, which was all removable. They might use this treasure in self-defense, but they were bound to replace all that they had taken. By this estimate of their wealth he strove to encourage them. He added that they had thirteen thousand hoplites, besides the sixteen thousand who occupied the fortresses or who manned the walls of the city. For this was the number engaged on garrison duty at the beginning of the war, whenever the enemy invaded Attica; they were made up of the elder and younger men, and of such metics as bore heavy arms. The Phaleric wall extended four miles from Phalerum to the city walls: the portion of the city wall which was guarded was somewhat less than five miles; that between the Long Wall and the Phaleric requiring no guard. The Long Walls running down to the Piraeus were rather more than four and a half miles in length; the outer only was guarded. The whole circuit of the Piraeus and of Munychia was not quite seven miles, of which half required a guard. The Athenian cavalry, so Pericles pointed out, numbered twelve hundred, including mounted archers; the foot-archers, sixteen hundred; of triremes fit for service the city had three hundred.—The forces of various kinds which Athens possessed at the commencement of the war, when the first Peloponnesian invasion was impending, cannot be estimated at less.—To these Pericles added other arguments, such as he was fond of using, which were intended to prove to the Athenians that victory was certain.

The citizens were persuaded, and brought into the city their children and wives, their household goods, and even the wood-work of their houses, which they took down. Their flocks and beasts of burden they conveyed to Euboea and the adjacent islands.

The removal of the inhabitants was painful; for the Athenians had always been accustomed to reside in the country. . . . (*II, 13-14*)

[*Pericles' Funeral Oration. Plague at Athens.*]

During the same winter, in accordance with an old national custom, the funeral of those who first fell in this war was celebrated by the Athenians at the public charge. The ceremony is as follows: Three days before the celebration they erect a tent in which the bones of the dead are laid out, and every one brings to his own dead any offering which he pleases. At the time of the funeral the bones are placed in chests of cypress wood, which are conveyed on hearses; there is one chest for each tribe. They also carry a single empty litter decked with a pall for all whose bodies are missing, and cannot be recovered after the battle. The procession is accompanied by any one who chooses, whether citizen or stranger, and the female relatives of the deceased are present at the place of interment and make lamentation. The public sepulcher is situated in the most beautiful spot outside the walls; there they always bury those who fall in war; only after the battle of Marathon the dead, in recognition of their pre-eminent valor, were interred on the field. When the remains have been laid in the earth, some man of known ability and high reputation, chosen by the city, delivers a suitable oration over them; after which the people depart. Such is the manner of interment; and the ceremony was repeated from time to time throughout the war. Over those who were the first buried Pericles was chosen to speak. At the fitting moment he advanced from the sepulcher to a lofty stage, which had been erected in order that he might be heard as far as possible by the multitude, and spoke as follows:—

"Most of those who have spoken here before me have commended the lawgiver who added this oration to our other funeral customs; it seemed to them a worthy thing that such an honor should be given at their burial to the dead who have fallen on the field of battle. But I should have preferred that, when men's deeds have been brave, they should be honored in deed only, and with such an honor as this public funeral, which you are now witnessing. Then the reputation of many would not have been imperiled on the eloquence or want of eloquence of one, and their virtues believed or not as he spoke well or ill. For it is difficult to say neither too little nor too much; and even moderation is apt not to give the impression of truthfulness. The friend of the dead who knows the facts is likely to think that the words of the speaker fall short of his knowledge and of his wishes; another who is not so well informed, when he hears of anything which surpasses his own powers, will be envious and will suspect exaggeration. Mankind are tolerant of the praises of others so long as each hearer thinks that he can do as well or nearly as well himself, but, when the speaker rises above him, jealousy is aroused and he begins to be incredulous. However, since our ancestors have set the seal of their approval upon the practice, I must obey, and to the utmost of my power shall endeavor to satisfy the wishes and beliefs of all who hear me.

"I will speak first of our ancestors, for it is right and seemly that now, when we are lamenting the dead, a tribute should be paid to their memory. There has never been a time when they did not inhabit this land, which by their valor they have handed down from generation to generation, and we have received from them a free state. But if they were worthy of praise, still more were our fathers, who added to their inheritance, and after many a struggle transmitted to us their sons this great empire. And we ourselves assembled here to-day, who are still most of us in the vigor of life, have carried the work of improvement further, and have richly endowed our city with all things, so that she is sufficient for herself both in peace and war. Of the military exploits by which our various possessions were acquired, or of the energy with which we or our fathers drove back the tide of war, Hellenic or Barbarian, I will not speak; for the tale would be long and is familiar to you. But before I praise the dead, I should like to point out by what principles of action we rose to power, and under what institutions and through what manner of life our empire became great. For I conceive that such thoughts are not unsuited to the occasion, and that this numerous assembly of citizens and strangers may profitably listen to them.

"Our form of government does not enter into rivalry with the institutions of others. We do not copy our neighbors, but are an example to them. It is true that we are called a democracy, for the administration is in the hands of the many and not of the few. But while the law secures equal justice to all alike in their private disputes, the claim of excellence is also recognized; and when a citizen is in any way distinguished, he is preferred to the public service, not as a matter of privilege, but as the reward of merit. Neither is poverty a bar, but a man may benefit his country whatever be the obscurity of his condition. There is no exclusiveness in our public life, and in our private intercourse we are not suspicious of one another, nor angry with our neighbor if he does what he likes; we do not put on sour looks at him which, though harmless, are not pleasant. While we are thus unconstrained in our private intercourse, a spirit of reverence pervades our public acts; we are prevented from doing wrong by respect for the authorities and for the laws, having an especial regard to those which are ordained for the protection of the injured as well as to those unwritten laws which bring upon the transgressor of them the reprobation of the general sentiment.

"And we have not forgotten to provide for our weary spirits many relaxations from toil; we have regular games and sacrifices throughout the year; our homes are beautiful and elegant; and the delight which we daily feel in all these things helps to banish melancholy. Because of the greatness of our city the fruits of the whole earth flow in upon us; so that we enjoy the goods of other countries as freely as of our own.

"Then, again, our military training is in many respects superior to that of our adversaries. Our city is thrown open to the world, and we never expel a foreigner or prevent him from seeing or learning anything of which the secret if revealed to an enemy might profit him. We rely not upon management or trickery, but upon our own hearts and hands. And in the matter of education, whereas they from early youth are always undergoing laborious exercises which are to make them brave, we live at ease, and yet are equally ready to face the perils which they face. And here is the proof. The Lacedaemonians come into Attica not by themselves, but with their whole confederacy following; we go alone into a neighbor's country; and although our opponents are fighting for their homes and we on a foreign soil, we have seldom any difficulty in overcoming them. Our enemies have never yet felt our united strength; the care of a navy divides our attention, and on land we are obliged to send our own citizens everywhere. But they, if they meet and defeat a part of our army, are as proud as if they had routed us all, and when defeated they pretend to have been vanquished by us all.

"If then we prefer to meet danger with a light heart but without laborious training, and with a courage which is gained by habit and not enforced by law, are we not greatly the gainers? Since we do not anticipate the pain, although, when the hour comes, we can be as brave as those who never allow themselves to rest; and thus too our city is equally admirable in peace and in war. For we are lovers of the beautiful, yet simple in our tastes, and we cultivate the mind without loss of manliness. Wealth we employ, not for talk and ostentation, but when there is a real use for it. To avow poverty with us is no disgrace; the true disgrace is in doing nothing to avoid it. An Athenian citizen does not neglect the state because he takes care of his own household; and even those of us who are engaged in business have a very fair idea of politics. We alone regard a man who takes no interest in public affairs, not as a harmless, but as a useless character; and if few of us are originators, we are all sound judges of a policy. The great impediment to ac-

tion is, in our opinion, not discussion, but the want of that knowledge which is gained by discussion preparatory to action. For we
have a peculiar power of thinking before we act and of acting too,
whereas other men are courageous from ignorance but hesitate
upon reflection. And they are surely to be esteemed the bravest
spirits who, having the clearest sense both of the pains and pleasures of life, do not on that account shrink from danger. In doing
good, again, we are unlike others; we make our friends by conferring, not by receiving favors. Now he who confers a favor is
the firmer friend, because he would fain by kindness keep alive
the memory of an obligation; but the recipient is colder in his
feelings, because he knows that in requiting another's generosity
he will not be winning gratitude but only paying a debt. We alone
do good to our neighbors not upon a calculation of interest, but
in the confidence of freedom and in a frank and fearless spirit.
To sum up: I say that Athens is the school of Hellas, and that the
individual Athenian in his own person seems to have the power of
adapting himself to the most varied forms of action with the utmost
versatility and grace. This is no passing and idle word, but truth
and fact; and the assertion is verified by the position to which
these qualities have raised the state. For in the hour of trial Athens
alone among her contemporaries is superior to the report of her. No
enemy who comes against her is indignant at the reverses which
he sustains at the hands of such a city; no subject complains that
his masters are unworthy of him. And we shall assuredly not be
without witnesses; there are mighty monuments of our power
which will make us the wonder of this and of succeeding ages;
we shall not need the praises of Homer or of any other panegyrist
whose poetry may please for the moment, although his representa-
tion of the facts will not bear the light of day. For we have compelled every land and every sea to open a path for our valor, and
have everywhere planted eternal memorials of our friendship and
of our enmity. Such is the city for whose sake these men nobly
fought and died; they could not bear the thought that she might
be taken from them; and every one of us who survive should
gladly toil on her behalf.

"I have dwelt upon the greatness of Athens because I want

to show you that we are contending for a higher prize than those who enjoy none of these privileges, and to establish by manifest proof the merit of these men whom I am now commemorating. Their loftiest praise has been already spoken. For in magnifying the city I have magnified them, and men like them whose virtues made her glorious. And of how few Hellenes can it be said as of them, that their deeds when weighed in the balance have been found equal to their fame! Methinks that a death such as theirs has been given the true measure of a man's worth; it may be the first revelation of his virtues, but is at any rate their final seal. For even those who come short in other ways may justly plead the valor with which they have fought for their country; they have blotted out the evil with the good, and have benefited the state more by their public services than they have injured her by their private actions. None of these men were enervated by wealth or hesitated to resign the pleasures of life; none of them put off the evil day in the hope, natural to poverty, that a man, though poor, may one day become rich. But, deeming that the punishment of their enemies was sweeter than any of these things, and that they could fall in no nobler cause, they determined at the hazard of their lives to be honorably avenged, and to leave the rest. They resigned to hope their unknown chance of happiness; but in the face of death they resolved to rely upon themselves alone. And when the moment came they were minded to resist and suffer, rather than to fly and save their lives; they ran away from the word of dishonor, but on the battle-field their feet stood fast, and in an instant, at the height of their fortune, they passed away from the scene, not of their fear, but of their glory.

"Such was the end of these men; they were worthy of Athens, and the living need not desire to have a more heroic spirit, although they may pray for a less fatal issue. The value of such a spirit is not to be expressed in words. Any one can discourse to you for ever about the advantages of a brave defense, which you know already. But instead of listening to him I would have you day by day fix your eyes upon the greatness of Athens, until you become filled with the love of her; and when you are impressed by the spectacle of her glory, reflect that this empire has been acquired by men who knew their duty and had the courage to do it, who in the hour of conflict had the fear of dishonor always present to them, and who, if ever they failed in an enterprise, would not allow their virtues to be lost to their country, but freely gave their lives to her as the fairest offering which they could present at her feast. The sacrifice which they collectively made was individually repaid to them; for they received again each one for himself a praise which grows not old, and the noblest of all sepulchers—I speak not of that in which their remains are laid, but of that in which their glory survives, and is proclaimed always and on every fitting occasion both in word and deed. For the whole earth is the sepulcher of famous men; not only are they commemorated by columns and inscriptions in their own country, but in foreign lands there dwells also an unwritten memorial of them, graven not on stone but in the hearts of men. Make them your examples, and, esteeming courage to be freedom and freedom to be happiness, do not weigh too nicely the perils of war. The unfortunate who has no hope of a change for the better has less reason to throw away his life than the prosperous who, if he survive, is always liable to a change for the worse, and to whom any accidental fall makes the most serious difference. To a man of spirit, cowardice and disaster coming together are far more bitter than death striking him unperceived at a time when he is full of courage and animated by the general hope.

"Wherefore I do not now commiserate the parents of the dead who stand here; I would rather comfort them. You know that your life has been passed amid manifold vicissitudes; and that they may be deemed fortunate who have gained most honor, whether an honorable death like theirs, or an honorable sorrow like yours, and whose days have been so ordered that the term of their happiness is likewise the term of their life. I know how hard it is to make you feel this, when the good fortune of others will too often remind you of the gladness which once lightened your hearts. And sorrow is felt at the want of those blessings, not which a man never knew, but which were a part of his life before they were taken from him. Some of you are of an age at which they may hope to have other children, and they ought to bear their sorrow better; not only will the children who may hereafter be born make them forget their own lost ones, but the city will be doubly a gainer. She will not be left desolate, and she will be safer. For a man's counsel cannot have equal weight or worth, when he alone has no children to risk in the general danger. To those of you who have passed their prime, I say: 'Congratulate yourselves that you have been happy during the greater part of your days; remember that your life of sorrow will not last long, and be comforted by the glory of those who are gone. For the love of honor alone is ever young, and not riches, as some say, but honor is the delight of men when they are old and useless.'

"To you who are the sons and brothers of the departed, I see that the struggle to emulate them will be an arduous one. For all men praise the dead, and, however pre-eminent your virtue may be, hardly will you be thought, I do not say to equal, but even to approach them. The living have their rivals and detractors, but when a man is out of the way, the honor and good-will which he receives is unalloyed. And, if I am to speak of womanly virtues to those of you who will henceforth be widows, let me sum them up in one short admonition: To a woman not to show more weakness than is natural to her sex is a great glory, and not to be talked about for good or for evil among men.

"I have paid the required tribute, in obedience to the law, making use of such fitting words as I had. The tribute of deeds has been paid in part; for the dead have been honorably interred, and it remains only that their children should be maintained at the public charge until they are grown up: this is the solid prize with which, as with a garland, Athens crowns her sons living and dead, after a struggle like theirs. For where the rewards of virtue are greatest, there the noblest citizens are enlisted in the service of the state. And now, when you have duly lamented, every one his own dead, you may depart."

Such was the order of the funeral celebrated in this winter, with the end of which ended the first year of the Peloponnesian War. As soon as summer returned, the Peloponnesian army, comprising as before two-thirds of the force of each confederate state, under the command of the Lacedaemonian king Archidamus, the son of Zeuxidamus, invaded Attica, where they established themselves and ravaged the country. They had not been there many days when the plague broke out at Athens for the first time. A similar disorder is said to have previously smitten many places, particularly Lemnos, but there is no record of such a pestilence occurring elsewhere, or of so great a destruction of human life. For a while physicians, in ignorance of the nature of the disease, sought to apply remedies; but it was in vain, and they themselves were among the first victims, because they oftenest came into contact with it. No human art was of any avail, and as to supplications in temples, inquiries of oracles, and the like, they were utterly useless, and at last men were overpowered by the calamity and gave them all up.

The disease is said to have begun south of Egypt in Aethiopia; thence it descended into Egypt and Libya, and after spreading over the greater part of the Persian empire, suddenly fell upon Athens. It first attacked the inhabitants of the Piraeus, and it was supposed that the Peloponnesians had poisoned the cisterns, no conduits having as yet been made there. It afterward reached the upper city, and then the mortality became far greater. As to its probable origin or the causes which might or could have produced such a disturbance of nature, every man, whether a physician or not, will give his own opinion. But I shall describe its actual course, and the symptoms by which any one who knows them beforehand may recognize the disorder should it ever reappear. For I was myself attacked, and witnessed the sufferings of others.

The season was admitted to have been remarkably free from ordinary sickness; and if anybody was already ill of any other disease, it was absorbed in this. Many who were in perfect health, all in a moment, and without any apparent reason, were seized with violent heats in the head and with redness and inflammation of the eyes. Internally the throat and the tongue were quickly suffused with blood, and the breath became unnatural and fetid. There followed sneezing and hoarseness; in a short time the disorder, accompanied by a violent cough, reached the chest; then fastening lower down, it would move the stomach and bring on all the vomits of bile to which physicians have ever given names; and they were very distressing. An ineffectual retching producing violent convulsions attacked most of the sufferers; some as soon as the previous symptoms had abated, others not until long afterward. The body externally was not so very hot to the touch, nor yet pale; it was of a livid color inclining to red, and breaking out in pustules and ulcers. But the internal fever was intense; the sufferers could not bear to have on them even the finest linen garment; they insisted on being naked, and there was nothing which they longed for more eagerly than to throw themselves into cold water. And many of those who had no one to look after them actually plunged into the cisterns, for they were tormented by unceasing thirst, which was not in the least assuaged whether they drank little or much. They could not sleep; a restlessness which was intolerable never left them. While the disease was at its height the body, instead of wasting away, held out amid these sufferings in a marvelous manner, and either they died on the seventh or ninth day, not of weakness, for their strength was not exhausted, but of internal fever, which was the end of most; or, if they survived, then the disease descended into the bowels and there produced violent ulceration; severe diarrhoea at the same time set in, and at a later stage caused exhaustion, which finally with few exceptions carried them off. For the disorder which had originally settled in the head passed gradually through the whole body, and, if a person got over the worst, would often seize the extremities and leave its mark, attacking the privy parts and the fingers and the toes; and some escaped with the loss of these, some with the loss of their eyes. Some again had no sooner recovered than they were seized with a forgetfulness of all things and knew neither themselves nor their friends.

The general character of the malady no words can describe, and the fury with which it fastened upon each sufferer was too much for human nature to endure. There was one circumstance in particular which distinguished it from ordinary diseases. The birds and animals which feed on human flesh, although so many bodies were lying unburied, either never came near them, or died if they touched them. This was proved by a remarkable disappearance of the birds of prey, which were not to be seen either about the bodies or anywhere else; while in the case of the dogs the result was even more obvious, because they live with man.

Such was the general nature of the disease: I omit many strange peculiarities which characterized individual cases. None of the ordinary sicknesses attacked any one while it lasted, or, if they did, they ended in the plague. Some of the sufferers died from want of care, others equally who were receiving the greatest attention. No single remedy could be deemed a specific; for that which did good to one did harm to another. No constitution was of itself strong enough to resist or weak enough to escape the attacks; the disease carried off all alike and defied every mode of treatment. Most appalling was the despondency which seized upon any one who felt himself sickening; for he instantly abandoned his mind to despair and, instead of holding out, absolutely threw away his chance of life. Appalling too was the rapidity with which men caught the infection; dying like sheep if they attended on one another; and this was the principal cause of mortality. When they were afraid to visit one another, the sufferers died in their solitude, so that many houses were empty because there had been no one left to take care of the sick; or if they ventured they perished, especially those who aspired to heroism. For they went to see their friends without thought of themselves and were ashamed to leave them, at a time when the very relations of the dying were at last growing weary and ceased even to make lamentations, overwhelmed by the vastness of the calamity. But whatever instances there may have been of such devotion, more often the sick and the dying were tended by the pitying care of those who had recovered, because they knew the course of the disease and were themselves free from apprehension. For no one was ever attacked a second time, or not with a fatal result. All men congratulated them, and they themselves, in the excess of their joy at the moment, had an innocent fancy that they could not die of any other sickness.

The crowding of the people out of the country into the city aggravated the misery; and the newly-arrived suffered most. For, having no houses of their own, but inhabiting in the height of summer stifling huts, the mortality among them was dreadful, and they perished in wild disorder. The dead lay as they had died, one upon another, while others hardly alive wallowed in the streets and crawled about every fountain craving for water. The temples in which they lodged were full of the corpses of those who died in them; for the violence of the calamity was such that men, not knowing where to turn, grew reckless of all law, human and divine. The customs which had hitherto been observed at funerals were universally violated, and they buried their dead each one as best he could. Many, having no proper appliances, because the deaths in their household had been so numerous already, lost all shame in the burial of the dead. When one man had raised a funeral pile, others would come, and throwing on their dead first, set fire to it; or when some other corpse was already burning, before they could be stopped, would throw their own dead upon it and depart.

There were other and worse forms of lawlessness which the plague introduced at Athens. Men who had hitherto concealed what they took pleasure in, now grew bolder. For, seeing the sudden change,—how the rich died in a moment, and those who had nothing immediately inherited their property,—they reflected that life and riches were alike transitory, and they resolved to enjoy themselves while they could, and to think only of pleasure. Who would be willing to sacrifice himself to the law of honor when he knew not whether he would ever live to be held in honor? The pleasure of the moment and any sort of thing which conduced to it took the place both of honor and of expediency. No fear of Gods or law of man deterred a criminal. Those who saw all perishing alike, thought that the worship or neglect of the Gods made no difference. For offenses against human law no punishment was to be feared; no one would live long enough to be called to account. Already a far heavier sentence had been passed and was hanging over a man's head; before that fell, why should he not take a little pleasure?

Such was the grievous calamity which now afflicted the Athenians; within the walls their people were dying, and without,

their country was being ravaged. In their troubles they naturally
called to mind a verse which the elder men among them declared
to have been current long ago:—

"A Dorian war will come and a plague with it."

There was a dispute about the precise expression; some saying
that *limos,* a famine, and not *loimos,* a plague, was the original
word. Nevertheless, as might have been expected, for men's
memories reflected their sufferings, the argument in favor of
loimos prevailed at the time. But if ever in future years another
Dorian war arises which happens to be accompanied by a famine,
they will probably repeat the verse in the other form. The answer
of the oracle to the Lacedaemonians when the God was asked
"whether they should go to war or not," and he replied "that if
they fought with all their might, they would conquer, and that
he himself would take their part," was not forgotten by those who
had heard of it, and they quite imagined that they were witnessing the fulfillment of his words. The disease certainly did set in
immediately after the invasion of the Peloponnesians, and did not
spread into Peloponnesus in any degree worth speaking of, while
Athens felt its ravages most severely, and next to Athens the
places which were most populous. Such was the history of the
plague. (*II, 34-54*)

[*Pericles fell a victim to the plague in 429 B.C. An estimate
of him.*]

. . . In the conduct of public affairs [the Athenians] took [Peri-
cles'] advice, and sent no more embassies to Sparta; they were
again eager to prosecute the war. Yet in private they felt their
sufferings keenly; the common people had been deprived even
of the little which they possessed, while the upper class had lost
fair estates in the country with all their houses and rich furniture.
Worst of all, instead of enjoying peace, they were now at war.
The popular indignation was not pacified until they had fined
Pericles; but, soon afterward, with the usual fickleness of a multi-

tude, they elected him general and committed all their affairs to his charge. Their private sorrows were beginning to be less acutely felt, and for a time of public need they thought that there was no man like him. During the peace while he was at the head of affairs he ruled with prudence; under his guidance Athens was safe, and reached the height of her greatness in his time. When the war began he showed that here too he had formed a true estimate of the Athenian power. He survived the commencement of hostilities two years and six months; and, after his death, his foresight was even better appreciated than during his life. For he had told the Athenians that if they would be patient and would attend to their navy, and not seek to enlarge their dominion while the war was going on, nor imperil the existence of the city, they would be victorious; but they did all that he told them not to do, and in matters which seemingly had nothing to do with the war, from motives of private ambition and private interest they adopted a policy which had disastrous effects in respect both of themselves and of their allies; their measures, had they been successful, would only have brought honor and profit to individuals, and, when unsuccessful, crippled the city in the conduct of the war. The reason of the difference was that he, deriving authority from his capacity and acknowledged worth, being also a man of transparent integrity, was able to control the multitude in a free spirit; he led them rather than was led by them; for, not seeking power by dishonest arts, he had no need to say pleasant things, but, on the strength of his own high character, could venture to oppose and even to anger them. When he saw them unseasonably elated and arrogant, his words humbled and awed them; and, when they were depressed by groundless fears, he sought to re-animate their confidence. Thus Athens, though still in name a democracy, was in fact ruled by her greatest citizen. But his successors were more on an equality with one another, and, each one struggling to be first himself, they were ready to sacrifice the whole conduct of affairs to the whims of the people. Such weakness in a great and imperial city led to many errors, of which the greatest was the Sicilian expedition; not that the Athenians miscalculated their enemy's power, but they themselves, instead of consulting for the interests of the expedition which they had sent out, were occupied in intriguing against one another for the leadership of the democracy, and not only hampered the operations of the army, but became embroiled, for the first time, at home. And yet after they had lost in the Sicilian expedition the greater part of their fleet and army, and were now distracted by revolution, still they held out three years not only against their former enemies, but against the Sicilians who had combined with them, and against most of their own allies who had risen in revolt. Even when Cyrus the son of the King joined in the war and supplied the Peloponnesian fleet with money, they continued to resist, and were at last overthrown, not by their enemies, but by themselves and their own internal dissensions. So that at the time Pericles was more than justified in the conviction at which his foresight had arrived, that the Athenians would win an easy victory over the unaided forces of the Peloponnesians. (*II,* 65)

[*After Pericles' death, leadership at Athens fell to demagogues, such as Cleon the tanner. Debate on the treatment to be accorded rebellious Mytilene, the chief city of Lesbos, 427 B.C.*]

. . . Concerning the other captives a discussion was held, and in their indignation the Athenians determined to put to death not only the men then at Athens, but all the grown-up citizens of Mytilene, and to enslave the women and children; the act of the Mytilenaeans appeared inexcusable, because they were not subjects like the other states which had revolted, but free. That Peloponnesian ships should have had the audacity to find their way to Ionia and assist the rebels contributed to increase their fury; and the action showed that the revolt was a long premeditated affair. So they sent a trireme to Paches announcing their determination, and bidding him put the Mytilenaeans to death at once. But on the following day a kind of remorse seized them; they began to reflect that a decree which doomed to destruction not only the guilty, but a whole city, was cruel and monstrous. The Mytilenaean envoys who were at Athens perceived the change of feeling, and they and the Athenians who were in their interest prevailed on the magistrates to bring the question again before the people; this they were the more willing to do, because they saw themselves that the majority of the citizens were anxious to have an opportunity given them of reconsidering their decision. An assembly was again summoned, and different opinions were expressed by different speakers. In the former assembly, Cleon the son of Cleaenetus had carried the decree condemning the Mytilenaeans to death. He was the most violent of the citizens, and at that time exercised by far the greatest influence over the people. And now he came forward a second time and spoke as follows:—

"I have remarked again and again that a democracy cannot manage an empire, but never more than now, when I see you regretting your condemnation of the Mytilenaeans. Having no fear or suspicion of one another in daily life, you deal with your allies upon the same principle, and you do not consider that whenever you yield to them out of pity or are misled by their specious tales, you are guilty of a weakness dangerous to yourselves, and receive no thanks from them. You should remember that your empire is a despotism exercised over unwilling subjects, who are always conspiring against you; they do not obey in return for any kindness which you do them to your own injury, but in so far as you are their masters; they have no love of you, but they are held down by force. Besides, what can be more detestable than to be perpetually changing our minds? We forget that a state in which the laws, though imperfect, are inviolable, is better off than one in which the laws are good but ineffective. Dullness and modesty are a more useful combination than cleverness and license; and the more simple sort generally make better citizens than the more astute. For the latter desire to be thought wiser than the laws; they want to be always getting their own way in public discussions; they think that they can nowhere have a finer opportunity of displaying their intelligence, and their folly generally ends in the ruin of their country; whereas the others, mistrusting their own capacity, admit that the laws are wiser than themselves: they do not pretend to criticize the arguments of a great speaker; and being impartial judges, not ambitious rivals, they hit the mark. That is the spirit in which we should act; not suffering ourselves to be so excited by our own cleverness in a war of wits as to advise the Athenian people contrary to our own better judgment. (*III, 36-37*)

"I want you to put aside this trifling, and therefore I say to you that no single city has ever injured us so deeply as Mytilene. I can excuse those who find our rule too heavy to bear, or who have revolted because the enemy has compelled them. But islanders who had walls, and were unassailable by our enemies, except at sea, and on that element were sufficiently protected by a fleet of their own, who were independent and treated by us with the highest regard, when they act thus, they have not revolted (that word would imply that they were oppressed), but they have rebelled, and entering the ranks of our bitterest enemies have conspired with them to seek our ruin. And surely this is far more atrocious than if they had been led by motives of ambition to take up arms against us on their own account. They learned nothing from the misfortunes of their neighbors who had already revolted and been subdued by us, nor did the happiness of which they were in the enjoyment make them hesitate to court destruction. They trusted recklessly to the future, and cherishing hopes which, if less than their wishes, were greater than their powers, they went to war, preferring might to right. No sooner did they seem likely to win than they set upon us, although we were doing them no wrong. Too swift and sudden a rise is apt to make cities insolent and, in general, ordinary good-fortune is safer than extraordinary. Mankind apparently find it easier to drive away adversity than to retain prosperity. We should from the first have made no difference between the Mytilenaeans and the rest of our allies, and then their insolence would never have risen to such a height, for men naturally despise those who court them, but respect those who do not give way to them. Yet it is not too late to punish them as their crimes deserve. . . .

"Do not then hold out a hope, which eloquence can secure or money buy, that they are to be excused and that their error is to be deemed human and venial. Their attack was not unpremeditated; that might have been an excuse for them; but they knew what they were doing. This was my original contention, and I still maintain that you should abide by your former decision, and not be misled either by pity, or by the charm of words, or by a too forgiving temper. There are no three things more prejudicial to your power. Mercy should be reserved for the merciful, and not thrown away upon those who will have no compassion on us, and who must by the force of circumstances always be our enemies. And our charming orators will still have an arena, but one in which the questions at stake will not be so grave, and the city will not pay so dearly for her brief pleasure in listening to them, while they for a good speech get a good fee. Lastly, forgiveness is naturally shown to those who, being reconciled, will continue friends, and not to those who will always remain what they were, and will abate nothing of their enmity. In one word, if you do as I say, you will do what is just to the Mytilenaeans, and also what is expedient for yourselves; but, if you take the opposite course, they will not be grateful to you, and you will be self-condemned. For, if they were right in revolting, you must be wrong in maintaining your empire. But if, right or wrong, you are resolved to rule, then rightly or wrongly they must be chastised for your good. Otherwise you must give up your empire, and, when virtue is no longer dangerous, you may be as virtuous as you please. Punish them as they would have punished you; let not those who have escaped appear to have less feeling than those who conspired against them. Consider: what might not they have been expected to do if they had conquered?—especially since they were the aggressors. For those who wantonly attack others always rush into extremes, and sometimes, like these Mytilenaeans, to their own destruction. They know the fate which is reserved for them by an enemy who is spared: when a man is injured wantonly he is more dangerous if he escape than the enemy who has only suffered what he has inflicted. Be true then to yourselves, and recall as vividly as you can what you felt at the time; think how you would have given the world to crush your enemies, and now take your revenge. Do not be soft-hearted at the sight of their distress, but remember the danger which was once hanging over your heads. Chastise them as they deserve, and prove by an example to your other allies that rebellion will be punished with death. If this is made quite clear to them, your attention will no longer be diverted from your enemies by wars against your own allies."

Such were the words of Cleon; and after him Diodotus the son of Eucrates, who in the previous assembly had been the chief opponent of the decree which condemned the Mytilenaeans, came forward again and spoke as follows:—(III, 39-41)

"I do not come forward either as an advocate of the Mytilenaeans or as their accuser; the question for us rightly considered is not, what are their crimes? but, what is for our interest? If I prove them ever so guilty, I will not on that account bid you put them to death, unless it is expedient. Neither, if perchance there be some degree of excuse for them, would I have you spare them, unless it be clearly for the good of the state. For I conceive that we are now concerned, not with the present, but with the future. When Cleon insists that the infliction of death will be expedient and will secure you against revolt in time to come, I, like him taking the ground of future expediency, stoutly maintain the contrary position; and I would not have you be misled by the apparent fairness of his proposal, and reject the solid advantages of mine. You are angry with the Mytilenaeans, and the superior justice of his argument may for the moment attract you; but we are not at law with them, and do not want to be told what is just; we are considering a question of policy, and desire to know how we can turn them to account.

"To many offenses less than theirs states have affixed the punishment of death; nevertheless, excited by hope, men still risk their lives. No one when venturing on a perilous enterprise ever yet passed a sentence of failure on himself. And what city when entering on a revolt ever imagined that the power which she had, whether her own or obtained from her allies, did not justify the attempt? All are by nature prone to err both in public and in private life, and no law will prevent them. Men have gone through the whole catalogue of penalties in the hope that, by increasing their severity, they may suffer less at the hands of evildoers. In early ages the punishments, even of the worst offenses, would naturally be milder; but as time went on and mankind continued to transgress, they seldom stopped short of death. And still there are transgressors. Some greater terror then has yet to be discovered; certainly death is no deterrent. For poverty inspires necessity with daring; and wealth engenders avarice in pride and insolence; and the various conditions of human life, as they severally fall under the sway of some mighty and fatal power, lure men through their passions to destruction. Desire and hope are never wanting, the one leading, the other following, the one devising the enterprise, the other suggesting that fortune will be kind; and they are the most ruinous, for, being unseen, they far outweigh the dangers which are seen. Fortune too assists the illusion, for she often presents herself unexpectedly, and induces states as well as individuals to run into peril, however inadequate their means; and states even more than individuals, because they are throwing for a higher stake, freedom or empire, and because when a man has a whole people acting with him, he magnifies himself out of all reason. In a word then, it is impossible and simply absurd to suppose that human nature when bent upon some favorite project can be restrained either by the strength of law or by any other terror." (*III, 44-45*)

Thus spoke Diodotus, and such were the proposals on either side which most nearly represented the opposing parties. In spite of the reaction, there was a struggle between the two opinions; the show of hands was very near, but the motion of Diodotus prevailed. The Athenians instantly dispatched another trireme, hoping that, if the second could overtake the first, which had a start of about twenty-four hours, it might be in time to save the city. The Mytilenaean envoys provided wine and barley for the crew, and promised them great rewards if they arrived first. And such was their energy that they continued rowing whilst they ate their barley, kneaded with wine and oil, and slept and rowed by turns. Fortunately no adverse wind sprang up, and, the first of the two ships sailing in no great hurry on her untoward errand, and the second hastening as I have described, the one did indeed arrive sooner than the other, but not much sooner. Paches had read the decree and was about to put it into execution, when the second appeared and arrested the fate of the city.

So near was Mytilene to destruction.

The captives whom Paches had sent to Athens as being the most guilty numbered about a thousand, or rather more; these the Athenians, upon the motion of Cleon, put to death. They razed the walls of the Mytilenaeans and took away their fleet. Then, instead of imposing tribute on them, they divided the whole island, exclusive of the territory of Methymna, into three thousand portions, of which they dedicated three hundred to the Gods; the remainder they let out to cleruchi taken from their own citizens, whom they chose by lot and sent to Lesbos. The Lesbians undertook to pay them a yearly rent of two minae for each portion and cultivated the land themselves. The Athenians also took possession of the towns on the continent which the Mytilenaeans held, and these henceforward were subject to Athens.

Thus ended the revolt of Lesbos. (*III, 49-50*)

[*The effect of war on man's character: revolution at Corcyra, 427* B.C.]

. . . When the Corcyraeans perceived that the Athenian fleet was approaching, while that of the enemy had disappeared, they took the Messenian troops, who had hitherto been outside the walls, into the city, and ordered the ships which they had manned to sail round into the Hyllaic harbor. These proceeded on their way. Meanwhile they killed any of their enemies whom they caught in the city. On the arrival of the ships they disembarked those whom they had induced to go on board, and dispatched them; they also went to the temple of Hera, and persuading about fifty of the suppliants to stand their trial condemned them all to death. The majority would not come out, and, when they saw what was going on, destroyed one another in the enclosure of the temple where they were, except a few who hung themselves on trees, or put an end to their own lives in any other way which they could. And, during the seven days which Eurymedon after his arrival remained with his sixty ships, the Corcyraeans continued slaughtering those of their fellow-citizens whom they deemed their enemies; they professed to punish them for their designs against the democracy, but in fact some were killed from motives of personal enmity, and some because money was owing to them, by the hands of their debtors. Every form of death was to be seen; and everything, and more than everything, that commonly happens in revolutions, happened then. The father slew the son, and the suppliants were torn from the temples and slain near them; some of them were even walled up in the temple of Dionysus, and there perished. To such extremes of cruelty did revolution go; and this seemed to be the worst of revolutions, because it was the first.

For not long afterward nearly the whole Hellenic world was in commotion; in every city the chiefs of the democracy and of the oligarchy were struggling, the one to bring in the Athenians, the other the Lacedaemonians. Now in time of peace, men would have had no excuse for introducing either, and no desire to do so; but, when they were at war, the introduction of a foreign alliance on one side or the other to the hurt of their enemies and the advantage of themselves was easily effected by the dissatisfied party. And revolution brought upon the cities of Hellas many terrible calamities, such as have been and always will be while human nature remains the same, but which are more or less aggravated and differ in character with every new combination of circumstances. In peace and prosperity both states and individuals are actuated by higher motives, because they do not fall under the dominion of imperious necessities; but war, which takes away the comfortable provision of daily life, is a hard master and tends to assimilate men's characters to their conditions.

When troubles had once begun in the cities, those who followed carried the revolutionary spirit further and further, and determined to outdo the report of all who had preceded them by the ingenuity of their enterprises and the atrocity of their revenges. The meaning of words had no longer the same relation to things, but was changed by them as they thought proper. Reckless daring was held to be loyal courage; prudent delay was the excuse of a coward; moderation was the disguise of unmanly weakness; to know everything was to do nothing. Frantic energy was the true quality of a man. A conspirator who wanted to be safe was a recreant in disguise. The lover of violence was always trusted, and his opponent suspected. He who succeeded in a plot was deemed knowing, but a still greater master in craft was he who detected one. On the other hand, he who plotted from the first to have nothing to do with plots was a breaker up of parties and a poltroon who was afraid of the enemy. In a word, he who could outstrip another in a bad action was applauded, and so was he who encouraged to evil one who had no idea of it. The tie of party was stronger than the tie of blood, because a partisan was more ready to dare without asking why. (For party associations are not based upon any established law, nor do they seek the public good; they are formed in defiance of the laws and from self-interest.) The seal of good faith was not divine law, but fellowship in crime. If an enemy when he was in the ascendant offered fair words, the opposite party received them not in a generous spirit, but by a jealous watchfulness of his actions. Revenge was dearer than self-preservation. Any agreements sworn to by either party, when they could do nothing else, were binding as long as both were powerless. But he who on a favorable opportunity first took courage, and struck at his enemy when he saw him off his guard, had greater pleasure in a perfidious than he would have had in an open act of revenge; he congratulated himself that he had taken the safer course, and also that he had overreached his enemy and gained the prize of superior ability. In general the dishonest more easily gain credit for cleverness than the simple for goodness; men take a pride in the one, but are ashamed of the other.

The cause of all these evils was the love of power, originating in avarice and ambition, and the party-spirit which is engendered by them when men are fairly embarked in a contest. For the leaders on either side used specious names, the one party professing to uphold the constitutional equality of the many, the other the wisdom of an aristocracy, while they made the public interests, to which in name they were devoted, in reality their prize. Striving in every way to overcome each other, they committed the most monstrous crimes; yet even these were surpassed by the magnitude of their revenges which they pursued to the very utmost, neither party observing any definite limits either of justice or public expediency, but both alike making the caprice of the moment their law. Either by the help of an unrighteous sentence, or grasping power with the strong hand, they were eager to satiate the impatience of party-spirit. Neither faction cared for religion; but any fair pretense which succeeded in effecting some odious purpose was greatly lauded. And the citizens who were of neither party fell a prey to both; either they were disliked because they held aloof, or men were jealous of their surviving.

Thus revolution gave birth to every form of wickedness in Hellas. The simplicity which is so large an element in a noble nature was laughed to scorn and disappeared. An attitude of perfidious antagonism everywhere prevailed; for there was no word binding enough, nor oath terrible enough to reconcile enemies. Each man was strong only in the conviction that nothing was secure; he must look to his own safety, and could not afford to trust others. Inferior intellects generally succeeded best. For, aware of their own deficiencies, and fearing the capacity of their opponents, for whom they were no match in powers of speech, and whose subtle wits were likely to anticipate them in contriving evil, they struck boldly and at once. But the cleverer sort, presuming in their arrogance that they would be aware in time, and disdaining to act when they could think, were taken off their guard and easily destroyed. (*III, 81-83*)

[*The policy that "Might makes Right": the Melian Dialogue, 416* B.C.]

. . . The Athenians next made an expedition against the island of Melos with thirty ships of their own, six Chian, and two Lesbian, twelve hundred hoplites and three hundred archers besides twenty mounted archers of their own, and about fifteen hundred hoplites furnished by their allies in the islands. The Melians are colonists of the Lacedaemonians who would not submit to Athens like the other islanders. At first they were neutral and took no part.

But when the Athenians tried to coerce them by ravaging their lands, they were driven into open hostilities. The generals, Cleomedes the son of Lycomedes and Tisias the son of Tisimachus, encamped with the Athenian forces on the island. But before they did the country any harm they sent envoys to negotiate with the Melians. Instead of bringing these envoys before the people, the Melians desired them to explain their errand to the magistrates and to the dominant class. They spoke as follows:—

"Since we are not allowed to speak to the people, lest, forsooth, a multitude should be deceived by seductive and unanswerable arguments which they would hear set forth in a single uninterrupted oration (for we are perfectly aware that this is what you mean in bringing us before a select few), you who are sitting here may as well make assurance yet surer. Let us have no set speeches at all, but do you reply to each several statement of which you disapprove, and criticize it at once. Say first of all how you like this mode of proceeding."

The Melian representatives answered:—"The quiet interchange of explanations is a reasonable thing, and we do not object to that. But your warlike movements, which are present not only to our fears but to our eyes, seem to belie your words. We see that, although you may reason with us, you mean to be our judges; and that at the end of the discussion, if the justice of our cause prevail and we therefore refuse to yield, we may expect war; if we are convinced by you, slavery."

Ath. "Nay, but if you are only going to argue from fancies about the future, or if you meet us with any other purpose than that of looking your circumstances in the face and saving your city, we have done; but if this is your intention we will proceed."

Mel. "It is an excusable and natural thing that men in our position should neglect no argument and no view which may avail. But we admit that this conference has met to consider the question of our preservation; and therefore let the argument proceed in the manner which you propose."

Ath. "Well, then, we Athenians will use no fine words; we will not go out of our way to prove at length that we have a right to rule, because we overthrew the Persians; or that we attack you now because we are suffering any injury at your hands. We should not convince you if we did; nor must you expect to convince us by arguing that, although a colony of the Lacedaemonians, you have taken no part in their expeditions, or that you have never done us any wrong. But you and we should say what we really think, and aim only at what is possible, for we both alike know that into the discussion of human affairs the question of justice only enters where there is equal power to enforce it, and that the powerful exact what they can, and the weak grant what they must."

Mel. "Well, then, since you set aside justice and invite us to speak of expediency, in our judgment it is certainly expedient that you should respect a principle which is for the common good; that to every man when in peril a reasonable claim should be accounted a claim of right, and that any plea which he is disposed to urge, even if failing of the point a little, should help his cause. Your interest in this principle is quite as great as ours, inasmuch as you, if you fall, will incur the heaviest vengeance, and will be the most terrible example to mankind."

Ath. "The fall of our empire, if it should fall, is not an event to which we look forward with dismay; for ruling states such as Lacedaemon are not cruel to their vanquished enemies. With the Lacedaemonians, however, we are not now contending; the real danger is from our many subject states, who may of their own motion rise up and overcome their masters. But this is a danger which you may leave to us. And we will now endeavor to show that we have come in the interests of our empire, and that in what we are about to say we are only seeking the preservation of your city. For we want to make you ours with the least trouble to ourselves, and it is for the interests of us both that you should not be destroyed."

Mel. "It may be your interest to be our masters, but how can it be ours to be your slaves?"

Ath. "To you the gain will be that by submission you will avert the worst; and we shall be all the richer for your preservation."

Mel. "But must we be your enemies? Will you not receive

us as friends if we are neutral and remain at peace with you?"

Ath. "No, your enmity is not half so mischievous to us as your friendship; for the one is in the eyes of our subjects an argument of our power, the other of our weakness."

Mel. "But are your subjects really unable to distinguish between states in which you have no concern, and those which are chiefly your own colonies, and in some cases have revolted and been subdued by you?"

Ath. "Why, they do not doubt that both of them have a good deal to say for themselves on the score of justice, but they think that states like yours are left free because they are able to defend themselves, and that we do not attack them because we dare not. So that your subjection will give us an increase of security, as well as an extension of empire. For we are masters of the sea, and you who are islanders, and insignificant islanders too, must not be allowed to escape us."

Mel. "But do you not recognize another danger? For, once more, since you drive us from the plea of justice and press upon us your doctrine of expediency, we must show you what is for our interest, and, if it be for yours also, may hope to convince you:— Will you not be making enemies of all who are now neutrals? When they see how you are treating us they will expect you some day to turn against them; and if so, are you not strengthening the enemies whom you already have, and bringing upon you others who, if they could help, would never dream of being your enemies at all?"

Ath. "We do not consider our really dangerous enemies to be any of the peoples inhabiting the mainland who, secure in their freedom, may defer indefinitely any measures of precaution which they take against us, but islanders who, like you, happen to be under no control, and all who may be already irritated by the necessity of submission to our empire—these are our real enemies, for they are the most reckless and most likely to bring themselves as well as us into a danger which they cannot but foresee."

Mel. "Surely then, if you and your subjects will brave all this risk, you to preserve your empire and they to be quit of it, how base and cowardly would it be in us, who retain our freedom, not to do and suffer anything rather than be your slaves."

Ath. "Not so, if you calmly reflect: for you are not fighting against equals to whom you cannot yield without disgrace, but you are taking counsel whether or no you shall resist an overwhelming force. The question is not one of honor but of prudence."

Mel. "But we know that the fortune of war is sometimes impartial, and not always on the side of numbers. If we yield now, all is over; but if we fight, there is yet a hope that we may stand upright."

Ath. "Hope is a good comforter in the hour of danger, and when men have something else to depend upon, although hurtful, she is not ruinous. But when her spendthrift nature has induced them to stake their all, they see her as she is in the moment of their fall, and not till then. While the knowledge of her might enable them to be ware of her, she never fails. You are weak and a single turn of the scale might be your ruin. Do not you be thus deluded; avoid the error of which so many are guilty, who, although they might still be saved if they would take the natural means, when visible grounds of confidence forsake them, have recourse to the invisible, to prophecies and oracles and the like, which ruin men by the hopes which they inspire in them."

Mel. "We know only too well how hard the struggle must be against your power, and against fortune, if she does not mean to be impartial. Nevertheless we do not despair of fortune; for we hope to stand as high as you in the favor of heaven, because we are righteous, and you against whom we contend are unrighteous; and we are satisfied that our deficiency in power will be compensated by the aid of our allies the Lacedaemonians; they cannot refuse to help us, if only because we are their kinsmen, and for the sake of their own honor. And therefore our confidence is not so utterly blind as you suppose."

Ath. "As for the Gods, we expect to have quite as much of their favor as you: for we are not doing or claiming anything which goes beyond common opinion about divine or men's desires about human things. For of the Gods we believe, and of men we know, that by a law of their nature wherever they can rule they will. This law was not made by us, and we are not the first who have acted upon it; we did but inherit it, and shall bequeath it to all time, and we know that you and all mankind, if you were as strong as we are, would do as we do. So much for the Gods; we have told you why we expect to stand as high in their good opinion as you. And then as to the Lacedaemonians—when you imagine that out of very shame they will assist you, we admire the innocence of your idea, but we do not envy you the folly of it. The Lacedaemonians are exceedingly virtuous among themselves, and according to their national standard of morality. But, in respect of their dealings with others, although many things might be said, they can be described in few words—of all men whom we know they are the most notorious for identifying what is pleasant with what is honorable, and what is expedient with what is just. But how inconsistent is such a character with your present blind hope of deliverance!"

Mel. "That is the very reason why we trust them; they will look to their interest, and therefore will not be willing to betray the Melians, who are their own colonists, lest they should be distrusted by their friends in Hellas and play into the hands of their enemies."

Ath. "But do you not see that the path of expediency is safe, whereas justice and honor involve danger in practice, and such dangers the Lacedaemonians seldom care to face?"

Mel. "On the other hand, we think that whatever perils there may be, they will be ready to face them for our sakes, and will consider danger less dangerous where we are concerned. For if they need our aid we are close at hand, and they can better trust our loyal feeling because we are their kinsmen."

Ath. "Yes, but what encourages men who are invited to join in a conflict is clearly not the good-will of those who summon them to their side, but a decided superiority in real power. To this no men look more keenly than the Lacedaemonians; so little confidence have they in their own resources, that they only attack their neighbors when they have numerous allies, and therefore they are not likely to find their way by themselves to an island, when we are masters of the sea."

Mel. "But they may send their allies: the Cretan sea is a large place; and the masters of the sea will have more difficulty in overtaking vessels which want to escape than the pursued in escaping. If the attempt should fail they may invade Attica itself, and find their way to allies of yours whom Brasidas did not reach: and then you will have to fight, not for the conquest of a land in which you have no concern, but nearer home, for the preservation of your confederacy and of your own territory."

Ath. "Help may come from Lacedaemon to you as it has come to others, and should you ever have actual experience of it, then you will know that never once have the Athenians retired from a siege through fear of a foe elsewhere. You told us that the safety of your city would be your first care, but we remark that, in this long discussion, not a word has been uttered by you which would give a reasonable man expectation of deliverance. Your strongest grounds are hopes deferred, and what power you have is not to be compared with that which is already arrayed against you. Unless after we have withdrawn you mean to come, as even now you may, to a wiser conclusion, you are showing a great want of sense. For surely you cannot dream of flying to that false sense of honor which has been the ruin of so many when danger and dishonor were staring them in the face. Many men with their eyes still open to the consequences have found the word 'honor' too much for them, and have suffered a mere name to lure them on, until it has drawn down upon them real and irretrievable calamities; through their own folly they have incurred a worse dishonor than fortune would have inflicted upon them. If you are wise you will not run this risk; you ought to see that there can be no disgrace in yielding to a great city which invites you to become her ally on reasonable terms, keeping your own land, and merely paying tribute; and that you will certainly gain no honor if, having to choose between two alternatives, safety and war, you obstinately prefer the worse. To maintain our rights against equals, to be politic with superiors, and to be moderate toward inferiors is the path of safety. Reflect once more when we have withdrawn, and say to yourselves over and over again that you are deliberating about your one and only country, which may be saved or may be destroyed by a single decision."

The Athenians left the conference: the Melians, after consulting among themselves, resolved to persevere in their refusal, and made answer as follows:—"Men of Athens, our resolution is unchanged; and we will not in a moment surrender that liberty which our city, founded seven hundred years ago, still enjoys; we will trust to the good fortune which, by the favor of the Gods, has hitherto preserved us, and for human help to the Lacedaemonians, and endeavor to save ourselves. We are ready however to be your friends, and the enemies neither of you nor of the Lacedaemonians, and we ask you to leave our country when you have made such a peace as may appear to be in the interest of both parties."

Such was the answer of the Melians; the Athenians, as they quitted the conference, spoke as follows:—"Well, we must say, judging from the decision at which you have arrived, that you are the only men who deem the future to be more certain than the present, and regard things unseen as already realized in your fond anticipation, and that the more you cast yourselves upon the Lacedaemonians and fortune and hope, and trust them, the more complete will be your ruin."

The Athenian envoys returned to the army; and the generals, when they found that the Melians would not yield, immediately commenced hostilities. They surrounded the town of Melos with a wall, dividing the work among the several contingents. They then left troops of their own and of their allies to keep guard both by land and by sea, and retired with the greater part of their army; the remainder carried on the blockade.

. . . The Melians took that part of the Athenian wall which looked toward the agora by a night assault, killed a few men, and brought in as much grain and other necessaries as they could; they then retreated and remained inactive. After this the Athenians set a better watch. . . .

About the same time the Melians took another part of the Athenian wall; for the fortifications were insufficiently guarded.

Whereupon the Athenians sent fresh troops, under the command of Philocrates the son of Demeas. The place was now closely invested, and there was treachery among the citizens themselves. So the Melians were induced to surrender at discretion. The Athenians thereupon put to death all who were of military age, and made slaves of the women and children. They then colonized the island, sending thither five hundred settlers of their own. (*V, 84-116*)

[*The Athenians prepare an expedition against Sicily, 415 B.C. The leaders chosen: Nicias, an aristocrat who opposed the imperialistic venture; Lamachus, a fighter of the old school, who is soon killed; and Alcibiades—the brilliant, self-seeking nephew of Pericles—who is recalled on reaching Sicily and immediately deserts to Sparta.*]

During the same winter the Athenians conceived a desire of sending another expedition to Sicily, larger than those commanded by Laches and Eurymedon. They hoped to conquer the island. Of its great size and numerous population, barbarian as well as Hellenic, most of them knew nothing, and they never reflected that they were entering on a struggle almost as arduous as the Peloponnesian War. The voyage in a merchant-vessel round Sicily takes up nearly eight days, and this great island is all but a part of the mainland, being divided from it by a sea not much more than two miles in width. (*VI, 1*)

. . . The Athenians called an assembly, and when they heard both from their own and from the Egestaean envoys, among other inviting but untrue statements, that there was abundance of money lying ready in the temples and in the treasury of Egesta, they passed a vote that sixty ships should be sent to Sicily; Alcibiades the son of Cleinias, Nicias the son of Niceratus, and Lamachus the son of Xenophanes were appointed commanders with full powers. They were to assist Egesta against Selinus; if this did not demand all their military strength they were empowered to restore the Leontines, and generally to further in such manner as they deemed best the Athenian interests in Sicily. Five days afterward another assembly was called to consider what steps should be taken for the immediate equipment of the expedition, and to vote any additional supplies which the generals might require. Nicias, who had been appointed general against his will, thought that the people had come to a wrong conclusion, and that upon slight if specious grounds they were aspiring to the conquest of Sicily, which was no easy task. So, being desirous of diverting the Athenians from their purpose, he came forward and admonished them . . . . (VI, 8)

. . . Most of the Athenians who came forward to speak were in favor of war, and reluctant to rescind the vote which had been already passed, although a few took the other side. The most enthusiastic supporter of the expedition was Alcibiades the son of Cleinias; he was determined to oppose Nicias, who was always his political enemy and had just now spoken of him in disparaging terms; but the desire to command was even a stronger motive with him. He was hoping that he might be the conqueror of Sicily and Carthage; and that success would repair his private fortunes, and gain him money as well as glory. He had a great position among the citizens and was devoted to horse-racing and other pleasures which outran his means. And in the end his wild courses went far to ruin the Athenian state. For the people feared the extremes to which he carried the lawlessness of his personal habits, and the far-reaching purposes which invariably animated him in all his actions. They thought that he was aiming at a tyranny and set themselves against him. And therefore, although his talents as a military commander were unrivaled, they entrusted the administration of the war to others, because they personally objected to his private habits; and so they speedily shipwrecked the state. . . . (VI, 15)

The people were more than ever resolved upon war. Nicias, seeing that his old argument would no longer deter them, but that he might possibly change their minds if he insisted on the magnitude of the force which would be required, came forward again and spoke. (VI, 19)

. . . He meant either to deter the Athenians by bringing home to them the vastness of the undertaking, or to provide as far as he could for the security of the expedition if he were compelled to proceed. The result disappointed him. Far from losing their enthusiasm at the disagreeable prospect, they were more determined than ever; they approved of his advice, and were confident that every chance of danger was now removed. All alike were seized with a passionate desire to sail, the elder among them convinced that they would achieve the conquest of Sicily,— at any rate such an armament could suffer no disaster; the youth were longing to see with their own eyes the marvels of a distant land, and were confident of a safe return; the main body of the troops expected to receive present pay, and to conquer a country which would be an inexhaustible mine of pay for the future. The enthusiasm of the majority was so overwhelming that, although some disapproved, they were afraid of being thought unpatriotic if they voted on the other side, and therefore held their peace.

At last an Athenian came forward and, calling upon Nicias, said that they would have no more excuses and delays; he must speak out and say what forces the people were to vote him. He replied, with some unwillingness, that he would prefer to consider the matter at leisure with his colleagues, but that, as far as he could see at present, they ought to have at least a hundred triremes of their own; of these a certain number might be used as transports, and they must order more triremes from their allies. Of heavy-armed troops they would require in all, including Athenians and allies, not less than five thousand, and more if they could possibly have them; the rest of the armament must be in proportion, and should comprise archers to be procured both at home and from Crete, and slingers. These forces, and whatever else seemed to be required, the generals would make ready before they started.

Upon this the Athenians at once decreed that the generals should be empowered to act as they thought best in the interest of the state respecting the numbers of the army and the whole management of the expedition. Then the preparations began. Lists for service were made up at home and orders given to the allies. The city had newly recovered from the plague and from the constant pressure of war; a new population had grown up; there had been time for the accumulation of money during the peace; so that there was abundance of everything at command.

While they were in the midst of their preparations, the Hermae or square stone figures carved after the ancient Athenian fashion, and standing everywhere at the doorways both of temples and private houses, in one night had nearly all of them throughout the city their faces mutilated. The offenders were not known, but great rewards were publicly offered for their detection, and a decree was passed that any one, whether citizen, stranger, or slave, might without fear of punishment disclose this or any other profanation of which he was cognizant. The Athenians took the matter greatly to heart—it seemed to them ominous of the fate of the expedition; and they ascribed it to conspirators who wanted to effect a revolution and to overthrow the democracy.

Certain metics and servants gave information, not indeed about the Hermae, but about the mutilation of other statues which had shortly before been perpetrated by some young men in a drunken frolic: they also said that the mysteries were repeatedly profaned by the celebration of them in private houses, and of this impiety they accused, among others, Alcibiades. A party who were jealous of his influence over the people, which interfered with the permanent establishment of their own, thinking that if they could get rid of him they would be supreme, took up and exaggerated the charges against him, clamorously insisting that both the mutilation of the Hermae and the profanation of the mysteries were part of a conspiracy against the democracy, and that he was at the bottom of the whole affair. In proof they alleged the excesses of his ordinary life, which were unbecoming in the citizen of a free state.

He strove then and there to clear himself of the charges, and also offered to be tried before he sailed (for all was now ready), in order that, if he were guilty, he might be punished, and if acquitted, might retain his command. He adjured his countrymen to listen to no calumnies which might be propagated against him in his absence; and he protested that they would be wiser in not sending a man who had so serious an imputation hanging over him on a command so important. But his enemies feared that if the trial took place at once he would have the support of the army; and that the people would be lenient, and would not forget that he had induced the Argives and some Mantineans to join in the expedition. They therefore exerted themselves to postpone the trial. To this end they suborned fresh speakers, who proposed that he should sail now and not delay the expedition, but should return and stand his trial within a certain number of days. Their intention was that he should be recalled and tried when they had stirred up a stronger feeling against him, which they could better do in his absence. So it was decided that Alcibiades should sail.

About the middle of summer the expedition started for Sicily. Orders had been previously given to most of the allies, to the grain-ships, the smaller craft, and generally to the vessels in attendance on the armament, that they should muster at Corcyra, whence the whole fleet was to strike across the Ionian gulf to the promontory of Iapygia. Early in the morning of the day appointed for their departure, the Athenian forces and such of their allies as had already joined them went down to the Piraeus and began to man the ships. Almost the entire population of Athens accompanied them, citizens and strangers alike. The citizens came to take farewell, one of an acquaintance, another of a kinsman, another of a son, and as they passed along were full of hope and full of tears; hope of conquering Sicily, tears because they doubted whether they would ever see their friends again, when they thought of the long voyage on which they were going away. At the last moment of parting the danger was nearer; and terrors which had never occurred to them when they were voting the expedition now entered into their souls. Nevertheless their spirits revived at the sight of the armament in all its strength and of the abundant provision which they had made. The strangers and the rest of the multitude came out of curiosity, desiring to witness an enterprise of which the greatness exceeded belief.

No armament so magnificent or costly had ever been sent out by any single Hellenic power, though in mere number of ships and hoplites that which sailed to Epidaurus under Pericles and afterward under Hagnon to Potidaea was not inferior. For that expedition consisted of a hundred Athenian and fifty Chian and Lesbian triremes, conveying four thousand hoplites all Athenian citizens, three hundred cavalry, and a multitude of allied troops. Still the voyage was short and the equipments were poor, whereas this expedition was intended to be long absent, and was thoroughly provided both for sea and land service, wherever its presence might be required. On the fleet the greatest pains and expense had been lavished by the trierarchs and the state. The public treasury gave a drachma a day to each sailor, and furnished empty hulls for sixty swift-sailing vessels, and for forty transports carrying hoplites. All these were manned with the best crews which could be obtained. The trierarchs, besides the pay given by the state, added somewhat more out of their own means to the wages of the upper ranks of rowers and of the petty officers. The figure-heads and other fittings provided by them were of the most costly description. Every one strove to the utmost that his own ship might excel both in beauty and swiftness. The infantry had been well selected and the lists carefully made up. There was the keenest rivalry among the soldiers in the matter of arms and personal equipment. And while at home the Athenians were thus competing with one another in the performance of their several duties, to the rest of Hellas the expedition seemed to be a grand display of their power and greatness, rather than a preparation for war. If any one had reckoned up the whole expenditure, both of the state and of individual soldiers and others, including in the first not only what the city had already laid out, but what was entrusted to the generals, and in the second what either at the time or afterward private persons spent upon their outfit, or the trierarchs upon their ships, the provision for the long voyage which every one may be supposed to have carried with him over and above his public pay, and what soldiers or traders may have taken for purposes of exchange, he would have found that altogether an immense sum amounting to many talents was withdrawn from the city. Men were quite amazed at the boldness of the scheme and the magnificence of the spectacle, which were everywhere spoken of, no less than at the great disproportion of the force when compared with that of the enemy against whom it was intended. Never had a greater expedition been sent to a foreign land; never was there an enterprise in which the hope of future success seemed to be better justified by actual power.

When the ships were manned and everything required for the voyage had been placed on board, silence was proclaimed by the sound of the trumpet, and all with one voice before setting sail offered up the customary prayers; these were recited, not in each ship separately, but by a single herald, the whole fleet accompanying him. On every deck both the officers and the marines, mingling wine in bowls, made libations from vessels of gold and silver. The multitude of citizens and other well-wishers who were looking on from the land joined in the prayer. The crews raised the paean and, when the libations were completed, put to sea. After sailing out for some distance in single file, the ships raced with one another as far as Aegina; thence they hastened onward to Corcyra, where the allies who formed the rest of the army were assembling. (VI, 24-32)

[The sea battle at Syracuse and the ensuing retreat by land, 413 B.C. Almost all of the 45,000 Athenians and their allies, who had sailed in two glorious fleets against Sicily with high hopes, were annihilated.]

When Gylippus and the other Syracusan generals had, like Nicias, encouraged their troops, perceiving the Athenians to be manning their ships, they presently did the same. Nicias, overwhelmed by the situation, and seeing how great and how near the peril was (for the ships were on the very point of rowing out), feeling too, as men do on the eve of a great struggle, that all which he had done was nothing, and that he had not said half enough, again addressed the trierarchs, and calling each of them by his father's name, and his own name, and the name of his tribe, he entreated those who had made any reputation for themselves not to be false to it, and those whose ancestors were eminent not to tarnish their hereditary fame. He reminded them that they were the inhabitants of the freest country in the world, and how in Athens there was no interference with the daily life of any man. He spoke to them of their wives and children and their fathers' Gods, as men will at such a time; for then they do not care whether their common-place phrases seem to be out of date or not, but loudly reiterate the old appeals, believing that they may be of some service at the awful moment. When he thought that he had exhorted them, not enough, but as much as the scanty time allowed, he retired, and led the land-forces to the shore, extending the line as far as he could, so that they might be of the greatest use in encouraging the combatants on board ship. Demosthenes, Menander, and Euthydemus. who had gone on board the Athenian fleet to take the command, now quitted their own station, and proceeded straight to the closed mouth of the harbor, intending to force their way to the open sea where a passage was still left.

The Syracusans and their allies had already put out with nearly the same number of ships as before. A detachment of them guarded the entrance of the harbor; the remainder were disposed all round it in such a manner that they might fall on the Athenians from every side at once, and that their land-forces might at the same time be able to co-operate wherever the ships retreated to the shore. Sicanus and Agatharchus commanded the Syracusan fleet, each of them a wing; Pythen and the Corinthians occupied the center. When the Athenians approached the closed mouth of the harbor the violence of their onset overpowered the ships which were stationed there; they then attempted to loosen the fastenings. Whereupon from all sides the Syracusans and their allies came bearing down upon them, and the conflict was no longer confined to the entrance, but extended throughout the harbor. No previous engagement had been so fierce and obstinate. Great was the eagerness with which the rowers on both sides rushed upon their enemies whenever the word of command was given; and keen was the contest between the pilots as they maneuvered one against another. The marines too were full of anxiety that, when ship struck ship, the service on deck should not fall short of the rest; every one in the place assigned to him was eager to be foremost among his fellows. Many vessels meeting—and never did so many fight in so small a space, for the two fleets together amounted to nearly two hundred—they were seldom able to strike in the regular manner, because they had no opportunity of first retiring or breaking the line; they generally fouled one another as ship dashed against ship in the hurry of flight or pursuit. All the time that another vessel was bearing down, the men on deck poured showers of javelins and arrows and stones upon the enemy; and when the two closed, the marines fought hand to hand, and endeavored to board. In many places, owing to the want of room, they who had struck another found that they were struck themselves; often two or even more vessels were unavoidably entangled about one, and the pilots had to make plans of attack and defense, not against one adversary only, but against several coming from different sides. The crash of so many ships dashing against one another took away the wits of the crews, and made it impossible to hear the boatswains, whose voices in both fleets rose high, as they gave directions to the rowers, or cheered them on in the excitement of the struggle. On the Athenian side they were shouting to their men that they must force a passage and seize the opportunity now or never of returning in safety to their native land. To the Syracusans and their allies was represented the glory of preventing the escape of their enemies, and of a victory by which every man would exalt the honor of his own city. The commanders too, when they saw any ship backing without necessity, would call the captain by his name, and ask, of the Athenians, whether they were retreating because they expected to be more at home upon the land of their bitterest foes than upon that sea which had been their own so long; on the Syracusan side, whether, when they knew perfectly well that the Athenians were only eager to find some means of flight, they would themselves fly from the fugitives.

While the naval engagement hung in the balance the two armies on shore had great trial and conflict of soul. The Sicilian soldier was animated by the hope of increasing the glory which he had already won, while the invader was tormented by the fear that his fortunes might sink lower still. The last chance of the Athenians lay in their ships, and their anxiety was dreadful. The fortune of the battle varied; and it was not possible that the spectators on the shore should all receive the same impression of it.

Being quite close and having different points of view, they would some of them see their own ships victorious; their courage would then revive, and they would earnestly call upon the Gods not to take from them their hope of deliverance. But others, who saw their ships worsted, cried and shrieked aloud, and were by the sight alone more utterly unnerved than the defeated combatants themselves. Others again, who had fixed their gaze on some part of the struggle which was undecided, were in a state of excitement still more terrible; they kept swaying their bodies to and fro in an agony of hope and fear as the stubborn conflict went on and on; for at every instant they were all but saved or all but lost. And while the strife hung in the balance you might hear in the Athenian army at once lamentation, shouting, cries of victory or defeat, and all the various sounds which are wrung from a great host in extremity of danger. Not less agonizing were the feelings of those on board. At length the Syracusans and their allies, after a protracted struggle, put the Athenians to flight, and triumphantly bearing down upon them, and encouraging one another with loud cries and exhortations, drove them to land. Then that part of the navy which had not been taken in the deep water fell back in confusion to the shore, and the crews rushed out of the ships into the camp. And the land-forces, no longer now divided in feeling, but uttering one universal groan of intolerable anguish, ran, some of them to save the ships, others to defend what remained of the wall; but the greater number began to look to themselves and to their own safety. Never had there been a greater panic in an Athenian army than at that moment. They now suffered what they had done to others at Pylos. For at Pylos the Lacedaemonians, when they saw their ships destroyed, knew that their friends who had crossed over into the island of Sphacteria were lost with them. And so now the Athenians, after the rout of their fleet, knew that they had no hope of saving themselves by land unless events took some extraordinary turn.

Thus, after a fierce battle and a great destruction of ships and men on both sides, the Syracusans and their allies gained the victory. They gathered up the wrecks and bodies of the dead, and sailing back to the city, erected a trophy. The Athenians, overwhelmed by their misery, never so much as thought of recovering their wrecks or of asking leave to collect their dead. Their intention was to retreat that very night. Demosthenes came to Nicias and proposed that they should once more man their remaining vessels and endeavor to force the passage at daybreak, saying that they had more ships fit for service than the enemy. For the Athenian fleet still numbered sixty, but the enemy had less than fifty. Nicias approved of his proposal, and they would have manned the ships, but the sailors refused to embark; for they were paralyzed by their defeat, and had no longer any hope of succeeding. So the Athenians all made up their minds to escape by land.

Hermocrates the Syracusan suspected their intention, and dreading what might happen if their vast army, retreating by land and settling somewhere in Sicily, should choose to renew the war, he went to the authorities, and represented to them that they ought not to allow the Athenians to withdraw by night (mentioning his own suspicion of their intentions), but that all the Syracusans and their allies should go out in advance, wall up the roads, and occupy the passes with a guard. They thought very much as he did, and wanted to carry out his plan, but doubted whether their men, who were too glad to repose after a great battle, and in time of festival—for there happened on that very day to be a sacrifice to Heracles—could be induced to obey. Most of them, in the exultation of victory, were drinking and keeping holiday, and at such a time how could they ever be expected to take up arms and go forth at the order of the generals? On these grounds the authorities decided that the thing was impossible. Whereupon Hermocrates himself, fearing lest the Athenians should gain a start and quietly pass the most difficult places in the night, contrived the following plan: when it was growing dark he sent certain of his own acquaintance, accompanied by a few horsemen, to the Athenian camp. They rode up within earshot, and pretending to be friends (there were known to be men in the city who gave information to Nicias of what went on) called to some of the soldiers, and bade them tell him not to withdraw his army during the night, for the Syracusans were guarding the roads; he should make preparation at leisure and retire by day. Having delivered their message they departed, and those who had heard them informed the Athenian generals.

On receiving this message, which they supposed to be genuine, they remained during the night. And having once given up the intention of starting immediately, they decided to remain during the next day, that the soldiers might, as well as they could, put together their baggage in the most convenient form, and depart, taking with them the bare necessaries of life, but nothing else.

Meanwhile the Syracusans and Gylippus, going forth before them with their land-forces, blocked the roads in the country by which the Athenians were likely to pass, guarded the fords of the rivers and streams, and posted themselves at the best points for receiving and stopping them. Their sailors rowed up to the beach and dragged away the Athenian ships. The Athenians themselves had burnt a few of them, as they had intended, but the rest the Syracusans towed away, unmolested and at their leisure, from the places where they had severally run aground, and conveyed them to the city.

On the third day after the sea-fight, when Nicias and Demosthenes thought that their preparations were complete, the army began to move. They were in a dreadful condition; not only was there the great fact that they had lost their whole fleet, and instead of their expected triumph had brought the utmost peril upon Athens as well as upon themselves, but also the sights which presented themselves as they quitted the camp were painful to every eye and mind. The dead were unburied, and when any one saw the body of a friend lying on the ground he was smitten with sorrow and dread, while the sick or wounded who still survived but had to be left were even a greater trial to the living, and more to be pitied than those who were gone. Their prayers and lamentations drove their companions to distraction; they would beg that they might be taken with them, and call by name any friend or relation whom they saw passing; they would hang upon their departing comrades and follow as far as they could, and, when their limbs and strength failed them, and they dropped behind, many were the imprecations and cries which they uttered. So that the whole army was in tears, and such was their despair that they could hardly make up their minds to stir, although they were leaving an enemy's country, having suffered calamities too great for tears already, and dreading miseries yet greater in the unknown future. There was also a general feeling of shame and self-reproach,—indeed they seemed, not like an army, but like the fugitive population of a city captured after a siege; and of a great city too. For the whole multitude who were marching together numbered not less than forty thousand. Each of them took with him anything he could carry which was likely to be of use. Even the heavy-armed and cavalry, contrary to their practice when under arms, conveyed about their persons their own food, some because they had no attendants, others because they could not trust them; for they had long been deserting, and most of them had gone off all at once. Nor was the food which they carried sufficient; for the supplies of the camp had failed. Their disgrace and the universality of the misery, although there might be some consolation in the very community of suffering, were nevertheless at that moment hard to bear, especially when they remembered from what pride and splendor they had fallen into their present low estate. Never had an Hellenic army experienced such a reverse. They had come intending to enslave others, and they were going away in fear that they would be themselves enslaved. Instead of the prayers and hymns with which they had put to sea, they were now departing amid appeals to heaven of another sort. They were no longer sailors but landsmen, depending, not upon their fleet, but upon their infantry. Yet in face of the great danger which still threatened them all these things appeared endurable.

Nicias, seeing the army disheartened at their terrible fall, went along the ranks and encouraged and consoled them as well as he could. In his fervor he raised his voice as he passed from one to another and spoke louder and louder, desiring that the benefit of his words might reach as far as possible.

"Even now, Athenians and allies, we must hope: men have been delivered out of worse straits than these, and I would not have you judge yourselves too severely on account either of the reverses which you have sustained or of your present undeserved miseries. I too am as weak as any of you; for I am quite prostrated by my disease, as you see. And although there was a time when I might have been thought equal to the best of you in the happiness of my private and public life, I am now in as great danger, and as much at the mercy of fortune, as the meanest. Yet my days have been passed in the performance of many a religious duty, and of many a just and blameless action. Therefore my hope of the future is still courageous, and our calamities do not appall me as they might. Who knows that they may not be lightened? For our enemies have had their full share of success, and if we were under the jealousy of any God when our fleet started, by this time we have been punished enough. Others ere now have attacked their neighbors; they have done as men will do, and suffered what men can bear. We may therefore begin to hope that the Gods will be more merciful to us; for we now invite their pity rather than their jealousy. And look at your own well-armed ranks; see how many brave soldiers you are, marching in solid array, and do not be dismayed; bear in mind that wherever you plant yourselves you are a city already, and that no city in Sicily will find it easy to resist your attack, or can dislodge you if you choose to settle. Provide for the safety and good order of your own march, and remember every one of you that on whatever spot a man is compelled to fight, there if he conquer he may find a native land and a fortress. We must press forward day and night, for our supplies are but scanty. The Sicels through fear of the Syracusans still adhere to us, and if we can only reach any part of their territory we shall be among friends, and you may consider yourselves secure. We have sent to them, and they have been told to meet us and bring food. In a word, soldiers, let me tell you that you must be brave; there is no place near to which a coward can fly. And if you now escape your enemies, those of you who are not Athenians will see once more the home for which they long, while you Athenians will again rear aloft the fallen greatness of Athens. For men, and not walls or ships in which are no men, constitute a state."

Thus exhorting his troops Nicias passed through the army, and wherever he saw gaps in the ranks or the men dropping out of line, he brought them back to their proper place. Demosthenes did the same for the troops under his command, and gave them similar exhortations. The army marched disposed in a hollow oblong: the division of Nicias leading, and that of Demosthenes following; the hoplites enclosed within their ranks the baggage-bearers and the rest of the host. When they arrived at the ford of the river Anapus they found a force of the Syracusans and of their allies drawn up to meet them; these they put to flight, and getting command of the ford, proceeded on their march. The Syracusans continually harassed them, the cavalry riding alongside, and the light-armed troops hurling darts at them. On this day the Athenians proceeded about four and a half miles and encamped at a hill. On the next day they started early, and, having advanced more than two miles, descended into a level plain, and encamped. The country was inhabited, and they were desirous of obtaining food from the houses, and also water which they might carry with them, as there was little to be had for many miles in the country which lay before them. Meanwhile the Syracusans had gone forward, and at a point where the road ascends a steep hill called the Acraean height, and there is a precipitous ravine on either side, were blocking up the pass by a wall. On the next day the Athenians advanced, although again impeded by the numbers of the enemy's cavalry who rode alongside, and of their javelin-men who threw darts at them. For a long time the Athenians maintained the struggle, but at last retired to their own encampment. Their supplies were now cut off, because the horsemen circumscribed their movements.

In the morning they started early and resumed their march. They pressed onward to the hill where the way was barred, and found in front of them the Syracusan infantry drawn up to defend the wall, in deep array, for the pass was narrow. Whereupon the Athenians advanced and assaulted the barrier, but the enemy, who were numerous and had the advantage of position, threw missiles upon them from the hill, which was steep, and so, not being able to force their way, they again retired and rested. During the conflict, as is often the case in the fall of the year, there came on a storm of rain and thunder, whereby the Athenians were yet more disheartened, for they thought that everything was conspiring to their destruction. While they were resting, Gylippus and the Syracusans dispatched a division of their army to raise a wall behind them across the road by which they had come; but the Athenians sent some of their own troops and frustrated their intention. They then retired with their whole army in the direction of the plain and passed the night. On the following day they again advanced. The Syracusans now surrounded and attacked them on every side, and wounded many of them. If the Athenians advanced they retreated, but charged them when they retired, falling especially upon the hindermost of them, in the hope that, if they could put to flight a few at a time, they might strike a panic into the whole army. In this fashion the Athenians struggled on for a long time, and having advanced about three-quarters of a mile rested in the plain. The Syracusans then left them and returned to their own encampment.

The army was now in a miserable plight, being in want of every necessary; and by the continual assaults of the enemy great numbers of the soldiers had been wounded. Nicias and Demosthenes, perceiving their condition, resolved during the night to light as many watch-fires as possible and to lead off their forces. They intended to take another route and march toward the sea in the direction opposite to that from which the Syracusans were watching them. Now their whole line of march lay, not toward Catana, but toward the other side of Sicily, in the direction of Camarina and Gela, and the cities, Hellenic or Barbarian, of that region. So they lighted numerous fires and departed in the night. And then, as constantly happens in armies, especially in very great ones, and as might be expected when they were marching by night in an enemy's country, and with the enemy from whom they were flying not far off, there arose a panic among them, and they fell into confusion. The army of Nicias, which was leading the way, kept together, and got on considerably in advance, but that of Demosthenes, which was the larger half, was severed from the other division, and marched in worse order. At daybreak, however, they succeeded in reaching the sea, and striking into the Helorine road marched along it, intending as soon as they arrived at the Cacyparis to follow up the course of the river through the interior of the island. They were expecting that the Sicels for whom they had sent would meet them on this road. When they had reached the river they found there also a guard of the Syracusans cutting off the passage by a wall and palisade. They forced their way through and, crossing the river, passed on toward another river which is called the Erineus, this being the direction in which their guides led them.

When daylight broke and the Syracusans and their allies saw that the Athenians had departed, most of them thought that Gylippus had let them go on purpose, and were very angry with him. They easily found the line of their retreat, and quickly following, came up with them about the time of the midday meal. The troops of Demosthenes were last; they were marching slowly and in disorder, not having recovered from the panic of the previous night, when they were overtaken by the Syracusans, who immediately fell upon them and fought. Separated as they were from the others, they were easily hemmed in by the Syracusan cavalry and driven into a narrow space. The division of Nicias was now as much as six miles in advance, for he marched faster, thinking that their safety depended at such a time, not in remaining and fighting, if they could avoid it, but in retreating as quickly as they could, and resisting only when they were positively compelled. Demosthenes, on the other hand, who had been more incessantly harassed throughout the retreat, because marching last he was first attacked by the enemy, now, when he saw the Syracusans pursuing him, instead of pressing onward, ranged his army in order of battle. Thus lingering he was surrounded, and he and the Athenians under his command were in the greatest confusion. For they were crushed into a walled enclosure, having a road on both sides and planted thickly with olive-trees, and missiles were hurled at them from all points. The Syracusans naturally preferred this mode of attack to a regular engagement. For to risk themselves against desperate men would have been only playing into the hands of the Athenians. Moreover, every one was sparing of his life; their good fortune was already assured, and they did not want to fall in the hour of victory. Even by this irregular mode of fighting they thought that they could overpower and capture the Athenians.

And so when they had gone on all day assailing them with missiles from every quarter, and saw that they were quite worn out with their wounds and all their other sufferings, Gylippus and the Syracusans made a proclamation, first of all to the islanders, that any of them who pleased might come over to them and have their freedom. But only a few cities accepted the offer. At length an agreement was made for the entire force under Demosthenes. Their arms were to be surrendered, but no one was to suffer death, either from violence or from imprisonment, or from want of the bare means of life. So they all surrendered, being in number six thousand, and gave up what money they had. This they threw into the hollows of shields and filled four. The captives were at once taken to the city. On the same day Nicias and his division reached the river Erineus, which he crossed, and halted his army on a rising ground.

On the following day he was overtaken by the Syracusans, who told him that Demosthenes had surrendered, and bade him do the same. He, not believing them, procured a truce while he sent a horseman to go and see. Upon the return of the horseman bringing assurance of the fact, he sent a herald to Gylippus and the Syracusans, saying that he would agree, on behalf of the Athenian state, to pay the expenses which the Syracusans had incurred in the war, on condition that they should let his army go; until the money was paid he would give Athenian citizens as hostages, a man for a talent. Gylippus and the Syracusans would not accept these proposals, but attacked and surrounded this division of the army as they had the other, and hurled missiles at them from every side until the evening. They too were grievously in want of food and necessaries. Nevertheless they meant to wait for the dead of the night and then to proceed. They were just resuming their arms, when the Syracusans discovered them and raised the Paean. The Athenians, perceiving that they were detected, laid down their arms again, with the exception of about three hundred men who broke through the enemy's guard, and made their escape in the darkness as best they could.

When the day dawned Nicias led forward his army, and the Syracusans and the allies again assailed them on every side, hurling javelins and other missiles at them. The Athenians hurried on to the river Assinarus. They hoped to gain a little relief if they forded the river, for the mass of horsemen and other troops overwhelmed and crushed them; and they were worn out by fatigue and thirst. But no sooner did they reach the water than they lost all order and rushed in; every man was trying to cross first, and, the enemy pressing upon them at the same time, the passage of the river became hopeless. Being compelled to keep close together they fell one upon another, and trampled each other under foot: some at once perished, pierced by their own spears; others got entangled in the baggage and were carried down the stream. The Syracusans stood upon the further bank of the river, which was steep, and hurled missiles from above on the Athenians, who were huddled together in the deep bed of the stream and for the most part were drinking greedily. The Peloponnesians came down the bank and slaughtered them, falling chiefly upon those who were in the river. Whereupon the water at once became foul, but was drunk all the same, although muddy and dyed with blood, and the crowd fought for it.

At last, when the dead bodies were lying in heaps upon one another in the water and the army was utterly undone, some perishing in the river, and any who escaped being cut off by the cavalry, Nicias surrendered to Gylippus, in whom he had more confidence than in the Syracusans. He entreated him and the Lacedaemonians to do what they pleased with himself, but not to go on killing the men. So Gylippus gave the word to make prisoners. Thereupon the survivors, not including however a large number whom the soldiers concealed, were brought in alive. As for the three hundred who had broken through the guard in the night, the Syracusans sent in pursuit and seized them. The total of the public prisoners when collected was not great; for many were appropriated by the soldiers, and the whole of Sicily was full of them, they not having capitulated like the troops under Demosthenes. A large number also perished; the slaughter at the river being very great, quite as great as any which took place in the Sicilian war; and not a few had fallen in the frequent attacks which were made upon the Athenians during their march. Still many escaped, some at the time, others ran away after an interval of slavery, and all these found refuge at Catana.

The Syracusans and their allies collected their forces and returned with the spoil, and as many prisoners as they could take with them, into the city. The captive Athenians and allies they deposited in the quarries, which they thought would be the safest place of confinement. Nicias and Demosthenes they put to the sword, although against the will of Gylippus. For Gylippus thought that to carry home with him to Lacedaemon the generals of the enemy, over and above all his other successes, would be a brilliant triumph. One of them, Demosthenes, happened to be the greatest foe, and the other the greatest friend of the Lacedaemonians, both in the same matter of Pylos and Sphacteria. For Nicias had taken up their cause, and had persuaded the Athenians to make the peace which set at liberty the prisoners taken in the island. The Lacedaemonians were grateful to him for the service, and this was the main reason why he trusted Gylippus and surrendered himself to him. But certain Syracusans, who had been in communication with him, were afraid (such was the report) that on some suspicion of their guilt he might be put to the torture and bring trouble on them in the hour of their prosperity. Others, and especially the Corinthians, feared that, being rich, he might by bribery escape and do them further mischief. So the Syracusans gained the consent of the allies and had him executed. For these or the like reasons he suffered death. No one of the Hellenes in my time was less deserving of so miserable an end; for he lived in the practice of every virtue.

Those who were imprisoned in the quarries were at the beginning of their captivity harshly treated by the Syracusans. There were great numbers of them, and they were crowded in a deep and narrow place. At first the sun by day was still scorching and suffocating, for they had no roof over their heads, while the autumn nights were cold, and the extremes of temperature engendered violent disorders. Being cramped for room they had to do everything on the same spot. The corpses of those who died from their wounds, exposure to heat and cold, and the like, lay heaped one upon another. The smells were intolerable; and they were at the same time afflicted by hunger and thirst. During eight months they were allowed only about half a pint of water and a pint of food a day. Every kind of misery which could befall man in such a place befell them. This was the condition of all the captives for about ten weeks. At length the Syracusans sold them, with the exception of the Athenians and of any Sicilian or Italian Greeks who had sided with them in the war. The whole number of the public prisoners is not accurately known, but they were not less than seven thousand.

Of all the Hellenic actions which took place in this war, or indeed, as I think, of all Hellenic actions which are on record, this was the greatest—the most glorious to the victors, the most ruinous to the vanquished; for they were utterly and at all points defeated, and their sufferings were prodigious. Fleet and army perished from the face of the earth; nothing was saved, and of the many who went forth few returned home.

Thus ended the Sicilian expedition. (*VII, 69-87*)

XENOPHON

Translated by H. G. Dakyns

THE HELLENICA

[*The state trireme Paralus reaches Piraeus, Athens' harbor, with the news that the Athenian fleet has been destroyed at the River Aegospotami by the Spartan Lysander. The fall of Athens, 404 B.C.*]

. . . It was night when the *Paralus* reached Athens with her evil tidings, on receipt of which a bitter wail of woe broke forth. From Piraeus, following the line of the long walls up to the heart of the city, it swept and swelled, as each man to his neighbor passed on the news. On that night no man slept. There was mourning and sorrow for those that were lost, but the lamentation for the dead was merged in even deeper sorrow for themselves, as they pictured the evils they were about to suffer, the like of which they had themselves inflicted upon the men of Melos, who were colonists of the Lacedaemonians, when they mastered them by siege. Or on the men of Histiaea; on Scione and Torone; on the Aeginetans, and many another Hellenic city. On the following day the public assembly met, and, after debate, it was resolved to block up all the harbors save one, to put the walls in a state of defense, to post guards at various points, and to make all other necessary preparation for a siege. Such were the concerns of the men of Athens.

Lysander presently left the Hellespont with two hundred sail and arrived at Lesbos, where he established a new order of things in Mytilene and the other cities of the island. Meanwhile he dispatched Eteonicus with a squadron of ten ships to the northern coasts, where that officer brought about a revolution of affairs

From *The Works of Xenophon,* translated by H. G. Dakyns, London, 1890, through the courtesy of Macmillan & Co. Ltd.

which placed the whole region in the hands of Lacedaemon. Indeed, in a moment of time, after the sea-fight, the whole of Hellas had revolted from Athens, with the solitary exception of the men of Samos. These, having massacred the notables, held the state under their control. After a while Lysander sent messages to Agis at Deceleia, and to Lacedaemon, announcing his approach with a squadron of two hundred sail.

In obedience to a general order of Pausanias, the other king of Lacedaemon, a levy in force of the Lacedaemonians and all the rest of Peloponnesus, except the Argives, was set in motion for a campaign. As soon as the several contingents had arrived, the king put himself at their head and marched against Athens, encamping in the gymnasium of the Academy, as it is called. Lysander had now reached Aegina, where, having got together as many of the former inhabitants as possible, he formally reinstated them in their city; and what he did in behalf of the Aeginetans, he did also in behalf of the Melians, and of the rest who had been deprived of their countries. He then pillaged the island of Salamis, and finally came to moorings off Piraeus with one hundred and fifty ships of the line, and established a strict blockade against all merchant ships entering that harbor.

The Athenians, finding themselves besieged by land and sea, were in sore perplexity what to do. Without ships, without allies, without provisions, the belief gained hold upon them that there was no way of escape. They must now, in their turn, suffer what they had themselves inflicted upon others; not in retaliation, indeed, for ills received, but out of sheer insolence, overriding the citizens of petty states, and for no better reason than that these were allies of the very men now at their gates. In this frame of mind they enfranchised those who at any time had lost their civil rights, and schooled themselves to endurance; and, albeit many succumbed to starvation, no thought of truce or reconciliation with their foes was breathed. But when the stock of grain was absolutely insufficient, they sent an embassy to Agis, proposing to become allies of the Lacedaemonians on the sole condition of keeping their fortification walls and Piraeus; and to draw up articles of treaty on these terms. Agis bade them betake themselves to Lacedaemon, seeing that he had no authority to act himself. With this answer the ambassadors returned to Athens, and were forthwith sent on to Lacedaemon. On reaching Sellasia, a town in Laconian territory, they waited till they got their answer from the ephors, who, having learnt their terms (which were identical with those already proposed to Agis), bade them instantly to be gone, and, if they really desired peace, to come with other proposals, the fruit of happier reflection. Thus the ambassadors returned home, and reported the result of their embassy, whereupon despondency fell upon all. It was a painful reflection that in the end they would be sold into slavery; and meanwhile, pending the return of a second embassy, many must needs fall victims to starvation. The razing of their fortifications was not a solution which any one cared to recommend. A person, Archestratus, had indeed put the question in the Council, whether it were not best to make peace with the Lacedaemonians on such terms as they were willing to propose; but he was thrown into prison. The Laconian proposals referred to involved the destruction of both long walls for a space of more than a mile. And a decree had been passed, making it illegal to submit any such proposition about the walls. Things having reached this pass, Theramenes made a proposal in the public assembly as follows: If they chose to send him as an ambassador to Lysander, he would go and find out why the Lacedaemonians were so unyielding about the walls; whether it was they really intended to enslave the city, or merely that they wanted a guarantee of good faith. Dispatched accordingly, he lingered on with Lysander for three whole months and more, watching for the time when the Athenians, at the last pinch of starvation, would be willing to accede to any terms that might be offered. At last, in the fourth month, he returned and reported to the public assembly that Lysander had detained him all this while, and had ended by bidding him betake himself to Lacedaemon, since he had no authority himself to answer his questions, which must be addressed directly to the ephors. After this Theramenes was chosen with nine others to go to Lacedaemon as ambassadors with full powers. Meanwhile Lysander had sent an Athenian exile, named Aristoteles, in company of certain Lacedaemonians, to Sparta to report to the board of ephors how he had answered Theramenes, that they, and they alone, had supreme authority in matters of peace and war.

Theramenes and his companions presently reached Sellasia, and being here questioned as to the reason of their visit, replied that they had full powers to treat of peace. After which the ephors ordered them to be summoned to their presence. On their arrival a general assembly was convened, in which the Corinthians and Thebans more particularly, though their views were shared by many other Hellenes also, urged the meeting not to come to terms with the Athenians, but to destroy them. The Lacedaemonians replied that they would never reduce to slavery a city which was itself an integral portion of Hellas, and had performed a great and noble service to Hellas in the most perilous of emergencies. On the contrary, they were willing to offer peace on the terms now specified—namely, "That the long walls and the fortifications of Piraeus should be destroyed; that the Athenian fleet, with the exception of twelve vessels, should be surrendered; that the exiles should be restored; and lastly, that the Athenians should acknowledge the headship of Sparta in peace and war, leaving to her the choice of friends and foes, and following her lead by land and sea." Such were the terms which Theramenes and the rest who acted with him were able to report on their return to Athens. As they entered the city, a vast crowd met them, trembling lest their mission should have proved fruitless. For indeed delay was no longer possible, so long already was the list of victims daily perishing from starvation. On the day following, the ambassadors delivered their report, stating the terms upon which the Lacedaemonians were willing to make peace. Theramenes acted as spokesman, insisting that they ought to obey the Lacedaemonians and pull down the walls. A small minority raised their voice in opposition, but the majority were strongly in favor of the proposition, and the resolution was passed to accept the peace. After that, Lysander sailed into the Piraeus, and the exiles were readmitted. And so they fell to leveling the fortifications and walls with much enthusiasm, to the accompaniment of female flute-players, deeming that day the beginning of liberty to Greece. (*II*, 2)

POLYBIUS

Translated by Evelyn S. Shuckburgh

THE HISTORIES

Preface. Constitutions in general, especially those of Greece and Rome.
A comparison of constitutions.

> [Preface. Constitutions in general, and particularly those
> of Sparta and Rome.]

I am aware that some will be at a loss to account for my in-
terrupting the course of my narrative for the sake of entering upon
the following disquisition on the Roman constitution. But I
think that I have already in many passages made it fully evident
that this particular branch of my work was one of the necessities
imposed on me by the nature of my original design; and I pointed
this out with special clearness in the preface which explained the
scope of my history. I there stated that the feature of my work
which was at once the best in itself, and the most instructive to
the students of it, was that it would enable them to know and
fully realize in what manner, and under what kind of constitution,
it came about that nearly the whole world fell under the power
of Rome in somewhat less than fifty-three years,—an event certainly without precedent. This being my settled purpose, I could
see no more fitting period than the present for making a pause,
and examining the truth of the remarks about to be made on this
constitution. In private life if you wish to satisfy yourself as to
the badness or goodness of particular persons, you would not, if
you wish to get a genuine test, examine their conduct at a time of
uneventful repose, but in the hour of brilliant success or conspicuous reverse. For the true test of a perfect man is the power

of bearing with spirit and dignity violent changes of fortune. An examination of a constitution should be conducted in the same way: and therefore being unable to find in our day a more rapid or more signal change than that which has happened to Rome, I reserved my disquisition on its constitution for this place.

What is really educational and beneficial to students of history is the clear view of the causes of events, and the consequent power of choosing the better policy in a particular case. Now in every practical undertaking by a state we must regard as the most powerful agent for success or failure the form of its constitution; for from this as from a fountain-head all conceptions and plans of action not only proceed, but attain their consummation. (VI, 1)

Of the Greek republics, which have again and again risen to greatness and fallen into insignificance, it is not difficult to speak, whether we recount their past history or venture an opinion on their future. For to report what is already known is an easy task, nor is it hard to guess what is to come from our knowledge of what has been. But in regard to the Romans it is neither an easy matter to describe their present state, owing to the complexity of their constitution; nor to speak with confidence of their future, from our inadequate acquaintance with their peculiar institutions in the past whether affecting their public or their private life. It will require then no ordinary attention and study to get a clear and comprehensive conception of the distinctive features of this constitution.

Now, it is undoubtedly the case that most of those who profess to give us authoritative instruction on this subject distinguish three kinds of constitutions, which they designate *kingship, aristocracy, democracy*. But in my opinion the question might fairly be put to them, whether they name these as being the *only* ones, or as the *best*. In either case I think they are wrong. For it is plain that we must regard as the *best* constitution that which partakes of all these three elements. And this is no mere assertion, but has been proved by the example of Lycurgus, who was the first to construct a constitution—that of Sparta—on this principle. Nor can we admit that these are the *only* forms: for we have had before now examples of absolute and tyrannical forms of government, which, while differing as widely as possible from kingship, yet appear to have some points of resemblance to it; on which account all absolute rulers falsely assume and use, as far as they can, the title of king. Again there have been many instances of oligarchical governments having in appearance some analogy to aristocracies, which are, if I may say so, as different from them as it is possible to be. The same also holds good about democracy.

I will illustrate the truth of what I say. We cannot hold every absolute government to be a kingship, but only that which is accepted voluntarily, and is directed by an appeal to reason rather than to fear and force. Nor again is every oligarchy to be regarded as an aristocracy; the latter exists only where the power is wielded by the justest and wisest men selected on their merits. Similarly, it is not enough to constitute a democracy that the whole crowd of citizens should have the right to do whatever they wish or propose. But where reverence to the gods, succor of parents, respect to elders, obedience to laws, are traditional and habitual, in such communities, if the will of the majority prevail, we may speak of the form of government as a democracy. So then we enumerate six forms of government,—the three commonly spoken of which I have just mentioned, and three more allied forms, I mean *despotism, oligarchy* and *mob-rule*. The first of these arises without artificial aid and in the natural order of events. Next to this, and produced from it by the aid of art and adjustment, comes *kingship;* which degenerating into the evil form allied to it, by which I mean *tyranny,* both are once more destroyed and *aristocracy* produced. Again the latter being in the course of nature perverted to *oligarchy,* and the people passionately avenging the unjust acts of their rulers, *democracy* comes into existence; which again by its violence and contempt of law becomes sheer *mob-rule*. No clearer proof of the truth of what I say could be obtained than by a careful observation of the natural origin, genesis, and decadence of these several forms of government. For it is only by seeing distinctly how each of them is produced that a distinct view can also be obtained of its growth, zenith, and decadence, and the time, circumstance, and place in which each of these may be expected to recur. This method I have assumed to be especially applicable to the Roman constitution, because its origin and growth have from the first followed natural causes.

Now the natural laws which regulate the merging of one form of government into another are perhaps discussed with greater accuracy by Plato and some other philosophers. But their treatment, from its intricacy and exhaustiveness, is only within the capacity of a few. I will therefore endeavor to give a summary of the subject, just so far as I suppose it to fall within the scope of a practical history and the intelligence of ordinary people. For if my exposition appear in any way inadequate, owing to the general terms in which it is expressed, the details contained in what is immediately to follow will amply atone for what is left for the present unsolved.

What is the origin then of a constitution, and whence is it produced? Suppose that from floods, pestilences, failure of crops, or some such causes the race of man is reduced almost to extinction. Such things we are told have happened, and it is reasonable to think will happen again. Suppose accordingly all knowledge of social habits and arts to have been lost. Suppose that from the survivors, as from seeds, the race of man to have again multiplied. In that case I presume they would, like the animals, herd together; for it is but reasonable to suppose that bodily weakness would induce them to seek those of their own kind to herd with. And in that case too, as with the animals, he who was superior to the rest in strength of body or courage of soul would lead and rule them. For what we see happen in the case of animals that are without the faculty of reason, such as bulls, goats, and cocks,— among whom there can be no dispute that the strongest take the lead,—that we must regard as in the truest sense the teaching of nature. Originally then it is probable that the condition of life among men was this,—herding together like animals and following the strongest and bravest as leaders. The limit of this authority would be physical strength, and the name we should give it would be despotism. But as soon as the idea of family ties and social relation has arisen among such agglomerations of men, then is born also the idea of kingship, and then for the first time mankind conceives the notion of goodness and justice and their reverse.

The way in which such conceptions originate and come into existence is this. The intercourse of the sexes is an instinct of nature, and the result is the birth of children. Now, if any one of these children who have been brought up, when arrived at maturity, is ungrateful and makes no return to those by whom he was nurtured, but on the contrary presumes to injure them by word and deed, it is plain that he will probably offend and annoy such as are present, and have seen the care and trouble bestowed by the parents on the nurture and bringing up of their children. For seeing that men differ from the other animals in being the only creatures possessed of reasoning powers, it is clear that such a difference of conduct is not likely to escape their observation; but that they will remark it when it occurs, and express their displeasure on the spot: because they will have an eye to the future, and will reason on the likelihood of the same occurring to each of themselves. Again, if a man has been rescued or helped in an hour of danger, and, instead of showing gratitude to his preserver, seeks to do him harm, it is clearly probable that the rest will be displeased and offended with him, when they know it: sympathizing with their neighbor and imagining themselves in his case. Hence arises a notion in every breast of the meaning and theory of duty, which is in fact the beginning and end of justice. Similarly, again, when any one man stands out as the champion of all in a time of danger, and braves with firm courage the onslaught of the most powerful wild beasts, it is probable that such a man would meet with marks of favor and pre-eminence from the common people; while he who acted in a contrary way would fall under their contempt and dislike. From this, once more, it is reasonable to suppose that there would arise in the minds of the multitude a theory of the disgraceful and the honorable, and of the difference between them; and that one should be sought and imitated for its advantages, the other shunned. When, therefore, the leading and most powerful man among his people ever encourages such persons in accordance with the popular sentiment, and thereby assumes in the eyes of his subject the appearance of being the distributor to each man according to his deserts, they no longer obey him and support his rule from fear of violence, but rather from conviction of its utility, however old he may be, rallying round him with one heart and soul, and fighting against all who form designs against his government. In this way he becomes a *king* instead of a *despot* by imperceptible degrees, reason having ousted brute courage and bodily strength from their supremacy.

This then is the natural process of formation among mankind of the notion of goodness and justice, and their opposites; and this is the origin and genesis of genuine kingship: for people do not only keep up the government of such men personally, but for their descendants also for many generations; from the conviction that those who are born from and educated by men of this kind will have principles also like theirs. But if they subsequently become displeased with their descendants, they do not any longer decide their choice of rulers and kings by their physical strength or brute courage; but by the differences of their intellectual and reasoning faculties, from practical experience of the decisive importance of such a distinction. In old times, then, those who were once thus selected, and obtained this office, grew old in their royal functions, making magnificent strongholds and surrounding them with walls and extending their frontiers, partly for the security of their subjects, and partly to provide them with abundance of the necessaries of life; and while engaged in these works they were exempt from all vituperation or jealousy; because they did not make their distinctive dress, food, or drink, at all conspicuous, but lived very much like the rest, and joined in the everyday employments of the common people. But when their royal power became hereditary in their family, and they found every necessary for security ready to their hands, as well as more than was necessary for their personal support, then they gave the rein to their appetites; imagined that rulers must needs wear different clothes from those of subjects; have different and elaborate luxuries of the table; and must even seek sensual indulgence, however unlawful the source, without fear of denial. These things having given rise in the one case to jealousy and offense, in the other to outburst of hatred and passionate resentment, the kingship became a tyranny: the first step in disintegration was taken; and plots began to be formed against the government, which did not now proceed from the worst men but from the noblest, most high-minded, and most courageous, because these are the men who can least submit to the tyrannical acts of their rulers.

But as soon as the people got leaders, they co-operated with them against the dynasty for the reasons I have mentioned; and then *kingship* and *despotism* were alike entirely abolished, and *aristocracy* once more began to revive and start afresh. For in their immediate gratitude to those who had deposed the despots, the people employed them as leaders, and entrusted their interests to them; who, looking upon this charge at first as a great privilege, made the public advantage their chief concern, and conducted all kinds of business, public or private, with diligence and caution. But when the sons of these men received the same position of authority from their fathers,—having had no experience of misfortunes, and none at all of civil equality and freedom of speech, but having been bred up from the first under the shadow of their fathers' authority and lofty position,—some of them gave themselves up with passion to avarice and unscrupulous love of money, others to drinking and the boundless debaucheries which accompany it, and others to the violation of women or the forcible appropriation of boys; and so they turned an *aristocracy* into an *oligarchy*. But it was not long before they roused in the minds of the people the same feelings as before; and their fall therefore was very like the disaster which befell the tyrants.

For no sooner had the knowledge of the jealousy and hatred existing in the citizens against them emboldened some one to oppose the government by word or deed, than he was sure to find the whole people ready and prepared to take his side. Having then got rid of these rulers by assassination or exile, they do not venture to set up a king again, being still in terror of the injustice to which this led before; nor dare they entrust the common interests again to more than one, considering the recent example of their misconduct: and therefore, as the only sound hope left them is that which depends upon themselves, they are driven to take refuge in that; and so changed the constitution from an oligarchy to a *democracy*, and took upon themselves the superintendence and charge of the state. And as long as any survive who have had experience of oligarchical supremacy and domination, they regard their present constitution as a blessing, and hold equality and freedom as of the utmost value. But as soon as a new generation has arisen, and the democracy has descended to their children's children, long association weakens their value for equality and freedom, and some seek to become more powerful than the ordinary citizens; and the most liable to this temptation are the rich. So when they begin to be fond of office, and find themselves unable to obtain it by their own unassisted efforts and their own merits, they ruin their estates, while enticing and corrupting the common people in every possible way. By which means when, in their senseless mania for reputation, they have made the populace ready and greedy to receive bribes, the virtue of democracy is destroyed, and it is transformed into a government of violence and the strong hand. For the mob, habituated to feed at the expense of others, and to have its hopes of a livelihood in the property of its neighbors, as soon as it has got a leader sufficiently ambitious and daring, being excluded by poverty from the sweets of civil honors, produces a reign of mere violence. Then come tumultuous assemblies, massacres, banishments, re-divisions of land; until, after losing all trace of civilization, it has once more found a master and a despot.

This is the regular cycle of constitutional revolutions, and the natural order in which constitutions change, are transformed, and return again to their original stage. If a man have a clear grasp of these principles he may perhaps make a mistake as to the dates at which this or that will happen to a particular constitution; but he will rarely be entirely mistaken as to the stage of growth or decay at which it has arrived, or as to the point at which it will undergo some revolutionary change. However, it is in the case of the Roman constitution that this method of inquiry will most fully teach us its formation, its growth, and zenith, as well as the changes awaiting it in the future; for this, if any constitution ever did, owed, as I said just now, its original foundation and growth to natural causes, and to natural causes will owe its decay. My subsequent narrative will be the best illustration of what I say.

For the present I will make a brief reference to the legislation of Lycurgus: for such a discussion is not at all alien to my subject.

That statesman was fully aware that all those changes which I have enumerated come about by an undeviating law of nature; and reflected that every form of government that was unmixed, and rested on one species of power, was unstable; because it was swiftly perverted into that particular form of evil peculiar to it and inherent in its nature. For just as rust is the natural dissolvent of iron, wood-worms and grubs to timber, by which they are destroyed without any external injury, but by that which is engendered in themselves; so in each constitution there is naturally engendered a particular vice inseparable from it: in kingship it is absolutism; in aristocracy it is oligarchy; in democracy lawless ferocity and violence; and to these vicious states all these forms of government are, as I have lately shown, inevitably transformed. Lycurgus, I say, saw all this, and accordingly combined together all the excellences and distinctive features of the best constitutions, that no part should become unduly predominant, and be perverted into its kindred vice; and that, each power being checked by the others, no one part should turn the scale or decisively out-balance the others; but that, by being accurately adjusted and in exact equilibrium, the whole might remain long steady like a ship sailing close to the wind. The royal power was prevented from growing insolent by fear of the people, which had also assigned to it an adequate share in the constitution. The people in their turn were restrained from a bold contempt of the kings by fear of the Gerusia: the members of which, being selected on grounds of merit, were certain to throw their influence on the side of justice in every question that arose; and thus the party placed at a disadvantage by its conservative tendency was always strengthened and supported by the weight and influence of the Gerusia. The result of this combination has been that the Lacedaemonians retained their freedom for the longest period of any people with which we are acquainted.

Lycurgus however established his constitution without the discipline of adversity, because he was able to foresee by the light of reason the course which events naturally take and the source from which they come. But though the Romans have arrived at the same result in framing their commonwealth, they have not done so by means of abstract reasoning, but through many struggles and difficulties, and by continually adopting reforms from knowledge gained in disaster. The result has been a constitution like that of Lycurgus, and the best of any existing in my time. . . .

I have given an account of the constitution of Lycurgus. I will now endeavor to describe that of Rome at the period of their disastrous defeat at Cannae.

I am fully conscious that to those who actually live under this constitution I shall appear to give an inadequate account of it by the omission of certain details. Knowing accurately every portion of it from personal experience, and from having been bred up in its customs and laws from childhood, they will not be struck so much by the accuracy of the description, as annoyed by its omissions; nor will they believe that the historian has purposely omitted unimportant distinctions, but will attribute his silence upon the origin of existing institutions or other important facts to ignorance. What is told they depreciate as insignificant or beside the purpose; what is omitted they desiderate as vital to the question: their object being to appear to know more than the writers. But a good critic should not judge a writer by what he leaves unsaid, but from what he says: if he detects mis-statement in the latter, he may then feel certain that ignorance accounts for the former; but if what he says is accurate, his omissions ought to be attributed to deliberate judgment and not to ignorance. So much for those whose criticisms are prompted by personal ambition rather than by justice. . . .

Another requisite for obtaining a judicious approval for an historical disquisition, is that it should be germane to the matter in hand; if this is not observed, though its style may be excellent and its matter irreproachable, it will seem out of place, and disgust rather than please. . . .

As for the Roman constitution, it had three elements, each of them possessing sovereign powers: and their respective share of power in the whole state had been regulated with such a scrupulous regard to equality and equilibrium, that no one could say for certain, not even a native, whether the constitution as a whole were an aristocracy or democracy or despotism. And no wonder: for if we confine our observation to the power of the Consuls we should be inclined to regard it as despotic; if on that of the Senate, as aristocratic; and if finally one looks at the power possessed by the people it would seem a clear case of a democracy. What the exact powers of these several parts were, and still, with slight modifications, are, I will now state.

The Consuls, before leading out the legions, remain in Rome and are supreme masters of the administration. All other magistrates, except the Tribunes, are under them and take their orders. They introduce foreign ambassadors to the Senate; bring matters requiring deliberation before it; and see to the execution of its decrees. If, again, there are any matters of state which require the authorization of the people, it is their business to see to them, to summon the popular meetings, to bring the proposals before them, and to carry out the decrees of the majority. In the preparations for war also, and in a word in the entire administration of a campaign, they have all but absolute power. It is competent to them to impose on the allies such levies as they think good, to appoint the Military Tribunes, to make up the roll for soldiers and select those that are suitable. Besides they have absolute power of inflicting punishment on all who are under their command while on active service: and they have authority to expend as much of the public money as they choose, being accompanied by a quaestor who is entirely at their orders. A survey of these powers would in fact justify our describing the constitution as despotic,—a clear case of royal government. Nor will it affect the truth of my description, if any of the institutions I have described are changed in our time, or in that of our posterity: and the same remarks apply to what follows.

The Senate has first of all the control of the treasury, and regulates the receipts and disbursements alike. For the Quaestors cannot issue any public money for the various departments of the state without a decree of the Senate, except for the service of the Consuls. The Senate controls also what is by far the largest and most important expenditure, that, namely, which is made by the censors every *lustrum* for the repair or construction of public buildings; this money cannot be obtained by the censors except by the grant of the Senate. Similarly all crimes committed in Italy requiring a public investigation, such as treason, conspiracy, poisoning, or willful murder, are in the hands of the Senate. Besides, if any individual or state among the Italian allies requires a controversy to be settled, a penalty to be assessed, help or protection to be afforded,—all this is the province of the Senate. Or again, outside Italy, if it is necessary to send an embassy to reconcile warring communities, or to remind them of their duty, or sometimes to impose requisitions upon them, or to receive their submission, or finally to proclaim war against them,—this too is the business of the Senate. In like manner the reception to be given to foreign ambassadors in Rome, and the answers to be returned to them, are decided by the Senate. With such business the people have nothing to do. Consequently, if one were staying at Rome when the Consuls were not in town, one would imagine the constitution to be a complete aristocracy: and this has been the idea entertained by many Greeks, and by many kings as well, from the fact that nearly all the business they had with Rome was settled by the Senate.

After this one would naturally be inclined to ask what part is left for the people in the constitution, when the Senate has these various functions, especially the control of the receipts and expenditure of the exchequer; and when the Consuls, again, have absolute power over the details of military preparation, and an absolute authority in the field? There is, however, a part left the people, and it is a most important one. For the people is the sole fountain of honor and of punishment; and it is by these two things and these alone that dynasties and constitutions and, in a word, human society are held together: for where the distinction between them is not sharply drawn both in theory and practice, there no undertaking can be properly administered,—as indeed we might expect when good and bad are held in exactly the same honor. The people then are the only court to decide matters of life and death; and even in cases where the penalty is money, if the sum to be assessed is sufficiently serious, and especially when the accused have held the higher magistracies. And in regard to this arrangement there is one point deserving especial commendation and record. Men who are on trial for their lives at Rome, while sentence is in process of being voted,—if even only one of the tribes whose votes are needed to ratify the sentence has not voted,—have the privilege at Rome of openly departing and condemning themselves to a voluntary exile. Such men are safe at Naples or Praeneste or at Tibur, and at other towns with which this arrangement has been duly ratified on oath.

Again, it is the people who bestow offices on the deserving, which are the most honorable rewards of virtue. It has also the absolute power of passing or repealing laws; and, most important of all, it is the people who deliberate on the question of peace or war. And when provisional terms are made for alliance, suspension of hostilities, or treaties, it is the people who ratify them or the reverse.

These considerations again would lead one to say that the chief power in the state was the people's, and that the constitution was a democracy.

Such, then, is the distribution of power between the several parts of the state. I must now show how each of these several parts can, when they choose, oppose or support each other.

The Consul, then, when he has started on an expedition with the powers I have described, is to all appearance absolute in the administration of the business in hand; still he has need of the support both of people and Senate, and, without them, is quite unable to bring the matter to a successful conclusion. For it is plain that he must have supplies sent to his legions from time to time; but without a decree of the Senate they can be supplied neither with grain, nor clothes, nor pay, so that all the plans of a commander must be futile, if the Senate is resolved either to shrink from danger or hamper his plans. And again, whether a Consul shall bring any undertaking to a conclusion or no depends entirely upon the Senate: for it has absolute authority at the end of a year to send another Consul to supersede him, or to continue the existing one in his command. Again, even to the successes of the generals the Senate has the power to add distinction and glory, and on the other hand to obscure their merits and lower their credit. For these high achievements are brought in tangible form

before the eyes of the citizens by what are called "triumphs." But these triumphs the commanders cannot celebrate with proper pomp, or in some cases celebrate at all, unless the Senate concurs and grants the necessary money. As for the people, the Consuls are pre-eminently obliged to court their favor, however distant from home may be the field of their operations; for it is the people, as I have said before, that ratifies, or refuses to ratify, terms of peace and treaties; but most of all because when laying down their office they have to give an account of their administration before it. Therefore in no case is it safe for the Consuls to neglect either the Senate or the good-will of the people.

As for the Senate, which possesses the immense power I have described, in the first place it is obliged in public affairs to take the multitude into account, and respect the wishes of the people; and it cannot put into execution the penalty for offenses against the republic, which are punishable with death, unless the people first ratify its decrees. Similarly even in matters which directly affect the senators,—for instance, in the case of a law diminishing the Senate's traditional authority, or depriving senators of certain dignities and offices, or even actually cutting down their property, —even in such cases the people have the sole power of passing or rejecting the law. But most important of all is the fact that, if the Tribunes interpose their veto, the Senate not only are unable to pass a decree, but cannot even hold a meeting at all, whether formal or informal. Now, the Tribunes are always bound to carry out the decree of the people, and above all things to have regard to their wishes: therefore, for all these reasons the Senate stands in awe of the multitude, and cannot neglect the feelings of the people.

In like manner the people on its part is far from being independent of the Senate, and is bound to take its wishes into account both collectively and individually. For contracts, too numerous to count, are given out by the censors in all parts of Italy for the repairs or construction of public buildings; there is also the collection of revenue from many rivers, harbors, gardens, mines, and land—everything, in a word, that comes under the control of the Roman government: and in all these the people at large are engaged; so that there is scarcely a man, so to speak, who is not interested either as a contractor or as being employed in the works. For some purchase the contracts from the censors for themselves; and others go partners with them; while others again go security for these contractors, or actually pledge their property to the treasury for them. Now over all these transactions the Senate has absolute control. It can grant an extension of time; and in case of unforeseen accident can relieve the contractors from a portion of their obligation, or release them from it altogether, if they are absolutely unable to fulfill it. And there are many details in which the Senate can inflict great hardships, or, on the other hand, grant great indulgences to the contractors: for in every case the appeal is to it. But the most important point of all is that the judges are taken from its members in the majority of trials, whether public or private, in which the charges are heavy. Consequently, all citizens are much at its mercy; and being alarmed at the uncertainty as to when they may need its aid, are cautious about resisting or actively opposing its will. And for a similar reason men do not rashly resist the wishes of the Consuls, because one and all may become subject to their absolute authority on a campaign.

The result of this power of the several estates for mutual help or harm is a union sufficiently firm for all emergencies, and a constitution than which it is impossible to find a better. For whenever any danger from without compels them to unite and work together, the strength which is developed by the State is so extraordinary, that everything required is unfailingly carried out by the eager rivalry shown by all classes to devote their whole minds to the need of the hour, and to secure that any determination come to should not fail for want of promptitude; while each individual works, privately and publicly alike, for the accomplishment of the business in hand. Accordingly, the peculiar constitution of the State makes it irresistible, and certain of obtaining whatever it determines to attempt. Nay, even when these external alarms are past, and the people are enjoying their good fortune and the fruits of their victories, and, as usually happens, growing corrupted by flattery and idleness, show a tendency to violence and arro-

gance,—it is in these circumstances, more than ever, that the
constitution is seen to possess within itself the power of correcting
abuses. For when any one of the three classes becomes puffed up,
and manifests an inclination to be contentious and unduly encroaching, the mutual interdependency of all the three, and the
possibility of the pretensions of any one being checked and
thwarted by the others, must plainly check this tendency: and
so the proper equilibrium is maintained by the impulsiveness of
the one part being checked by its fear of the other. (*VI, 3-18*)

[*A comparison of constitutions.*]

Nearly all historians have recorded as constitutions of eminent
excellence those of Lacedaemonia, Crete, Mantinea, and Carthage.
Some have also mentioned those of Athens and Thebes. The
former I may allow to pass; but I am convinced that little need
be said of the Athenian and Theban constitutions: their growth
was abnormal, the period of their zenith brief, and the changes
they experienced unusually violent. Their glory was a sudden and
fortuitous flash, so to speak; and while they still thought themselves prosperous, and likely to remain so, they found themselves
involved in circumstances completely the reverse. The Thebans
got their reputation for valor among the Greeks, by taking advantage of the senseless policy of the Lacedaemonians, and the
hatred of the allies toward them, owing to the valor of one, or
at most two, men who were wise enough to appreciate the situation. Since fortune quickly made it evident that it was not the
peculiarity of their constitution, but the valor of their leaders,
which gave the Thebans their success. For the great power of
Thebes notoriously took its rise, attained its zenith, and fell to
the ground with the lives of Epaminondas and Pelopidas. We
must therefore conclude that it was not its constitution, but its
men, that caused the high fortune which it then enjoyed.

A somewhat similar remark applies to the Athenian constitution also. For though it perhaps had more frequent interludes of
excellence, yet its highest perfection was attained during the
brilliant career of Themistocles; and having reached that point

it quickly declined, owing to its essential instability. For the Athenian demos is always in the position of a ship without a commander. In such a ship, if fear of the enemy, or the occurrence of a storm induce the crew to be of one mind and to obey the helmsman, everything goes well; but if they recover from this fear, and begin to treat their officers with contempt, and to quarrel with each other because they are no longer all of one mind,—one party wishing to continue the voyage, and the other urging the steersman to bring the ship to anchor; some letting out the sheets, and others hauling them in, and ordering the sails to be furled,— their discord and quarrels make a sorry show to lookers on; and the position of affairs is full of risk to those on board engaged on the same voyage: and the result has often been that, after escaping the dangers of the widest seas, and the most violent storms, they wreck their ship in harbor and close to shore. And this is what has often happened to the Athenian constitution. For, after repelling, on various occasions, the greatest and most formidable dangers by the valor of its people and their leaders, there have been times when, in periods of secure tranquillity, it has gratuitously and recklessly encountered disaster. Therefore I need say no more about either it, or the Theban constitution: in both of which a mob manages everything on its own unfettered impulse—a mob in the one city distinguished for headlong outbursts of fiery temper, in the other trained in long habits of violence and ferocity. (VI, 43-44)

. . . Nor again would it be fair to introduce the Republic of Plato, which is also spoken of in high terms by some philosophers. For just as we refuse admission to the athletic contests to those actors or athletes who have not acquired a recognized position or trained for them, so we ought not to admit this Platonic constitution to the contest for the prize of merit unless it can first point to some genuine and practical achievement. Up to this time the notion of bringing it into comparison with the constitutions of Sparta, Rome, and Carthage would be like putting up a statue to compare with living and breathing men. Even if such a statue were faultless in point of art, the comparison of the life-

less with the living would naturally leave an impression of imperfection and incongruity upon the minds of the spectators.

I shall therefore omit these, and proceed with my description of the Laconian constitution. Now it seems to me that for securing unity among the citizens, for safe-guarding the Laconian territory, and preserving the liberty of Sparta inviolate, the legislation and provisions of Lycurgus were so excellent, that I am forced to regard his wisdom as something superhuman. For the equality of landed possessions, the simplicity in their food, and the practice of taking it in common, which he established, were well calculated to secure morality in private life and to prevent civil broils in the State; as also their training in the endurance of labors and dangers to make men brave and noble minded: but when both these virtues, courage and high morality, are combined in one soul or in one state, vice will not readily spring from such a soil, nor will such men easily be overcome by their enemies. By constructing his constitution therefore in this spirit, and of these elements, he secured two blessings to the Spartans,—safety for their territory, and a lasting freedom for themselves long after he was gone. He appears however to have made no one provision whatever, particular or general, for the acquisition of the territory of their neighbors; or for the assertion of their supremacy; or, in a word, for any policy of aggrandizement at all. What he had still to do was to impose such a necessity, or create such a spirit among the citizens, that, as he had succeeded in making their individual lives independent and simple, the public character of the state should also become independent and moral. But the actual fact is, that, though he made them the most disinterested and sober-minded men in the world, as far as their own ways of life and their national institutions were concerned, he left them in regard to the rest of Greece ambitious, eager for supremacy, and encroaching in the highest degree. (VI, 47-48)

My object, then, in this digression is to make it manifest by actual facts that, for guarding their own country with absolute safety, and for preserving their own freedom, the legislation of Lycurgus was entirely sufficient; and for those who are content with these objects we must concede that there neither exists, nor ever has existed, a constitution and civil order preferable to that of Sparta. But if any one is seeking aggrandizement, and believes that to be a leader and ruler and despot of numerous subjects, and to have all looking and turning to him, is a finer thing than that, —in this point of view we must acknowledge that the Spartan constitution is deficient, and that of Rome superior and better constituted for obtaining power. And this has been proved by actual facts. For when the Lacedaemonians strove to possess themselves of the supremacy in Greece, it was not long before they brought their own freedom itself into danger. Whereas the Romans, after obtaining supreme power over the Italians themselves, soon brought the whole world under their rule,—in which achievement the abundance and availability of their supplies largely contributed to their success.

Now the Carthaginian constitution seems to me originally to have been well contrived in these most distinctively important particulars. For they had kings, and the Gerusia had the powers of an aristocracy, and the multitude were supreme in such things as affected them; and on the whole the adjustment of its several parts was very like that of Rome and Sparta. But about the period of its entering on the Hannibalian war the political state of Carthage was on the decline, that of Rome improving. For whereas there is in every body, or polity, or business a natural stage of growth, zenith, and decay; and whereas everything in them is at its best at the zenith; we may thereby judge of the difference between these two constitutions as they existed at that period. For exactly so far as the strength and prosperity of Carthage preceded that of Rome in point of time, by so much was Carthage then past its prime, while Rome was exactly at its zenith, as far as its political constitution was concerned. In Carthage therefore the influence of the people in the policy of the state had already risen to be supreme, while at Rome the Senate was at the height of its power: and so, as in the one measures were deliberated upon by the many, in the other by the best men, the policy of the Romans in all public undertakings proved the stronger; on which account,

though they met with capital disasters, by force of prudent counsels they finally conquered the Carthaginians in the war.

If we look however at separate details, for instance at the
provisions for carrying on a war, we shall find that whereas for a
naval expedition the Carthaginians are the better trained and
prepared,—as it is only natural with a people with whom it has
been hereditary for many generations to practice this craft, and
to follow the seaman's trade above all nations in the world,—yet,
in regard to military service on land, the Romans train themselves
to a much higher pitch than the Carthaginians. The former bestow
their whole attention upon this department: whereas the Carthaginians wholly neglect their infantry, though they do take some
slight interest in the cavalry. The reason of this is that they employ
foreign mercenaries, the Romans native and citizen levies. It is
in this point that the latter polity is preferable to the former. They
have their hopes of freedom ever resting on the courage of mercenary troops: the Romans on the valor of their own citizens and
the aid of their allies. The result is that even if the Romans have
suffered a defeat at first, they renew the war with undiminished
forces, which the Carthaginians cannot do. For, as the Romans
are fighting for country and children, it is impossible for them to
relax the fury of their struggle; but they persist with obstinate
resolution until they have overcome their enemies. What has
happened in regard to their navy is an instance in point. In skill
the Romans are much behind the Carthaginians, as I have already
said; yet the upshot of the whole naval war has been a decided
triumph for the Romans, owing to the valor of their men. For
although nautical science contributes largely to success in sea-
fights, still it is the courage of the marines that turns the scale
most decisively in favor of victory. The fact is that Italians as a
nation are by nature superior to Phoenicians and Libyans both
in physical strength and courage; but still their habits also do
much to inspire the youth with enthusiasm for such exploits.
One example will be sufficient of the pains taken by the Roman
state to turn out men ready to endure anything to win a reputation
in their country for valor.

Whenever one of their illustrious men dies, in the course of his funeral, the body with all its paraphernalia is carried into the forum to the Rostra, as a raised platform there is called, and sometimes is propped upright upon it so as to be conspicuous, or, more rarely, is laid upon it. Then with all the people standing round, his son, if he has left one of full age and he is there, or, failing him, one of his relations, mounts the Rostra and delivers a speech concerning the virtues of the deceased, and the successful exploits performed by him in his lifetime. By these means the people are reminded of what has been done, and made to see it with their own eyes,—not only such as were engaged in the actual transactions but those also who were not;—and their sympathies are so deeply moved, that the loss appears not to be confined to the actual mourners, but to be a public one affecting the whole people. After the burial and all the usual ceremonies have been performed, they place the likeness of the deceased in the most conspicuous spot in his house, surmounted by a wooden canopy or shrine. This likeness consists of a mask made to represent the deceased with extraordinary fidelity both in shape and color. These likenesses they display at public sacrifices adorned with much care. And when any illustrious member of the family dies, they carry these masks to the funeral, putting them on men whom they thought as like the originals as possible in height and other personal peculiarities. And these substitutes assume clothes according to the rank of the person represented: if he was a consul or praetor, a toga with purple stripes; if a censor, whole purple; if he had also celebrated a triumph or performed any exploit of that kind, a toga embroidered with gold. These representatives also ride themselves in chariots, while the fasces and axes, and all the other customary insignia of the particular offices, lead the way, according to the dignity of the rank in the state enjoyed by the deceased in his lifetime; and on arriving at the Rostra they all take their seats on ivory chairs in their order. There could not easily be a more inspiring spectacle than this for a young man of noble ambitions and virtuous aspirations. For can we conceive any one to be unmoved at the sight of all the likenesses collected together of the

jecting them. This is the reason why, apart from anything else, Greek statesmen, if entrusted with a single talent, though protected by ten checking-clerks, as many seals, and twice as many witnesses, yet cannot be induced to keep faith: whereas among the Romans, in their magistracies and embassies, men have the handling of a great amount of money, and yet from pure respect to their oath keep their faith intact. And, again, in other nations it is a rare thing to find a man who keeps his hands out of the public purse, and is entirely pure in such matters: but among the Romans it is a rare thing to detect a man in the act of committing such a crime. . . .

That to all things, then, which exist there is ordained decay and change I think requires no further arguments to show: for the inexorable course of nature is sufficient to convince us of it.

But in all polities we observe two sources of decay existing from natural causes, the one external, the other internal and self-produced. The external admits of no certain or fixed definition, but the internal follows a definite order. What kind of polity, then, comes naturally first, and what second, I have already stated in such a way, that those who are capable of taking in the whole drift of my argument can henceforth draw their own conclusions as to the future of the Roman polity. For it is quite clear, in my opinion. When a commonwealth, after warding off many great dangers, has arrived at a high pitch of prosperity and undisputed power, it is evident that, by the lengthened continuance of great wealth within it, the manner of life of its citizens will become more extravagant; and that the rivalry for office, and in other spheres of activity, will become fiercer than it ought to be. And as this state of things goes on more and more, the desire of office and the shame of losing reputation, as well as the ostentation and extravagance of living, will prove the beginning of a deterioration. And of this change the people will be credited with being the authors, when they become convinced that they are being cheated by some from avarice, and are puffed up with flattery by others from love of office. For when that comes about, in their passionate resentment and acting under the dictates of anger, they will refuse to obey any longer, or to be content with having equal powers with their leaders, but will demand to have all or far the greatest themselves. And when that comes to pass the constitution will receive a new name, which sounds better than any other in the world, liberty or democracy; but, in fact, it will become that worst of all governments, mob-rule.

With this description of the formation, growth, zenith, and present state of the Roman polity, and having discussed also its difference, for better and worse, from other polities, I will now at length bring my essay on it to an end. (*VI, 50-57*)

LIVY

Translated by D. Spillan and Cyrus Edmonds

[*Book I translated by D. Spillan; the remainder by both*]

THE HISTORY OF ROME

Preface. The founding of Rome. Hannibal invades Italy. The Battle at Lake Trasimenus. The Battle at Cannae. Confusion at Rome. Death of Hasdrubal. Publius Cornelius Scipio "Africanus" gives Carthage peace terms and returns to Rome.

[Preface.]

Whether in tracing the history of the Roman people, from the foundation of the city, I shall employ myself to a useful purpose, I am neither very certain, nor, if I were, dare I say: inasmuch as I observe, that it is both an old and hackneyed practice, later authors always supposing that they will either adduce something more authentic in the facts, or, that they will excel the less polished ancients in their style of writing. Be that as it may, it will, at all events, be a satisfaction to me, that I too have contributed my share to perpetuate the achievements of a people, the lords of the world; and if, amidst so great a number of historians, my reputation should remain in obscurity, I may console myself with the celebrity and luster of those who shall stand in the way of my fame. Moreover, the subject is both of immense labor, as being one which must be traced back for more than seven hundred years, and which, having set out from small beginnings, has increased to such a degree that it is now distressed by its own magnitude. And, to most readers, I doubt not but that the first origin and the events immediately succeeding, will afford but little pleasure, while they will be hastening to these later times, in which the strength of this overgrown people has for a long period been working its own destruction. I, on the contrary, shall seek this, as a reward of my labor, viz., to withdraw myself from the view of the calamities, which our age has witnessed for so many years, so long as I am reviewing with my whole attention these ancient times, being free from every care that may distract a writer's mind, though it can not warp it from the truth. The traditions which have come down to us of what happened before the building of the city, or before its building was contemplated, as being suitable rather to the fictions of poetry than to the genuine records of history, I have no intention either to affirm or refute. This indulgence is conceded to antiquity, that by blending things human with divine, it may make the origin of cities appear more venerable: and if any people might be allowed to consecrate their origin, and to ascribe it to the gods as its authors, such is the renown of the Roman people in war, that when they represent Mars, in particular, as their own parent and that of their founder, the nations of the world may submit to this as patiently as they submit to their sovereignty. But in whatever way these and such like matters shall be attended to, or judged of, I shall not deem of great importance. I would have every man apply his mind seriously to consider these points, viz., what their life and what their manners were; through what men and by what measures, both in peace and in war, their empire was acquired and extended; then, as discipline gradually declined, let him follow in his thoughts their morals, at first as slightly giving way, anon how they sunk more and more, then began to fall headlong, until he reaches the present times, when we can neither endure our vices, nor their remedies. This it is which is particularly salutary and profitable in the study of history, that you behold instances of every variety of conduct displayed on a conspicuous monument; that from thence you may select for yourself and for your country that which you may imitate; thence *note* what is shameful in the undertaking, and shameful in the result, which you may avoid. But either a fond partiality for the task I have undertaken deceives me, or there never was any state either greater, or more moral, or richer in good examples, nor one into which luxury and avarice made their entrance so late, and where poverty and frugality were so much and so long honored; so that the less wealth there was, the less desire was there. Of late, riches have introduced avarice, and excessive pleasures a longing for them, amidst luxury and a passion for ruining ourselves and destroying every thing else. But let complaints, which will not be agreeable even then, when perhaps they will be also necessary, be kept aloof at least from the first stage of commencing so great a work. We should rather, if it was usual with us [historians] as it is with poets, begin with good omens, vows, and prayers to the gods and goddesses to vouchsafe good success to our efforts in so arduous an undertaking. (*I, Preface*)

[The founding of Rome.]

. . . On this point the tradition is twofold: some say that Latinus, after being overcome in battle, made first a peace, and then an alliance with Aeneas: others that, when the armies were drawn out in battle-array, before the signals were sounded, Latinus advanced to the front of the troops and invited the leader of the adventurers to a conference. That he then inquired who they were, whence [they had come], or by what casualty they had left their home, and in quest of what they had landed on the Laurentine territory: after he heard that the host were Trojans, their chief Aeneas, the son of Anchises and Venus, and that, driven from their own country and their homes, which had been destroyed by fire, they were seeking a settlement and a place for building a town, struck with admiration of the noble origin of the nation and of the hero, and their spirit, alike prepared for peace or war, he confirmed the assurance of future friendship by giving his right hand: that upon this a compact was struck between the chiefs, and mutual greetings passed between the armies: that Aeneas was hospitably entertained by Latinus: that Latinus, in the presence of his household gods, added a family league to the public one, by giving Aeneas his daughter in marriage. This event confirms the Trojans in the hope of at length terminating their wanderings by a fixed and permanent settlement. They build a town. Aeneas calls it Lavinium, after the name of his wife. In a short time, too, a son was the issue of the new marriage, to whom his parents gave the name of Ascanius. (I, 1)

. . . This Ascanius, wheresoever and of whatever mother born (it is at least certain that he was the son of Aeneas), Lavinium being overstocked with inhabitants, left that flourishing and, considering these times, wealthy city to his mother or stepmother, and built for himself a new one at the foot of Mount Alba, which, being extended on the ridge of a hill, was, from its situation, called Alba Longa. Between the founding of Lavinium and the transplanting this colony to Alba Longa about thirty years intervened. Yet its power had increased to such a degree, especially after the defeat of the Etrurians, that not even upon the death of Aeneas, nor after that, during the regency of Lavinia, and the first essays of the young prince's reign, did Mezentius, the Etrurians, or any other of its neighbors dare to take up arms against it. A peace had been concluded between the two nations on these terms, that the River Albula, now called Tiber, should be the common boundary between the Etrurians and Latins. . . .

But, in my opinion, the origin of so great a city, and the establishment of an empire next in power to that of the gods, was due to the Fates. The vestal Rhea, being deflowered by force, when she had brought forth twins, declares Mars to be the father of her illegitimate offspring, either because she believed it to be so, or because a god was a more creditable author of her offense. But neither gods nor men protect her or her children from the king's cruelty: the priestess is bound and thrown into prison: the children he commands to be thrown into the current of the river. By some interposition of providence, the Tiber having overflowed its banks in stagnant pools, did not admit of any access to the regular bed of the river; and the bearers supposed that the infants could be drowned in water however still; thus, as if they had effectually executed the king's orders, they expose the boys in the nearest land-flood, where now stands the ficus Ruminalis (they say that it was called Romularis). The country thereabout was then a vast wilderness. The tradition is, that when the water, subsiding, had left the floating trough, in which the children had been exposed, on dry ground, a thirsty she-wolf, coming from the neighboring

mountains, directed her course to the cries of the infants, and
that she held down her dugs to them with so much gentleness,
that the keeper of the king's flock found her licking the boys
with her tongue. It is said his name was Faustulus; and that they
were carried by him to his homestead to be nursed by his wife
Laurentia. Some are of opinion that she was called Lupa among
the shepherds, from her being a common prostitute, and that this
gave rise to the surprising story. The children thus born and thus
brought up, when arrived at the years of manhood, did not loiter
away their time in tending the folds or following the flocks, but
roamed and hunted in the forests. Having by this exercise im-
proved their strength and courage, they not only encountered wild
beasts, but even attacked robbers laden with plunder, and afterward divided the spoil among the shepherds. And in company with
these, the number of their young associates daily increasing, they
carried on their business and their sports. (*I, 3-4*)

   . . . Thus the government of Alba being committed to Nu-
mitor, a desire seized Romulus and Remus to build a city on the
spot where they had been exposed and brought up. And there
was an overflowing population of Albans and of Latins. The
shepherds too had come into that design, and all these readily
inspired hopes that Alba and Lavinium would be but petty places
in comparison with the city which they intended to build. But
ambition of the sovereignty, the bane of their grandfather, interrupted these designs, and thence arose a shameful quarrel from a
beginning sufficiently amicable. For as they were twins, and the
respect due to seniority could not determine the point, they agreed
to leave to the tutelary gods of the place to choose, by augury,
which should give a name to the new city, which govern it when
built.

   Romulus chose the Palatine and Remus the Aventine hill as
their stands to make their observations. It is said, that to Remus
an omen came first, six vultures; and now, the omen having been
declared, when double the number presented itself to Romulus,
his own party saluted each king; the former claimed the kingdom
on the ground of priority of time, the latter on account of the
number of birds. Upon this, having met in an altercation, from

the contest of angry feelings they turn to bloodshed; there Remus fell from a blow received in the crowd. A more common account is, that Remus, in derision of his brother, leaped over his new-built wall, and was, for that reason, slain by Romulus in a passion; who, after sharply chiding him, added words to this effect: "So shall every one fare who shall dare to leap over my fortifications." Thus Romulus got the sovereignty to himself; the city, when built, was called after the name of its founder. His first work was to fortify the Palatine hill where he had been educated. To the other gods he offers sacrifices according to the Alban rite; to Hercules, according to the Grecian rite, as they had been instituted by Evander. (*I, 6-7*)

[*The Second Punic War, 218-201* B.C. *Hannibal prepares to invade Italy. The crossing of the Alps.*]

I may be permitted to premise at this division of my work, what most historians have professed at the beginning of their whole undertaking; that I am about to relate the most memorable of all wars that were ever waged: the war which the Carthaginians, under the conduct of Hannibal, maintained with the Roman people. For never did any states and nations more efficient in their resources engage in contest, nor had they themselves at any other period so great a degree of power and energy. They brought into action, too, no arts of war unknown to each other, but those which had been tried in the first Punic war; and so various was the fortune of the conflict, and so doubtful the victory, that they who conquered were more exposed to danger. The hatred with which they fought also was almost greater than their resources; the Romans being indignant that the conquered aggressively took up arms against their victors; the Carthaginians, because they considered that in their subjection it had been lorded over them with haughtiness and avarice. There is besides a story, that Hannibal, when about nine years old, while he boyishly coaxed his father Hamilcar that he might be taken to Spain (at the time when the African war was completed, and he was employed in sacrificing previously to transporting his army thither), was conducted to the altar, and, having laid his hand on the offerings, was bound by an oath to prove himself, as soon as he could, an enemy to the Roman people. The loss of Sicily and Sardinia grieved the high spirit of Hamilcar: for he deemed that Sicily had been given up through a premature despair of their affairs, and that Sardinia, during the disturbances in Africa, had been treacherously taken by the Romans, while, in addition, the payment of a tribute had been imposed. (*XXI, 1*)

. . . Hannibal, having been sent into Spain, from his very first arrival drew the eyes of the whole army upon him. The veteran soldiers imagined that Hamilcar, in his youth, was restored to them; they remarked the same vigor in his looks and animation in his eye, the same features and expression of countenance; and then, in a short time, he took care that his father should be of the least powerful consideration in conciliating their esteem. There never was a genius more fitted for the two most opposite duties of obeying and commanding; so that you could not easily decide whether he were dearer to the general or the army: and neither did Hasdrubal prefer giving the command to any other, when any thing was to be done with courage and activity; nor did the soldiers feel more confidence and boldness under any other leader. His fearlessness in encountering dangers, and his prudence when in the midst of them, were extreme. His body could not be exhausted, nor his mind subdued, by any toil. He could alike endure either heat or cold. The quantity of his food and drink was determined by the wants of nature, and not by pleasure. The seasons of his sleeping and waking were distinguished neither by day nor night. The time that remained after the transaction of business was given to repose; but that repose was neither invited by a soft bed nor by quiet. Many have seen him, wrapped in a military cloak, lying on the ground amid the watches and outposts of the soldiers. His dress was not at all superior to that of his equals: his arms and his horses were conspicuous. He was at once by far the first of the cavalry and infantry; and, foremost to advance to the charge, was last to leave the engagement. Excessive vices counterbalanced these high virtues of the hero; inhuman cruelty, more than Punic perfidy, no

truth, no reverence for things sacred, no fear of the gods, no respect for oaths, no sense of religion. With a character thus made
up of virtue and vices, he served for three years under the command of Hasdrubal, without neglecting any thing which ought to
be done or seen by one who was to become a great general.
(XXI, 4)

Hannibal, therefore, when his own resolution was fixed to
proceed in his course and advance on Italy, having summoned an
assembly, works upon the minds of the soldiers in various ways,
by reproof and exhortation. He said that "he wondered what
sudden fear had seized breasts ever before undismayed; that
through so many years they had made their campaigns with conquest; nor had departed from Spain before all the nations and
countries which two opposite seas embrace were subjected to the
Carthaginians. That then, indignant that the Romans demanded
those, whosoever had besieged Saguntum, to be delivered up to
them, as on account of a crime, they had passed the Iberus to
blot out the name of the Romans, and to emancipate the world.
That then the way seemed long to no one, though they were pursuing it from the setting to the rising of the sun. That now, when
they saw by far the greater part of their journey accomplished, the
passes of the Pyrenees surmounted, amidst the most ferocious nations, the Rhone, that mighty river, crossed, in spite of the opposition of so many thousand Gauls, the fury of the river itself
having been overcome, when they had the Alps in sight, the
other side of which was Italy, should they halt through weariness
at the very gates of the enemy, imagining the Alps to be—what
else than lofty mountains? That supposing them to be higher
than the summits of the Pyrenees, assuredly no part of the earth
reached the sky, nor was insurmountable by mankind. The Alps,
in fact, were inhabited and cultivated—produced and supported
living beings. Were they passable by a few men and impassable to
armies? That those very ambassadors whom they saw before them
had not crossed the Alps borne aloft through the air on wings;
neither were their ancestors indeed natives of the soil, but settling
in Italy from foreign countries, had often as emigrants safely
crossed these very Alps in immense bodies, with their wives and

children. To the armed soldier, carrying nothing with him but the instruments of war, what in reality was impervious or insurmountable? That Saguntum might be taken, what dangers, what toils were for eight months undergone! Now, when their aim was Rome, the capital of the world, could any thing appear so dangerous or difficult as to delay their undertaking? That the Gauls had formerly gained possession of that very country which the Carthaginian despairs of being able to approach. That they must, therefore, either yield in spirit and valor to that nation which they had so often during those times overcome; or look forward, as the end of their journey, to the plain which spreads between the Tiber and the walls of Rome."

He orders them, roused by these exhortations, to refresh themselves and prepare for the journey. Next day, proceeding upward along the bank of the Rhone, he makes for the inland part of Gaul: not because it was the more direct route to the Alps, but believing that the farther he retired from the sea, the Romans would be less in his way; with whom, before he arrived in Italy, he had no intention of engaging. . . .

Publius Cornelius the consul, about three days after Hannibal moved from the bank of the Rhone, had come to the camp of the enemy, with his army drawn up in square, intending to make no delay in fighting; but when he saw the fortifications deserted, and that he could not easily come up with them so far in advance before him, he returned to the sea and his fleet, in order more easily and safely to encounter Hannibal when descending from the Alps. But that Spain, the province which he had obtained by lot, might not be destitute of Roman auxiliaries, he sent his brother Cneius Scipio, with the principal part of his forces, against Hasdrubal, not only to defend the old allies and conciliate new, but also to drive Hasdrubal out of Spain. He himself, with a very small force, returned to Genoa, intending to defend Italy with the army which was around the Po. From the Druentia, by a road that lay principally through plains, Hannibal arrived at the Alps without molestation from the Gauls that inhabit those regions. Then, though the scene had been previously anticipated from report (by which uncertainties are wont to be exaggerated), yet the height of the mountains when viewed so near, and the snows almost mingling with the sky, the shapeless huts situated on the cliffs, the cattle and beasts of burden withered by the cold, the men unshorn and wildly dressed, all things, animate and inanimate, stiffened with frost, and other objects more terrible to be seen than described, renewed their alarm. To them, marching up the first acclivities, the mountaineers appeared occupying the heights overhead; who, if they had occupied the more concealed valleys, might, by rushing out suddenly to the attack, have occasioned great flight and havoc. Hannibal orders them to halt, and having sent forward Gauls to view the ground, when he found there was no passage that way, he pitches his camp in the widest valley he could find, among places all rugged and precipitous. Then, having learned from the same Gauls, when they had mixed in conversation with the mountaineers, from whom they differed little in language and manners, that the pass was only beset during the day, and that at night each withdrew to his own dwelling, he advanced at the dawn to the heights, as if designing openly and by day to force his way through the defile. The day then being passed in feigning a different attempt from that which was in preparation, when they had fortified the camp in the same place where they had halted, as soon as he perceived that the mountaineers had descended from the heights, and that the guards were withdrawn, having lighted for show a greater number of fires than was proportioned to the number that remained, and having left the baggage in the camp, with the cavalry and the principal part of the infantry, he himself with a party of light-armed, consisting of all the most courageous of his troops, rapidly cleared the defile, and took post on those very heights which the enemy had occupied.

At dawn of light the next day the camp broke up, and the rest of the army began to move forward. The mountaineers, on a signal being given, were now assembling from their forts to their usual station, when they suddenly behold part of the enemy overhanging them from above, in possession of their former position, and the others passing along the road. Both these objects, presented at the same time to the eye and the mind, made them

stand motionless for a little while; but when they afterward saw
the confusion in the pass, and that the marching body was thrown
into disorder by the tumult which itself created, principally from
the horses being terrified, thinking that whatever terror they added
would suffice for the destruction of the enemy, they scramble
along the dangerous rocks, as being accustomed alike to pathless
and circuitous ways. Then indeed the Carthaginians were opposed at once by the enemy and by the difficulties of the ground;
and each striving to escape first from the danger, there was more
fighting among themselves than with their opponents. The horses,
in particular, created danger in the lines, which, being terrified
by the discordant clamors which the groves and re-echoing valleys
augmented, fell into confusion; and if by chance struck or
wounded, they were so dismayed that they occasioned a great
loss both of men and baggage of every description: and as the pass
on both sides was broken and precipitous, this tumult threw many
down to an immense depth, some even of the armed men; but
the beasts of burden, with their loads, were rolled down like the
fall of some vast fabric. Though these disasters were shocking to
view, Hannibal, however, kept his place for a little, and kept his
men together, lest he might augment the tumult and disorder;
but afterward, when he saw the line broken, and that there was
danger that he should bring over his army preserved to no purpose if deprived of their baggage, he hastened down from the
higher ground; and though he had routed the enemy by the first
onset alone, he at the same time increased the disorder in his own
army: but that tumult was composed in a moment, after the roads
were cleared by the flight of the mountaineers; and presently the
whole army was conducted through, not only without being disturbed, but almost in silence. He then took a fortified place, which
was the capital of that district, and the little villages that lay
around it, and fed his army for three days with the grain and
cattle he had taken; and during these three days, as the soldiers
were neither obstructed by the mountaineers, who had been
daunted by the first engagement, nor yet much by the ground, he
made considerable way.

He then came to another state, abounding, for a mountainous

country, with inhabitants; where he was nearly overcome, not by open war, but by his own arts of treachery and ambuscade. Some old men, governors of forts, came as deputies to the Carthaginian, professing, "that having been warned by the useful example of the calamities of others, they wished rather to experience the friendship than the hostilities of the Carthaginians: they would, therefore, obediently execute his commands, and begged that he would accept of a supply of provisions, guides of his march, and hostages for the sincerity of their promises." Hannibal, when he had answered them in a friendly manner, thinking that they should neither be rashly trusted nor yet rejected, lest if repulsed they might openly become enemies, having received the hostages whom they proffered, and made use of the provisions which they of their own accord brought down to the road, follows their guides, by no means as among a people with whom he was at peace, but with his line of march in close order. The elephants and cavalry formed the van of the marching body; he himself, examining every thing around, and intent on every circumstance, followed with the choicest of the infantry. When they came into a narrower pass, lying on one side beneath an overhanging eminence, the barbarians, rising at once on all sides from their ambush, assail them in front and rear, both at close quarters and from a distance, and roll down huge stones on the army. The most numerous body of men pressed on the rear; against whom the infantry facing about and directing their attack made it very obvious that, had not the rear of the army been well supported, a great loss must have been sustained in that pass. Even as it was, they came to the extremity of danger, and almost to destruction; for while Hannibal hesitates to lead down his division into the defile, because, though he himself was a protection to the cavalry, he had not in the same way left any aid to the infantry in the rear; the mountaineers, charging obliquely, and on having broken through the middle of the army, took possession of the road; and one night was spent by Hannibal without his cavalry and baggage.

Next day, the barbarians running in to the attack between [the two divisions] less vigorously, the forces were reunited, and the defile passed, not without loss, but yet with a greater destruction of beasts of burden than of men. From that time the mountaineers fell upon them in smaller parties, more like an attack of robbers than war, sometimes on the van, sometimes on the rear, according as the ground afforded them advantage, or stragglers advancing or loitering gave them an opportunity. Though the elephants were driven through steep and narrow roads with great loss of time, yet wherever they went they rendered the army safe from the enemy, because men unacquainted with such animals were afraid of approaching too nearly. On the ninth day they came to a summit of the Alps, chiefly through places trackless; and after many mistakes of their way, which were caused either by the treachery of the guides, or, when they were not trusted, by entering valleys at random on their own conjectures of the route. For two days they remained encamped on the summit; and rest was given to the soldiers, exhausted with toil and fighting; and several beasts of burden, which had fallen down among the rocks, by following the track of the army arrived at the camp. A fall of snow, it being now the season of the setting of the constellation of the Pleiades, caused great fear to the soldiers, already worn out with weariness of so many hardships. On the standards being moved forward at day-break, when the army proceeded slowly over all places entirely blocked up with snow, and languor and despair strongly appeared in the countenances of all, Hannibal, having advanced before the standards, and ordered the soldiers to halt on a certain eminence, whence there was a prospect far and wide, points out to them Italy and the plains of the Po, extending themselves beneath the Alpine mountains; and said "that they were now surmounting not only the ramparts of Italy, but also of the city of Rome; that the rest of the journey would be smooth and down-hill; that after one, or, at most, a second battle, they would have the citadel and capital of Italy in their power and possession." The army then began to advance, the enemy now making no attempts beyond petty thefts, as opportunity offered. But the journey proved much more difficult than it had been in the ascent, as the declivity of the Alps, being generally shorter on the side of Italy, is consequently steeper; for nearly all the road was precipitous, narrow, and slippery, so that neither those who made the least stumble could prevent themselves from falling, nor, when fallen, remain in the same place, but rolled, both men and beasts of burden, one upon another.

They then came to a rock much more narrow, and formed of such perpendicular ledges that a light-armed soldier, carefully making the attempt, and clinging with his hands to the bushes and roots around, could with difficulty lower himself down. The ground, even before very steep by nature, had been broken by a recent falling away of the earth into a precipice of nearly a thousand feet in depth. Here when the cavalry had halted, as if at the end of their journey, it is announced to Hannibal, wondering what obstructed the march, that the rock was impassable. Having then gone himself to view the place, it seemed clear to him that he must lead his army round it, by however great a circuit, through the pathless and untrodden regions around. But this route also proved impracticable; for while the new snow of a moderate depth remained on the old, which had not been removed, their footsteps were planted with ease as they walked upon the new snow, which was soft and not too deep; but when it was dissolved by the trampling of so many men and beasts of burden, they then walked on the bare ice below, and through the dirty fluid formed by the melting snow. Here there was a wretched struggle, both on account of the slippery ice not affording any hold to the step, and giving way beneath the foot more readily by reason of the slope; and whether they assisted themselves in rising by their hands or their knees, their supports themselves giving way, they would tumble again; nor were there any stumps or roots near by pressing against which one might with hand or foot support himself; so that they only floundered on the smooth ice and amidst the melted snow. The beasts of burden sometimes also cut into this lower ice by merely treading upon it, at others they broke it completely through, by the violence with which they struck in their hoofs in their struggling, so that most of them, as if taken in a trap, stuck in the hardened and deeply frozen ice.

At length, after the men and beasts of burden had been fatigued to no purpose, the camp was pitched on the summit, the ground being cleared for that purpose with great difficulty, so much snow was there to be dug out and carried away. The soldiers being then set to make a way down the cliff, by which alone a passage could be effected, and it being necessary that they should cut through the rocks, having felled and lopped a number of large trees which grew around, they make a huge pile of timber; and as soon as a strong wind fit for exciting the flames arose, they set fire to it, and, pouring vinegar on the heated stones, they render them soft and crumbling. They then open a way with iron instruments through the rock thus heated by the fire, and soften its declivities by gentle windings, so that not only the beasts of burden, but also the elephants, could be led down it. Four days were spent about this rock, the beasts nearly perishing through hunger; for the summits of the mountains are for the most part bare, and if there is any pasture the snows bury it. The lower parts contain valleys, and some sunny hills, and rivulets flowing beside woods, and scenes more worthy of the abode of man. There the beasts of burden were sent out to pasture, and rest given for three days to the men, fatigued with forming the passage: they then descended into the plains, the country and the dispositions of the inhabitants being now less rugged.

In this manner chiefly they came to Italy, in the fifth month (as some authors relate) after leaving New Carthage, having crossed the Alps in fifteen days. What number of forces Hannibal had when he had passed into Italy is by no means agreed upon by authors. Those who state them at the highest, make mention of a hundred thousand foot and twenty thousand horse; those who state them at the lowest, of twenty thousand foot and six thousand horse. Lucius Cincius Alimentus, who relates that he was made prisoner by Hannibal, would influence me most as an authority, did he not confound the number by adding the Gauls and Ligurians. Including these (who, it is more probable, flocked to him afterward, and so some authors assert), he says that eighty thousand foot and ten thousand horse were brought into Italy; and that he had heard from Hannibal himself that, after crossing the Rhone, he had lost thirty-six thousand men, and an immense number of horses and other beasts of burden, among the Taurini, the next nation to the Gauls, as he descended into Italy. As this circumstance is agreed on by all, I am the more surprised that it should be doubtful by what road he crossed the Alps; and that it should commonly be believed that he passed over the Pennine mountain, and that thence the name was given to that ridge of the Alps. Coelius says that he passed over the top of Mount Cremo; both which passes would have brought him, not to the Taurini, but through the Salassian mountaineers to the Libuan Gauls. Neither is it probable that these roads into Gaul were then open, especially since those which lead to the Pennine mountain would have been blocked up by nations half German; nor by Hercules (if this argument has weight with any one) do the Veragri, the inhabitants of this ridge, know of the name being given to these mountains from the passage of the Carthaginians, but from the divinity, whom the mountaineers style Penninus, worshiped on the highest summit. (*XXI, 30-38*)

[*Hannibal wins at Lake Trasimenus in Etruria, 217* B.C. *Fabius Maximus, "the Delayer," appointed to save Rome.*]

While the consul employs himself at Rome in appeasing the gods and holding the levy, Hannibal, setting out from his winter-quarters, because it was reported that the consul Flaminius had now arrived at Arretium, although a longer but more commodious route was pointed out to him, takes the nearer road through a marsh where the Arno had, more than usual, overflowed its banks. He ordered the Spaniards and Africans (in these lay the strength of his veteran army) to lead, their own baggage being intermixed with them, lest, being compelled to halt anywhere, they should want what might be necessary for their use: the Gauls he ordered to go next, that they might form the middle of the marching body, the cavalry to march in the rear; next, Mago, with the light-armed Numidians, to keep the army together, particularly coercing the Gauls, if, fatigued with exertion and the length of the march, as that nation is wanting in vigor for such exertions, they should fall away or halt. The van still followed the standards wherever the guides did but lead them, through the exceedingly deep and almost fathomless eddies of the river, nearly swallowed up in mud, and

plunging themselves in. The Gauls could neither support themselves when fallen, nor raise themselves from the eddies. Nor did
they sustain their bodies with spirit nor their minds with hope,
some scarce dragging on their wearied limbs; others dying where
they had once fallen, their spirits being subdued with fatigue,
among the beasts which themselves also lay prostrate in every
place. But chiefly watching wore them out, endured now for
four days and three nights. When, the water covering every place,
not a dry spot could be found where they might stretch their weary
bodies, they laid themselves down upon their baggage, thrown
in heaps into the waters. Piles of beasts, which lay everywhere
through the whole route, afforded a necessary bed for temporary
repose to those seeking any place which was not under water.
Hannibal himself, riding on the only remaining elephant, to be
the higher from the water, contracted a disorder in his eyes, at
first from the unwholesomeness of the vernal air, which is attended with transitions from heat to cold; and at length, from
watching, nocturnal damps, the marshy atmosphere disordering
his head, and because he had neither opportunity nor leisure for
remedies, loses one of them.

Many men and cattle having been lost thus wretchedly,
when at length he had emerged from the marshes, he pitches his
camp as soon as he could on dry ground. And here he received
information, through the scouts sent in advance, that the Roman
army was round the walls of Arretium. Next the plans and temper
of the consul, the situation of the country, the roads, the sources
from which provisions might be obtained, and whatever else it
was useful to know; all these things he ascertained by the most
diligent inquiry. The country was among the most fertile of Italy,
the plains of Etruria, between Faesulae and Arretium, abundant
in its supply of grain, cattle, and every other requisite. The consul
was haughty from his former consulship, and felt no proper degree
of reverence not only for the laws and the majesty of the fathers,
but even for the gods. This temerity, inherent in his nature, fortune had fostered by a career of prosperity and success in civil
and military affairs. Thus it was sufficiently evident that, heedless
of gods and men, he would act in all cases with presumption and

precipitation; and, that he might fall the more readily into the errors natural to him, the Carthaginian begins to fret and irritate him; and leaving the enemy on his left, he takes the road to Faesulae, and marching through the center of Etruria, with intent to plunder, he exhibits to the consul, in the distance, the greatest devastation he could with fires and slaughters. Flaminius, who would not have rested even if the enemy had remained quiet; then, indeed, when he saw the property of the allies driven and carried away almost before his eyes, considering that it reflected disgrace upon him that the Carthaginian was now roaming at large through the heart of Italy and marching without resistance to storm the very walls of Rome, though every other person in the council advised safe rather than showy measures, urging that he should wait for his colleague, in order that, joining their armies, they might carry on the war with united courage and counsels; and that, meanwhile, the enemy should be prevented from his unrestrained freedom in plundering by the cavalry and the light-armed auxiliaries, in a fury hurried out of the council, and at once gave out the signal for marching and for battle. "Nay, rather," says he, "let us lie before the walls of Arretium, for here is our country, here our household gods. Let Hannibal, slipping through our fingers, waste Italy through and through; and, ravaging and burning every thing, let him arrive at the walls of Rome; nor let us move hence till the fathers shall have summoned Flaminius from Arretium, as they did Camillus of old from Veii." While reproaching them thus, and in the act of ordering the standards to be speedily pulled up, when he had sprung upon his horse, the animal fell suddenly, and threw the unseated consul over his head. All the by-standers being alarmed at this as an unhappy omen in the commencement of the affair, in addition word is brought that the standard could not be pulled up, though the standard-bearer strove with all his force. Flaminius, turning to the messenger, says, "Do you bring, too, letters from the Senate, forbidding me to act. Go, tell them to dig up the standard, if, through fear, their hands are so benumbed that they can not pluck it up." Then the army began to march; the chief officers, besides that they dissented from the plan, being terrified by the twofold prodigy; while the soldiery in general were elated by the confidence of their leader, since they regarded merely the hope he entertained, and not the reasons of the hope.

Hannibal lays waste the country between the city Cortona and the lake Trasimenus with all the devastation of war, the more to exasperate the enemy to revenge the injuries inflicted on his allies. They had now reached a place formed by nature for an ambuscade, where the Trasimenus comes nearest to the mountains of Cortona. A very narrow passage only intervenes, as though room enough just for that purpose had been left designedly; after that a somewhat wider plain opens itself, and then some hills rise up. On these he pitches his camp, in full view, where he himself, with his Spaniards and Africans, only might be posted. The Baliares and his other light troops he leads round the mountains; his cavalry he posts at the very entrance of the defile, some eminences conveniently concealing them; in order that when the Romans had entered, the cavalry advancing, every place might be enclosed by the lake and the mountains. Flaminius, passing the defiles before it was quite daylight, without reconnoitering, though he had arrived at the lake the preceding day at sunset, when the troops began to be spread into the wider plain, saw that part only of the enemy which was opposite to him; the ambuscade in his rear and overhead escaped his notice. And when the Carthaginian had his enemy enclosed by the lake and mountains, and surrounded by his troops, he gives the signal to all to make a simultaneous charge; and each running down the nearest way, the suddenness and unexpectedness of the event was increased to the Romans by a mist rising from the lake, which had settled thicker on the plain than on the mountains; and thus the troops of the enemy ran down from the various eminences, sufficiently well discerning each other, and therefore with the greater regularity. A shout being raised on all sides, the Roman found himself surrounded before he could well see the enemy; and the attack on the front and flank had commenced ere his line could be well formed, his arms prepared for action, or his swords unsheathed.

The consul, while all were panic-struck, himself sufficiently undaunted, though in so perilous a case, marshals, as well as the time and place permitted, the lines which were thrown into confusion by each man's turning himself toward the various shouts; and wherever he could approach or be heard, exhorts them, and bids them stand and fight: for that they could not escape thence by vows and prayers to the gods, but by exertion and valor; that a way was sometimes opened by the sword through the midst of marshaled armies, and that generally the less the fear the less the danger. However, from the noise and tumult, neither his advice nor command could be caught; and so far were the soldiers from knowing their own standards, and ranks, and position, that they had scarce sufficient courage to take up arms and make them ready for battle; and certain of them were surprised before they could prepare them, being burdened rather than protected by them; while in so great darkness there was more use of ears than of eyes. They turned their faces and eyes in every direction toward the groans of the wounded, the sounds of blows upon the body or arms, and the mingled clamors of the menacing and the affrighted. Some, as they were making their escape, were stopped, having encountered a body of men engaged in fight; and bands of fugitives returning to the battle, diverted others. After charges had been attempted unsuccessfully in every direction, and on their flanks the mountains and the lake, on the front and rear the lines of the enemy enclosed them, when it was evident that there was no hope of safety but in the right hand and the sword; then each man became to himself a leader and encourager to action; and an entirely new contest arose, not a regular line, with principes, hastati, and triarii; nor of such a sort as that the van-guard should fight before the standards, and the rest of the troops behind them; nor such that each soldier should be in his own legion, cohort, or company: chance collects them into bands; and each man's own will assigned to him his post, whether to fight in front or rear; and so great was the ardor of the conflict, so intent were their minds upon the battle, that not one of the combatants felt an earthquake which threw down large portions of many of the cities of Italy, turned rivers from their rapid courses, carried the sea up into rivers, and leveled mountains with a tremendous crash.

The battle was continued near three hours, and in every

quarter with fierceness; around the consul, however, it was still hotter and more determined. Both the strongest of the troops, and himself too, promptly brought assistance wherever he perceived his men hard-pressed and distressed. But, distinguished by his armor, the enemy attacked him with the utmost vigor, while his countrymen defended him; until an Insubrian horseman, named Ducarius, knowing him also by his face, says to his countrymen, "Lo, this is the consul who slew our legions and laid waste our fields and city. Now will I offer this victim to the shades of my countrymen, miserably slain;" and putting spurs to his horse, he rushes through a very dense body of the enemy; and first slaying his armor-bearer, who had opposed himself to his attack as he approached, ran the consul through with his lance; the triarii, opposing their shields, kept him off when seeking to despoil him. Then first the flight of a great number began; and now neither the lake nor the mountains obstructed their hurried retreat; they run through all places, confined and precipitous, as though they were blind; and arms and men are tumbled one upon another. A great many, when there remained no more space to run, advancing into the water through the first shallows of the lake, plunge in, as far as they could stand above it with their heads and shoulders. Some there were whom inconsiderate fear induced to try to escape even by swimming; but as that attempt was inordinate and hopeless, they were either overwhelmed in the deep water, their courage failing, or, wearied to no purpose, made their way back, with extreme difficulty, to the shallows; and there were cut up on all hands by the cavalry of the enemy, which had entered the water. Near upon six thousand of the foremost body, having gallantly forced their way through the opposing enemy, entirely unacquainted with what was occurring in their rear, escaped from the defile; and having halted on a certain rising ground, and hearing only the shouting and clashing of arms, they could not know nor discern, by reason of the mist, what was the fortune of the battle. At length, the affair being decided, when the mist, dispelled by the increasing heat of the sun, had cleared the atmosphere, then, in the clear light, the mountains and plains showed their ruin, and the Roman army miserably destroyed:

and thus, lest being descried at a distance, the cavalry should be sent against them, hastily snatching up their standards, they hurried away with all possible expedition. On the following day, when in addition to their extreme sufferings in other respects, famine also was at hand, Maharbal, who had followed them during the night with the whole body of cavalry, pledging his honor that he would let them depart with single garments if they would deliver up their arms, they surrendered themselves; which promise was kept by Hannibal with Punic fidelity, and he threw them all into chains.

This is the celebrated battle at the Trasimenus, and recorded among the few disasters of the Roman people. Fifteen thousand Romans were slain in the battle. Ten thousand, who had been scattered in the flight through all Etruria, returned to the city by different roads. One thousand five hundred of the enemy perished in the battle; many on both sides died afterward of their wounds. The carnage on both sides is related, by some authors, to have been many times greater. I, besides that I would relate nothing drawn from a worthless source, to which the minds of historians generally incline too much, have as my chief authority Fabius, who was contemporary with the events of this war. Such of the captives as belonged to the Latin confederacy being dismissed without ransom, and the Romans thrown into chains, Hannibal ordered the bodies of his own men to be gathered from the heaps of the enemy and buried: the body of Flaminius too, which was searched for with great diligence for burial, he could not find. On the first intelligence of this defeat at Rome, a concourse of the people, dismayed and terrified, took place in the Forum. The matrons, wandering through the streets, ask all they meet, what sudden disaster was reported? what was the fate of the army? And when the multitude, like a full assembly, having directed their course to the comitium and Senate-house, were calling upon the magistrates, at length, a little before sunset, Marcus Pomponius, the praetor, declares, "We have been defeated in a great battle;" and though nothing more definite was heard from him, yet, full of the rumors which they had caught one from another, they carry back to their homes intelligence that the consul, with a great part of his troops, was slain; that a few only survived, and these either widely dispersed in flight through Etruria, or else captured by the enemy. As many as had been the calamities of the vanquished army, into so many anxieties were the minds of those distracted whose relations had served under Flaminius, and who were uninformed of what had been the fate of their friends; nor does any one know certainly what he should either hope or fear. During the next and several successive days a greater number of women almost than men stood at the gates, waiting either for some one of their friends or for intelligence of them, surrounding and earnestly interrogating those they met: nor could they be torn away from those they knew especially, until they had regularly inquired into everything. Then, as they retired from the informants, you might discern their various expressions of countenance, according as intelligence, pleasing or sad, was announced to each; and those who congratulated or condoled on their return home. The joy and grief of the women were especially manifested. They report that one, suddenly meeting her son, who had returned safe, expired at the very door before his face; that another, who sat grieving at her house at the falsely reported death of her son, became a corpse, from excessive joy, at the first sight of him on his return. The praetors detained the Senators in the house for several days, from sunrise to sunset, deliberating under whose conduct, and by what forces, the victorious Carthaginians could be opposed.

Before their plans were sufficiently determined another unexpected defeat is reported: four thousand horse, sent under the conduct of C. Centenius, propraetor, by Servilius to his colleague, were cut off by Hannibal in Umbria, to which place, on hearing of the battle at Trasimenus, they had turned their course. The report of this event variously affected the people. Some, having their minds preoccupied with heavier grief, considered the recent loss of cavalry trifling, in comparison with their former losses; others did not estimate what had occurred by itself, but considered that, as in a body already laboring under disease, a slight cause would be felt more violently than a more powerful one in a robust constitution; so, whatever adverse event befell the state in its then sickly and impaired condition ought to be estimated, not by the magnitude of the event itself, but with reference to its exhausted strength, which could endure nothing that could oppress it. The state, therefore, took refuge in a remedy for a long time before neither wanted nor employed, the appointment of a dictator; and because the consul was absent, by whom alone it appeared he could be nominated; and because neither message nor letter could easily be sent to him through the country occupied by Punic troops; and because the people could not appoint a dictator, which had never been done to that day, the people created Quintus Fabius Maximus pro-dictator, and Marcus Minucius Rufus master of the horse. To them the Senate assigned the task of strengthening the walls and towers of the city; of placing guards in such quarters as seemed good, and breaking down the bridges of the river, considering that they must now fight at home in defense of their city, since they were unable to protect Italy. (*XXII, 2-8*)

[*The new Roman consuls, Lucius Aemilius Paulus and Gaius Terentius Varro, meet Hannibal at Cannae in Apulia, 216 B.C., probably antiquity's most terrible battle.*]

When the consuls, employing sufficient diligence in exploring the road in pursuit of the Carthaginian, had arrived at Cannae, where they had the enemy in the sight of them, having divided their forces, they fortify two camps, with nearly the same interval as before, at Geronium. The river Aufidus, which flowed by both the camps, afforded approach to the watering-parties of each, as opportunity served, though not without contest. The Romans in the lesser camp, however, which was on the other side the Aufidus, were more freely furnished with water, because the farther bank had no guard of the enemy. Hannibal, entertaining a hope that the consuls would not decline a battle in this tract, which was naturally adapted to a cavalry engagement, in which portion of his forces he was invincible, formed his line, and provoked the enemy by a skirmishing attack with his Numidians. Upon this the Roman camp began again to be embroiled by a mutiny among the soldiers, and the disagreement of the consuls: since Paulus instanced to Varro the temerity of Sempronius and

Flaminius; while Varro pointed to Fabius, as a specious example
to timid and inactive generals. The latter called both gods and
men to witness "that no part of the blame attached to him, that
Hannibal had now made Italy his own, as it were, by right of
possession; that he was held bound by his colleague; that the
swords and arms were taken out of the hands of the indignant
soldiers who were eager to fight." The former declared "that, if
any disaster should befall the legions thus exposed and betrayed
into an ill-advised and imprudent battle, he should be exempt
from any blame, though the sharer of all the consequences. That
he must take care that their hands were equally energetic in the
battle, whose tongues were so forward and impetuous."

While time is thus consumed in altercation rather than
deliberating, Hannibal, who had kept his troops drawn up in
order of battle till late in the day, when he had led the rest of
them back into the camp, sends Numidians across the river to
attack a watering-party of the Romans from the lesser camp.
Having routed this disorderly band by shouting and tumult, before they had well reached the opposite bank, they advanced even
to an outpost which was before the rampart, and near the very
gates of the camp. It seemed so great an indignity, that now even
the camp of the Romans should be terrified by a tumultuary band
of auxiliaries, that this cause alone kept back the Romans from
crossing the river forthwith, and forming their line, that the chief
command was on that day held by Paulus. Accordingly, Varro, on
the following day, on which it was his turn to hold the command, without consulting his colleague, displayed the signal for
battle, and, forming his troops, led them across the river. Paulus
followed, because he could better disapprove of the proceeding
than withhold his assistance. Having crossed the river, they add
to their forces those which they had in the lesser camp; and thus
forming their line, place the Roman cavalry in the right wing,
which was next the river; and next them the infantry: at the
extremity of the left wing the allied cavalry; within them the allied
infantry, extending to the center, and contiguous to the Roman
legions. The darters, and the rest of the light-armed auxiliaries,
formed the van. The consuls commanded the wings; Varro the

left; Paulus the right. To Geminus Servilius was committed the charge of maintaining the battle in the center.

Hannibal, at break of day, having sent before him the Baliares and other light-armed troops, crossed the river, and placed his troops in line of battle, as he had conveyed them across the river. The Gallic and Spanish cavalry he placed in the left wing, opposite the Roman cavalry: the right wing was assigned to the Numidian cavalry, the center of the line being strongly formed by the infantry, so that both extremities of it were composed of Africans, between which Gauls and Spaniards were placed. One would suppose the Africans were for the most part Romans, they were so equipped with arms captured at the Trebia, and for the greater part at the Trasimenus. The shields of the Gauls and Spaniards were of the same shape; their swords unequal and dissimilar. The Gauls had very long ones, without points. The Spaniards, who were accustomed to stab more than to cut their enemy, had swords convenient, from their shortness, and with points. The aspect of these nations in other respects was terrific, both as to the appearance they exhibited and the size of their persons. The Gauls were naked above the navel: the Spaniards stood arrayed in linen vests resplendent with surprising whiteness, and bordered with purple. The whole amount of infantry standing in battle-array was forty thousand; of cavalry ten. The generals who commanded the wings were, on the left, Hasdrubal; on the right, Maharbal: Hannibal himself, with his brother Mago, commanded the center. The sun very conveniently shone obliquely upon both parties—the Romans facing the south, and the Carthaginians the north; either placed so designedly, or having stood thus by chance. The wind, which the inhabitants of the district call the Vulturnus, blowing violently in front of the Romans, prevented their seeing far by rolling clouds of dust into their faces.

The shout being raised, the auxiliaries charged, and the battle commenced, in the first place, with the light-armed troops: then the left wing, consisting of the Gallic and Spanish cavalry, engages with the Roman right wing, by no means in the manner of a cavalry battle; for they were obliged to engage front to front;

for, as on one side the river, on the other the line of infantry
hemmed them in, there was no space left at their flanks for evolu-
tion, but both parties were compelled to press directly forward.
At length the horses standing still, and being crowded together,
man grappling with man, dragged him from his horse. The contest
now came to be carried on principally on foot. The battle, however,
was more violent than lasting; and the Roman cavalry being repulsed, turn their backs. About the conclusion of the contest between the cavalry, the battle between the infantry commenced.
At first the Gauls and Spaniards preserved their ranks unbroken,
not inferior in strength or courage; but at length the Romans,
after long and repeated efforts, drove in with their even front and
closely-compacted line, that part of the enemy's line in the form
of a wedge, which projected beyond the rest, which was too thin,
and therefore deficient in strength. These men, thus driven back
and hastily retreating, they closely pursued; and as they urged
their course without interruption through this terrified band, as it
fled with precipitation, were borne first upon the center line of
the enemy; and, lastly, no one opposing them, they reached the
African reserve troops. These were posted at the two extremities
of the line, where it was depressed; while the center, where the
Gauls and Spaniards were placed, projected a little. When the
wedge thus formed being driven in, at first rendered the line level,
but afterward, by the pressure, made a curvature in the center,
the Africans, who had now formed wings on each side of them,
surrounded the Romans on both sides, who incautiously rushed
into the intermediate space; and presently extending their wings,
enclosed the enemy on the rear also. After this the Romans, who
had in vain finished one battle, leaving the Gauls and Spaniards,
whose rear they had slaughtered, in addition commence a fresh
encounter with the Africans, not only disadvantageous, because,
being hemmed in, they had to fight against troops who surrounded
them, but also because, fatigued, they fought with those who were
fresh and vigorous.

Now also in the left wing of the Romans, in which the allied
cavalry were opposed to the Numidians, the battle was joined,
which was at first languid, commencing with a stratagem on the

part of the Carthaginians. About five hundred Numidians, who, besides their usual arms, had swords concealed beneath their coats of mail, quitting their own party, and riding up to the enemy under the semblance of deserters, with their bucklers behind them, suddenly leap down from their horses, and, throwing down their bucklers and javelins at the feet of their enemies, are received into their center, and, being conducted to the rear, ordered to remain there; and there they continued until the battle became general. But afterward, when the thoughts and attention of all were occupied with the contest, snatching up the shields which lay scattered on all hands among the heaps of slain, they fell upon the rear of the Roman line, and striking their backs and wounding their hams, occasioned vast havoc, and still greater panic and confusion. While in one part terror and flight prevailed, in another the battle was obstinately persisted in, though with little hope. Hasdrubal, who was then commanding in that quarter, withdrawing the Numidians from the center of the army, as the conflict with their opponents was slight, sends them in pursuit of the scattered fugitives, and joining the Africans, now almost weary with slaying rather than fighting the Spanish and Gallic infantry.

On the other side of the field, Paulus, though severely wounded from a sling in the very commencement of the battle, with a compact body of troops, frequently opposed himself to Hannibal, and in several quarters restored the battle, the Roman cavalry protecting him; who, at length, when the consul had not strength enough even to manage his horse, dismounted from their horses. And when some one brought intelligence that the consul had ordered the cavalry to dismount, it is said that Hannibal observed, "How much rather would I that he delivered them to me in chains." The fight maintained by the dismounted cavalry was such as might be expected, when the victory was undoubtedly on the side of the enemy, the vanquished preferring death in their places to flight; and the conquerors, who were enraged at them for delaying the victory, butchering those whom they could not put to flight. They at length, however, drove the few who remained away, worn out with exertion and wounds. After that they were all dispersed, and such as could sought to regain their horses for flight. Cneius Lentulus, a military tribune, seeing, as he rode by, the consul sitting upon a stone and covered with blood, said to him: "Lucius Aemilius! the only man whom the gods ought to regard as being guiltless of this day's disaster, take this horse, while you have any strength remaining, and I am with you to raise you up and protect you. Make not this battle more calamitous by the death of a consul. There is sufficient matter for tears and grief without this addition." In reply the consul said: "Do thou, indeed, go on and prosper, Cneius Lentulus, in your career of virtue! But beware lest you waste in bootless commiseration the brief opportunity of escaping from the hands of the enemy. Go and tell the fathers publicly to fortify the city of Rome, and garrison it strongly before the victorious enemy arrive; and tell Quintus Fabius, individually, that Lucius Aemilius lived, and now dies, mindful of his injunctions. Allow me to expire amidst these heaps of my slaughtered troops, that I may not a second time be accused after my consulate, or stand forth as the accuser of my colleague, in order to defend my own innocence by criminating another." While finishing these words, first a crowd of their flying countrymen, after that the enemy, came upon them; they overwhelm the consul with their weapons, not knowing who he was: in the confusion his horse rescued Lentulus. After that they fly precipitately. Seven thousand escaped to the lesser camp, ten to the greater, about two thousand to the village itself of Cannae, who were immediately surrounded by Carthalo and the cavalry, no fortifications protecting the village. The other consul, whether by design or by chance, made good his escape to Venusia with about seventy horse, without mingling with any party of the flying troops. Forty thousand foot, two thousand seven hundred horse, there being an equal number of citizens and allies, are said to have been slain. Among these both the quaestors of the consuls, Lucius Atilius and Lucius Furius Bibaculus; twenty-one military tribunes; several who had passed the offices of consul, praetor, and aedile; among these they reckon Cneius Servilius Germinus, and Marcus Minucius, who had been master of the horse on a former year, and consul some years before: moreover, eighty, either Sena-

tors, or who had borne those offices by which they might be elected
into the Senate, and who had voluntarily enrolled themselves in
the legions. Three thousand infantry and three hundred cavalry
are said to have been captured in that battle.

Such is the battle of Cannae, equal in celebrity to the defeat
at the Allia; but as it was less important in respect to those things
which happened after it, because the enemy did not follow up the
blow, so was it more important and more horrible with respect to
the slaughter of the army; for with respect to the flight at the Allia,
as it betrayed the city, so it preserved the army. At Cannae, scarcely
seventy accompanied the flying consul: almost the whole army
shared the fate of the other who died. (*XXII, 44-50*)

[*Confusion in Rome on the approach of Hannibal.*]

On the day he crossed the Vulturnus, Hannibal pitched his camp
at a small distance from the river. The next day, passing by Cales,
he reached the Sidicinian territory, and having spent a day there
in devastating the country, he led his troops along the Latin Way
through the territory of Suessa, Allifae, and Casinum. Under the
walls of Casinum he remained encamped for two days, ravaging
the country all around; thence passing by Interamna and Aqui-
num, he came into the Fregellan territory, to the river Liris, where
he found the bridge broken down by the Fregellans in order to
impede his progress. Fulvius also was detained at the Vulturnus,
in consequence of Hannibal's having burnt the ships, and
the difficulty he had in procuring rafts to convey his troops
across that river from the great scarcity of materials. The army
having been conveyed across by rafts, the remainder of the march
of Fulvius was uninterrupted, a liberal supply of provisions having
been prepared for him, not only in all the towns, but also on the
sides of the road; while his men, who were all activity, exhorted
each other to quicken their pace, remembering that they were
going to defend their country. A messenger from Fregella, who
had traveled a day and a night without intermission, arriving at
Rome, caused the greatest consternation; and the whole city was

thrown into a state of alarm by the running up and down of persons who made vague additions to what they heard, and thus increased the confusion which the original intelligence created. The lamentations of women were not only heard from private houses, but the matrons from every quarter, rushing into the public streets, ran up and down around the shrines of the gods, sweeping the altars with their disheveled hair, throwing themselves upon their knees and stretching their uplifted hands to heaven and the gods, imploring them to rescue the city of Rome out of the hands of their enemies, and preserve the Roman mothers and their children from harm. The Senate sat in the Forum near the magistrates, in case they should wish to consult them. Some were receiving orders and departing to their own department of duty; others were offering themselves wherever there might be occasion for their aid. Troops were posted in the citadel, in the Capitol, upon the walls around the city, and also on the Alban mount and the fort of Aesula. During this confusion, intelligence was brought that Quintus Fulvius, the proconsul, had set out from Capua with an army; when the Senate decreed that Quintus Fulvius should have equal authority with the consuls, lest, on entering the city, his power should cease. Hannibal, having most destructively ravaged the Fregellan territory, on account of the bridge having been broken down, came into the territory of the Lavici, passing through those of Frusino, Ferentinum, and Anagnia; thence passing through Algidum, he directed his course to Tusculum; but not being received within the walls, he went down to the right below Tusculum to Gabii; and marching his army down thence into the territory of the Pupinian tribe, he pitched his camp eight miles from the city. The nearer the enemy came, the greater was the number of fugitives slain by the Numidians who preceded him, and the greater the number of prisoners made of every rank and age.

During this confusion, Fulvius Flaccus entered the city with his troops through the Capuan gate, passed through the midst of the city, and through Carinae, to Esquiliae; and going out thence, pitched his camp between the Esquiline and Colline gates. The plebeian aediles brought a supply of provisions there. The consuls and the Senate came to the camp, and a consultation was held on the state of the republic. It was resolved that the consuls should encamp in the neighborhood of the Colline and Esquiline gates; that Caius Calpurnius, the city praetor, should have the command of the Capitol and the citadel; and that a full Senate should be continually assembled in the Forum, in case it should be necessary to consult them amidst such sudden emergencies. Meanwhile, Hannibal advanced his camp to the Anio, three miles from the city, and fixing his position there, he advanced with two thousand horse from the Colline gate as far as the Temple of Hercules, and, riding up, took as near a view as he could of the walls and site of the city. Flaccus, indignant that he should do this so freely and so much at his ease, sent out a party of cavalry, with orders to displace and drive back to their camp the cavalry of the enemy. After the fight had begun, the consuls ordered the Numidian deserters, who were on the Aventine, to the number of twelve hundred, to march through the midst of the city to the Esquiline, judging that no troops were better calculated to fight among the hollows, the garden walls, and tombs, or in the enclosed roads which were on all sides. But some persons, seeing them from the citadel and Capitol as they filed off on horseback down the Publician hill, cried out that the Aventine was taken. This circumstance occasioned such confusion and terror, that if the Carthaginian camp had not been without the city, the whole multitude, such was their alarm, would have rushed out. They then fled for refuge into their houses and upon the roofs, where they threw stones and weapons on their own soldiers as they passed along the streets, taking them for enemies. Nor could the tumult be repressed, or the mistake explained, as the streets were thronged with crowds of rustics and cattle, which the sudden alarm had driven into the city. The battle between the cavalry was successful, and the enemy were driven away; and as it was necessary to repress the tumults which were arising in several quarters without any cause, it was resolved that all who had been dictators, consuls, or censors should be invested with authority till

such time as the enemy had retired from the walls. During the
remainder of the day and the following night, several tumults arose
without any foundation, and were repressed.

The next day Hannibal, crossing the Anio, drew out all his
forces in order of battle; nor did Flaccus and the consuls decline
to fight. When the troops on both sides were drawn up to try the
issue of a battle, in which Rome was to be the prize of the victors,
a violent shower of rain, mingled with hail, created such disorder
in both the lines, that the troops, scarcely able to hold their arms,
retired to their camps, less through fear of the enemy than of any
thing else. On the following day, likewise, a similar tempest separated the armies marshaled on the same ground; but after they
had retired to their camps the weather became wonderfully serene
and tranquil. The Carthaginians considered this circumstance as
a Divine interposition, and it is reported that Hannibal was heard
to say, "that sometimes he wanted the will to make himself master
of Rome, at other times the opportunity." Two other circumstances
also, one inconsiderable, the other important, diminished his
hopes. The important one was, that while he lay with his armed
troops near the walls of the city, he was informed that troops had
marched out of it with colors flying, as a reinforcement for Spain;
that of less importance was, that he was informed by one of his
prisoners that the very ground on which his camp stood was sold
at this very time, without any diminution in its price. Indeed, so
great an insult and indignity did it appear to him that a purchaser should be found at Rome for the very soil which he held
and possessed by right of conquest, that he immediately called
a crier, and ordered that the silversmiths' shops which at that time
stood around the Roman Forum should be put up for sale. Induced
by these circumstances, he retired to the river Tutia, six miles
from the city, whence he proceeded to the grove of Feronia, where
was a temple at that time celebrated for its riches. The Capena-
tians and other states in the neighborhood, by bringing here their
first-fruits and other offerings according to their abilities, kept it
decorated with abundance of gold and silver. Of all these offerings
the temple was now despoiled. After the departure of Hannibal,

vast heaps of brass were found there, as the soldiers, from a religious feeling, had thrown in pieces of uncoined brass. . . .
(XXVI, 9-11)

[Hannibal's brother, Hasdrubal, leaves the Carthaginian base in Spain with desperately needed reinforcements. His messengers, however, are captured. The Roman consuls then secretly join forces and destroy Hasdrubal at the Metaurus River in northern Italy, 207 B.C. This presaged the doom of Hannibal and his city.]

Meanwhile four Gallic horsemen and two Numidians, who were sent to Hannibal with a letter from Hasdrubal, after he had retired from the siege of Placentia, having traversed nearly the whole length of Italy through the midst of enemies, while following Hannibal as he was retiring to Metapontum, were taken to Tarentum by mistaking the roads; where they were seized by some Roman foragers, who were straggling through the fields, and brought before the propraetor, Caius Claudius. At first they endeavored to baffle him by evasive answers, but threats of applying torture being held out to them, they were compelled to confess the truth; when they fully admitted that they were the bearers of a letter from Hasdrubal to Hannibal. They were delivered into the custody of Lucius Virginius, a military tribune, together with the letter sealed as it was, to be conveyed to the consul Claudius. At the same time two troops of Samnites were sent with them as an escort. Having made their way to the consul, the letter was read by means of an interpreter, and the captives were interrogated; when Claudius, coming to the conclusion that the predicament of the state was not such as that her generals should carry on the war, each within the limits of his own province, and with his own troops, according to the customary plans of warfare, and with an enemy marked out for him by the Senate, but that some unlooked-for and unexpected enterprise must be attempted, which, in its commencement, might cause no less dread among their countrymen than their enemies, but which, when accomplished, might convert

their great fear into great joy, sent the letter of Hasdrubal to
Rome to the Senate; and at the same time informed the conscript
fathers what his intentions were; and recommended that, as Hasdrubal had written to his brother that he should meet him in
Umbria, they should send for the legion from Capua to Rome,
enlist troops at Rome, and oppose the city forces to the enemy at
Narnia. Such was his letter to the Senate. Messengers were sent
in advance through the territory of Larinum, Marrucia, Frentana,
and Praetutia, where he was about to march his army, with orders
that they should all bring down from their farms and towns to the
road-side provisions ready dressed for the soldiers to eat; and that
they should bring out horses and other beasts of burden, so that
those who were tired might have plenty of conveyances. He then
selected the choicest troops out of the whole army of the Romans
and allies, to the amount of six thousand infantry and one thousand horse; and gave out that he intended to seize on the nearest
town in Lucania and the Carthaginian garrison in it, and that they
should all be in readiness to march. Setting out by night he turned
off toward Picenum, and, making his marches as long as possible,
led his troops to join his colleague, having left Quintus Catius,
lieutenant-general, in command of the camp. (*XXVII, 43*)

The Carthaginians were already standing before their camp
in battle-array. This circumstance delayed the battle: Hasdrubal,
who had advanced before the line with a few horsemen, remarked
some old shields among the enemy which he had not seen before,
and some horses leaner than the rest; their numbers also appeared
greater than usual. Suspecting, therefore, what was really the case,
he hastily sounded a retreat, and sent a party to the river from
which they got their water, where some of them might be intercepted, and notice taken whether there were perchance any there
whose complexions were more than ordinarily sun-burnt, as from
a recent march. At the same time, he ordered a party to ride round
the camp at a distance and note whether the rampart was extended
in any part, and also observe whether the signal sounded once or
twice. Having received a report of all these particulars, the fact
of the camp's not being enlarged led him into error. There were

now two camps, as there were before the other consul arrived, one belonging to Marcus Livius, the other to Lucius Porcius, and to neither of them had any addition been made to give more room for the tents. But the veteran general, who was accustomed to a Roman enemy, was much struck by their reporting that the signal sounded once in the praetor's camp, and twice in the consul's; there must, therefore, be two consuls, and he felt the most painful anxiety as to the manner in which the other had got away from Hannibal. Least of all could he suspect, what was really the case, that he had got away from Hannibal by deceiving him to such an extent as that he knew not where the general was, and where the army whose camp stood opposite to his own. Surely, he concluded, deterred by a defeat of no ordinary kind, he has not dared to pursue him; and he began to entertain the most serious fears that he had himself come too late with assistance, now that affairs were desperate, and lest the same good-fortune attended the Roman arms in Italy which they had experienced in Spain. Sometimes he imagined that his letter could not have reached him, and that, it having been intercepted, the consul had hastened to overpower him. Thus anxious and perplexed, having put out the fires, he issued a signal at the first watch to collect the baggage in silence, and gave orders to march. In the hurry and confusion occasioned by a march by night, their guides were not watched with sufficient care and attention. One of them stopped in a place of concealment which he had beforehand fixed upon in his mind, the other swam across the river Metaurus, at a ford with which he was acquainted. The troops, thus deserted by their guides, at first wandered up and down through the fields; and some of them, overpowered with sleep, and fatigued with watching, stretched themselves on the ground here and there, leaving their standards thinly attended. Hasdrubal gave orders to march along the bank of the river until the light should discover the road; but pursuing a circuitous and uncertain course along the turnings and windings of that tortuous river, with the intention of crossing it as soon as the first light should discover a place convenient for the purpose, he made but little progress; but wasting the day in a fruitless attempt to discover a ford—for, the farther he went from the sea, the higher he found the banks which kept the river in its course—he gave the enemy time to overtake him.

First Nero arrived with the whole body of his cavalry; then Porcius came up with him, with the light-infantry. And while these were harassing his weary troops on every side, and charging them, and the Carthaginian, stopping his march, which resembled a flight, was desirous of encamping on an eminence, on the bank of the river, Livius came up with all his foot forces, not after the manner of troops on march, but armed and marshaled for immediate action. When they had united all their forces, and the line was drawn out, Claudius took the direction of the battle in the right wing, Livius in the left; the management of the center was given to the praetor. Hasdrubal, when he saw that an engagement was inevitable, giving over the fortification of a camp, placed his elephants in the front line, before the standards; on either side these he placed in the left wing the Gauls to oppose Claudius, not so much from any confidence he reposed in them as because he believed them to be dreaded by the enemy; the right wing he took to himself against M. Livius, together with the Spaniards, in whom, as being veteran troops, he placed his greatest hopes. Behind the elephants, in the center, the Ligurians were posted; but his line was rather long than deep. The Gauls were covered by a hill, which extended in front. That part of the line which was occupied by the Spaniards engaged the left wing of the Romans, the whole of whose right wing, extending beyond the line of battle, was unengaged. The hill before them prevented their making an attack either in front or flank. Between Livius and Hasdrubal a furious contest arose, and the slaughter on both sides was dreadful. Here were both the generals, here the major part of the Roman horse and infantry, here the Spaniards, veteran troops, and experienced in the Roman manner of fighting, and the Ligurians, a nation inured to war. The elephants were also driven to the same part, which, on the first onset, disordered the van, and had now even dislodged the standards; but afterward, the contest growing hotter, and the shout increasing, they became less submissive to their riders, and ranged to and fro between the two lines, as if not knowing to which side they belonged, like ships floating about without rudders. Claudius, when he had striven in vain to advance up the hill, repeatedly calling out to his soldiers, "To what purpose, then, have we performed so long a march with such expedition?" when he found it impossible to make his way to the enemy in that quarter, withdrawing several cohorts from the right wing, where he saw they would occupy an inactive station, rather than join in the fight, led them round the rear of the line, and, to the surprise not only of the enemy but his own party, charged their right flank; and such was their rapidity, that, after showing themselves on their flank, they almost immediately made an attack on their rear. Thus on all sides, in front, flank, and rear, the Spaniards and Ligurians were cut to pieces; and now the carnage had even reached the Gauls. Here the least opposition was found; for a great number of them had quitted their standards, having slunk off during the night, and laid themselves down to sleep up and down the fields, while even those who were present, being tired with marching and watching, for their bodies are most intolerant of fatigue, could scarcely carry their arms upon their shoulders. And now it was midday, and thirst and heat gave them over to the enemy to be killed or captured in multitudes.

More elephants were killed by their guides than by the enemy. They used to have with them a workman's knife, with a mallet. When these beasts began to grow furious, and attack their own party, the rider, placing this knife between the ears, just on the joint by which the neck is connected with the head, used to drive it in, striking it with all the force he could. This was found to be the most expeditious mode of putting these bulky animals to death, when they had destroyed all hope of governing them. This method was first practiced by Hasdrubal, a general whose conduct both frequently on other occasions, and especially in this battle, deserved to be recorded. By encouraging the men when fighting, and sharing equally in every danger, he kept up the battle. Sometimes by entreating, at other times by rebuking, the troops, when tired and indisposed to fight from weariness and over-exertion, he rekindled their spirits. He called back the flying, and restored the battle in many places when it had been given up. At length, when fortune decidedly declared for the Romans, lest he should survive so great an army which had been collected under the influence of his name, he put spurs to his horse and rushed upon a Roman cohort, where he fell fighting, as was worthy of the son of Hamilcar and the brother of Hannibal. At no time during that war were so many of the enemy slain in one battle; so that a defeat equal to that sustained at Cannae, whether in respect of the loss of the general or the troops, was considered to have been retorted upon him. Fifty-six thousand of the enemy were slain, five thousand four hundred captured. The other booty was great, both of every other kind, and also of gold and silver. In addition to the rest, there were recovered above four thousand Roman citizens, who had been taken by the enemy, which formed some consolation for the soldiers lost in that battle. For the victory was by no means bloodless. Just about eight thousand of the Romans and the allies were slain; and so completely were even the victors satiated with blood and slaughter, that the next day, when Livius the consul received intelligence that the Cisalpine Gauls and Ligurians, who had either not been present at the battle or had made their escape from the carnage, were marching off in one body without a certain leader, without standards, without any discipline or subordination; that if one squadron of horse were sent against them they might be all destroyed, he replied, "Let some survive to bear the news of the enemy's losses and of our valor."

Nero set out on the night following the battle, and marching at a more rapid rate than when he came, arrived at his camp before the enemy on the sixth day. As he was not preceded by a messenger, fewer people attended him on his march; but the joy felt was so great, that they were almost insane with delight. Neither state of feeling at Rome can be well described or told, whether that in which the citizens were when in doubtful expectation of the issue, or when they received the intelligence of victory. Every day, from the time that news arrived that the consul Claudius had set out, from sunrise to sunset, none of the Senators ever quitted the Senate-house, nor did the people depart from the Forum. The matrons, as they had themselves no means of affording assistance, had recourse to prayers and entreaties, and, going about to all the temples, wearied the gods with vows and supplications. While the city was in this state of solicitude and suspense, a vague report first arrived that two Narnian horsemen had come from the field of battle into the camp which stood as a defense in the entrance to Umbria, with intelligence that the enemy were cut to pieces. At first they rather heard than credited this news, as being too great and too joyful for the mind to take in, or obtain a firm belief. Even the very rapidity with which it had arrived formed an obstacle to its reception; for it was stated that the battle took place two days before. After this a letter was brought which had been sent by Lucius Manlius Acidinus, from his camp, on the subject of the arrival of the Narnian horsemen. This letter being conveyed through the Forum to the tribunal of the praetor, drew the Senators out of the Senate-house; and with such eagerness and hurry did the people crowd to the doors of the Senate-house, that the messenger could not approach, but was dragged off by persons who asked him questions, and demanded vociferously that the letter should be read on the rostrum before it was read in the Senate. At length they were put back and restrained by the magistrates; and thus the joy was gradually dispensed to their over-powered spirits. The letter was read first in the Senate, and then in the assembly of the people. The effect was various, according to the difference in the cast of men's minds, some thinking that there were already sure grounds for rejoicing, while others would place no confidence in the news till they listened to ambassadors or a letter from the consuls. (*XXVII, 47-50*)

[*After his defeat of Hannibal at Zama in Africa, 202* B.C., *Publius Cornelius Scipio "Africanus" lays down peace terms for Carthage and returns to Rome.*]

Immediately after the battle, Scipio, having taken and plundered the enemy's camp, returned to the sea and his ships, with an immense booty, news having reached him that Publius Lentulus had arrived at Utica with fifty men-of-war, and a hundred transports laden with every kind of stores. Concluding that he ought to bring before Carthage every thing which could increase the con-

sternation already existing there, after sending Laelius to Rome
to report his victory, he ordered Cneius Octavius to conduct the
legions thither by land; and, setting out himself from Utica with
the fresh fleet of Lentulus added to his former one, made for the
harbor of Carthage. When he had arrived within a short distance,
he was met by a Carthaginian ship decked with fillets and
branches of olive. There were ten deputies, the leading men in
the state, sent at the instance of Hannibal to solicit peace; to
whom, when they had come up to the stern of the general's ship,
holding out the badges of suppliants, entreating and imploring
the protection and compassion of Scipio, the only answer given
was, that they must come to Tunes, to which place he would move
his camp. After taking a view of the site of Carthage, not so much
for the sake of acquainting himself with it for any present object
as to dispirit the enemy, he returned to Utica, having recalled
Octavius to the same place. As they were proceeding thence to
Tunes, they received intelligence that Vermina, the son of Syphax,
with a greater number of horse than foot, was coming to the assistance of the Carthaginians. A part of his infantry, with all the
cavalry, having attacked them on their march on the first day of
the Saturnalia, routed the Numidians with little opposition; and
as every way by which they could escape in flight was blocked up,
for the cavalry surrounded them on all sides, fifteen thousand men
were slain, twelve hundred were taken alive, with fifteen hundred
Numidian horses, and seventy-two military standards. The prince
himself fled from the field, with a few attendants, during the confusion. The camp was then pitched near Tunes, in the same place
as before, and thirty ambassadors came to Scipio from Carthage.
These behaved in a manner even more calculated to excite compassion than the former, in proportion as their situation was
more pressing; but from the recollection of their recent perfidy,
they were heard with considerably less pity. In the council, though
all were impelled by just resentment to demolish Carthage, yet,
when they reflected upon the magnitude of the undertaking, and
the length of time which would be consumed in the siege of so
well fortified and strong a city, while Scipio himself was uneasy in
consequence of the expectation of a successor, who would come

in for the glory of having terminated the war, though it was accomplished already by the exertions and danger of another, the minds of all were inclined to peace.

The next day the ambassadors being called in again, and, with many rebukes for their perfidy, warned that, instructed by so many disasters, they would at length believe in the existence of the gods and the obligation of an oath, these conditions of the peace were stated to them: "That they should enjoy their liberty and live under their own laws; that they should possess such cities and territories as they had enjoyed before the war, and with the same boundaries, and that the Romans should on that day desist from devastation. That they should restore to the Romans all deserters and fugitives, giving up all their ships of war except ten triremes, with such tamed elephants as they had, and that they should not tame any more. That they should not carry on war in or out of Africa without the permission of the Roman people. That they should make restitution to Masinissa, and form a league with him. That they should furnish grain, and pay for the auxiliaries until the ambassadors had returned from Rome. That they should pay ten thousand talents of silver, in equal annual installments distributed over fifty years. That they should give a hundred hostages, according to the pleasure of Scipio, not younger than fourteen nor older than thirty. That he would grant them a truce on condition that the transports, together with their cargoes, which had been seized during the former truce, were restored. Otherwise they would have no truce, nor any hope of a peace." When the ambassadors who were ordered to bear these conditions home reported them in an assembly, and Gisgo had stood forth to dissuade them from the terms, and was being listened to by the multitude, who were at once indisposed for peace and unfit for war, Hannibal, indignant that such language should be held and listened to at such a juncture, laid hold of Gisgo with his own hand, and dragged him from his elevated position. This unusual sight in a free state having raised a murmur among the people, the soldier, disconcerted at the liberties which the citizens took, thus addressed them: "Having left you when nine years old, I have returned after a lapse of thirty-six years. I flatter myself

I am well acquainted with the qualifications of a soldier, having been instructed in them from my childhood, sometimes by my own situation, and sometimes by that of my country. The privileges, the laws, and customs of the city and the Forum you ought to teach me." Having thus apologized for his indiscretion, he discoursed largely concerning the peace, showing how inoppressive the terms were, and how necessary it was. The greatest difficulty was, that of the ships which had been seized during the truce nothing was to be found except the ships themselves: nor was it easy to collect the property, because those who were charged with having it were opposed to the peace. It was resolved that the ships should be restored, and that the men, at least, should be looked up; and as to whatever else was missing, that it should be left to Scipio to put a value upon it, and that the Carthaginians should make compensation accordingly in money. There are those who say that Hannibal went from the field of battle to the sea-coast; whence he immediately sailed in a ship, which he had ready for the purpose, to King Antiochus; and that when Scipio demanded above every thing that Hannibal should be given up to him, answer was made that Hannibal was not in Africa. (XXX, 36-37)

Peace having been established by sea and land, [Scipio] embarked his troops and crossed over to Lilybaeum in Sicily; whence, having sent a great part of his soldiers by ships, he himself proceeded through Italy, which was rejoicing, not less on account of the peace than the victory; while not only the inhabitants of the cities poured out to show him honor, but crowds of rustics thronged the roads. He arrived at Rome and entered the city in a triumph of unparalleled splendor. He brought into the treasury one hundred and twenty-three thousand pounds of silver. He distributed to each of his soldiers four hundred *asses* out of the spoils. By the death of Syphax, which took place but a short time before at Tibur, whither he had been removed from Alba, a diminution was occasioned in the interest of the pageant rather than in the glory of him who triumphed. His death, however, was attended with circumstances which produced a strong sensation, for he was buried at the public expense. Polybius, an author by no means to be despised, asserts that this king was led in the triumph.

Quintus Terentius Culleo followed Scipio in his triumph with a cap of liberty on his head, and during the remainder of his life treated him with the respect due to him as the author of his freedom. I have not been able to ascertain whether the partiality of the soldiers or the favor of the people fixed upon him the surname of Africanus, or whether, in the same manner as Felix was applied to Sulla, and Magnus to Pompey, in the memory of our fathers, it originated in the flattery of his friends. He was, doubtless, the first general who was distinguished by a name derived from the nation which he had conquered. Afterward, in imitation of his example, some, by no means his equals in his victories, affixed splendid inscriptions on their statues and gave honorable surnames to their families. (*XXX, 45*)

SALLUST

Translated by John Selby Watson

THE JUGURTHINE WAR

Jugurtha, the threatening king of Numidia. Rome's plight is apparently due to party strife and especially to the corrupt upper classes. An estimate of Marius, the future leader of the popular party.

[Having thwarted the Gracchan democratic reforms, the Senate further revealed its incapacity and corruption in North Africa. There the grandson of Rome's former ally Masinissa, Jugurtha by name, after killing the rightful heirs, had himself usurped the throne of the client state of Numidia.]

I am about to relate the war which the Roman people carried on with Jugurtha, King of the Numidians; first, because it was great, sanguinary, and of varied fortune; and secondly, because then, for the first time, opposition was offered to the power of the nobility; a contest which threw every thing, religious and civil, into confusion, and was carried to such a height of madness, that nothing but war, and the devastation of Italy, could put an end to civil dissensions. But before I fairly commence my narrative, I will take a review of a few preceding particulars, in order that the whole subject may be more clearly and distinctly understood.

In the second Punic war, in which Hannibal, the leader of the Carthaginians, had weakened the power of Italy more than any other enemy since the Roman name became great, Masinissa, King of the Numidians, being received into alliance by Publius Scipio, who, from his merits was afterward surnamed Africanus, had performed for us many eminent exploits in the field. In return for which services, after the Carthaginians were subdued, and after Syphax, whose power in Italy was great and extensive, was taken prisoner, the Roman people presented to Masinissa, as a free gift, all the cities and lands that they had captured. Masinissa's friendship for us, accordingly, remained faithful and inviolate; his reign and his life ended together. His son, Micipsa, alone succeeded to his kingdom; Mastanabal and Gulussa, his two brothers, having been carried off by disease. Micipsa had two sons, Adherbal and Hiempsal, and had brought up in his house, with the same care as his own children, a son of his brother Mastanabal, named Jugurtha, whom Masinissa, as being the son of a concubine, had left in a private station.

Jugurtha, as he grew up, being strong in frame, graceful in person, but, above all, vigorous in understanding, did not allow himself to be enervated by pleasure and indolence, but, as is the usage of his country, exercised himself in riding, throwing the javelin, and contending in the race with his equals in age; and, though he excelled them all in reputation, he was yet beloved by all. He also passed much of his time in hunting; he was first, or among the first, to wound the lion and other beasts; he performed very much, but spoke very little of himself.

Micipsa, though he was at first gratified with these circumstances, considering that the merit of Jugurtha would be an honor to his kingdom, yet, when he reflected that the youth was daily increasing in popularity, while he himself was advanced in age, and his children but young, he was extremely disturbed at the state of things, and revolved it frequently in his mind. The very nature of man, ambitious of power, and eager to gratify its desires, gave him reason for apprehension, as well as the opportunity afforded by his own age and that of his children, which was sufficient, from the prospect of such a prize, to lead astray even men of moderate desires. The affection of the Numidians, too, which was strong toward Jugurtha, was another cause for alarm; among whom, if he should cut off such a man, he feared that some insurrection or war might arise.

Surrounded by such difficulties, and seeing that a man, so

popular among his countrymen, was not to be destroyed either by force or by fraud, he resolved, as Jugurtha was of an active disposition, and eager for military reputation, to expose him to dangers in the field, and thus make trial of fortune. During the Numantine war, therefore, when he was sending supplies of horse and foot to the Romans, he gave him the command of the Numidians, whom he dispatched into Spain, hoping that he would certainly perish, either by an ostentatious display of his bravery, or by the merciless hand of the enemy. But this project had a very different result from that which he had expected. For when Jugurtha, who was of an active and penetrating intellect, had learned the disposition of Publius Scipio, the Roman general, and the character of the enemy, he quickly rose, by great exertion and vigilance, by modestly submitting to orders, and frequently exposing himself to dangers, to such a degree of reputation, that he was greatly beloved by our men, and extremely dreaded by the Numantines. He was indeed, what is peculiarly difficult, both brave in action, and wise in counsel; qualities, of which the one, from forethought, generally produces fear, and the other, from confidence, rashness. The general, accordingly, managed almost every difficult matter by the aid of Jugurtha, numbered him among his friends, and grew daily more and more attached to him, as a man whose advice and whose efforts were never useless. With such merits were joined generosity of disposition, and readiness of wit, by which he united to himself many of the Romans in intimate friendship.

There were at that time, in our army, a number of officers, some of low, and some of high birth, to whom wealth was more attractive than virtue or honor; men who were attached to certain parties, and of consequence in their own country; but, among the allies, rather distinguished than respected. These persons inflamed the mind of Jugurtha, of itself sufficiently aspiring, by assuring him, "that if Micipsa should die, he might have the kingdom of Numidia to himself; for that he was possessed of eminent merit, and that any thing might be purchased at Rome."

When Numantia, however, was destroyed, and Scipio had determined to dismiss the auxiliary troops, and to return to Rome, he led Jugurtha, after having honored him, in a public assembly, with the noblest presents and applauses, into his own tent; where he privately admonished him "to court the friendship of the Romans rather by attention to them as a body, than by practicing on individuals; to bribe no one, as what belonged to many could not without danger be bought from a few; and adding that, if he would but trust to his own merits, glory and regal power would spontaneously fall to his lot; but, should he proceed too rashly, he would only, by the influence of his money, hasten his own ruin."

Having thus spoken, he took leave of him, giving him a letter, which he was to present to Micipsa. . . .

Micipsa, when he found, from the letter of the general, that what he had already heard reported was true, being moved, both by the merit of the youth and by the interest felt for him by Scipio, altered his purpose, and endeavored to win Jugurtha by kindness. He accordingly, in a short time, adopted him as his son, and made him, by his will, joint-heir with his own children.

A few years afterward, when, being debilitated by age and disease, he perceived that the end of his life was at hand, he is said, in the presence of his friends and relations, and of Adherbal and Hiempsal his sons, to have spoken with Jugurtha in the following manner:

"I received you, Jurgurtha, at a very early age, into my kingdom, at a time when you had lost your father, and were without prospects or resources, expecting that, in return for my kindness, I should not be less loved by you than by my own children, if I should have any. Nor have my anticipations deceived me; for, to say nothing of your other great and noble deeds, you have lately, on your return from Numantia, brought honor and glory both to me and my kingdom; by your bravery, you have rendered the Romans, from being previously our friends, more friendly to us than ever; the name of our family is revived in Spain; and, finally, what is most difficult among mankind, you have suppressed envy by pre-eminent merit.

"And now, since nature is putting a period to my life, I exhort and conjure you, by this right hand, and by the fidelity which you owe to my kingdom, to regard these princes, who are your cousins by birth, and your brothers by my generosity, with sincere affection; and not to be more anxious to attach to yourself strangers, than to retain the love of those connected with you by blood. It is not armies, or treasures, that form the defenses of a kingdom, but friends, whom you can neither command by force nor purchase with gold; for they are acquired only by good offices and integrity. And who can be a greater friend than one brother to another? Or what stranger will you find faithful, if you are at enmity with your own family? I leave you a kingdom, which will be strong if you act honorably, but weak, if you are ill-affected to each other; for by concord even small states are increased, but by discord, even the greatest fall to nothing.

"But on you, Jugurtha, who are superior in age and wisdom, it is incumbent, more than on your brothers, to be cautious that nothing of a contrary tendency may arise; for, in all disputes, he that is the stronger, even though he receive the injury, appears, because his power is greater, to have inflicted it. And do you, Adherbal and Hiempsal, respect and regard a kinsman of such a character; imitate his virtues, and make it your endeavor to show that I have not adopted a better son than those whom I have begotten."

. . . A few days afterward Micipsa died.

When the princes had performed his funeral with due magnificence, they met together to hold a discussion on the general condition of their affairs. Hiempsal, the youngest, who was naturally violent, and who had previously shown contempt for the mean birth of Jugurtha, as being inferior on his mother's side, sat down on the right hand of Adherbal, in order to prevent Jugurtha from being the middle one of the three, which is regarded by the Numidians as the seat of honor. Being urged by his brother, however, to yield to superior age, he at length removed, but with reluctance, to the other seat.

In the course of this conference, after a long debate about the administration of the kingdom, Jugurtha suggested, among other measures, "that all the acts and decrees made in the last five years should be annulled, as Micipsa, during that period, had been enfeebled by age, and scarcely sound in intellect." Hiempsal replied, "that he was exceedingly pleased with the proposal, since Jugurtha himself, within the last three years, had been adopted as joint-heir to the throne." This repartee sunk deeper into the mind of Jugurtha than any one imagined. From that very time, accordingly, being agitated with resentment and jealousy, he began to meditate and concert schemes, and to think of nothing but projects for secretly cutting off Hiempsal. But his plans proving slow in operation, and his angry feelings remaining unabated, he resolved to execute his purpose by any means whatsoever.

At the first meeting of the princes, of which I have just spoken, it had been resolved, in consequence of their disagreement, that the treasures should be divided among them, and that limits should be set to the jurisdiction of each. Days were accordingly appointed for both these purposes, but the earlier of the two for the division of the money. The princes, in the meantime, retired into separate places of abode in the neighborhood of the treasury. Hiempsal, residing in the town of Thirmida, happened to occupy the house of a man, who, being Jugurtha's chief lictor, had always been liked and favored by his master. This man, thus opportunely presented as an instrument, Jugurtha loaded with promises, and induced him to go to his house, as if for the purpose of looking over it, and provide himself with false keys to the gates; for the true ones used to be given to Hiempsal; adding, that he himself, when circumstances should call for his presence, would be at the place with a large body of men. This commission the Numidian speedily executed, and, according to his instructions, admitted Jugurtha's men in the night, who, as soon as they had entered the house, went different ways in quest of the prince; some of his attendants they killed while asleep, and others as they met them; they searched into secret places, broke open those that were shut, and filled the whole premises with uproar and tumult. Hiempsal, after a time, was found concealed in the hut of a maid-servant, where, in his alarm and ignorance of the locality, he had at first taken refuge. The Numidians, as they had been ordered, brought his head to Jugurtha.

The report of so atrocious an outrage was soon spread through Africa. Fear seized on Adherbal, and on all who had been subject to Micipsa. The Numidians divided into two parties, the greater number following Adherbal, but the more warlike, Jugurtha; who, accordingly, armed as large a force as he could, brought several cities, partly by force and partly by their own consent, under his power, and prepared to make himself sovereign of the whole of Numidia. Adherbal, though he had sent ambassadors to Rome, to inform the senate of his brother's murder and his own circumstances, yet, relying on the number of his troops, prepared for an armed resistance. When the matter, however, came to a contest, he was defeated, and fled from the field of battle into our province, and from thence hastened to Rome.

Jugurtha, having thus accomplished his purposes, and reflecting, at leisure, on the crime which he had committed, began to feel a dread of the Roman people, against whose resentment he had no hopes of security but in the avarice of the nobility, and in his own wealth. A few days afterward, therefore, he dispatched ambassadors to Rome, with a profusion of gold and silver, whom he directed, in the first place, to make abundance of presents to his old friends, and then to procure him new ones; and not to hesitate, in short, to effect whatever could be done by bribery.

When these deputies had arrived at Rome, and had sent large presents, according to the prince's direction, to his intimate friends, and to others whose influence was at that time powerful, so remarkable a change ensued, that Jugurtha, from being an object of the greatest odium, grew into great regard and favor with the nobility; who, partly allured with hope, and partly with actual largesses, endeavored, by soliciting the members of the senate individually, to prevent any severe measures from being adopted against him. When the ambassadors, accordingly, felt sure of success, the senate, on a fixed day, gave audience to both parties. . . . (5-13)

When the prince had concluded his speech, the ambassadors of Jugurtha, depending more on their money than their cause, replied, in a few words, "that Hiempsal had been put to death by the Numidians for his cruelty; that Adherbal, commencing war of his own accord, complained, after he was defeated, of being unable to do injury; and that Jugurtha entreated the senate not to consider him a different person from what he had been known to be at Numantia, nor to set the assertions of his enemy above his own conduct."

Both parties then withdrew from the senate-house, and the senate immediately proceeded to deliberate. The partisans of the ambassadors, with a great many others, corrupted by their influence, expressed contempt for the statements of Adherbal, extolled with the highest encomiums the merits of Jugurtha, and exerted themselves as strenuously, with their interest and eloquence, in defense of the guilt and infamy of another, as they would have striven for their own honor. A few, however, on the other hand, to whom right and justice were of more estimation than wealth, gave their opinion that Adherbal should be assisted, and the murder of Hiempsal severely avenged. Of all these the most forward was Aemilius Scaurus, a man of noble birth and great energy, but factious, and ambitious of power, honor, and wealth; yet an artful concealer of his own vices. He, seeing that the bribery of Jugurtha was notorious and shameless, and fearing that, as in such cases often happens, its scandalous profusion might excite public odium, restrained himself from the indulgence of his ruling passion.

Yet that party gained the superiority in the senate, which preferred money and interest to justice. A decree was made, "that ten commissioners should divide the kingdom, which Micipsa had possessed, between Jugurtha and Adherbal." Of this commission the leading person was Lucius Opimius, a man of distinction, and of great influence at that time in the senate, from having in his consulship, on the death of Caius Gracchus and Marcus Fulvius Flaccus, prosecuted the victory of the nobility over the plebeians with great severity.

Jugurtha, though he had already counted Scaurus among his friends at Rome, yet received him with the most studied ceremony, and, by presents and promises, wrought on him so effectually, that he preferred the prince's interest to his own character, honor, and all other considerations. The rest of the commissioners he assailed in a similar way, and gained over most of them; by a few only integrity was more regarded than lucre. In the division of the kingdom, that part of Numidia which borders on Mauretania, and which is superior in fertility and population, was allotted to Jugurtha; of the other part, which, though better furnished with harbors and buildings, was more valuable in appearance than in reality, Adherbal became the possessor. (15-16)

[*Jugurtha's excesses and bribery of Roman envoys finally forced the Senate to declare war, 111 B.C., a step welcomed by the knights—the equestrian, or business, class at Rome. Coming to Rome on the promise of safe conduct, Jugurtha murdered a rival to the Numidian throne. On leaving, he said, "Here is a city for sale and doomed to speedy ruin, if only a purchaser appears!" Party strife, and especially the corrupt upper classes, were apparently the cause of Rome's plight.*]

The prevalence of parties among the people, and of factions in the senate, and of all evil practices attendant on them, had its origin at Rome, a few years before, during a period of tranquillity, and amid the abundance of all that mankind regarded as desirable. For, before the destruction of Carthage, the senate and people managed the affairs of the republic with mutual moderation and forbearance; there were no contests among the citizens for honor or ascendency; but the dread of an enemy kept the state in order. When that fear, however, was removed from their minds, licentiousness and pride, evils which prosperity loves to foster, immediately began to prevail; and thus peace, which they had so eagerly desired in adversity, proved, when they had obtained it, more grievous and fatal than adversity itself. The patricians carried their authority, and the people their liberty, to excess; every man took, snatched, and seized what he could. There was a complete division into two factions, and the republic was torn in pieces between them. Yet the nobility still maintained an ascendency by conspiring together; for the strength of the people, being disunited and dispersed among a multitude, was less able to exert itself. Things were accordingly directed, both at home and in the field, by the will of a small number of men, at whose disposal were the

the treasury, the provinces, offices, honors, and triumphs; while the people were oppressed with military service and with poverty, and the generals divided the spoils of war with a few of their friends. The parents and children of the soldiers, meantime, if they chanced to dwell near a powerful neighbor, were driven from their homes. Thus avarice, leagued with power, disturbed, violated, and wasted every thing, without moderation or restraint; disregarding alike reason and religion, and rushing headlong, as it were, to its own destruction. For whenever any arose among the nobility, who preferred true glory to unjust power, the state was immediately in a tumult, and civil discord spread with as much disturbance as attends a convulsion of the earth. (41)

[Jugurtha continued to bribe Roman generals sent against him, until the energetic consul, Metellus, took command in 109 B.C. Gaius Marius, future leader of the popular party, went with him to Africa as an officer: a sketch of his character.]

About the same time, as Gaius Marius, who happened to be at Utica, was sacrificing to the gods, an augur told him that great and wonderful things were presaged to him; that he might therefore pursue whatever designs he had formed, trusting to the gods for success; and that he might try fortune as often as he pleased, for that all his undertakings would prosper. Previously to this period an ardent longing for the consulship had possessed him; and he had, indeed, every qualification for obtaining it, except antiquity of family; he had industry, integrity, great knowledge of war, and a spirit undaunted in the field; he was temperate in private life, superior to pleasure and riches, and ambitious only of glory. Having been born at Arpinum, and brought up there during his boyhood, he employed himself, as soon as he was of age to bear arms, not in the study of Greek eloquence, nor in learning the refinements of the city, but in military service; and thus, amid the strictest discipline, his excellent genius soon attained full vigor. When he solicited the people, therefore, for the military tribuneship, he was well known by name, though most were strangers to his face, and unanimously elected by the tribes. After this office he attained others in succession, and conducted himself so well in his public duties, that he was always deemed worthy of a higher station than he had reached. Yet, though such had been his character hitherto (for he was afterward carried away by ambition), he had not ventured to stand for the consulship. The people, at that time, still disposed of other civil offices, but the nobility transmitted the consulship from hand to hand among themselves. Nor had any commoner appeared, however famous or distinguished by his achievements, who would not have been thought unworthy of that honor, and, as it were, a disgrace to it.

But when Marius found that the words of the augur pointed in the same direction as his own inclinations prompted him, he requested of Metellus leave of absence, that he might offer himself a candidate for the consulship. Metellus, though eminently distinguished by virtue, honor, and other qualities valued by the good, had yet a haughty and disdainful spirit, the common failing of the nobility. He was at first, therefore, astonished at so extraordinary an application, expressed surprise at Marius's views, and advised him, as if in friendship, "not to indulge such unreasonable expectations, or elevate his thoughts above his station. that all things were not to be coveted by all men; that his present condition ought to satisfy him; and, finally, that he should be cautious of asking from the Roman people what they might justly refuse him." Having made these and similar remarks, and finding that the resolution of Marius was not at all affected by them, he told him "that he would grant what he desired as soon as the public business would allow him." On Marius repeating his request several times afterward, he is reported to have said, "that he need not be in a hurry to go, as he would be soon enough if he became a candidate with his own son." Metellus's son was then on service in the camp with his father, and was about twenty years old.

This taunt served only to rouse the feelings of Marius, as well for the honor at which he aimed, as against Metellus. He suffered himself to be actuated, therefore, by ambition and resentiment, the worst of counselors. He omitted nothing hence-forward, either in deeds or words, that could increase his own popularity. He allowed the soldiers, of whom he had the command in the winter quarters, more relaxation of discipline than he had ever granted them before. He talked of the war among the merchants, of whom there was a great number at Utica, censoriously with respect to Metellus, and vauntingly with regard to himself; saying "that if but half of the army were granted him, he would in a few days have Jugurtha in chains; but that the war was purposely protracted by the consul, because, being a man of vanity and regal pride, he was too fond of the delights of power." All these assertions appeared the more credible to the merchants, as, by the long continuance of the war, they had suffered in their fortunes; and to impatient minds no haste is sufficient. (63-64)

SUETONIUS

Translated by Alexander Thomson; revised by T. Forester

JULIUS CAESAR

[Suetonius' biography of Caesar may not penetrate to the depths, nor explain his genius, but it does provide a wealth of information for a judgment of him.]

Julius Caesar, the Divine, lost his father when he was in the sixteenth year of his age; and the year following, being nominated to the office of high-priest of Jupiter, he repudiated Cossutia, who was very wealthy, although her family belonged only to the equestrian order, and to whom he had been contracted when he was a mere boy. He then married Cornelia, the daughter of Cinna, who was four times consul; and had by her, shortly afterward, a daughter named Julia. Resisting all the efforts of the dictator Sulla to induce him to divorce Cornelia, he suffered the penalty of being stripped of his sacerdotal office, his wife's dowry, and his own patrimonial estates; and, being identified with the adverse faction, was compelled to withdraw from Rome. After changing his place of concealment nearly every night, although he was suffering from a quartan ague, and having effected his release by bribing the officers who had tracked his footsteps, he at length obtained a pardon through the intercession of the vestal virgins, and of Mamercus Aemilius and Aurelius Cotta, his near relatives. We are assured that when Sulla, having withstood for a while the entreaties of his own best friends, persons of distinguished rank, at last yielded to their importunity, he exclaimed—either by a divine impulse, or from a shrewd conjecture: "Your suit is granted, and you may take him among you; but know," he added, "that this man, for whose safety you are so extremely anxious, will, some day or other, be the ruin of the party of the nobles, in defense of which you are leagued with me; for in this one Caesar, you will find many a Marius." (1)

In his aedileship, he not only embellished the Comitium, and the rest of the Forum, with the adjoining halls, but adorned the Capitol also, with temporary piazzas, constructed for the purpose of displaying some part of the superabundant collections he had made for the amusement of the people. He entertained them with the hunting of wild beasts, and with games, both alone and in conjunction with his colleague. On this account, he obtained the whole credit of the expense to which they had jointly contributed; insomuch that his colleague, Marcus Bibulus, could not forbear remarking, that he was served in the manner of Pollux. For as the temple erected in the Forum to the two brothers, went by the name of Castor alone, so his and Caesar's joint munificence was imputed to the latter only. To the other public spectacles exhibited to the people, Caesar added a fight of gladiators, but with fewer pairs of combatants than he had intended. For he had collected from all parts so great a company of them, that his enemies became alarmed; and a decree was made, restricting the number of gladiators which any one was allowed to retain at Rome. (10)

After he was chosen praetor, the conspiracy of Catiline was discovered; and while every other member of the senate voted for inflicting capital punishment on the accomplices in that crime, he alone proposed that the delinquents should be distributed for safe custody among the towns of Italy, their property being confiscated. He even struck such terror into those who were advocates for greater severity, by representing to them what universal odium would be attached to their memories by the Roman people, that Decius Silanus, consul-elect, did not hesitate to qualify his proposal, it not being very honorable to change it, by a lenient interpretation; as if it had been understood in a harsher sense than he intended, and Caesar would certainly have carried his point, having brought over to his side a great number of the senators, among whom was Cicero, the consul's brother, had not a speech by Marcus Cato infused new vigor into the resolutions of the senate. He persisted, however, in obstructing the measure, until a body of the Roman knights, who stood under arms as a guard, threat-

ened him with instant death, if he continued his determined opposition. They even thrust at him with their drawn swords, so
that those who sat next him moved away; and a few friends, with
no small difficulty, protected him, by throwing their arms round
him, and covering him with their togas. At last, deterred by this
violence, he not only gave way, but absented himself from the
senate-house during the remainder of that year. (14)

Of the two other competitors for the consulship, Lucius Luceius and Marcus Bibulus, he joined with the former, upon condition that Luceius, being a man of less interest but greater
affluence, should promise money to the electors, in their joint
names. Upon which the party of the nobles, dreading how far
he might carry matters in that high office, with a colleague disposed
to concur in and second his measures, advised Bibulus to promise
the voters as much as the other; and most of them contributed
toward the expense, Cato himself admitting that bribery, under
such circumstances, was for the public good. He was accordingly
elected consul jointly with Bibulus. Actuated still by the same
motives, the prevailing party took care to assign provinces of small
importance to the new consuls, such as the care of the woods and
roads. Caesar, incensed at this indignity, endeavored by the most
assiduous and flattering attentions to gain to his side Cneius Pompey, at that time dissatisfied with the senate for the backwardness
they showed to confirm his acts, after his victories over Mithridates.
He likewise brought about a reconciliation between Pompey and
Marcus Crassus, who had been at variance from the time of their
joint consulship, in which office they were continually clashing;
and he entered into an agreement with both, that nothing should
be transacted in the government, which was displeasing to any
of the three.

Having entered upon his office, he introduced a new regulation, that the daily acts both of the senate and people should be
committed to writing, and published. He also revived an old custom, that an officer should precede him, and his lictors follow
him, on the alternate months when the fasces were not carried
before him. Upon preferring a bill to the people for the division
of some public lands, he was opposed by his colleague, whom he

violently drove out of the forum. Next day the insulted consul made a complaint in the senate of this treatment; but such was the consternation, that no one having the courage to bring the matter forward or move a censure, which had been often done under outrages of less importance, he was so much dispirited, that until the expiration of his office he never stirred from home, and did nothing but issue edicts to obstruct his colleague's proceedings. From that time, therefore, Caesar had the sole management of public affairs; insomuch that some wags, when they signed any instrument as witnesses, did not add "in the consulship of Caesar and Bibulus," but, "of Julius and Caesar;" putting the same person down twice, under his name and surname. The following verses likewise were currently repeated on this occasion:

> Nothing was done in Bibulus's year:
> No; Caesar only then was consul here.

The land of Stellas, consecrated by our ancestors to the gods, with some other lands in Campania left subject to tribute, for the support of the expenses of the government, he divided, but not by lot, among upward of twenty thousand freemen, who had each of them three or more children. He eased the publicans, upon their petition, of a third part of the sum which they had engaged to pay into the public treasury; and openly admonished them not to bid so extravagantly upon the next occasion. He made various profuse grants to meet the wishes of others, no one opposing him; or if any such attempt was made, it was soon suppressed. Marcus Cato, who interrupted him in his proceedings, he ordered to be dragged out of the senate-house by a lictor, and carried to prison. Lucius Lucullus, likewise, for opposing him with some warmth, he so terrified with the apprehension of being criminated, that, to deprecate the consul's resentment, he fell on his knees. And upon Cicero's lamenting in some trial the miserable condition of the times, he the very same day, by nine o'clock, transferred his enemy, Publius Clodius, from a patrician to a plebeian family; a change which he had long solicited in vain. At last, effectually to intimidate all those of the opposite party, he by great rewards prevailed upon Vettius to declare, that he had been solicited by certain persons to assassinate Pompey; and when he was brought before the rostra to name those who had been concerted between them, after naming one or two to no purpose, not without great suspicion of subornation, Caesar, despairing of success in this rash stratagem, is supposed to have taken off his informer by poison. (19-20)

Being, therefore, now supported by the interest of his father-in-law and son-in-law, of all the provinces he made choice of Gaul, as most likely to furnish him with matter and occasion for triumphs. At first indeed he received only Cisalpine Gaul, with the addition of Illyricum, by a decree proposed by Vatinius to the people; but soon afterward obtained from the senate Gallia Comata also, the senators being apprehensive, that if they should refuse it him, that province, also, would be granted him by the people. Elated now with his success, he could not refrain from boasting, a few days afterward, in a full senate-house, that he had, in spite of his enemies, and to their great mortification, obtained all he desired, and that for the future he would make them, to their shame, submissive to his pleasure. One of the senators observing, sarcastically: "That will not be very easy for a woman to do," he jocosely replied, "Semiramis formerly reigned in Assyria, and the Amazons possessed great part of Asia." (22)

During nine years in which he held the government of the province, his achievements were as follows: he reduced all Gaul, bounded by the Pyrenean forest, the Alps, mount Gebenna, and the two rivers, the Rhine and the Rhone, and being about three thousand two hundred miles in compass, into the form of a province, excepting only the nations in alliance with the republic, and such as had merited his favor; imposing upon this new acquisition an annual tribute of forty millions of sesterces. He was the first of the Romans who, crossing the Rhine by a bridge, attacked the Germanic tribes inhabiting the country beyond that river, whom he defeated in several engagements. He also invaded the Britons, a people formerly unknown, and having vanquished them, exacted from them contributions and hostages. Amidst such a series of successes, he experienced thrice only any signal disaster; once in Britain, when his fleet was nearly wrecked in a storm; in Gaul, at Gergovia, where one of his legions was put to the rout; and in the territory of the Germans, his lieutenants Titurius and Aurunculeius were cut off by an ambuscade. (25)

He endeavored with equal assiduity to engage in his interest princes and provinces in every part of the world; presenting some with thousands of captives, and sending to others the assistance of troops, at whatever time and place they desired, without any authority from either the senate or people of Rome. He likewise embellished with magnificent public buildings the most powerful cities not only of Italy, Gaul, and Spain, but of Greece and Asia; until all people being now astonished, and speculating on the obvious tendency of these proceedings, Claudius Marcellus, the consul, declaring first by proclamation, that he intended to propose a measure of the utmost importance to the state, made a motion in the senate that some person should be appointed to succeed Caesar in his province, before the term of his command was expired; because the war being brought to a conclusion, peace was restored, and the victorious army ought to be disbanded. He further moved, that Caesar being absent, his claims to be a candidate at the next election of consuls should not be admitted, as Pompey himself had afterward abrogated that privilege by a decree of the people. The fact was, that Pompey, in his law relating to the choice of chief magistrates, had forgot to except Caesar, in the article in which he declared all such as were not present incapable of being candidates for any office; but soon afterward, when the law was inscribed on brass, and deposited in the treasury, he corrected his mistake. Marcellus, not content with depriving Caesar of his provinces, and the privilege intended him by Pompey, likewise moved the senate, that the freedom of the city should be taken from those colonists whom, by the Vatinian law, he had settled at New Como; because it had been conferred upon them with ambitious views, and by a stretch of the laws. (28)

When intelligence, therefore, was received, that the interposition of the tribunes in his favor had been utterly rejected, and that they themselves had fled from the city, he immediately sent forward some cohorts, but privately, to prevent any suspicion of his design; and, to keep up appearances, attended at a public spectacle, examined the model of a fencing-school which he proposed to build, and, as usual, sat down to table with a numerous party of his friends. But after sun-set, mules being put to his carriage from a neighboring mill, he set forward on his journey with all possible privacy, and a small retinue. The lights going out, he lost his way, and wandered about a long time, until at length, by the help of a guide, whom he found toward day-break, he proceeded on foot through some narrow paths, and again reached the road. Coming up with his troops on the banks of the Rubicon, which was the boundary of his province, he halted for a while, and, revolving in his mind the importance of the step he was on the point of taking, he turned to those about him, and said: "We may still retreat; but if we pass this little bridge, nothing is left for us but to fight it out in arms."

While he was thus hesitating, the following incident occurred. A person remarkable for his noble mien and graceful aspect, appeared close at hand, sitting and playing upon a pipe. When, not only the shepherds, but a number of soldiers also flocked from their posts to listen to him, and some trumpeters among them, he snatched a trumpet from one of them, ran to the river with it, and sounding the advance with a piercing blast, crossed to the other side. Upon this, Caesar exclaimed, "Let us go whither the omens of the Gods and the iniquity of our enemies call us. The die is now cast." (31-32)

Of his subsequent proceedings I shall give a cursory detail, in the order in which they occurred. He took possession of Picenum, Umbria, and Etruria; and having obliged Lucius Domitius, who had been tumultuously nominated his successor, and held Corfinium with a garrison, to surrender, and dismissed him, he marched along the coast of the Adriatic, to Brundisium, to which place the consuls and Pompey were fled with the intention of crossing the sea as soon as possible. After vain attempts, by all the obstacles he could oppose, to prevent their leaving the harbor, he turned his steps toward Rome, where he appealed to the senate on the present state of public affairs; and then set out for Spain, in which province Pompey had a numerous army, under the command of three lieutenants, Marcus Petreius, Lucius Afranius, and

Marcus Varro; declaring among his friends, before he set forward, "That he was going against an army without a general, and should return thence against a general without an army." Though his progress was retarded both by the siege of Marseilles, which shut her gates against him, and a very great scarcity of grain, yet in a short time he bore down all before him.

Thence he returned to Rome, and crossing the sea to Macedonia, blocked up Pompey during almost four months, within a line of ramparts of prodigious extent; and at last defeated him in the battle of Pharsalia. Pursuing him in his flight to Alexandria, where he was informed of his murder, he presently found himself also engaged, under all the disadvantages of time and place, in a very dangerous war, with king Ptolemy, who, he saw, had treacherous designs upon his life. It was winter, and he, within the walls of a well-provided and subtle enemy, was destitute of every thing, and wholly unprepared for such a conflict. He succeeded, however, in his enterprise, and put the kingdom of Egypt into the hands of Cleopatra and her younger brother; being afraid to make it a province, lest, under an aspiring prefect, it might become the center of revolt. From Alexandria he went into Syria, and thence to Pontus, induced by intelligence which he had received respecting Pharnaces. This prince, who was son of the great Mithridates, had seized the opportunity which the distraction of the times offered for making war upon his neighbors, and his insolence and fierceness had grown with his success. Caesar, however, within five days after entering his country, and four hours after coming in sight of him, overthrew him in one decisive battle. Upon which, he frequently remarked to those about him the good fortune of Pompey, who had obtained his military reputation, chiefly, by victory over so feeble an enemy. He afterward defeated Scipio and Juba, who were rallying the remains of the party in Africa, and Pompey's sons in Spain. (34-35)

Turning afterward his attention to the regulation of the commonwealth, he corrected the calendar, which had for some time become extremely confused, through the unwarrantable liberty which the pontiffs had taken in the article of intercalation. To such a height had this abuse proceeded, that neither the festivals designed for the harvest fell in summer, nor those for the vintage in autumn. He accommodated the year to the course of the sun, ordaining that in future it should consist of three hundred and sixty-five days without any intercalary month; and that every fourth year an intercalary day should be inserted. That the year might thenceforth commence regularly with the calends, or first of January, he inserted two months between November and December; so that the year in which this regulation was made consisted of fifteen months, including the month of intercalation, which, according to the division of time then in use, happened that year.

He filled up the vacancies in the senate, by advancing several plebeians to the rank of patricians, and also increased the number of praetors, aediles, quaestors, and inferior magistrates; restoring, at the same time, such as had been degraded by the censors, or convicted of bribery at elections. The choice of magistrates he so divided with the people, that, excepting only the candidates for the consulship, they nominated one half of them, and he the other. The method which he practiced in those cases was, to recommend such persons as he had pitched upon, by bills dispersed through the several tribes to this effect: "Caesar the dictator to such a tribe (naming it). I recommend to you ——— (naming likewise the persons), that by the favor of your votes they may attain to the honors for which they sue." He likewise admitted to offices the sons of those who had been proscribed. The trial of causes he restricted to two orders of judges, the equestrian and senatorial; excluding the tribunes of the treasury who had before made a third class. The revised census of the people he ordered to be taken neither in the usual manner or place, but street by street, by the principal inhabitants of the several quarters of the city; and he reduced the number of those who received grain at the public cost, from three hundred and twenty, to a hundred and fifty, thousand. To prevent any tumults on account of the census, he ordered that the praetor should every year fill up by lot the vacancies occasioned by death, from those who were not enrolled for the receipt of grain.

Eighty thousand citizens having been distributed into foreign colonies, he enacted, in order to stop the drain on the population, that no freeman of the city above twenty, and under forty, years of age, who was not in the military service, should absent himself from Italy for more than three years at a time; that no senator's son should go abroad, unless in the retinue of some high officer; and as to those whose pursuit was tending flocks and herds, that no less than a third of the number of their shepherds free-born should be youths. He likewise made all those who practiced physic in Rome, and all teachers of the liberal arts, free of the city, in order to fix them in it, and induce others to settle there. With respect to debts, he disappointed the expectation which was generally entertained, that they would be totally canceled; and ordered that the debtors should satisfy their creditors, according to the valuation of their estates, at the rate at which they were purchased before the commencement of the civil war; deducting from the debt what had been paid for interest either in money or by bonds; by virtue of which provision about a fourth part of the debt was lost. He dissolved all the guilds, except such as were of ancient foundation. Crimes were punished with greater severity; and the rich being more easily induced to commit them because they were only liable to banishment, without the forfeiture of their property, he stripped murderers, as Cicero observes, of their whole estates, and other offenders of one half. (40-42)

His thoughts were now fully employed from day to day on a variety of great projects for the embellishment and improvement of the city, as well as for guarding and extending the bounds of the empire. In the first place, he meditated the construction of a temple to Mars, which should exceed in grandeur every thing of that kind in the world. For this purpose, he intended to fill up the lake on which he had entertained the people with the spectacle of a sea-fight. He also projected a most spacious theater adjacent to the Tarpeian mount; and also proposed to reduce the civil law to a reasonable compass, and out of that immense and un-digested mass of statutes to extract the best and most necessary parts into a few books; to make as large a collection as possible of works in the Greek and Latin languages, for the public use; the province of providing and putting them in proper order being assigned to Marcus Varro. He intended likewise to drain the Pomptine marshes, to cut a channel for the discharge of the waters of the lake Fucinus, to form a road from the Adriatic through the ridge of the Apennine to the Tiber; to make a cut through the isthmus of Corinth, to reduce the Dacians, who had over-run Pontus and Thrace, within their proper limits, and then to make war upon the Parthians, through the Lesser Armenia, but not to risk a general engagement with them, until he had made some trial of their prowess in war. But in the midst of all his undertakings and projects, he was carried off by death; before I speak of which, it may not be improper to give an account of his person, dress, and manners, together with what relates to his pursuits, both civil and military.

It is said that he was tall, of a fair complexion, round limbed, rather full faced, with eyes black and piercing; and that he enjoyed excellent health, except toward the close of his life, when he was subject to sudden fainting-fits, and disturbance in his sleep. He was likewise twice seized with the falling sickness while engaged in active service. He was so nice in the care of his person, that he not only kept the hair of his head closely cut and had his face smoothly shaved, but even caused the hair on other parts of the body to be plucked out by the roots, a practice for which some persons rallied him. His baldness gave him much uneasiness, having often found himself upon that account exposed to the jibes of his enemies. He therefore used to bring forward the hair from the crown of his head; and of all the honors conferred upon him by the senate and people, there was none which he either accepted or used with greater pleasure, than the right of wearing constantly a laurel crown. It is said that he was particular in his dress. For he used the Latus Clavus with fringes about the wrists, and always had it girded about him, but rather loosely. This circumstance gave origin to the expression of Sulla, who often advised the nobles to beware of "the ill-girt boy." (44-45)

In eloquence and warlike achievements, he equaled at least, if he did not surpass, the greatest of men. After his prosecution of Dolabella, he was indisputably reckoned one of the most distinguished advocates. Cicero, in recounting to Brutus the famous orators, declares, "that he does not see that Caesar was inferior to any one of them;" and says, "that he had an elegant, splendid, noble, and magnificent vein of eloquence." And in a letter to Cornelius Nepos, he writes of him in the following terms: "What! Of all the orators, who, during the whole course of their lives, have done nothing else, which can you prefer to him? Which of them is more pointed or terse in his periods, or employs more polished and elegant language?" In his youth, he seems to have chosen Strabo Caesar for his model; from whose oration in behalf of the Sardinians he has transcribed some passages literally into his Divination. In his delivery he is said to have had a shrill voice, and his action was animated, but not ungraceful. He has left behind him some speeches, among which are ranked a few that are not genuine, such as that on behalf of Quintus Metellus. These Augustus supposes, with reason, to be rather the production of blundering short-hand writers, who were not able to keep pace with him in the delivery, than publications of his own. For I find in some copies that the title is not "For Metellus," but "What he wrote to Metellus;" whereas the speech is delivered in the name of Caesar, vindicating Metellus and himself from the aspersions cast upon them by their common defamers. The speech addressed "To his soldiers in Spain," Augustus considers likewise as spurious. We meet with two under this title; one made, as is pretended, in the first battle, and the other in the last; at which time, Asinius Pollio says, he had not leisure to address the soldiers, on account of the suddenness of the enemy's attack. (55)

He was perfect in the use of arms, an accomplished rider, and able to endure fatigue beyond all belief. On a march, he used to go at the head of his troops, sometimes on horseback, but oftener on foot, with his head bare in all kinds of weather. He would travel post in a light carriage without baggage, at the rate of a hundred miles a day; and if he was stopped by floods in the rivers, he swam across, or floated on skins inflated with wind, so that he often anticipated intelligence of his movements.

In his expeditions, it is difficult to say whether his caution or his daring was most conspicuous. He never marched his army by roads which were exposed to ambuscades, without having previously examined the nature of the ground by his scouts. Nor did he cross over to Britain, before he had carefully examined, in person, the navigation, the harbors, and the most convenient point of landing in the island. When intelligence was brought to him of the siege of his camp in Germany, he made his way to his troops, through the enemy's stations, in a Gaulish dress. He crossed the sea from Brundisium to Dyrrachium, in the winter, through the midst of the enemy's fleets; and the troops, under orders to join him, being slow in their movements, notwithstanding repeated messages to hurry them, but to no purpose, he at last went privately, and alone, aboard a small vessel in the night time, with his head muffled up; nor did he make himself known, or suffer the master to put about, although the wind blew strong against them, until they were ready to sink. (57-58)

But what brought upon him the greatest odium, and was thought an unpardonable insult, was his receiving the whole body of the conscript fathers sitting, before the temple of Venus, when they waited upon him with a number of decrees, conferring on him the highest dignities. Some say that, on his attempting to rise, he was held down by Cornelius Balbus; others, that he did not attempt to rise at all, but frowned on Caius Trebatius, who suggested to him that he should stand up to receive the senate. This behavior appeared the more intolerable in him, because, when one of the tribunes of the people, Pontius Aquila, would not rise up to him, as he passed by the tribunes' seat during his triumph, he was so much offended, that he cried out, "Well then, you tribune, Aquila, oust me from the government." And for some days afterward, he never promised a favor to any person, without this proviso, "if Pontius Aquila will give me leave." (78)

For this reason the conspirators precipitated the execution of their design, that they might not be obliged to give their assent to the proposal. Instead, therefore, of caballing any longer separately, in small parties, they now united their counsels; the people themselves being dissatisfied with the present state of affairs, both privately and publicly condemning the tyranny under which they lived, and calling on patriots to assert their cause against the

usurper. Upon the admission of foreigners into the senate, a hand-
bill was posted up in these words: "A good deed! let no one show
a new senator the way to the house." These verses were likewise
currently repeated:

> The Gauls he dragged in triumph through the town,
> Caesar has brought into the senate-house,
> And changed their *plaids* for the patrician gown.

When Quintus Maximus, who had been his deputy in the consulship for the last three months, entered the theater, and the lictor,
according to custom, bid the people take notice who was coming,
they all cried out, "He is no consul." After the removal of Caese-
tius and Marullus from their office, they were found to have
a great many votes at the next election of consuls. Some one wrote
under the statue of Lucius Brutus, "Would you were now alive!"
and under the statue of Caesar himself these lines:

> Because he drove from Rome the royal race,
> Brutus was first made consul in their place.
> This man, because he put the consuls down,
> Has been rewarded with a royal crown.

About sixty persons were engaged in the conspiracy against
him, of whom Caius Cassius, and Marcus and Decimus Brutus
were the chief. It was at first debated among them, whether they
should attack him in the Campus Martius when he was taking the
votes of the tribes, and some of them should throw him off the
bridge, while others should be ready to stab him upon his fall; or
else in the Via Sacra, or at the entrance of the theater. But after
public notice had been given by proclamation for the senate to
assemble upon the ides of March [15th March], in the senate-
house built by Pompey, they approved both of the time and place,
as most fitting for their purpose.

Caesar had warning given him of his fate by indubitable
omens. A few months before, when the colonists settled at Capua,
by virtue of the Julian law, were demolishing some old sepulchers
in building country-houses, and were the more eager at the work,
because they discovered certain vessels of antique workmanship,

a tablet of brass was found in a tomb, in which Capys, the founder of Capua, was said to have been buried, with an inscription in the Greek language to this effect: "Whenever the bones of Capys come to be discovered, a descendant of Iulus will be slain by the hands of his kinsmen, and his death revenged by fearful disasters throughout Italy." Lest any person should regard this anecdote as a fabulous or silly invention, it was circulated upon the authority of Caius Balbus, an intimate friend of Caesar's. A few days likewise before his death, he was informed that the horses, which, upon his crossing the Rubicon, he had consecrated, and turned loose to graze without a keeper, abstained entirely from eating, and shed floods of tears. The soothsayer Spurinna, observing certain ominous appearances in a sacrifice which he was offering, advised him to beware of some danger, which threatened to befall him before the ides of March were past. The day before the ides, birds of various kinds from a neighboring grove, pursuing a wren which flew into Pompey's senate-house, with a sprig of laurel in its beak, tore it in pieces. Also, in the night on which the day of his murder dawned, he dreamt at one time that he was soaring above the clouds, and, at another, that he had joined hands with Jupiter. His wife Calpurnia fancied in her sleep that the pediment of the house was falling down, and her husband stabbed on her bosom; immediately upon which the chamber doors flew open. On account of these omens, as well as his infirm health, he was in some doubt whether he should not remain at home, and defer to some other opportunity the business which he intended to propose to the senate; but Decimus Brutus advising him not to disappoint the senators, who were numerously assembled, and waited his coming, he was prevailed upon to go, and accordingly set forward about the fifth hour. In his way, some person having thrust into his hand a paper, warning him against the plot, he mixed it with some other documents which he held in his left hand, intending to read it at leisure. Victim after victim was slain, without any favorable appearances in the entrails; but still, disregarding all omens, he entered the senate-house, laughing at Spurinna as a false prophet, because the ides of March were come, without any mischief having befallen him. To which the soothsayer replied, "They are come, indeed, but not past."

When he had taken his seat, the conspirators stood round him, under color of paying their compliments; and immediately Tullius Cimber, who had engaged to commence the assault, advancing nearer than the rest, as if he had some favor to request, Caesar made signs that he should defer his petition to some other time. Tullius immediately seized him by the toga, on both shoulders; at which Caesar crying out, "Violence is meant!" one of the Cassii wounded him a little below the throat. Caesar seized him by the arm, and ran it through with his stylus; and endeavoring to rush forward was stopped by another wound. Finding himself now attacked on all hands with naked poniards, he wrapped the toga about his head, and at the same moment drew the skirt round his legs with his left hand, that he might fall more decently with the lower part of his body covered. He was stabbed with three and twenty wounds, uttering a groan only, but no cry, at the first wound; although some authors relate, that when Marcus Brutus fell upon him, he exclaimed, "What! art thou, too, one of them? Thou, my son!" The whole assembly instantly dispersing, he lay for some time after he expired, until three of his slaves laid the body on a litter, and carried it home, with one arm hanging down over the side. Among so many wounds, there was none that was mortal, in the opinion of the surgeon Antistius, except the second, which he received in the breast. The conspirators meant to drag his body into the Tiber as soon as they had killed him; to confiscate his estate, and rescind all his enactments; but they were deterred by fear of Mark Antony, and Lepidus, Caesar's master of the horse, and abandoned their intentions. (80-82)

Notice of his funeral having been solemnly proclaimed, a pile was erected in the Campus Martius, near the tomb of his daughter Julia; and before the Rostra was placed a gilded tabernacle, on the model of the temple of Venus Genetrix; within which was an ivory bed, covered with purple and cloth of gold. At the head was a trophy, with the [blood-stained] robe in which he was slain. It being considered that the whole day would not suffice for carrying the funeral oblations in solemn procession before the corpse, directions were given for every one, without regard to order, to carry them from the city into the Campus Martius, by what way they pleased. To raise pity and indignation for his murder, in the plays acted at the funeral, a passage was sung from Pacuvius's tragedy, entitled, "The Trial for Arms":

> "That ever I, unhappy man, should save
>   Wretches, who thus have brought me to the grave!"

And some lines also from Acilius's tragedy of "Electra," to the same effect. Instead of a funeral panegyric, the consul Antony ordered a herald to proclaim to the people the decree of the senate, in which they had bestowed upon him all honors, divine and human; with the oath by which they had engaged themselves for the defense of his person; and to these he added only a few words of his own. The magistrates and others, who had formerly filled the highest offices, carried the bier from the Rostra into the Forum. While some proposed that the body should be burnt in the sanctuary of the temple of Jupiter Capitolinus, and others in Pompey's senate-house; on a sudden, two men, with swords by their sides, and spears in their hands, set fire to the bier with lighted torches. The throng around immediately heaped upon it dry faggots, the tribunals and benches of the adjoining courts, and whatever else came to hand. Then the musicians and players stripped off the dresses they wore on the present occasion, taken from the wardrobe of his triumph at spectacles, rent them, and threw them into the flames. The legionaries, also, of his veteran bands, cast in their armor, which they had put on in honor of his funeral. Most of the ladies did the same by their ornaments, with the bullae, and mantles of their children. In this public mourning there joined a multitude of foreigners, expressing their sorrow according to the fashion of their respective countries; but especially the Jews, who for several nights together frequented the spot where the body was burnt. (84)

He died in the fifty-sixth year of his age, and was ranked among the Gods, not only by a formal decree, but in the belief of the vulgar. For during the first games which Augustus, his heir consecrated to his memory, a comet blazed for seven days together, rising always about eleven o'clock; and it was supposed to be the soul of Caesar, now received into heaven: for which reason, likewise, he is represented on his statue with a star on his brow. The senate-house in which he was slain, was ordered to be shut up, and a decree made that the ides of March should be called parricidal, and the senate should never more assemble on that day. (88)

TACITUS

Translated by Alfred John Church and William Jackson Brodribb

THE ANNALS

The death of Augustus and the accession of Tiberius. Enforcement of the law of treason. The death of Germanicus. His funeral. Sejanus procures the death of Drusus. The inglorious nature of the present. The plans of Sejanus. Tiberius retires to Capri. Tiberius a tyrant; his death. Nero's accession. His early acts. Nero causes the murders of his mother and former wife. Nero on the stage. The great fire at Rome and the persecution of the Christians. Conspiracy of Piso. Death of Seneca. Death of Petronius.

[*Early Rome. The death of Augustus,* A.D. *14. The start of Tiberius' reign,* A.D. *14-37.*]

Rome at the beginning was ruled by kings. Freedom and the consulship were established by Lucius Brutus. Dictatorships were held for a temporary crisis. The power of the decemvirs did not last beyond two years, nor was the consular jurisdiction of the military tribunes of long duration. The despotisms of Cinna and Sulla were brief; the rule of Pompeius and of Crassus soon yielded before Caesar; the arms of Lepidus and Antonius before Augustus; who, when the world was wearied by civil strife, subjected it to empire under the title of "Prince." But the successes and reverses of the old Roman people have been recorded by famous historians; and fine intellects were not wanting to describe the times of Augustus, till growing sycophancy scared them away. The histories of Tiberius, Caius, Claudius, and Nero, while they were in power, were falsified through terror, and after their death were written under the irritation of a recent hatred. Hence my purpose is to relate a few facts about Augustus—more particularly his last acts, then the reign of Tiberius, and all which follows, without either bitterness or partiality, from any motives to which I am far removed.

When after the destruction of Brutus and Cassius there was no longer any army of the Commonwealth, when Pompeius was crushed in Sicily, and when, with Lepidus pushed aside and Antonius slain, even the Julian faction had only Caesar left to lead it, then, dropping the title of triumvir, and giving out that he was a Consul, and was satisfied with a tribune's authority for the protection of the people, Augustus won over the soldiers with gifts, the populace with cheap grain, and all men with the sweets of repose, and so grew greater by degrees, while he concentrated in himself the functions of the Senate, the magistrates, and the laws. He was wholly unopposed, for the boldest spirits had fallen in battle, or in the proscription, while the remaining nobles, the readier they were to be slaves, were raised the higher by wealth and promotion, so that, aggrandized by revolution, they preferred the safety of the present to the dangerous past. Nor did the provinces dislike that condition of affairs, for they distrusted the government of the Senate and the people, because of the rivalries between the leading men and the rapacity of the officials, while the protection of the laws was unavailing, as they were continually deranged by violence, intrigue, and finally by corruption.

Augustus meanwhile, as supports to his despotism, raised to the pontificate and curule aedileship Claudius Marcellus, his sister's son, while a mere stripling, and Marcus Agrippa, of humble birth, a good soldier, and one who had shared his victory, to two consecutive consulships, and as Marcellus soon afterward died, he also accepted him as his son-in-law. Tiberius Nero and Claudius Drusus, his stepsons, he honored with imperial titles, although his own family was as yet undiminished. For he had admitted the children of Agrippa, Caius and Lucius, into the house of the Caesars; and before they had yet laid aside the dress of boyhood he had most fervently desired, with an outward show of reluctance, that they should be entitled "princes of the youth," and be consuls-elect. When Agrippa died, and Lucius Caesar as he was on his

way to our armies in Spain, and Caius while returning from
Armenia, still suffering from a wound, were prematurely cut off
by destiny, or by their step-mother Livia's treachery, Drusus too
having long been dead, Nero remained alone of the stepsons, and
in him everything tended to center. He was adopted as a son, as
a colleague in empire and a partner in the tribunician power, and
paraded through all the armies, no longer through his mother's
secret intrigues, but at her open suggestion. For she had gained
such a hold on the aged Augustus that he drove out as an exile
into the island of Planasia, his only grandson, Agrippa Postumus,
who, though devoid of worthy qualities, and having only the brute
courage of physical strength, had not been convicted of any gross
offense. And yet Augustus had appointed Germanicus, Drusus's
offspring, to the command of eight legions on the Rhine, and required Tiberius to adopt him, although Tiberius had a son, now
a young man, in his house; but he did it that he might have several
safeguards to rest on. He had no war at the time on his hands
except against the Germans, which was rather to wipe out the
disgrace of the loss of Quintilius Varus and his army than out
of an ambition to extend the empire, or for any adequate recompense. At home all was tranquil, and there were magistrates with
the same titles; there was a younger generation, sprung up since
the victory of Actium, and even many of the older men had been
born during the civil wars. How few were left who had seen the
republic!

Thus the State had been revolutionized, and there was
not a vestige left of the old sound morality. Stript of equality, all
looked up to the commands of a sovereign without the least apprehension for the present, while Augustus in the vigor of life could
maintain his own position, that of his house, and the general
tranquillity. When in advanced old age, he was worn out by a
sickly frame, and the end was near and new prospects opened, a
few spoke in vain of the blessings of freedom, but most people
dreaded and some longed for war. The popular gossip of the large
majority fastened itself variously on their future masters. "Agrippa
was savage, and had been exasperated by insult, and neither from
age nor experience in affairs was equal to so great a burden. Tibe-

rius Nero was of mature years, and had established his fame in war, but he had the old arrogance inbred in the Claudian family, and many symptoms of a cruel temper, though they were repressed, now and then broke out. He had also from earliest infancy been reared in an imperial house; consulships and triumphs had been heaped on him in his younger days; even in the years which, on the pretext of seclusion, he spent in exile at Rhodes, he had had no thoughts but of wrath, hypocrisy, and secret sensuality. There was his mother too with a woman's caprice. They must, it seemed, be subject to a female and to two striplings besides, who for a while would burden, and some day rend asunder the State."

While these and like topics were discussed, the infirmities of Augustus increased, and some suspected guilt on his wife's part. For a rumor had gone abroad that a few months before he had sailed to Planasia on a visit to Agrippa, with the knowledge of some chosen friends, and with one companion, Fabius Maximus; that many tears were shed on both sides, with expressions of affection, and that thus there was a hope of the young man being restored to the home of his grandfather. This, it was said, Maximus had divulged to his wife Marcia, she again to Livia. All was known to Caesar, and when Maximus soon afterward died, by a death some thought to be self-inflicted, there were heard at his funeral wailings from Marcia, in which she reproached herself for having been the cause of her husband's destruction. Whatever the fact was, Tiberius as he was just entering Illyria was summoned home by an urgent letter from his mother, and it has not been thoroughly ascertained whether at the city of Nola he found Augustus still breathing or quite lifeless. For Livia had surrounded the house and its approaches with a strict watch, and favorable bulletins were published from time to time, till, provision having been made for the demands of the crisis, one and the same report told men that Augustus was dead and that Tiberius Nero was master of the State.

The first crime of the new reign was the murder of Postumus Agrippa. Though he was surprised and unarmed, a centurion of the firmest resolution dispatched him with difficulty. Tiberius gave no explanation of the matter to the Senate; he pretended that there were directions from his father ordering the tribune in charge of the prisoner not to delay the slaughter of Agrippa, whenever he should himself have breathed his last. Beyond a doubt, Augustus had often complained of the young man's character, and had thus succeeded in obtaining the sanction of a decree of the Senate for his banishment. But he never was hard-hearted enough to destroy any of his kinsfolk, nor was it credible that death was to be the sentence of the grandson in order that the stepson might feel secure. It was more probable that Tiberius and Livia, the one from fear, the other from a stepmother's enmity, hurried on the destruction of a youth whom they suspected and hated. When the centurion reported, according to military custom, that he had executed the command, Tiberius replied that he had not given the command, and that the act must be justified to the Senate.

As soon as Sallustius Crispus who shared the secret (he had, in fact, sent the written order to the tribune) knew this, fearing that the charge would be shifted on himself, and that his peril would be the same whether he uttered fiction or truth, he advised Livia not to divulge the secrets of her house or the counsels of friends, or any services performed by the soldiers, nor to let Tiberius weaken the strength of imperial power by referring everything to the Senate, for "the condition," he said, "of holding empire is that an account cannot be balanced unless it be rendered to one person."

Meanwhile at Rome people plunged into slavery—consuls, senators, knights. The higher a man's rank, the more eager his hypocrisy, and his looks the more carefully studied, so as neither to betray joy at the decease of one emperor nor sorrow at the rise of another, while he mingled delight and lamentations with his flattery. Sextus Pompeius and Sextus Apuleius, the consuls, were the first to swear allegiance to Tiberius Caesar, and in their presence the oath was taken by Seius Strabo and Caius Turranius, respectively the commander of the praetorian cohorts and the superintendent of the grain supplies. Then the Senate, the soldiers and the people did the same. For Tiberius would inaugurate everything with the consuls, as though the ancient constitution remained, and he hesitated about being emperor. Even the proclamation by which he summoned the senators to their chamber, he issued merely with the title of Tribune, which he had received under Augustus. The wording of the proclamation was brief, and in a very modest tone. "He would," it said, "provide for the honors due to his father, and not leave the lifeless body, and this was the only public duty he now claimed."

As soon, however, as Augustus was dead, he had given the watchword to the praetorian cohorts, as commander-in-chief. He had the guard under arms, with all the other adjuncts of a court; soldiers attended him to the forum; soldiers went with him to the Senate House. He sent letters to the different armies, as though supreme power was now his, and showed hesitation only when he spoke in the Senate. His chief motive was fear that Germanicus, who had at his disposal so many legions, such vast auxiliary forces of the allies, and such wonderful popularity, might prefer the possession to the expectation of empire. He looked also at public opinion, wishing to have the credit of having been called and elected by the State rather than of having crept into power through the intrigues of a wife and a dotard's adoption. It was subsequently understood that he assumed a wavering attitude, to test likewise the temper of the nobles. For he would twist a word or a look into a crime and treasure it up in his memory.

On the first day of the Senate he allowed nothing to be discussed but the funeral of Augustus, whose will, which was brought in by the Vestal Virgins, named as his heirs Tiberius and Livia. The latter was to be admitted into the Julian family with the name of Augusta; next in expectation were the grand and great-grandchildren. In the third place, he had named the chief men of the State, most of whom he hated, simply out of ostentation and to win credit with posterity. His legacies were not beyond the scale of a private citizen, except a bequest of forty-three million five hundred thousand sesterces "to the people and populace of Rome," of one thousand to every praetorian soldier, and of three hundred to every man in the legionary cohorts composed of Roman citizens.

Next followed a deliberation about funeral honors. Of these the most imposing were thought fitting. The procession was to be conducted through "the gate of triumph," on the motion of Gallus

Asinius; the titles of the laws passed, the names of the nations conquered by Augustus were to be borne in front, on that of Lucius Arruntius. Messala Valerius further proposed that the oath of allegiance to Tiberius should be yearly renewed, and when Tiberius asked him whether it was at *his* bidding that he had brought forward this motion, he replied that he had proposed it spontaneously, and that in whatever concerned the State he would use only his own discretion, even at the risk of offending. This was the only style of adulation which yet remained. The Senators unanimously exclaimed that the body ought to be borne on their shoulders to the funeral pile. The emperor left the point to them with disdainful moderation, and he then admonished the people by a proclamation not to indulge in that tumultuous enthusiasm which had distracted the funeral of the Divine Julius, or express a wish that Augustus should be burnt in the Forum instead of in his appointed resting-place in the Campus Martius.

On the day of the funeral soldiers stood round as a guard, amid much ridicule from those who had either themselves witnessed or who had heard from their parents of the famous day when slavery was still something fresh, and freedom had been resought in vain, when the slaying of Caesar, the Dictator, seemed to some the vilest, to others, the most glorious of deeds. "Now," they said, "an aged sovereign, whose power had lasted long, who had provided his heirs with abundant means to coerce the State, requires forsooth the defense of soldiers that his burial may be undisturbed."

Then followed much talk about Augustus himself, and many expressed an idle wonder that the same day marked the beginning of his assumption of empire and the close of his life, and, again, that he had ended his days at Nola in the same house and room as his father Octavius. People extolled too the number of his consulships, in which he had equaled Valerius Corvus and Caius Marius combined, the continuance for thirty-seven years of the tribunician power, the title of Imperator twenty-one times earned, and his other honors which had been either frequently repeated or were wholly new. Sensible men, however, spoke variously of his life with praise and censure. Some said "that dutiful feeling toward a father, and the necessities of the State in which laws had then no place, drove him into civil war, which can neither be planned nor conducted on any right principles. He had often yielded to Antonius, while he was taking vengeance on his father's murderers, often also to Lepidus. When the latter sank into feeble dotage and the former had been ruined by his profligacy, the only remedy for his distracted country was the rule of a single man. Yet the State had been organized under the name neither of a kingdom nor a dictatorship, but under that of a prince. The ocean and remote rivers were the boundaries of the empire; the legions, provinces, fleets, all things were linked together; there was law for the citizens; there was respect shown to the allies. The capital had been embellished on a grand scale; only in a few instances had he resorted to force, simply to secure general tranquillity."

It was said, on the other hand, "that filial duty and State necessity were merely assumed as a mask. It was really from a lust of sovereignty that he had excited the veterans by bribery, had, when a young man and a subject, raised an army, tampered with the Consul's legions, and feigned an attachment to the faction of Pompeius. Then, when by a decree of the Senate he had usurped the high functions and authority of Praetor, when Hirtius and Pansa were slain—whether they were destroyed by the enemy, or Pansa by poison infused into a wound, Hirtius by his own soldiers and Caesar's treacherous machinations—he at once possessed himself of both their armies, wrested the consulate from a reluctant Senate, and turned against the State the arms with which he had been intrusted against Antonius. Citizens were proscribed, lands divided, without so much as the approval of those who executed these deeds. Even granting that the deaths of Cassius and of the Bruti were sacrifices to a hereditary enmity (though duty requires us to waive private feuds for the sake of the public welfare), still Pompeius had been deluded by the phantom of peace, and Lepidus by the mask of friendship. Subsequently, Antonius had been lured on by the treaties of Tarentum and Brundisium, and by his marriage with the sister, and paid by his death the penalty of a treacherous alliance. No doubt, there was peace after all this, but it was a peace stained with blood; there were the disasters of Lollius and Varus, the murders at Rome of the Varros, Egnatii, and Julii."

The domestic life too of Augustus was not spared. "Nero's wife had been taken from him, and there had been the farce of consulting the pontiffs, whether, with a child conceived and not yet born, she could properly marry. There were the excesses of Quintus Tedius and Vedius Pollio; last of all, there was Livia, terrible to the State as a mother, terrible to the house of the Caesars as a stepmother. No honor was left for the gods, when Augustus chose to be himself worshiped with temples and statues, like those of the deities, and with flamens and priests. He had not even adopted Tiberius as his successor out of affection or any regard to the State, but, having thoroughly seen his arrogant and savage temper, he had sought glory for himself by a contrast of extreme wickedness." For, in fact, Augustus, a few years before, when he was a second time asking from the Senate the tribunician power for Tiberius, though his speech was complimentary, had thrown out certain hints as to his manners, style, and habits of life, which he meant as reproaches, while he seemed to excuse. However, when his obsequies had been duly performed, a temple with a religious ritual was decreed him.

After this all prayers were addressed to Tiberius. He, on his part, urged various considerations, the greatness of the empire, his distrust of himself. "Only," he said, "the intellect of the Divine Augustus was equal to such a burden. Called as he had been by him to share his anxieties, he had learnt by experience how exposed to fortune's caprices was the task of universal rule. Consequently, in a state which had the support of so many great men, they should not put everything on one man, as many, by uniting their efforts, would more easily discharge public functions." There was more grand sentiment than good faith in such words. Tiberius's language even in matters which he did not care to conceal, either from nature or habit, was always hesitating and obscure, and now that he was struggling to hide his feelings completely, it was all the more involved in uncertainty and doubt. The Senators, however, whose only fear was lest they might seem to understand him, burst into complaints, tears, and prayers. They raised their hands to the gods, to the statue of Augustus, and to the knees of Tiberius, when he ordered a document to be produced and read. This contained a description of the resources of the State, of the number of citizens and allies under arms, of the fleets, subject kingdoms, provinces, taxes, direct and indirect, necessary expenses and customary bounties. All these details Augustus had written with his own hand, and had added a counsel, that the empire should be confined to its present limits, either from fear or out of jealousy.

Meantime, while the Senate stooped to the most abject supplication, Tiberius happened to say that although he was not equal to the whole burden of the State, yet he would undertake the charge of whatever part of it might be entrusted to him. Thereupon Asinius Gallus said, "I ask you, Caesar, what part of the State you wish to have entrusted to you?" Confounded by the sudden inquiry he was silent for a few moments; then, recovering his presence of mind, he replied that it would by no means become his modesty to choose or to avoid in a case where he would prefer to be wholly excused. Then Gallus again, who had inferred anger from his looks, said that the question had not been asked with the intention of dividing what could not be separated, but to convince him by his own admission that the body of the State was one, and must be directed by a single mind. He further spoke in praise of Augustus, and reminded Tiberius himself of his victories, and of his admirable deeds for many years as a civilian. Still, he did not thereby soften the emperor's resentment, for he had long been detested from an impression that, as he had married Vipsania, daughter of Marcus Agrippa, who had once been the wife of Tiberius, he aspired to be more than a citizen, and kept up the arrogant tone of his father, Asinius Pollio.

Next, Lucius Arruntius, who differed but little from the speech of Gallus, gave like offense, though Tiberius had no old grudge against him, but simply mistrusted him, because he was rich and daring, had brilliant accomplishments, and corresponding popularity. For Augustus, when in his last conversations he was discussing who would refuse the highest place, though sufficiently capable, who would aspire to it without being equal to it, and who would unite both the ability and ambition, had described Marcus Lepidus as able but contemptuously indifferent, Gallus Asinius as ambitious and incapable, Lucius Arruntius as not unworthy of it, and, should the chance be given him, sure to make the venture. About the two first there is a general agreement, but instead of Arruntius some have mentioned Cneius Piso, and all these men, except Lepidus, were soon afterward destroyed by various charges through the contrivance of Tiberius. Quintus Haterius too and Mamercus Scaurus ruffled his suspicious temper, Haterius by having said—"How long, Caesar, will you suffer the State to be without a head?" Scaurus by the remark that there was a hope that the Senate's prayers would not be fruitless, seeing that he had not used his right as Tribune to negative the motion of the Consuls. Tiberius instantly broke out into invective against Haterius; Scaurus, with whom he was far more deeply displeased, he passed over in silence. Wearied at last by the assembly's clamorous importunity and the urgent demands of individual Senators, he gave way by degrees, not admitting that he undertook empire, but yet ceasing to refuse it and to be entreated. It is known that Haterius having entered the palace to ask pardon, and thrown himself at the knees of Tiberius as he was walking, was almost killed by the soldiers, because Tiberius fell forward, accidentally or from being entangled by the suppliant's hands. Yet the peril of so great a man did not make him relent, till Haterius went with entreaties to Augusta, and was saved by her very earnest intercessions.

Great too was the Senate's sycophancy to Augusta. Some would have her styled "parent;" others "mother of the country," and a majority proposed that to the name of Caesar should be added "son of Julia." The emperor repeatedly asserted that there must be a limit to the honors paid to women, and that he would observe similar moderation in those bestowed on himself, but annoyed at the invidious proposal, and indeed regarding a woman's elevation as a slight to himself, he would not allow so much as a lictor to be assigned her, and forbade the erection of an altar in memory of her adoption, and any like distinction. But for Germanicus Caesar he asked pro-consular powers, and envoys were dispatched to confer them on him, and also to express sympathy with his grief at the death of Augustus. The same request was not made for Drusus, because he was consul elect and present at Rome. Twelve candidates were named for the praetorship, the number which Augustus had handed down, and when the Senate urged Tiberius to increase it, he bound himself by an oath not to exceed it.

It was then for the first time that the elections were transferred from the Campus Martius to the Senate. For up to that day, though the most important rested with the emperor's choice, some were settled by the partialities of the tribes. Nor did the people complain of having the right taken from them, except in mere idle talk, and the Senate, being now released from the necessity of bribery and of degrading solicitations, gladly upheld the change, Tiberius confining himself to the recommendation of only four candidates who were to be nominated without rejection or canvass. Meanwhile the tribunes of the people asked leave to exhibit at their own expense games to be named after Augustus and added to the Calendar as the Augustales. Money was, however, voted from the exchequer, and though the use of the triumphal robe in the circus was prescribed, it was not allowed them to ride in a chariot. Soon the annual celebration was transferred to the praetor, to whose lot fell the administration of justice between citizens and foreigners. (I, 1-15)

[Tiberius now rigorously enforces the law of treason, "lex de maiestate." This led to the rise of private informers, "delatores," for bringing accusations.]

. . . The title of "father of his country," which the people had so often thrust on him, Tiberius refused, nor would he allow obedience to be sworn to his enactments, though the Senate voted it, for he said repeatedly that all human things were uncertain, and that the more he had obtained, the more precarious was his position. But he did not thereby create a belief in his patriotism, for he had revived the law of treason, the name of which indeed was known in ancient times, though other matters came under its jurisdiction, such as the betrayal of an army, or seditious stirring up of the people, or, in short, any corrupt act by which a man had impaired "the majesty of the people of Rome." Deeds only were liable to accusation; words went unpunished. It was Augustus who first, under color of this law, applied legal inquiry to libelous writings, provoked, as he had been, by the licentious freedom with which Cassius Severus had defamed men and women of distinction in his insulting satires. Soon afterward, Tiberius, when consulted by Pompeius Macer, the praetor, as to whether prosecutions for treason should be revived, replied that the laws must be enforced. He too had been exasperated by the publication of verses of uncertain authorship, pointed at his cruelty, his arrogance, and his dissensions with his mother. (I, 72)

[Tiberius had planned to have Germanicus succeed him, but A.D. 19 his nephew died mysteriously in the East. Some people thought that he had been murdered by Piso, the Syrian governor. Germanicus' widow—Agrippina, the granddaughter of Augustus—suspected Tiberius.]

Germanicus meanwhile, as he was returning from Egypt, found that all his directions to the legions and to the various cities had been repealed or reversed. This led to grievous insults on Piso, while he as savagely assailed the prince. Piso then resolved to quit Syria. Soon he was detained there by the failing health of Germanicus, but when he heard of his recovery, while people were paying the vows they had offered for his safety, he went attended by his lictors, drove away the victims placed by the altars with all the preparations for sacrifice, and the festal gathering of the populace of Antioch. Then he left for Seleucia and awaited the result of the illness which had again attacked Germanicus. The terrible intensity of the malady was increased by the belief that he had been poisoned by Piso. And certainly there were found hidden in the floor and in the walls disinterred remains of human bodies, incantations and spells, and the name of Germanicus inscribed on leaden tablets, half-burnt cinders smeared with blood, and other horrors by which in popular belief souls are devoted to the infernal deities. Piso too was accused of sending emissaries to note curiously every unfavorable symptom of the illness.

Germanicus heard of all this with anger, no less than with fear. "If my doors," he said, "are to be besieged, if I must gasp out my last breath under my enemies' eyes, what will then be the lot of my most unhappy wife, of my infant children? Poisoning seems tedious; he is in eager haste to have the sole control of the province and the legions. But Germanicus is not yet fallen so low, nor will the murderer long retain the reward of the fatal deed."

He then addressed a letter to Piso, renouncing his friendship, and, as many also state, ordered him to quit the province. Piso without further delay weighed anchor, slackening his course that he might not have a long way to return should Germanicus' death leave Syria open to him.

For a brief space the prince's hopes rose; then his frame became exhausted, and, as his end drew near, he spoke as follows to the friends by his side:—

"Were I succumbing to nature, I should have just ground of complaint even against the gods for thus tearing me away in my youth by an untimely death from parents, children, country. Now, cut off by the wickedness of Piso and Plancina, I leave to your hearts my last entreaties. Describe to my father and brother, torn by what persecutions, entangled by what plots, I have ended by the worst of deaths the most miserable of lives. If any were touched by my bright prospects, by ties of blood, or even by envy toward me while I lived, they will weep that the once prosperous survivor of so many wars has perished by a woman's treachery. You will have the opportunity of complaint before the Senate, of an appeal to the laws. It is not the chief duty of friends to follow the dead with unprofitable laments, but to remember his wishes, to fulfill his commands. Tears for Germanicus even strangers will shed; vengeance must come from *you,* if you loved the man more than his fortune. Show the people of Rome her who is the grand-daughter of the Divine Augustus, as well as my consort; set before

them my six children. Sympathy will be on the side of the accusers,
and to those who screen themselves under infamous orders belief
or pardon will be refused."

His friends clasped the dying man's right hand, and swore
that they would sooner lose life than revenge.

He then turned to his wife and implored her by the memory
of her husband and by their common offspring to lay aside her
high spirit, to submit herself to the cruel blows of fortune, and
not, when she returned to Rome, to enrage by political rivalry
those who were stronger than herself. This was said openly; other
words were whispered, pointing, it was supposed, to his fears from
Tiberius. Soon afterward he expired, to the intense sorrow of the
province and of the neighboring peoples. Foreign nations and
kings grieved over him, so great was his courtesy to allies, his
humanity to enemies. He inspired reverence alike by look and
voice, and while he maintained the greatness and dignity of the
highest rank, he had escaped the hatred that waits on arrogance.

His funeral, though it lacked the family statues and procession, was honored by panegyrics and a commemoration of his
virtues. Some there were who, as they thought of his beauty, his
age, and the manner of his death, the vicinity too of the country
where he died, likened his end to that of Alexander the Great.
Both had a graceful person and were of noble birth; neither had
much exceeded thirty years of age, and both fell by the treachery
of their own people in strange lands. But Germanicus was gracious
to his friends, temperate in his pleasures, the husband of one wife,
with only legitimate children. He was too no less a warrior, though
rashness he had none, and, though after having cowed Germany
by his many victories, he was hindered from crushing it into
subjection. Had he had the sole control of affairs, had he possessed
the power and title of a king, he would have attained military glory
as much more easily as he had excelled Alexander in clemency,
in self-restraint, and in all other virtues.

As to the body which, before it was burnt, lay bare in the
forum at Antioch, its destined place of burial, it is doubtful
whether it exhibited the marks of poisoning. For men according

as they pitied Germanicus and were prepossessed with suspicion or were biased by partiality toward Piso, gave conflicting accounts.

Then followed a deliberation among the generals and other senators present about the appointment of a governor to Syria. The contest was slight among all but Vibius Marsus and Cneius Sentius, between whom there was a long dispute. Finally Marsus yielded to Sentius as an older and keener competitor. Sentius at once sent to Rome a woman infamous for poisonings in the province and a special favorite of Plancina, Martina by name, on the demand of Vitellius and Veranius and others, who were preparing the charges and the indictment as if a prosecution had already been commenced.

Agrippina meantime, worn out though she was with sorrow and bodily weakness, yet still impatient of everything which might delay her vengeance, embarked with the ashes of Germanicus and with her children, pitied by all. Here indeed was a woman of the highest nobility, and but lately because of her splendid union wont to be seen amid an admiring and sympathizing throng, now bearing in her bosom the mournful relics of death, with an uncertain hope of revenge, with apprehensions for herself, repeatedly at fortune's mercy by reason of the ill-starred fruitfulness of her marriage. Piso was at the island of Cos when tidings reached him that Germanicus was dead. He received the news with extravagant joy, slew victims, visited the temples, with no moderation in his transports; while Plancina's insolence increased, and she then for the first time exchanged for the gayest attire the mourning she had worn for her lost sister. (*II, 69-75*)

[*The funeral of Germanicus.*]

Without pausing in her winter voyage Agrippina arrived at the island of Corcyra, facing the shores of Calabria. There she spent a few days to compose her mind, for she was wild with grief and knew not how to endure. Meanwhile on hearing of her arrival, all her intimate friends and several officers, every one indeed who had served under Germanicus, many strangers too from the neighboring towns, some thinking it respectful to the emperor, and still more following their example, thronged eagerly to Brundisium, the nearest and safest landing place for a voyager.

As soon as the fleet was seen on the horizon, not only the harbor and the adjacent shores, but the city walls too and the roofs and every place which commanded the most distant prospect were filled with crowds of mourners, who incessantly asked one another, whether, when she landed, they were to receive her in silence or with some utterance of emotion. They were not agreed on what befitted the occasion when the fleet slowly approached, its crew, not joyous as is usual, but wearing all a studied expression of grief. When Agrippina descended from the vessel with her two children, clasping the funeral urn, with eyes riveted to the earth, there was one universal groan. You could not distinguish kinsfolk from strangers, or the laments of men from those of women; only the attendants of Agrippina, worn out as they were by long sorrow, were surpassed by the mourners who now met them, fresh in their grief.

The emperor had dispatched two praetorian cohorts with instructions that the magistrates of Calabria, Apulia, and Campania were to pay the last honors to his son's memory. Accordingly tribunes and centurions bore Germanicus's ashes on their shoulders. They were preceded by the standards unadorned and the fasces reversed. As they passed colony after colony, the populace in black, the knights in their state robes, burnt vestments and perfumes with other usual funeral adjuncts, in proportion to the wealth of the place. Even those whose towns were out of the route, met the mourners, offered victims and built altars to the dead, testifying their grief by tears and wailings. Drusus went as far as Tarracina with Claudius, brother of Germanicus, and the children who had been at Rome. Marcus Valerius and Caius Aurelius, the consuls, who had already entered on office, and a great number of the people thronged the road in scattered groups, every one weeping as he felt inclined. Flattery there was none, for all knew that Tiberius could scarcely dissemble his joy at the death of Germanicus.

Tiberius and Augusta refrained from showing themselves,

thinking it below their dignity to shed tears in public, or else fearing that, if all eyes scrutinized their faces, their hypocrisy would be revealed. I do not find in any historian or in the daily register that Antonia, Germanicus's mother, rendered any conspicuous honor to the deceased, though besides Agrippina, Drusus, and Claudius, all his other kinsfolk are mentioned by name. She may either have been hindered by illness, or with a spirit overpowered by grief she may not have had the heart to endure the sight of so great an affliction. But I can more easily believe that Tiberius and Augusta, who did not leave the palace, kept her within, that their sorrow might seem equal to hers, and that the grandmother and uncle might be thought to follow the mother's example in staying at home.

The day on which the remains were consigned to the tomb of Augustus, was now desolate in its silence, now distracted by lamentations. The streets of the city were crowded; torches were blazing throughout the Campus Martius. There the soldiers under arms, the magistrates without their symbols of office, the people in the tribes, were all incessantly exclaiming that the commonwealth was ruined, that not a hope remained, too boldly and openly to let one think that they remembered their rulers. But nothing impressed Tiberius more deeply than the enthusiasm kindled in favor of Agrippina, whom men spoke of as the glory of the country, the sole surviving offspring of Augustus, the solitary example of the old times, while looking up to heaven and the gods they prayed for the safety of her children and that they might outlive their oppressors.

Some there were who missed the grandeur of a state-funeral, and contrasted the splendid honors conferred by Augustus on Drusus, the father of Germanicus. "Then the emperor himself," they said, "went in the extreme rigor of winter as far as Ticinum, and never leaving the corpse entered Rome with it. Round the funeral bier were ranged the images of the Claudii and the Julii; there was weeping in the forum, and a panegyric before the rostra; every honor devised by our ancestors or invented by their descendants was heaped on him. But as for Germanicus, even the customary distinctions due to any noble had not fallen to his lot. Granting that his body, because of the distance of the journey, was burnt in any fashion in foreign lands, still all the more honors ought to have been afterward paid him, because at first chance had denied them. His brother had gone but one day's journey to meet him; his uncle, not even to the city gates. Where were all those usages of the past, the image at the head of the bier, the lays composed in commemoration of worth, the eulogies and laments, or at least the semblance of grief?"

All this was known to Tiberius, and, to silence popular talk, he reminded the people in a proclamation that many eminent Romans had died for their country and that none had been honored with such passionate regret. This regret was a glory both to himself and to all, provided only a due mean were observed; for what was becoming in humble homes and communities, did not befit princely personages and an imperial people. Tears and the solace found in mourning were suitable enough for the first burst of grief; but now they must brace their hearts to endurance, as in former days the Divine Julius after the loss of his only daughter, and the Divine Augustus when he was bereft of his grandchildren, had thrust away their sorrow. There was no need of examples from the past, showing how often the Roman people had patiently endured the defeats of armies, the destruction of generals, the total extinction of noble families. Princes were mortal; the State was everlasting. Let them then return to their usual pursuits, and, as the shows of the festival of the Great Goddess were at hand, even resume their amusements. (*III, 1-6*)

[*Sejanus, prefect of the praetorian guard, procures the death of Drusus, Tiberius' son, A.D. 23. The inglorious nature of the present. Sejanus, hoping to seize the Empire for himself, plans to persuade Tiberius to leave Rome. Tiberius retires to Campania and thence to the Island of Capri, in the Bay of Naples.*]

The year when Caius Asinius and Caius Antistius were consuls was the ninth of Tiberius's reign, a period of tranquillity for the State and prosperity for his own house, for he counted Germanicus's death a happy incident. Suddenly fortune deranged everything; the emperor became a cruel tyrant, as well as an abettor of cruelty in others. Of this the cause and origin was Aelius Sejanus, commander of the praetorian cohorts, of whose influence I have already spoken. I will now fully describe his extraction, his character, and the daring wickedness by which he grasped at power.

Born at Vulsinii, the son of Seius Strabo, a Roman knight, he attached himself in his early youth to Caius Caesar, grandson of the Divine Augustus, and the story went that he had sold his person to Apicius, a rich debauchee. Soon afterward he won the heart of Tiberius so effectually by various artifices that the emperor, ever dark and mysterious toward others, was with Sejanus alone careless and freespoken. It was not through his craft, for it was by this very weapon that he was overthrown; it was rather from heaven's wrath against Rome, to whose welfare his elevation and his fall were alike disastrous. He had a body which could endure hardships, and a daring spirit. He was one who screened himself, while he was attacking others; he was as cringing as he was imperious; before the world he affected humility; in his heart he lusted after supremacy, for the sake of which he was sometimes lavish and luxurious, but oftener energetic and watchful, qualities quite as mischievous when hypocritically assumed for the attainment of sovereignty.

He strengthened the hitherto moderate powers of his office by concentrating the cohorts scattered throughout the capital into one camp, so that they might all receive orders at the same moment, and that the sight of their numbers and strength might give confidence to themselves, while it would strike terror into the citizens. His pretexts were the demoralization incident to a dispersed soldiery, the greater effectiveness of simultaneous action in the event of a sudden peril, and the stricter discipline which would be ensured by the establishment of an encampment at a distance from the temptations of the city. As soon as the camp was completed, he crept gradually into the affections of the soldiers by mixing with them and addressing them by name, himself selecting the centurions and tribunes. With the Senate too he sought to ingratiate himself, distinguishing his partisans with offices and provinces, Tiberius readily yielding, and being so biased that not only in private conversation but before the senators and the people he spoke highly of him as the partner of his toils, and allowed his statues to be honored in theaters, in forums, and at the headquarters of our legions.

There were however obstacles to his ambition in the imperial house with its many princes, a son in youthful manhood and grown-up grandsons. As it would be unsafe to sweep off such a number at once by violence, while craft would necessitate successive intervals in crime, he chose, on the whole, the stealthier way, and to begin with Drusus, against whom he had the stimulus of a recent resentment. Drusus, who could not brook a rival and was somewhat irascible, had, in a casual dispute, raised his fist at Sejanus, and, when he defended himself, had struck him in the face. On considering every plan, Sejanus thought his easiest revenge was to turn his attention to Livia, Drusus's wife. She was a sister of Germanicus, and though she was not handsome as a girl, she became a woman of surpassing beauty. Pretending an ardent passion for her, he seduced her, and having won his first infamous triumph, and assured that a woman after having parted with her virtue will hesitate at nothing, he lured her on to thoughts of marriage, of a share in sovereignty, and of her husband's destruction. And she, the niece of Augustus, the daughter-in-law of Tiberius, the mother of children by Drusus, for a provincial paramour, foully disgraced herself, her ancestors, and her descendants, giving up honor and a sure position for prospects as base as they were uncertain. They took into their confidence Eudemus, Livia's friend and physician, whose profession was a pretext for frequent secret interviews. Sejanus, to avert his mistress's jealousy, divorced his wife Apicata, by whom he had had three children. Still the magnitude of the crime caused fear and delay, and sometimes a conflict of plans.

Meanwhile, at the beginning of this year, Drusus, one of the children of Germanicus, assumed the dress of manhood, with a repetition of the honors decreed by the Senate to his brother Nero. The emperor added a speech, with warm praise of his son for sharing a father's affection to his brother's children. Drusus indeed, difficult as it is for power and mutual harmony to exist side by side, had the character of being kindly disposed or at least not unfriendly toward the lads. And now the old plan, so often insincerely broached, of a progress through the provinces, was again discussed. The emperor's pretext was the number of veterans on the eve of discharge and the necessity of fresh levies for the army. Volunteers were not forthcoming, and even if they were sufficiently numerous, they had not the same bravery and discipline, as it is chiefly the needy and the homeless who adopt by their own choice a soldier's life. Tiberius also rapidly enumerated the legions and the provinces which they had to garrison. I too ought, I think, to go through these details, and thus show what forces Rome then had under arms, what kings were our allies, and how much narrower then were the limits of our empire.

Italy on both seas was guarded by fleets, at Misenum and at Ravenna, and the contiguous coast of Gaul by ships of war captured in the victory of Actium, and sent by Augustus powerfully manned to the town of Forojulium. But our chief strength was on the Rhine, as a defense alike against Germans and Gauls, and numbered eight legions. Spain, lately subjugated, was held by three. Mauretania was king Juba's, who had received it as a gift from the Roman people. The rest of Africa was garrisoned by two legions, and Egypt by the same number. Next, beginning with Syria, all within the entire tract of country stretching as far as the Euphrates, was kept in restraint by four legions, and on this frontier were Iberian, Albanian, and other kings, to whom our greatness was a protection against any foreign power. Thrace was held by Rhoemetalces and the children of Cotys; the bank of the Danube by two legions in Pannonia, two in Moesia, and two also were stationed in Dalmatia, which, from the situation of the country, were in the rear of the other four, and, should Italy suddenly require aid, not too distant to be summoned. But the capital was garrisoned by its own special soldiery, three city, nine praetorian cohorts, levied for the most part in Etruria and Umbria, or ancient Latium and the old Roman colonies. There were besides, in commanding positions in the provinces, allied fleets, cavalry and light infantry, of but little inferior strength. But any detailed account of them would be misleading, since they moved from place to place as circumstances required, and had their numbers increased and sometimes diminished.

It is however, I think, a convenient opportunity for me to review the hitherto prevailing methods of administration in the other departments of the State, inasmuch as that year brought with it the beginning of a change for the worse in Tiberius's policy. In the first place, public business and the most important private matters were managed by the Senate: the leading men were allowed freedom of discussion, and when they stooped to flattery, the emperor himself checked them. He bestowed honors with regard to noble ancestry, military renown, or brilliant accomplishments as a civilian, letting it be clearly seen that there were no better men to choose. The consul and the praetor retained their prestige; inferior magistrates exercised their authority; the laws too, with the single exception of cases of treason, were properly enforced.

As to the duties on grain, the indirect taxes and other branches of the public revenue, they were in the hands of companies of Roman knights. The emperor entrusted his own property to men of the most tried integrity or to persons known only by their general reputation, and once appointed they were retained without any limitation, so that most of them grew old in the same employments. The city populace indeed suffered much from high prices, but this was no fault of the emperor, who actually endeavored to counteract barren soils and stormy seas with every resource of wealth and foresight. And he was also careful not to distress the provinces by new burdens, and to see that in bearing the old they were safe from any rapacity or oppression on the part of governors. Corporal punishments and confiscations of property were unknown.

The emperor had only a few estates in Italy, slaves on a moderate scale, and his household was confined to a few freedmen. If ever he had a dispute with a private person, it was decided in the law courts. All this, not indeed with any graciousness, but in a blunt fashion which often alarmed, he still kept up, until the death of Drusus changed everything. While he lived, the system continued, because Sejanus, as yet only in the beginning of his power, wished to be known as an upright counselor, and there was one whose vengeance he dreaded, who did not conceal his hatred and incessantly complained "that a stranger was invited to assist in the government while the emperor's son was alive. How near was the step of declaring the stranger a colleague! Ambition at first had a steep path before it; when once the way had been entered, zealous adherents were forthcoming. Already, at the pleasure of the commander of the guards, a camp had been established; the soldiers were given into his hands; his statues were to be seen among the monuments of Cneius Pompeius; his grandsons would be of the same blood as the family of the Drusi. Henceforth they must pray that he might have self-control, and so be contented." So would Drusus talk, not infrequently, or only in the hearing of a few persons. Even his confidences, now that his wife had been corrupted, were betrayed.

Sejanus accordingly thought that he must be prompt, and chose a poison the gradual working of which might be mistaken for a natural disorder. It was given to Drusus by Lygdus, a eunuch, as was ascertained eight years later. As for Tiberius, he went to the Senate house during the whole time of the prince's illness, either because he was not afraid, or to show his strength of mind, and even in the interval between his death and funeral. Seeing the consuls, in token of their grief, sitting on the ordinary benches, he reminded them of their high office and of their proper place; and when the Senate burst into tears, suppressing a groan, he revived their spirits with a fluent speech. "He knew indeed that he might be reproached for thus encountering the gaze of the Senate after so recent an affliction. Most mourners could hardly bear even the soothing words of kinsfolk or to look on the light of day. And such were not to be condemned as weak. But he had sought a more manly consolation in the bosom of the commonwealth."

Then deploring the extreme age of Augusta, the childhood of his grandsons, and his own declining years, he begged the Senate to summon Germanicus's children, the only comfort under their present misery. The consuls went out, and having encouraged the young princes with kind words, brought them in and presented them to the emperor. Taking them by the hand he said: "Senators, when these boys lost their father, I committed them to their uncle, and begged him, though he had children of his own, to cherish and rear them as his own offspring, and train them for himself and for posterity. Drusus is now lost to us, and I turn my prayers to you, and before heaven and your country I adjure you to receive into your care and guidance the great-grandsons of Augustus, descendants of a most noble ancestry. So fulfill your duty and mine. To you, Nero and Drusus, these senators are as fathers. Such is your birth that your prosperity and adversity must alike affect the State."

There was great weeping at these words, and then many a benediction. Had the emperor set bounds to his speech, he must have filled the hearts of his hearers with sympathy and admiration. But he now fell back on those idle and often ridiculed professions about restoring the republic, and the wish that the consuls or some one else might undertake the government, and thus destroyed belief even in what was genuine and noble.

The same honors were decreed to the memory of Drusus as to that of Germanicus, and many more were added. Such is the way with flattery, when repeated. The funeral with its procession of statues was singularly grand. Aeneas, the father of the Julian house, all the Alban kings, Romulus, Rome's founder, then the Sabine nobility, Attus Clausus, and the busts of all the other Claudii were displayed in a long train.

In relating the death of Drusus I have followed the narrative of most of the best historians. But I would not pass over a rumor of the time, the strength of which is not even yet exhausted. Sejanus, it is said, having seduced Livia into crime, next secured, by the foulest means, the consent of Lygdus, the eunuch, as from his youth and beauty he was his master's favorite, and one of his principal attendants. When those who were in the secret had decided on the time and place of the poisoning, Sejanus, with the most consummate daring, reversed his plan, and, whispering an accusation against Drusus of intending to poison his father, warned Tiberius to avoid the first draught offered him as he was dining at his son's house. Thus deceived, the old emperor, on sitting down to the banquet, took the cup and handed it to Drusus. His suspicions were increased when Drusus, in perfect unconsciousness, drank it off with youthful eagerness, apparently, out of fear and shame, bringing on himself the death which he had plotted against his father.

These popular rumors, over and above the fact that they are not vouched for by any good writer, may be instantly refuted. For who, with moderate prudence, far less Tiberius with his great experience, would have thrust destruction on a son, without even hearing him, with his own hand too, and with an impossibility of returning to better thoughts? Surely he would rather have had the slave, who handed the poison, tortured, have sought to discover the traitor, in short, would have been as hesitating and tardy in the case of an only son hitherto unconvicted of any crime, as he was naturally even with strangers. But as Sejanus had the credit of contriving every sort of wickedness, the fact that he was the emperor's special favorite, and that both were hated by the rest of the world, procured belief for any monstrous fiction, and rumor too always has a dreadful side in regard to the deaths of men in power. Besides, the whole process of the crime was betrayed by Apicata, Sejanus's wife, and fully divulged, under torture, by Eudemus and Lygdus. No writer has been found sufficiently malignant to fix the guilt on Tiberius, though every circumstance was scrutinized and exaggerated. My object in mentioning and refuting this story is, by a conspicuous example, to put down hearsay, and to request all into whose hands my work shall come, not to catch eagerly at wild and improbable rumors in preference to genuine history which has not been perverted into romance. (IV, 1-11)

Much of what I have related and shall have to relate, may perhaps, I am aware, seem petty trifles to record. But no one must compare my annals with the writings of those who have described Rome in old days. They told of great wars, of the storming of cities, of the defeat and capture of kings, or whenever they turned by preference to home affairs, they related, with a free scope for digression, the strifes of consuls with tribunes, land and grain-laws, and the struggles between the commons and the aristocracy. My labors are circumscribed and inglorious; peace wholly unbroken or but slightly disturbed, dismal misery in the capital, an emperor careless about the enlargement of the empire, such is my theme. Still it will not be useless to study those at first sight trifling events out of which the movements of vast changes often take their rise.

All nations and cities are ruled by the people, the nobility, or by one man. A constitution, formed by selection out of these elements, it is easy to commend but not to produce; or, if it is produced, it cannot be lasting. Formerly, when the people had power or when the patricians were in the ascendant, the popular temper and the methods of controlling it, had to be studied, and those who knew most accurately the spirit of the Senate and aristocracy, had the credit of understanding the age and of being wise men. So now, after a revolution, when Rome is nothing but the realm of a single despot, there must be good in carefully noting and recording this period, for it is but few who have the foresight to distinguish right from wrong or what is sound from what is hurtful, while most men learn wisdom from the fortunes of others. Still, though this is instructive, it gives very little pleasure. Descriptions of countries, the various incidents of battles, glorious deaths of great generals, enchain and refresh a reader's mind. I have to present in succession the merciless biddings of a tyrant, incessant prosecutions, faithless friendships, the ruin of innocence, the same causes issuing in the same results, and I am everywhere confronted by a wearisome monotony in my subject matter. Then, again, an ancient historian has but few disparagers, and no one cares whether you praise more heartily the armies of Carthage or Rome. But of many who endured punishment or disgrace under Tiberius, the descendants yet survive; or even though the families themselves may be now extinct, you will find those who, from a resemblance of character, imagine that the evil deeds of others are a reproach to themselves. Again, even honor and virtue make enemies, condemning, as they do, their opposites by too close a contrast. But I return to my work. (*IV*, 32-33)

. . . Henceforth Tiberius even in private conversations persisted in showing contempt for such homage to himself. Some attributed this to modesty; many to self-distrust; a few to a mean spirit. "The noblest men," it was said, "have the loftiest aspirations, and so Hercules and Bacchus among the Greeks and Quirinus among us were enrolled in the number of the gods. Augustus did better, seeing that he had aspired. All other things princes have as a matter of course; one thing they ought insatiably to pursue, that their memory may be glorious. For to despise fame is to despise merit."

Sejanus meanwhile, dazed by his extravagant prosperity and urged on too by a woman's passion, Livia now insisting on his promise of marriage, addressed a memorial to the emperor. For it was then the custom to apply to him by writing, even though he was at Rome. This petition was to the following effect:—The kindness of Augustus, the father, and then the many favorable testimonies of Tiberius, the son, had engendered the habit of confiding his hopes and wishes to the ears of emperors as readily as to those of the gods. The splendor of high distinctions he had never craved; he had rather chosen watchings and hardships, like one of the common soldiers, for the emperor's safety. But there was one most glorious honor he had won, the reputation of being worthy of an alliance with a Caesar. This was the first motive of his ambition. As he had heard that Augustus, in marrying his daughter, had even entertained some thoughts of Roman knights, so if a husband were sought for Livia, he hoped Tiberius would bear in mind a friend who would find his reward simply in the glory of the alliance. He did not wish to rid himself of the duties imposed on him; he thought it enough for his family to be secured against the unjust displeasure of Agrippina, and this for the sake of his children. For, as for himself, enough and more than enough for him would be a life completed while such a sovereign still reigned.

Tiberius, in reply, after praising the loyal sentiments of Sejanus and briefly enumerating the favors he had bestowed on him, asked time for impartial consideration, adding that while other men's plans depended on their ideas of their own interest, princes, who had to regulate their chief actions by public opinion, were in a different position. . . .

Sejanus, no longer thinking of his marriage but filled with a deeper alarm, rejoined by deprecating the whispers of suspicion, popular rumor and the gathering storm of odium. That he might not impair his influence by closing his doors on the throngs of his many visitors or strengthen the hands of accusers by admitting them, he made it his aim to induce Tiberius to live in some charming spot at a distance from Rome. In this he foresaw several advantages. Access to the emperor would be under his own control, and letters, for the most part being conveyed by soldiers, would pass through his hands. Caesar too, who was already in the decline of life, would soon, when enervated by retirement, more readily transfer to him the functions of empire; envy toward himself would be lessened when there was an end to his crowded levees and the reality of power would be increased by the removal of its empty show. So he began to declaim against the laborious life of the capital, the bustling crowds and streaming multitudes, while he praised repose and solitude, with their freedom from vexations and misunderstandings, and their special opportunities for the study of the highest questions. (IV, 38-41)

Meanwhile, after long reflection on his purpose and frequent deferment of it, the emperor retired into Campania to dedicate, as he pretended, a temple to Jupiter at Capua and another to Augustus at Nola, but really resolved to live at a distance from Rome. Although I have followed most historians in attributing the cause of his retirement to the arts of Sejanus, still, as he passed six consecutive years in the same solitude after that minister's destruction, I am often in doubt whether it is not to be more truly ascribed to himself, and his wish to hide by the place of his retreat the cruelty and licentiousness which he betrayed by his actions. Some thought that in his old age he was ashamed of his personal appearance. He had indeed a tall, singularly slender and stooping figure, a bald head, a face full of eruptions, and covered here and there with plasters. In the seclusion of Rhodes he had habituated himself to shun society and to hide his voluptuous life.

According to one account his mother's domineering temper drove him away; he was weary of having her as his partner in power, and he could not thrust her aside, because he had received this very power as her gift. For Augustus had had thoughts of putting the Roman state under Germanicus, his sister's grandson, whom all men esteemed, but yielding to his wife's entreaties he left Germanicus to be adopted by Tiberius and adopted Tiberius himself. With this Augusta would taunt her son, and claim back what she had given.

His departure was attended by a small retinue, one senator, who was an ex-consul, Cocceius Nerva, learned in the laws, one Roman knight, besides Sejanus, of the highest order, Curtius Atticus, the rest being men of liberal culture, for the most part Greeks, in whose conversation he might find amusement. It was said by men who knew the stars that the motions of the heavenly bodies when Tiberius left Rome were such as to forbid the possibility of his return. This caused ruin to many who conjectured that his end was near and spread the rumor; for they never foresaw the very improbable contingency of his voluntary exile from his home for eleven years. Soon afterward it was clearly seen what a narrow margin there is between such science and delusion and in what obscurity truth is veiled. That he would not return to Rome was not a mere random assertion; as to the rest, they were wholly in the dark, seeing that he lived to extreme old age in the country or on the coast near Rome and often close to the very walls of the city. (IV, 57-58)

Caesar, meanwhile, after dedicating the temples in Campania, warned the public by an edict not to disturb his retirement and posted soldiers here and there to keep off the throngs of townsfolk. But he so loathed the towns and colonies and, in short, every place on the mainland, that he buried himself in the island of Capri which is separated by three miles of strait from the extreme point of the promontory of Sorrentum. The solitude of the place was, I believe, its chief attraction, for a harborless sea surrounds it and even for a small vessel it has but few safe retreats, nor can any one land unknown to the sentries. Its air in winter is soft, as it is screened by a mountain which is a protection against cutting

winds. In summer it catches the western breezes, and the open sea
round it renders it most delightful. It commanded too a prospect
of the most lovely bay, till Vesuvius, bursting into flames, changed
the face of the country. Greeks, so tradition says, occupied those
parts and Capri was inhabited by the Teleboi. Tiberius had by
this time filled the island with twelve country houses, each with
a grand name and a vast structure of its own. Intent as he had once
been on the cares of state, he was now for thoroughly unbending
himself in secret profligacy and a leisure of malignant schemes. For
he still retained that rash proneness to suspect and to believe,
which even at Rome Sejanus used to foster, and which he here
excited more keenly, no longer concealing his machinations against
Agrippina and Nero. Soldiers hung about them, and every message, every visit, their public and their private life were I may say
regularly chronicled. And persons were actually suborned to
advise them to flee to the armies of Germany, or when the Forum
was most crowded, to clasp the statue of the Divine Augustus and
appeal to the protection of the people and Senate. These counsels
they disdained, but they were charged with having had thoughts
of acting on them. (*IV, 67*)

[*Tiberius a tyrant. His death* A.D. *37.*]

In the consulship of Rubellius and Fufius, both of whom had
the surname Geminus, died in an advanced old age Julia Augusta.
A Claudia by birth and by adoption a Livia and a Julia, she united
the noblest blood of Rome. Her first marriage, by which she had
children, was with Tiberius Nero, who, an exile during the
Perusian war, returned to Rome when peace had been concluded
between Sextus Pompeius and the triumvirs. After this Caesar,
enamored of her beauty, took her away from her husband, whether
against her wish is uncertain. So impatient was he that he brought
her to his house actually pregnant, not allowing time for her
confinement. She had no subsequent issue, but allied as she was
through the marriage of Agrippina and Germanicus to the blood of
Augustus, her great-grandchildren were also his. In the purity of
her home life she was of the ancient type, but was more gracious

than was thought fitting in ladies of former days. An imperious mother and an amiable wife, she was a match for the diplomacy of her husband and the dissimulation of her son. Her funeral was simple, and her will long remained unexecuted. Her panegyric was pronounced from the Rostra by her great-grandson, Caius Caesar, who afterward succeeded to power.

Tiberius however, making no change in his voluptuous life, excused himself by letter for his absence from his last duty to his mother on the ground of the pressure of business. He even abridged, out of moderation, as it seemed, the honors which the Senate had voted on a lavish scale to her memory, allowing only a very few, and adding that no religious worship was to be decreed, this having been her own wish. In a part of the same letter he sneered at female friendships, with an indirect censure on the consul Fufius, who had risen to distinction through Augusta's partiality. Fufius was indeed a man well fitted to win the affection of a woman; he was witty too, and accustomed to ridicule Tiberius with those bitter jests which the powerful remember so long.

This at all events was the beginning of an unmitigated and grinding despotism. As long indeed as Augusta lived, there yet remained a refuge, for with Tiberius obedience to his mother was the habit of a life, and Sejanus did not dare to set himself above a parent's authority. Now, so to say, they threw off the reins and let loose their fury. A letter was sent, directed against Agrippina and Nero, which was popularly believed to have been long before forwarded and to have been kept back by Augusta, as it was publicly read soon after her death. It contained expressions of studied harshness, yet it was not armed rebellion or a longing for revolution, but unnatural passions and profligacy which the emperor imputed to his grandson. Against his daughter-in-law he did not dare to invent this much; he merely censured her insolent tongue and defiant spirit, amid the panic-stricken silence of the Senate, till a few who had no hope from merit (and public calamities are ever used by individuals for interested purposes) demanded that the question should be debated. The most eager was Cotta Messalinus, who made a savage speech. Still, the other principal senators, and especially the magistrates, were perplexed, for Tiberius, notwithstanding his furious invective, had left everything else in doubt.

There was in the Senate one Junius Rusticus, who having been appointed by the emperor to register its debates was therefore supposed to have an insight into his secret purposes. This man, whether through some fatal impulse (he had indeed never before given any evidence of courage) or a misdirected acuteness which made him tremble at the uncertain future, while he forgot impending perils, attached himself to the waverers, and warned the consuls not to enter on the debate. He argued that the highest issues turned on trivial causes, and that the fall of the house of Germanicus might one day move the old man's remorse. At the same moment the people, bearing the images of Agrippina and Nero, thronged round the Senate-house, and, with words of blessing on the emperor, kept shouting that the letter was a forgery and that it was not by the prince's will that ruin was being plotted against his house. And so that day passed without any dreadful result.

Fictitious speeches too against Sejanus were published under the names of ex-consuls, for several persons indulged, all the more recklessly because anonymously, the caprice of their imaginations. Consequently the wrath of Sejanus was the more furious, and he had ground for alleging that the Senate disregarded the emperor's trouble; that the people were in revolt; that speeches in a new style and new resolutions were being heard and read. What remained but to take the sword and choose for their generals and emperors those whose images they had followed as standards?

Upon this the emperor, after repeating his invectives against his grandson and his daughter-in-law and reprimanding the populace in an edict, complained to the Senate that by the trick of one senator the imperial dignity had been publicly flouted, and he insisted that, after all, the whole matter should be left to his exclusive decision. Without further deliberation, they proceeded, not indeed to pronounce the final sentence (for this was forbidden), but to declare that they were prepared for vengeance, and were restrained only by the strong hand of the sovereign. (V, 1-5)

Tiberius's bodily powers were now leaving him, but not his skill in dissembling. There was the same stern spirit; he had his words and looks under strict control, and occasionally would try to hide his weakness, evident as it was, by a forced politeness. After frequent changes of place, he at last settled down on the promontory of Misenum in a country-house once owned by Lucius Lucullus. It was there discovered that he was drawing near his end, and thus. There was a physician, distinguished in his profession, of the name of Charicles, usually employed, not indeed to have the direction of the emperor's varying health, but to put his advice at immediate disposal. This man, as if he were leaving on business of his own, clasped his hand, with a show of homage, and touched his pulse. Tiberius noticed it. Whether he was displeased and strove the more to hide his anger, is a question; at any rate, he ordered the banquet to be renewed, and sat at the table longer than usual, by way, apparently, of showing honor to his departing friend. Charicles, however, assured Macro that his breath was failing and that he would not last more than two days. All was at once hurry; there were conferences among those on the spot and dispatches to the generals and armies. On the 15th of March, his breath failing, he was believed to have expired, and Caius Caesar was going forth with a numerous throng of congratulating followers to take the first possession of the empire, when suddenly news came that Tiberius was recovering his voice and sight, and calling for persons to bring him food to revive him from his faintness. Then ensued a universal panic, and while the rest fled hither and thither, every one feigning grief or ignorance, Caius Caesar, in silent stupor, passed from the highest hopes to the extremity of apprehension. Macro, nothing daunted, ordered the old emperor to be smothered under a huge heap of clothes, and all to quit the entrance-hall.

And so died Tiberius, in the seventy-eighth year of his age. Nero was his father, and he was on both sides descended from the Claudian house, though his mother passed by adoption, first into the Livian, then into the Julian family. From earliest infancy, perilous vicissitudes were his lot. Himself an exile, he was the companion of a proscribed father, and on being admitted as a stepson into the house of Augustus, he had to struggle with many rivals, so long as Marcellus and Agrippa and, subsequently,

Caius and Lucius Caesar were in their glory. Again his brother
Drusus enjoyed in a greater degree the affection of the citizens.
But he was more than ever on dangerous ground after his marriage with Julia, whether he tolerated or escaped from his wife's
profligacy. On his return from Rhodes he ruled the emperor's
now heirless house for twelve years, and the Roman world, with
absolute sway, for about twenty-three. His character too had its
distinct periods. It was a bright time in his life and reputation,
while under Augustus he was a private citizen or held high offices; a time of reserve and crafty assumption of virtue, as long as
Germanicus and Drusus were alive. Again, while his mother
lived, he was a compound of good and evil; he was infamous for
his cruelty, though he veiled his debaucheries, while he loved or
feared Sejanus. Finally, he plunged into every wickedness and
disgrace, when fear and shame being cast off, he simply indulged
his own inclinations. (*VI, 50-51*)

[Nero commences his reign, A.D. 54-68. His early acts and
companions.]

The first death under the new emperor, that of Junius Silanus,
proconsul of Asia, was, without Nero's knowledge, planned by
the treachery of Agrippina. Not that Silanus had provoked destruction by any violence of temper, apathetic as he was, and so
utterly despised under former despotisms, that Caius Caesar used
to call him the golden sheep. The truth was that Agrippina, having contrived the murder of his brother Lucius Silanus, dreaded
his vengeance; for it was the incessant popular talk that preference
ought to be given over Nero, who was scarcely out of his boyhood
and had gained the empire by crime, to a man of mature age, of
blameless life, of noble birth, and, as a point then much regarded,
of the line of the Caesars. Silanus in fact was the son of a great-
grandson of Augustus. This was the cause of his destruction. The
agents of the deed were Publius Celer, a Roman knight, and He-
lius, a freedman, men who had the charge of the emperor's do-
mains in Asia. They gave the proconsul poison at a banquet, too
openly to escape discovery.

With no less precipitation, Narcissus, Claudius's freedman, whose quarrels with Agrippina I have mentioned, was driven to suicide by his cruel imprisonment and hopeless plight, even against the wishes of Nero, with whose yet concealed vices he was wonderfully in sympathy from his rapacity and extravagance.

And now they had proceeded to further murders but for the opposition of Afranius Burrus and Annaeus Seneca. These two men guided the emperor's youth with an unity of purpose seldom found where authority is shared, and though their accomplishments were wholly different, they had equal influence. Burrus, with his soldier's discipline and severe manners, Seneca, with lessons of eloquence and a dignified courtesy, strove alike to confine the frailty of the prince's youth, should he loathe virtue, within allowable indulgences. They had both alike to struggle against the domineering spirit of Agrippina, who inflamed with all the passions of an evil ascendency had Pallas on her side, at whose suggestion Claudius had ruined himself by an incestuous marriage and a fatal adoption of a son. Nero's temper however was not one to submit to slaves, and Pallas, by a surly arrogance quite beyond a freedman, had provoked disgust. Still every honor was openly heaped on Agrippina, and to a tribune who according to military custom asked the watchword, Nero gave "the best of mothers." The Senate also decreed her two lictors, with the office of priestess to Claudius, and voted to the late emperor a censor's funeral, which was soon followed by deification.

On the day of the funeral the prince pronounced Claudius's panegyric, and while he dwelt on the antiquity of his family and on the consulships and triumphs of his ancestors, there was enthusiasm both in himself and his audience. The praise of his graceful accomplishments, and the remark that during his reign no disaster had befallen Rome from the foreigner, were heard with favor. When the speaker passed on to his foresight and wisdom, no one could refrain from laughter, though the speech, which was composed by Seneca, exhibited much elegance, as indeed that famous man had an attractive genius which suited the popular ear of the time. Elderly men, who amuse their leisure with comparing the past and the present, observed that Nero was the first emperor who needed another man's eloquence. The dictator Caesar rivaled the greatest orators, and Augustus had an easy and fluent way of speaking, such as became a sovereign. Tiberius too thoroughly understood the art of balancing words, and was sometimes forcible in the expression of his thoughts, or else intentionally obscure. Even Caius Caesar's disordered intellect did not wholly mar his faculty of speech. Nor did Claudius, when he spoke with preparation, lack elegance. Nero from early boyhood turned his lively genius in other directions; he carved, painted, sang, or practiced the management of horses, occasionally composing verses which showed that he had the rudiments of learning. (XIII, 1-3)

Meanwhile the mother's influence was gradually weakened, as Nero fell in love with a freedwoman, Acte by name, and took into his confidence Otho and Claudius Senecio, two young men of fashion, the first of whom was descended from a family of consular rank, while Senecio's father was one of the emperor's freedmen. Without the mother's knowledge, then in spite of her opposition, they had crept into his favor by debaucheries and equivocal secrets, and even the prince's older friends did not thwart him, for here was a girl who without harm to any one gratified his desires, when he loathed his wife Octavia, high born as she was, and of approved virtue, either from some fatality, or because vice is overpoweringly attractive. It was feared too that he might rush into outrages on noble ladies, were he debarred from this indulgence.

Agrippina, however, raved with a woman's fury about having a freedwoman for a rival, a slave girl for a daughter-in-law, with like expressions. Nor would she wait till her son repented or wearied of his passion. The fouler her reproaches, the more powerfully did they inflame him, till completely mastered by the strength of his desire, he threw off all respect for his mother, and put himself under the guidance of Seneca, one of whose friends, Annaeus Serenus, had veiled the young prince's intrigue in its beginning by pretending to be in love with the same woman, and had lent his name as the ostensible giver of the presents secretly sent by the emperor to the girl. Then Agrippina, changing her tactics, plied the lad with various blandishments, and even offered the seclusion of her chamber for the concealment of indulgences which youth and the highest rank might claim. She went further; she pleaded guilty to an ill-timed strictness, and handed over to him the abundance of her wealth, which nearly approached the imperial treasures, and from having been of late extreme in her restraint of her son, became now, on the other hand, lax to excess. The change did not escape Nero; his most intimate friends dreaded it, and begged him to beware of the arts of a woman, who was always daring and was now false.

It happened at this time that the emperor after inspecting the apparel in which wives and mothers of the imperial house had been seen to glitter, selected a jeweled robe and sent it as a gift to his mother, with the unsparing liberality of one who was bestowing by preference on her a choice and much coveted present. Agrippina, however, publicly declared that so far from her wardrobe being furnished by these gifts, she was really kept out of the remainder, and that her son was merely dividing with her what he derived wholly from herself.

Some there were who put even a worse meaning on her words. And so Nero, furious with those who abetted such arrogance in a woman, removed Pallas from the charge of the business with which he had been entrusted by Claudius, and in which he acted, so to say, as the controller of the throne. The story went that as he was departing with a great retinue of attendants, the emperor rather wittily remarked that Pallas was going to swear himself out of office. Pallas had in truth stipulated that he should not be questioned for anything he had done in the past, and that his accounts with the State were to be considered as balanced. Thereupon, with instant fury, Agrippina rushed into frightful menaces, sparing not the prince's ears her solemn protest "that Britannicus was now of full age, he who was the true and worthy heir of his father's sovereignty, which a son, by mere admission and adoption, was abusing in outrages on his mother. She shrank not from an utter exposure of the wickedness of that ill-starred house, of her own marriage, to begin with, and of her poisoner's craft. All that the gods and she herself had taken care of was that her stepson was yet alive; with him she would go to the camp, where on one side should be heard the daughter of Germanicus; on the other, the crippled Burrus and the exile Seneca, claiming, forsooth, with disfigured hand, and a pedant's tongue, the government of the world." As she spoke, she raised her hand in menace and heaped insults on him, as she appealed to the deified Claudius, to the infernal shades of the Silani, and to those many fruitless crimes.

Nero was confounded at this, and as the day was near on which Britannicus would complete his fourteenth year, he reflected, now on the domineering temper of his mother, and now again on the character of the young prince, which a trifling circumstance had lately tested, sufficient however to gain for him wide popularity. During the feast of Saturn, amid other pastimes of his playmates, at a game of lot drawing for king, the lot fell to Nero, upon which he gave all his other companions different orders, and such as would not put them to the blush; but when he told Britannicus to step forward and begin a song, hoping for a laugh at the expense of a boy who knew nothing of sober, much less of riotous society, the lad with perfect coolness commenced some verses which hinted at his expulsion from his father's house and from supreme power. This procured him pity, which was the more conspicuous, as night with its merriment had stript off all disguise. Nero saw the reproach and redoubled his hate. Pressed by Agrippina's menaces, having no charge against his brother and not daring openly to order his murder, he meditated a secret device and directed poison to be prepared through the agency of Julius Pollio, tribune of one of the praetorian cohorts, who had in his custody a woman under sentence for poisoning, Locusta by name, with a vast reputation for crime. That every one about the person of Britannicus should care nothing for right or honor, had long ago been provided for. He actually received his first dose of poison from his tutors and passed it off his bowels, as it was rather weak or so qualified as not at once to prove deadly. But Nero, impatient at such slow progress in crime, threatened the tribune and ordered the poisoner to execution for prolonging his anxiety while they were thinking of the popular talk and planning their own defense. Then they promised that death should be as sudden as if it were the hurried work of the dagger, and a rapid poison of previously tested ingredients was prepared close to the emperor's chamber.

It was customary for the imperial princes to sit during their meals with other nobles of the same age, in the sight of their kinsfolk, at a table of their own, furnished somewhat frugally. There Britannicus was dining, and as what he ate and drank was always tested by the taste of a select attendant, the following device was contrived, that the usage might not be dropped or the crime betrayed by the death of both prince and attendant. A cup as yet harmless, but extremely hot and already tasted, was handed to Britannicus; then, on his refusing it because of its warmth, poison was poured in with some cold water, and this so penetrated his entire frame that he lost alike voice and breath. There was a stir among the company; some, taken by surprise, ran hither and thither, while those whose discernment was keener, remained motionless, with their eyes fixed on Nero, who, as he still reclined in seeming unconsciousness, said that this was a common occurrence, from a periodical epilepsy, with which Britannicus had been afflicted from his earliest infancy, and that his sight and senses would gradually return. As for Agrippina, her terror and confusion, though her countenance struggled to hide it, so visibly appeared, that she was clearly just as ignorant as was Octavia, Britannicus's own sister. She saw, in fact, that she was robbed of her only remaining refuge, and that here was a precedent for parricide. Even Octavia, not withstanding her youthful inexperience, had learnt to hide her grief, her affection, and indeed every emotion.

And so after a brief pause the company resumed its mirth. One and the same night witnessed Britannicus's death and funeral, preparations having been already made for his obsequies, which were on a humble scale. He was however buried in the Campus Martius, amid storms so violent, that in the popular belief they portended the wrath of heaven against a crime which many were even inclined to forgive when they remembered the immemorial feuds of brothers and the impossibility of a divided throne. It is

related by several writers of the period that many days before the
murder, Nero had offered the worst insult to the boyhood of
Britannicus; so that his death could no longer seem a premature or
dreadful event, though it happened at the sacred board, without
even a moment for the embraces of his sisters, hurried on too, as
it was, under the eyes of an enemy, on the sole surviving offspring
of the Claudii, the victim first of dishonor, then of poison. The
emperor apologized for the hasty funeral by reminding people
that it was the practice of our ancestors to withdraw from view
any grievously untimely death, and not to dwell on it with panegyrics or display. For himself, he said, that as he had now lost a
brother's help, his remaining hopes centered in the State, and
all the more tenderness ought to be shown by the Senate and
people toward a prince who was the only survivor of a family born
to the highest greatness. (*XIII, 12-17*)

A profligacy equally notorious in that same year proved the
beginning of great evils to the State. There was at Rome one
Sabina Poppaea; her father was Titus Ollius, but she had assumed the name of her maternal grandfather Poppaeus Sabinus,
a man of illustrious memory and pre-eminently distinguished by
the honors of a consulship and a triumph. As for Ollius, before
he attained promotion, the friendship of Sejanus was his ruin.
This Poppaea had everything but a right mind. Her mother, who
surpassed in personal attractions all the ladies of her day, had
bequeathed to her alike fame and beauty. Her fortune adequately
corresponded to the nobility of her descent. Her conversation was
charming and her wit anything but dull. She professed virtue,
while she practiced laxity. Seldom did she appear in public, and
it was always with her face partly veiled, either to disappoint men's
gaze or to set off her beauty. Her character she never spared,
making no distinction between a husband and a paramour, while
she was never a slave to her own passion or to that of her lover.
Wherever there was a prospect of advantage, there she transferred
her favors. And so while she was living as the wife of Rufius
Crispinus, a Roman knight, by whom she had a son, she was attracted by the youth and fashionable elegance of Otho, and by
the fact too that he was reputed to have Nero's most ardent friend-

ship. Without any delay the intrigue was followed by marriage.

Otho now began to praise his wife's beauty and accomplishments to the emperor, either from a lover's thoughtlessness or to inflame Nero's passion, in the hope of adding to his own influence by the further tie which would arise out of possession of the same woman. Often, as he rose from the emperor's table, was he heard repeatedly to say that he was going to her, to the high birth and beauty which had fallen to his lot, to that which all men pray for, the joy of the fortunate. These and like incitements allowed but of brief delay. Once having gained admission, Poppaea won her way by artful blandishments, pretending that she could not resist her passion and that she was captivated by Nero's person. Soon, as the emperor's love grew ardent, she would change and be supercilious, and, if she were detained more than one or two nights, would say again and again that she was a married woman and could not give up her husband attached as she was to Otho by a manner of life, which no one equaled. "His ideas and his style were grand; at his house everything worthy of the highest fortune was ever before her eyes. Nero, on the contrary, with his slave girl mistress, tied down by his attachment to Acte, had derived nothing from his slavish associations but what was low and degrading."

Otho was now cut off from Nero's usual familiar intercourse, and then even from interviews and from the royal suite, and at last was appointed governor of the province of Lusitania, that he might not be the emperor's rival at Rome. There he lived up to the time of the civil wars, not in the fashion of his disgraceful past, but uprightly and virtuously, a pleasure-loving man when idle, and self-restrained when in power (*XIII, 45-46*)

[Nero causes the murder of his mother, Agrippina the Younger. His excesses and amusements. Having married the beauteous Poppaea Sabina, Nero orders the murder of his divorced wife, Octavia.]

In the year of the consulship of Caius Vipstanus and Caius Fonteius, Nero deferred no more a long meditated crime. Length of power had matured his daring, and his passion for Poppaea daily grew more ardent. As the woman had no hope of marriage for herself or of Octavia's divorce while Agrippina lived, she would reproach the emperor with incessant vituperation and sometimes call him in jest a mere ward who was under the rule of others, and was so far from having empire that he had not even his liberty. "Why," she asked, "was her marriage put off? Was it, forsooth, her beauty and her ancestors, with their triumphal honors, that failed to please, or her being a mother, and her sincere heart? No; the fear was that as a wife at least she would divulge the wrongs of the Senate, and the wrath of the people at the arrogance and rapacity of his mother. If the only daughter-in-law Agrippina could bear was one who wished evil to her son, let her be restored to her union with Otho. She would go anywhere in the world, where she might hear of the insults heaped on the emperor, rather than witness them, and be also involved in his perils."

These and the like complaints, rendered impressive by tears and by the cunning of an adulteress, no one checked, as all longed to see the mother's power broken, while not a person believed that the son's hatred would steel his heart to her murder.

Cluvius relates that Agrippina in her eagerness to retain her influence went so far that more than once at midday, when Nero, even at that hour, was flushed with wine and feasting, she presented herself attractively attired to her half intoxicated son and offered him her person, and that when kinsfolk observed wanton kisses and caresses, portending infamy, it was Seneca who sought a female's aid against a woman's fascinations, and hurried in Acte, the freed girl, who alarmed at her own peril and at Nero's disgrace, told him that the incest was notorious, as his mother boasted of it, and that the soldiers would never endure the rule of an impious sovereign. Fabius Rusticus tells us that it was not Agrippina, but Nero, who lusted for the crime, and that it was frustrated by the adroitness of that same freed-girl. Cluvius's account, however, is also that of all other authors, and popular belief inclines to it, whether it was that Agrippina really conceived such a monstrous wickedness in her heart, or perhaps because the thought of a strange passion seemed comparatively credible in a woman, who in her girlish years had allowed herself to be seduced by Lepidus in the hope of winning power, had stooped with a like ambition to the lust of Pallas, and had trained herself for every infamy by her marriage with her uncle.

Nero accordingly avoided secret interviews with her, and when she withdrew to her gardens or to her estates at Tusculum and Antium, he praised her for courting repose. At last, convinced that she would be too formidable, wherever she might dwell, he resolved to destroy her, merely deliberating whether it was to be accomplished by poison, or by the sword, or by any other violent means. Poison at first seemed best, but, were it to be administered at the imperial table, the result could not be referred to chance after the recent circumstances of the death of Britannicus. Again, to tamper with the servants of a woman who, from her familiarity with crime, was on her guard against treachery, appeared to be extremely difficult, and then, too, she had fortified her constitution by the use of antidotes. How again the dagger and its work were to be kept secret, no one could suggest, and it was feared too that whoever might be chosen to execute such a crime would spurn the order.

An ingenious suggestion was offered by Anicetus, a freedman, commander of the fleet at Misenum, who had been tutor to Nero in boyhood and had a hatred of Agrippina which she reciprocated. He explained that a vessel could be constructed, from which a part might by a contrivance be detached, when out at sea, so as to plunge her unawares into the water. "Nothing," he said, "allowed of accidents so much as the sea, and should she be overtaken by shipwreck, who would be so unfair as to impute to crime an offense committed by the winds and waves? The emperor would add the honor of a temple and of shrines to the deceased lady, with every other display of filial affection."

Nero liked the device, favored as it also was by the particular time, for he was celebrating Minerva's five days' festival at Baiae. Thither he enticed his mother by repeated assurances that children ought to bear with the irritability of parents and to soothe their tempers, wishing thus to spread a rumor of reconciliation and to secure Agrippina's acceptance through the feminine credulity, which easily believes what gives joy. As she approached, he went to the shore to meet her (she was coming from Antium), welcomed her with outstretched hand and embrace, and conducted her to Bauli. This was the name of a country house, washed by a bay of the sea, between the promontory of Misenum and the lake of Baiae. Here was a vessel distinguished from others by its equipment, seemingly meant, among other things, to do honor to his mother; for she had been accustomed to sail in a trireme, with a crew of marines. And now she was invited to a banquet, that night might serve to conceal the crime. It was well known that somebody had been found to betray it, that Agrippina had heard of the plot, and in doubt whether she was to believe it, was conveyed to Baiae in her litter. There some soothing words allayed her fear; she was graciously received, and seated at table above the emperor. Nero prolonged the banquet with various conversation, passing from a youth's playful familiarity to an air of constraint, which seemed to indicate serious thought, and then, after protracted festivity, escorted her on her departure, clinging with kisses to her eyes and bosom, either to crown his hypocrisy or because the last sight of a mother on the eve of destruction caused a lingering even in that brutal heart.

A night of brilliant starlight with the calm of a tranquil sea was granted by heaven, seemingly, to convict the crime. The vessel had not gone far, Agrippina having with her two of her intimate attendants, one of whom, Crepereius Gallus, stood near the helm, while Acerronia, reclining at Agrippina's feet as she reposed herself, spoke joyfully of her son's repentance and of the recovery of the mother's influence, when at a given signal the ceiling of the place, which was loaded with a quantity of lead, fell in, and Crepereius was crushed and instantly killed. Agrippina and Acerronia were protected by the projecting sides of the couch, which happened to be too strong to yield under the weight. But this was not followed by the breaking up of the vessel; for all were bewildered, and those too, who were in the plot, were hindered by the unconscious majority. The crew then thought it best to throw the vessel on one side and so sink it, but they could not themselves promptly unite to face the emergency, and others, by counteracting the attempt, gave an opportunity of a gentler fall into the sea. Acerronia, however, thoughtlessly exclaiming that she was Agrippina, and imploring help for the emperor's mother, was dispatched with poles and oars, and such naval implements as chance offered. Agrippina was silent and was thus the less recognized; still, she received a wound in her shoulder. She swam, then met with some small boats which conveyed her to the Lucrine lake, and so entered her house.

There she reflected how for this very purpose she had been invited by a lying letter and treated with conspicuous honor, how also it was near the shore, not from being driven by winds or dashed on rocks, that the vessel had in its upper part collapsed, like a mechanism anything but nautical. She pondered too the death of Acerronia; she looked at her own wound, and saw that her only safeguard against treachery was to ignore it. Then she sent her freedman Agerinus to tell her son how by heaven's favor and his good fortune she had escaped a terrible disaster; that she begged him, alarmed, as he might be, by his mother's peril, to put off the duty of a visit, as for the present she needed repose. Meanwhile, pretending that she felt secure, she applied remedies to her wound, and fomentations to her person. She then ordered search to be made for the will of Acerronia, and her property to be sealed, in this alone throwing off disguise.

Nero, meantime, as he waited for tidings of the consummation of the deed, received information that she had escaped with the injury of a slight wound, after having so far encountered the peril that there could be no question as to its author. Then, paralyzed with terror and protesting that she would show herself the next moment eager for vengeance, either arming the slaves or stirring up the soldiery, or hastening to the Senate and the people, to charge him with the wreck, with her wound, and with the destruction of her friends, he asked what resource he had against all this, unless something could be at once devised by Burrus and Seneca. He had instantly summoned both of them, and possibly they were already in the secret. There was a long silence on their part; they feared they might remonstrate in vain, or believed the crisis to be such that Nero must perish, unless Agrippina were at once crushed. Thereupon Seneca was so far the more prompt as to glance back on Burrus, as if to ask him whether the bloody deed must be required of the soldiers. Burrus replied "that the praetorians were attached to the whole family of the Caesars, and remembering Germanicus would not dare a savage deed on his offspring. It was for Anicetus to accomplish his promise."

Anicetus, without a pause, claimed for himself the consummation of the crime. At those words, Nero declared that that day gave him empire, and that a freedman was the author of this mighty boon. "Go," he said, "with all speed and take with you the men readiest to execute your orders." He himself, when he had heard of the arrival of Agrippina's messenger, Agerinus, contrived a theatrical mode of accusation, and, while the man was repeating his message, threw down a sword at his feet, then ordered him to be put in irons, as a detected criminal, so that he might invent a story how his mother had plotted the emperor's destruction and in the shame of discovered guilt had by her own choice sought death.

Meantime, Agrippina's peril being universally known and taken to be an accidental occurrence, everybody, the moment he heard of it, hurried down to the beach. Some climbed projecting piers; some the nearest vessels; others, as far as their stature allowed, went into the sea; some, again, stood with outstretched arms, while the whole shore rung with wailings, with prayers and cries, as different questions were asked and uncertain answers given. A vast multitude streamed to the spot with torches, and as soon as all knew that she was safe, they at once prepared to wish her joy, till the sight of an armed and threatening force scared them away. Anicetus then surrounded the house with a guard, and having burst open the gates, dragged off the slaves who met him, till he came to the door of her chamber, where a few still stood, after the rest had fled in terror at the attack. A small lamp was in the room, and one slave-girl with Agrippina, who grew more and more anxious, as no messenger came from her son, not even Agerinus, while the appearance of the shore was changed, a solitude one moment, then sudden bustle and tokens of the worst catastrophe. As the girl rose to depart, she exclaimed, "Do you

too forsake me?" and looking round saw Anicetus, who had with
him the captain of the trireme, Herculeius, and Obaritus, a centurion of marines. "If," said she, "you have come to see me, take
back word that I have recovered, but if you are here to do a crime,
I believe nothing about my son; he has not ordered his mother's
murder."

The assassins closed in round her couch, and the captain of
the trireme first struck her head violently with a club. Then, as
the centurion bared his sword for the fatal deed, presenting her
person, she exclaimed, "Smite my womb," and with many wounds
she was slain. (*XIV, 1-8*)

While Nero was lingering in the towns of Campania, doubting how he should enter Rome, whether he would find the Senate
submissive and the populace enthusiastic, all the vilest courtiers,
and of these never had a court a more abundant crop, argued
against his hesitation by assuring him that Agrippina's name was
hated and that her death had heightened his popularity. "He
might go without a fear," they said, "and experience in his person
men's veneration for him." They insisted at the same time on
preceding him. They found greater enthusiasm than they had
promised, the tribes coming forth to meet him, the Senate in
holiday attire, troops of their children and wives arranged according to sex and age, tiers of seats raised for the spectacle, where
he was to pass, as a triumph is witnessed. Thus elated and exulting
over his people's slavery, he proceeded to the Capitol, performed
the thanksgiving, and then plunged into all the excesses, which,
though ill-restrained, some sort of respect for his mother had for
a while delayed.

He had long had a fancy for driving a four-horse chariot, and
a no less degrading taste for singing to the harp, in a theatrical
fashion, when he was at dinner. This he would remind people
was a royal custom, and had been the practice of ancient chiefs;
it was celebrated too in the praises of poets and was meant to
show honor to the gods. Songs indeed, he said, were sacred to
Apollo, and it was in the dress of a singer that that great and
prophetic deity was seen in Roman temples as well as in Greek
cities. He could no longer be restrained, when Seneca and Burrus

thought it best to concede one point that he might not persist in both. A space was enclosed in the Vatican valley where he might manage his horses, without the spectacle being public. Soon he actually invited all the people of Rome, who extolled him in their praises, like a mob which craves for amusements and rejoices when a prince draws them the same way. However, the public exposure of his shame acted on him as an incentive instead of sickening him, as men expected. Imagining that he mitigated the scandal by disgracing many others, he brought on the stage descendants of noble families, who sold themselves because they were paupers. As they have ended their days, I think it due to their ancestors not to hand down their names. And indeed the infamy is his who gave them wealth to reward their degradation rather than to deter them from degrading themselves. He prevailed too on some well-known Roman knights, by immense presents, to offer their services in the amphitheater; only pay from one who is able to command, carries with it the force of compulsion.

Still, not yet wishing to disgrace himself on a public stage, he instituted some games under the title of "juvenile sports," for which people of every class gave in their names. Neither rank nor age nor previous high promotion hindered any one from practicing the art of a Greek or Latin actor and even stooping to gestures and songs unfit for a man. Noble ladies too actually played disgusting parts, and in the grove, with which Augustus had surrounded the lake for the naval fight, there were erected places for meeting and refreshment, and every incentive to excess was offered for sale. Money too was distributed, which the respectable had to spend under sheer compulsion and which the profligate gloried in squandering. Hence a rank growth of abominations and of all infamy. Never did a more filthy rabble add a worse licentiousness to our long corrupted morals. Even, with virtuous training, purity is not easily upheld; far less amid rivalries in vice could modesty or propriety or any trace of good manners be preserved. Last of all, the emperor himself came on the stage, tuning his lute with elaborate care and trying his voice with his attendants. There were also present, to complete the show, a guard of soldiers with centurions and tribunes, and Burrus, who grieved and yet applauded. Then it was that Roman knights were first enrolled under the title of Augustani, men in their prime and remarkable for their strength, some, from a natural frivolity, others from the hope of promotion. Day and night they kept up a thunder of applause, and applied to the emperor's person and voice the epithets of deities. Thus they lived in fame and honor, as if on the strength of their merits.

Nero however, that he might not be known only for his accomplishments as an actor, also affected a taste for poetry, and drew round him persons who had some skill in such compositions, but not yet generally recognized. They used to sit with him, stringing together verses prepared at home, or extemporized on the spot, and fill up his own expressions, such as they were, just as he threw them off. This is plainly shown by the very character of the poems, which have no vigor or inspiration, or unity in their flow.

He would also bestow some leisure after his banquets on the teachers of philosophy, for he enjoyed the wrangles of opposing dogmatists. And some there were who liked to exhibit their gloomy faces and looks, as one of the amusements of the court. (*XIV,* 13-16)

Nero meanwhile declared by edict that the prefect had been corrupted into a design of gaining over the fleet, and added, in forgetfulness of his late charge of barrenness against Octavia, that, conscious of her profligacies, she had procured abortion, a fact he had himself ascertained. Then he confined her in the island of Pandataria. No exile ever filled the eyes of beholders with tears of greater compassion. Some still remembered Agrippina, banished by Tiberius, and the yet fresher memory of Julia, whom Claudius exiled, was present to men's thoughts. But they had life's prime for their stay; they had seen some happiness, and the horror of the moment was alleviated by recollections of a better lot in the past. For Octavia, from the first, her marriage-day was a kind of funeral, brought, as she was, into a house where she had nothing but scenes of mourning, her father and, an instant afterward, her brother, having been snatched from her by poison; then, a slave-girl raised above the mistress; Poppaea married only to ensure a wife's ruin, and, to end all, an accusation more horrible than any death.

And now the girl, in her twentieth year, with centurions and soldiers around her, already removed from among the living by the forecast of doom, still could not reconcile herself to death. After an interval of a few days, she received an order that she was to die, although she protested that she was now a widow and only a sister, and appealed to their common ancestors, the Germanici, and finally to the name of Agrippina, during whose life she had endured a marriage, which was miserable enough indeed, but not fatal. She was then tightly bound with cords, and the veins of every limb were opened; but as her blood was congealed by terror and flowed too slowly, she was killed outright by the steam of an intensely hot bath. To this was added the yet more appalling horror of Poppaea beholding the severed head which was conveyed to Rome.

And for all this offerings were voted to the temples. I record the fact with a special object. Whoever would study the calamities of that period in my pages or those of other authors, is to take it for granted that as often as the emperor directed banishments or executions, so often was there a thanksgiving to the gods, and what formerly commemorated some prosperous event, was then a token of public disaster. Still, if any decree of the Senate was marked by some new flattery, or by the lowest servility, I shall not pass it over in silence. (*XIV, 63-64*)

[*Nero on the stage. The great fire at Rome, A.D. 64; the persecution of the Christians—chosen as scapegoats—was the first in their history and was limited to those within Rome. The conspiracy of the senator Piso, and the death of Seneca, the Stoic philosopher.*]

In the year of the consulship of Caius Laecanius and Marcus Licinius a yet keener impulse urged Nero to show himself frequently on the public stage. Hitherto he had sung in private houses or gardens, during the Juvenile games, but these he now despised, as being but little frequented, and on too small a scale for so fine a voice. As, however, he did not venture to make a beginning at Rome, he chose Naples, because it was a Greek city. From this as his starting-point he might cross into Greece, and there, winning the well-known and sacred garlands of antiquity, evoke, with increased fame, the enthusiasm of the citizens. Accordingly, a rabble of the townsfolk was brought together, with those whom the excitement of such an event had attracted from the neighboring towns and colonies, and such as followed in the emperor's train to pay him honor or for various objects. All these, with some companies of soldiers, filled the theater at Naples.

There an incident occurred, which many thought unlucky, though to the emperor it seemed due to the providence of auspicious deities. The people who had been present, had quitted the theater, and the empty building then fell in without harm to anyone. Thereupon Nero in an elaborate ode thanked the gods, celebrating the good luck which attended the late downfall, and as he was on his way to cross the Adriatic sea, he rested awhile at Beneventum, where a crowded gladiatorial show was being exhibited by Vatinius. The man was one of the most conspicuously infamous sights in the imperial court, bred, as he had been, in a shoemaker's shop, of a deformed person and vulgar wit, originally introduced as a butt. After a time he grew so powerful by accusing all the best men, that in influence, wealth, and ability to injure, he was pre-eminent even in that bad company.

While Nero was frequently visiting the show, even amid his pleasures there was no cessation to his crimes. For during the very same period Torquatus Silanus was forced to die, because over and above his illustrious rank as one of the Junian family he claimed to be the great-grandson of Augustus. Accusers were ordered to charge him with prodigality in lavishing gifts, and with having no hope but in revolution. They said further that he had nobles about him for his letters, books, and accounts, titles all and rehearsals of supreme power. Then the most intimate of his freedmen were put in chains and torn from him, till, knowing the doom which impended, Torquatus divided the arteries in his arms. A speech from Nero followed, as usual, which stated that though he was guilty and with good reason distrusted his defense, he would yet have lived, had he awaited the clemency of the judge.

Soon afterward, giving up Greece for the present (his reasons were not certainly known), he returned to Rome, there dwelling in his secret imaginations on the provinces of the east, especially Egypt. Then having declared in a public proclamation that his absence would not be long and that all things in the State would remain unchanged and prosperous, he visited the temple of the Capitol for advice about his departure. There he adored the gods; then he entered also the temple of Vesta, and there feeling a sudden trembling throughout his limbs, either from terror inspired by the deity or because, from the remembrance of his crimes, he was never free from fear, he relinquished his purpose, repeatedly saying that all his plans were of less account than his love of his country. "He had seen the sad countenances of the citizens, he heard their secret complainings at the prospect of his entering on so long a journey, when they could not bear so much as his brief excursions, accustomed as they were to cheer themselves under mischances by the sight of the emperor. Hence, as in private relationships the closest ties were the strongest, so the people of Rome had the most powerful claims and must be obeyed in their wish to retain him."

These and the like sentiments suited the people, who craved amusement, and feared, always their chief anxiety, scarcity of grain, should he be absent. The Senate and leading citizens were in doubt whether to regard him as more terrible at a distance or among them. After a while, as is the way with great terrors, they thought what happened the worst alternative.

Nero, to win credit for himself of enjoying nothing so much as the capital, prepared banquets in the public places, and used the whole city, so to say, as his private house. Of these entertainments the most famous for their notorious profligacy were those furnished by Tigellinus, which I will describe as an illustration, that I may not have again and again to narrate similar extravagance. He had a raft constructed on Agrippa's lake, put the guests on board and set it in motion by other vessels towing it. These vessels glittered with gold and ivory; the crews were arranged according to age and experience in vice. Birds and beasts had been procured from remote countries, and sea monsters from the ocean. On the margin of the lake were set up brothels crowded with noble ladies, and on the opposite bank were seen naked prostitutes with obscene gestures and movements. As darkness approached, all the adjacent grove and surrounding buildings resounded with song, and shone brilliantly with lights. Nero, who polluted himself by every lawful or lawless indulgence, had not omitted a single abomination which could heighten his depravity, till a few days afterward he stooped to marry himself to one of that filthy herd, by name Pythagoras, with all the forms of regular wedlock. The bridal veil was put over the emperor; people saw the witnesses of the ceremony, the wedding dower, the couch and the nuptial torches; everything in a word was plainly visible, which, even when a woman weds, darkness hides.

A disaster followed, whether accidental or treacherously contrived by the emperor, is uncertain, as authors have given both accounts, worse, however, and more dreadful than any which have ever happened to this city by the violence of fire. It had its beginning in that part of the circus which adjoins the Palatine and Caelian hills, where, amid the shops containing inflamable wares, the conflagration both broke out and instantly became so fierce and so rapid from the wind that it seized in its grasp the entire length of the circus. For here there were no houses fenced in by solid masonry, or temples surrounded by walls, or any other obstacle to interpose delay. The blaze in its fury ran first through the level portions of the city, then rising to the hills, while it again devastated every place below them, it outstripped all preventive measures; so rapid was the mischief and so completely at its mercy the city, with those narrow winding passages and irregular streets, which characterized old Rome. Added to this were the wailings of terror-stricken women, the feebleness of age, the helpless inexperience of childhood, the crowds who sought to save themselves or others, dragging out the infirm or waiting for them, and by their hurry in the one case, by their delay in the other, aggravating the confusion. Often, while they looked behind them, they were intercepted by flames on their side or in their face. Or if they reached a refuge close at hand, when this too was seized by the fire, they found that, even places, which they had imagined to be remote, were involved in the same calamity. At last, doubting what they should avoid or whither betake themselves, they crowded the streets or flung themselves down in the fields, while some who had lost their all, even their very daily bread, and others out of love for their kinsfolk, whom they had been unable to rescue, perished, though escape was open to them. And no one dared to stop the mischief, because of incessant menaces from a number of persons who forbade the extinguishing of the flames, because again others openly hurled brands, and kept shouting that there was one who gave them authority, either seeking to plunder more freely, or obeying orders.

Nero at this time was at Antium, and did not return to Rome until the fire approached his house, which he had built to connect the palace with the gardens of Maecenas. It could not, however, be stopped from devouring the palace, the house, and everything around it. However, to relieve the people, driven out homeless as they were, he threw open to them the Campus Martius and the public buildings of Agrippa, and even his own gardens, and raised temporary structures to receive the destitute multitude. Supplies of food were brought up from Ostia and the neighboring towns, and the price of grain was reduced to three sesterces a peck. These acts, though popular, produced no effect, since a rumor had gone forth everywhere that, at the very time when the city was in flames, the emperor appeared on a private stage and sang of the destruction of Troy, comparing present misfortunes with the calamities of antiquity.

At last, after five days, an end was put to the conflagration at the foot of the Esquiline hill, by the destruction of all buildings on a vast space, so that the violence of the fire was met by clear ground and an open sky. But before people had laid aside their fears, the flames returned, with no less fury this second time, and especially in the spacious districts of the city. Consequently, though there was less loss of life, the temples of the gods, and the porticoes which were devoted to enjoyment, fell in a yet more widespread ruin. And to this conflagration there attached the greater infamy because it broke out on the Aemilian property of Tigellinus, and it seemed that Nero was aiming at the glory of founding a new city and calling it by his name. Rome, indeed, is divided into fourteen districts, four of which remained uninjured, three were leveled to the ground, while in the other seven were left only a few shattered, half-burnt relics of houses.

It would not be easy to enter into a computation of the private mansions, the blocks of tenements, and of the temples, which were lost. Those with the oldest ceremonial, as that dedicated by Servius Tullius to Luna, the great altar and shrine raised by the Arcadian Evander to the visibly appearing Hercules, the temple of Jupiter the Stayer, which was vowed by Romulus, Numa's royal palace, and the sanctuary of Vesta, with the tutelary deities of the Roman people, were burnt. So too were the riches acquired by our many victories, various beauties of Greek art, then again the ancient and genuine historical monuments of men of genius, and, notwithstanding the striking splendor of the restored city, old men will remember many things which could not be replaced. Some persons observed that the beginning of this conflagration was on the 19th of July, the day on which the Senones captured and fired Rome. Others have pushed a curious inquiry so far as to reduce the interval between these two conflagrations into equal numbers of years, months, and days.

Nero meanwhile availed himself of his country's desolation, and erected a mansion in which the jewels and gold, long familiar objects, quite vulgarized by our extravagance, were not so marvelous as the fields and lakes, with woods on one side to resemble a wilderness, and, on the other, open spaces and extensive views. The directors and contrivers of the work were Severus and Celer, who had the genius and the audacity to attempt by art even what nature had refused, and to fool away an emperor's resources. They had actually undertaken to sink a navigable canal from the lake Avernus to the mouths of the Tiber along a barren shore or through the face of hills, where one meets with no moisture which could supply water, except the Pomptine marshes. The rest of the country is broken rock and perfectly dry. Even if it could be cut through, the labor would be intolerable, and there would be no adequate result. Nero, however, with his love of the impossible, endeavored to dig through the nearest hills to Avernus, and there still remain the traces of his disappointed hope.

Of Rome meanwhile, so much as was left unoccupied by his mansion, was not built up, as it had been after its burning by the Gauls, without any regularity or in any fashion, but with rows of streets according to measurement, with broad thorough-fares, with a restriction on the height of houses, with open spaces, and the further addition of colonnades, as a protection to the frontage of the blocks of tenements. These colonnades Nero promised to erect at his own expense, and to hand óver the open spaces, when cleared of the debris, to the ground landlords. He also offered rewards proportioned to each person's position and property, and prescribed a period within which they were to obtain them on the completion of so many houses or blocks of building. He fixed on the marshes of Ostia for the reception of the rubbish, and arranged that the ships which had brought up grain by the Tiber, should sail down the river with cargoes of this rubbish. The buildings themselves, to a certain height, were to be solidly constructed, without wooden beams, of stone from Gabii or Alba, that material being impervious to fire. And to pro-vide that the water which individual license had illegally appro-priated, might flow in greater abundance in several places for the public use, officers were appointed, and everyone was to have in the open court the means of stopping a fire. Every building, too, was to be enclosed by its own proper wall, not by one common to others. These changes, which were liked for their utility, also added beauty to the new city. Some, however, thought that its old ar-rangement had been more conducive to health, inasmuch as the narrow streets with the elevation of the roofs were not equally penetrated by the sun's heat, while now the open space, un-sheltered by any shade, was scorched by a fiercer glow.

Such indeed were the precautions of human wisdom. The next thing was to seek means of propitiating the gods, and recourse was had to the Sibylline books, by the direction of which prayers were offered to Vulcanus, Ceres, and Proserpina. Juno, too, was entreated by the matrons, first, in the Capitol, then on the nearest part of the coast, whence water was procured to sprinkle the fane and image of the goddess. And there were sacred banquets and nightly vigils celebrated by married women. But all human efforts, all the lavish gifts of the emperor, and the propitiations of the gods, did not banish the sinister belief that the conflagration was the result of an order. Consequently, to get rid of the report, Nero fastened the guilt and inflicted the most exquisite tortures on a class hated for their abominations, called Christians by the populace. Christus, from whom the name had its origin, suffered the extreme penalty during the reign of Tiberius at the hands of one of our procurators, Pontius Pilatus, and a most mischievous superstition, thus checked for the moment, again broke out not only in Judaea, the first source of the evil, but even in Rome, where all things hideous and shameful from every part of the world find their center and become popular. Accordingly, an arrest was first made of all who pleaded guilty; then, upon their information, an immense multitude was convicted, not so much of the crime of firing the city, as of hatred against mankind. Mockery of every sort was added to their deaths. Covered with the skins of beasts, they were torn by dogs and perished, or were nailed to crosses, or were doomed to the flames and burnt, to serve as a nightly illumination, when daylight had expired.

Nero offered his gardens for the spectacle, and was exhibiting a show in the circus, while he mingled with the people in the dress of a charioteer or stood aloft on a car. Hence, even for criminals who deserved extreme and exemplary punishment, there arose a feeling of compassion; for it was not, as it seemed, for the public good, but to glut one man's cruelty, that they were being destroyed. (XV, 33-44)

Silius Nerva and Atticus Vestinus then entered on the consulship, and now a conspiracy was planned, and at once became formidable, for which senators, knights, soldiers, even women, had given their names with eager rivalry, out of hatred of Nero as well as a liking for Caius Piso. A descendant of the Calpurnian house, and embracing in his connections through his father's noble rank many illustrious families, Piso had a splendid reputation with the people from his virtue or semblance of virtue. His eloquence he exercised in the defense of fellow-citizens, his generosity toward friends, while even for strangers he had a courteous address and demeanor. He had, too, the fortuitous advantages of tall stature and a handsome face. But solidity of character and moderation in pleasure were wholly alien to him. He indulged in laxity, in display, and occasionally in excess. This suited the taste of that numerous class who, when the attractions of vice are so powerful, do not wish for strictness or special severity on the throne.

The origin of the conspiracy was not in Piso's personal ambition. But I could not easily narrate who first planned it or whose prompting inspired a scheme into which so many entered. . . .

. . . It was said that Subrius Flavus had formed a sudden resolution to attack Nero when singing on the stage, or when his house was in flames and he was running hither and thither, unattended, in the darkness. In the one case was the opportunity of solitude; in the other, the very crowd which would witness so glorious a deed, had roused a singularly noble soul; it was only the desire of escape, that foe to all great enterprises, which held him back.

Meanwhile, as [the conspirators] hesitated in prolonged suspense between hope and fear, a certain Epicharis (how she informed herself is uncertain, as she had never before had a thought of anything noble) began to stir and upbraid the conspirators. Wearied at last of their long delay, she endeavored, when staying in Campania, to shake the loyalty of the officers of the fleet at Misenum, and to entangle them in a guilty complicity. She began thus. There was a captain in the fleet, Volusius Proculus, who had been one of Nero's instruments in his mother's murder, and had not, as he thought, been promoted in proportion to the greatness of his crime. Either, as an old acquaintance of the woman, or on the strength of a recent intimacy, he divulged to her his services to Nero and their barren result to himself, adding complaints, and his determination to have vengeance, should the chance arise. He thus inspired the hope that he could be persuaded, and could secure many others. No small help was to be found in the fleet, and there would be numerous opportunities, as Nero delighted in frequent enjoyment of the sea off Puteoli and Misenum.

Epicharis accordingly said more, and began the history of all the emperor's crimes. "The Senate," she affirmed, "had no power left it; yet means had been provided whereby he might pay the penalty of having destroyed the State. Only let Proculus gird himself to do his part and bring over to their side his bravest soldiers, and then look for an adequate recompense." The conspirators' names, however, she withheld. Consequently the information of Proculus was useless, even though he reported what he had heard to Nero. For Epicharis being summoned and confronted with the informer easily silenced him, unsupported as he was by a single witness. But she was herself detained in custody, for Nero suspected that even what was not proved to be true, was not wholly false.

The conspirators, however, alarmed by the fear of disclosure, resolved to hurry on the assassination at Baiae, in Piso's villa, whither the emperor, charmed by its loveliness, often went, and where, unguarded and without the cumbrous grandeur of his rank, he would enjoy the bath and the banquet. But Piso refused, alleging the odium of an act which would stain with an emperor's blood, however bad he might be, the sanctity of the hospitable board and the deities who preside over it. "Better," he said, "in the capital, in that hateful mansion which was piled up with the plunder of the citizens, or in public, to accomplish what on the State's behalf they had undertaken."

So he said openly, with however a secret apprehension that Lucius Silanus might, on the strength of his distinguished rank and the teachings of Caius Cassius, under whom he had been trained, aspire to any greatness and seize on empire, which would be promptly offered him by all who had no part in the conspiracy, and who would pity Nero as the victim of a crime. Many thought that Piso shunned also the enterprising spirit of Vestinus, the consul, who might, he feared, rise up in the cause of freedom, or, by choosing another emperor, make the State his own gift. Vestinus, indeed, had no share in the conspiracy, though Nero on that charge gratified an old resentment against an innocent man.

At last they decided to carry out their design on that day of the circus games, which is celebrated in honor of Ceres, as the emperor, who seldom went out, and shut himself up in his house or gardens, used to go to the entertainments of the circus, and access to him was the easier from his keen enjoyment of the spectacle. They had so arranged the order of the plot, that Lateranus was to throw himself at the prince's knees in earnest entreaty, apparently craving relief for his private necessities, and, being a man of strong nerve and huge frame, hurl him to the ground and hold him down. When he was prostrate and powerless, the tribunes and centurions and all the others who had sufficient daring were to rush up and do the murder, the first blow being claimed by Scaevinus, who had taken a dagger from the Temple of Safety, or, according to another account, from that of Fortune, in the town of Ferentum, and used to wear the weapon as though dedicated to some noble deed. Piso, meanwhile, was to wait in the sanctuary of Ceres, whence he was to be summoned by Faenius, the commander of the guard, and by the others, and then conveyed into the camp, accompanied by Antonia, the daughter of Claudius Caesar, with a view to evoke the people's enthusiasm. So it is related by Caius Pliny. Handed down from whatever source, I had no intention of suppressing it, however absurd it may seem, either that Antonia should have lent her name at her life's peril to a hopeless project, or that Piso, with his well-known affection for his wife, should have pledged himself to another marriage, but for the fact that the lust of dominion inflames the heart more than any other passion.

It was however wonderful how among people of different class, rank, age, sex, among rich and poor, everything was kept in secrecy till betrayal began from the house of Scaevinus. The day before the treacherous attempt, after a long conversation with Antonius Natalis, Scaevinus returned home, sealed his will, and, drawing from its sheath the dagger of which I have already spoken, and complaining that it was blunted from long disuse, he ordered it to be sharpened on a stone to a keen and bright point. This task he assigned to his freedman Milichus. At the same time he sat down to a more than usually sumptuous banquet, and gave his favorite slaves their freedom, and money to others. He was himself depressed, and evidently in profound thought, though he affected gaiety in desultory conversation. Last of all, he directed ligatures for wounds and the means of stanching blood to be prepared by the same Milichus, who either knew of the conspiracy and was faithful up to this point, or was in complete ignorance and then first caught suspicions, as most authors have inferred from what followed. For when his servile imagination dwelt on the rewards of perfidy, and he saw before him at the same moment boundless wealth and power, conscience and care for his patron's life, together with the remembrance of the freedom he had received, fled from him. From his wife, too, he had adopted a womanly and yet baser suggestion; for she even held over him a dreadful thought, that many had been present, both freedmen and slaves, who had seen what he had; that one man's silence would be useless, whereas the rewards would be for him alone who was first with the information.

Accordingly at daybreak Milichus went to the Servilian gardens, and, finding the doors shut against him, said again and again that he was the bearer of important and alarming news. Upon this he was conducted by the gatekeepers to one of Nero's freedmen, Epaphroditus, and by him to Nero, whom he informed of the urgent danger, of the formidable conspiracy, and of all else which he had heard or inferred. He showed him too the weapon prepared for his destruction, and bade him summon the accused.

Scaevinus on being arrested by the soldiers began his defense with the reply that the dagger, about which he was accused, had of old been regarded with a religious sentiment by his ancestors, that it had been kept in his chamber, and been stolen by a trick of his freedman. He had often, he said, signed his will without heeding the observance of particular days, and had previously given presents of money as well as freedom to some of his slaves, only on this occasion he gave more freely, because, as his means were now impoverished and his creditors were pressing him, he distrusted the validity of his will. Certainly his table had always been profusely furnished, and his life luxurious, such as rigid censors would hardly approve. As to the bandages for wounds, none had been prepared at his order, but as all the man's other charges were absurd, he added an accusation in which he might make himself alike informer and witness.

He backed up his words by an air of resolution. Turning on his accuser, he denounced him as an infamous and depraved wretch, with so fearless a voice and look that the information was beginning to collapse, when Milichus was reminded by his wife that Antonius Natalis had had a long secret conversation with Scaevinus, and that both were Piso's intimate friends.

Natalis was therefore summoned, and they were separately asked what the conversation was, and what was its subject. Then a suspicion arose because their answers did not agree, and they were both put in irons. They could not endure the sight and the threat of torture. Natalis however, taking the initiative, knowing as he did more of the whole conspiracy, and being also more practiced in accusing, first confessed about Piso, next added the name of Annaeus Seneca, either as having been a messenger between him and Piso, or to win the favor of Nero, who hated Seneca and sought every means for his ruin. Then Scaevinus too, when he knew the disclosure of Natalis, with like pusillanimity, or under the impression that everything was now divulged, and that there could be no advantage in silence, revealed the other conspirators. Of these, Lucanus, Quintianus, and Senecio long persisted in denial; after a time, when bribed by the promise of impunity, anxious to excuse their reluctance, Lucanus named his mother Atilla, Quintianus and Senecio, their chief friends, respectively, Glitius Gallus and Annius Pollio.

Nero, meanwhile, remembering that Epicharis was in custody on the information of Volusius Proculus, and assuming that a woman's frame must be unequal to the agony, ordered her to be torn on the rack. But neither the scourge nor fire, nor the fury of the men as they increased the torture that they might not be a woman's scorn, overcame her positive denial of the charge. Thus the first day's inquiry was futile. On the morrow, as she was being dragged back on a chair to the same torments (for with her limbs all dislocated she could not stand), she tied a band, which she had stript off her bosom, in a sort of noose to the arched back of the chair, put her neck in it, and then straining with the whole weight of her body, wrung out of her frame its little remaining breath. All the nobler was the example set by a freedwoman at such a crisis in screening strangers and those whom she hardly knew, when freeborn men, Roman knights, and senators, yet unscathed by torture, betrayed, every one, his dearest kinsfolk. For even Lucanus and Senecio and Quintianus failed not to reveal their accomplices indiscriminately, and Nero was more and more alarmed, though he had fenced his person with a largely augmented guard.

Even Rome itself he put, so to say, under custody, garrisoning its walls with companies of soldiers and occupying with troops the coast and the river-banks. Incessantly were there flying through the public places, through private houses, country fields, and the neighboring villages, horse and foot soldiers, mixed with Germans, whom the emperor trusted as being foreigners. In long succession, troops of prisoners in chains were dragged along and stood at the gates of his gardens. When they entered to plead their cause, a smile of joy on any of the conspirators, a casual conversation, a sudden meeting, or the fact of having entered a banquet or a public show in company, was construed into a crime, while to the savage questionings of Nero and Tigellinus were added the violent menaces of Faenius Rufus, who had not yet been named by the informers, but who, to get the credit of complete ignorance, frowned fiercely on his accomplices. When Subius Flavus at his side asked him by a sign whether he should draw his sword in the middle of the trial and perpetrate the fatal deed, Rufus refused, and checked the man's impulse as he was putting his hand to his sword-hilt.

Some there were who, as soon as the conspiracy was betrayed, urged Piso, while Milichus' story was being heard and Scaevinus was hesitating, to go to the camp or mount the Rostra and test the feelings of the soldiers and of the people. "If," said they, "your accomplices join your enterprise, those also who are yet undecided will follow, and great will be the fame of the movement once started, and this in any new scheme is all-powerful. Against it Nero has taken no precaution. Even brave men are dismayed by sudden perils; far less will that stage-player, with Tigellinus forsooth and his concubines in his train, raise arms against you. Many things are accomplished on trial which cowards think arduous. It is vain to expect secrecy and fidelity from the varying tempers and bodily constitutions of such a host of accomplices. Torture or reward can overcome everything. Men will soon come to put you also in chains and inflict on you an ignominious death. How much more gloriously will you die while you cling to the State and invoke aid for liberty. Rather let the soldiers fail, the people be traitors, provided that you, if prematurely robbed of life, justify your death to your ancestors and descendants."

Unmoved by these considerations, Piso showed himself a few moments in public, then sought the retirement of his house, and there fortified his spirit against the worst, till a troop of soldiers arrived, raw recruits, or men recently enlisted, whom Nero had selected, because he was afraid of the veterans, imbued, though they were, with a liking for him. Piso expired by having the veins in his arms severed. His will, full of loathsome flatteries of Nero, was a concession to his love of his wife, a base woman, with only a beautiful person to recommend her, whom he had taken away from her husband, one of his friends. Her name was Atria Galla; that of her former husband, Domitius Silus. The tame spirit of the man, the profligacy of the woman, blazoned Piso's infamy.

In quick succession Nero added the murder of Plautius Lateranus, consul-elect, so promptly that he did not allow him to embrace his children or to have the brief choice of his own death. He was dragged off to a place set apart for the execution of slaves, and butchered by the hand of the tribune Statius, maintaining a resolute silence, and not reproaching the tribune with complicity in the plot.

Then followed the destruction of Annaeus Seneca, a special joy to the emperor, not because he had convicted him of the conspiracy, but anxious to accomplish with the sword what poison had failed to do. It was, in fact, Natalis alone who divulged Seneca's name, to this extent, that he had been sent to Seneca when ailing, to see him and remonstrate with him for excluding Piso from his presence, when it would have been better to have kept up their friendship by familiar intercourse; that Seneca's reply was that mutual conversations and frequent interviews were to the advantage of neither, but still that his own life depended on Piso's safety. Gavius Silvanus, tribune of a praetorian cohort, was ordered to report this to Seneca and to ask him whether he acknowledged what Natalis said and his own answer. Either by chance or purposely Seneca had returned on that day from Campania, and had stopped at a country-house four miles from Rome. Thither the tribune came next evening, surrounded the house with troops of soldiers, and then made known the emperor's message to Seneca as he was at dinner with his wife, Pompeia Paulina, and two friends.

Seneca replied that Natalis had been sent to him and had complained to him in Piso's name because of his refusal to see Piso, upon which he excused himself on the ground of failing health and the desire of rest. "He had no reason," he said, for "preferring the interest of any private citizen to his own safety, and he had no natural aptitude for flattery. No one knew this better than Nero, who had oftener experienced Seneca's freespokenness than his servility." When the tribune reported this answer in the presence of Poppaea and Tigellinus, the emperor's most confidential advisers in his moments of rage, he asked whether Seneca was meditating suicide. Upon this the tribune asserted that he saw no signs of fear, and perceived no sadness in his words or in his looks. He was accordingly ordered to go back and to announce sentence of death. Fabius Rusticus tells us that he did not return the way he came, but went out of his course to Faenius, the commander of the guard, and having explained to him the emperor's orders, and asked whether he was to obey them, was by him admonished to carry them out, for a fatal spell of cowardice was on them all. For this very Silvanus was one of the conspirators, and he was now abetting the crimes which he had united with them to avenge. But he spared himself the anguish of a word or of a look, and merely sent in to Seneca one of his centurions, who was to announce to him his last doom.

Seneca, quite unmoved, asked for tablets on which to inscribe his will, and, on the centurion's refusal, turned to his friends, protesting that as he was forbidden to requite them, he bequeathed to them the only, but still the noblest possession yet remaining to him, the pattern of his life, which, if they remembered, they would win a name for moral worth and steadfast friendship. At the same time he called them back from their tears to manly resolution, now with friendly talk, and now with the sterner language of rebuke. "Where," he asked again and again, "are your maxims of philosophy, or the preparation of so many years' study against evils to come? Who knew not Nero's cruelty? After a mother's and a brother's murder, nothing remains but to add the destruction of a guardian and a tutor."

Having spoken these and like words, meant, so to say, for all, he embraced his wife; then softening awhile from the stern resolution of the hour, he begged and implored her to spare herself the burden of perpetual sorrow, and, in the contemplation of a life virtuously spent, to endure a husband's loss with honorable consolations. She declared, in answer, that she too had decided to die, and claimed for herself the blow of the executioner. Thereupon Seneca, not to thwart her noble ambition, from an affection too which would not leave behind him for insult one whom he dearly loved, replied: "I have shown you ways of smoothing life; you prefer the glory of dying. I will not grudge you such a noble example. Let the fortitude of so courageous an end be alike in both of us, but let there be more in your decease to win fame."

Then by one and the same stroke they sundered with a dagger the arteries of their arms. Seneca, as his aged frame, attenuated by frugal diet, allowed the blood to escape but slowly, severed also the veins of his legs and knees. Worn out by cruel anguish, afraid too that his sufferings might break his wife's spirit, and that, as he looked on her tortures, he might himself sink into irresolution, he persuaded her to retire into another chamber. Even at the last moment his eloquence failed him not; he summoned his secretaries, and dictated much to them which, as it has been published for all readers in his own words, I forbear to paraphrase.

Nero meanwhile, having no personal hatred against Paulina and not wishing to heighten the odium of his cruelty, forbade her death. At the soldiers' prompting, her slaves and freedmen bound

up her arms, and stanched the bleeding, whether with her knowledge is doubtful. For as the vulgar are ever ready to think the worst,
there were persons who believed that, as long as she dreaded Nero's
relentlessness, she sought the glory of sharing her husband's death,
but that after a time, when a more soothing prospect presented
itself, she yielded to the charms of life. To this she added a few
subsequent years, with a most praiseworthy remembrance of her
husband, and with a countenance and frame white to a degree of
pallor which denoted a loss of much vital energy.

Seneca meantime, as the tedious process of death still lingered
on, begged Statius Annaeus, whom he had long esteemed for his
faithful friendship and medical skill, to produce a poison with
which he had some time before provided himself, the same drug
which extinguished the life of those who were condemned by a
public sentence of the people of Athens. It was brought to him
and he drank it in vain, chilled as he was throughout his limbs,
and his frame closed against the efficacy of the poison. At last he
entered a pool of heated water, from which he sprinkled the nearest
of his slaves, adding the exclamation, "I offer this liquid as a
libation to Jupiter the Deliverer." He was then carried into a
bath, with the steam of which he was suffocated, and he was
burnt without any of the usual funeral rites. So he had directed
in a codicil of his will, when even in the height of his wealth and
power he was thinking of his life's close. (XV, 48-64)

[The death of Petronius.]

With regard to Caius Petronius, I ought to dwell a little on his
antecedents. His days he passed in sleep, his nights in the business
and pleasures of life. Indolence had raised him to fame, as energy
raises others, and he was reckoned not a debauchee and spendthrift,
like most of those who squander their substance, but a man of refined luxury. And indeed his talk and his doings, the freer they
were and the more show of carelessness they exhibited, were the
better liked, for their look of natural simplicity. Yet as proconsul
of Bithynia and soon afterward as consul, he showed himself a
man of vigor and equal to business. Then falling back into vice

or affecting vice, he was chosen by Nero to be one of his few intimate associates, as a critic in matters of taste, while the emperor
thought nothing charming or elegant in luxury unless Petronius
had expressed to him his approval of it. Hence jealousy on the
part of Tigellinus, who looked on him as a rival and even his
superior in the science of pleasure. And so he worked on the
prince's cruelty, which dominated every other passion, charging
Petronius with having been the friend of Scaevinus, bribing a
slave to become informer, robbing him of the means of defense,
and hurrying into prison the greater part of his domestics.

It happened at the time that the emperor was on his way to
Campania and that Petronius, after going as far as Cumae, was
there detained. He bore no longer the suspense of fear or of hope.
Yet he did not fling away life with precipitate haste, but having
made an incision in his veins and then, according to his humor,
bound them up, he again opened them, while he conversed with
his friends, not in a serious strain or on topics that might win for
him the glory of courage. And he listened to them as they repeated, not thoughts on the immortality of the soul or on the
theories of philosophers, but light poetry and playful verses. To
some of his slaves he gave liberal presents, a flogging to others. He
dined, indulged himself in sleep, that death, though forced on
him, might have a natural appearance. Even in his will he did
not, as did many in their last moments, flatter Nero or Tigellinus
or any other of the men in power. On the contrary, he described
fully the prince's shameful excesses, with the names of his male
and female companions and their novelties in debauchery, and
sent the account under seal to Nero. Then he broke his signet-
ring, that it might not be subsequently available for imperiling
others. (*XVI, 18-19*)

THE HISTORIES

Rome after Nero's death. The fate of Galba.

[Nero's taxation and tyranny became unendurable. When
the tramp of approaching horses told him, as he hid in a
dingy cell, that the end was near, he ordered a faithful
freedman to stab him. His last words, declares Suetonius,
were, "A pity that such an artist should die." Here is the
situation at Rome a few months later, A.D. 69, known as
the Year of the Four Emperors.]

I begin my work with the time when Servius Galba was consul
for the second time with Titus Vinius for his colleague. Of the
former period, the 820 years dating from the founding of the city,
many authors have treated; and while they had to record the
transactions of the Roman people, they wrote with equal eloquence and freedom. After the conflict at Actium, and when it
became essential to peace, that all power should be centered in one
man, these great intellects passed away. Then too the truthfulness
of history was impaired in many ways; at first, through men's
ignorance of public affairs, which were now wholly strange to
them, then, through their passion for flattery, or, on the other
hand, their hatred of their masters. And so between the enmity of
the one and the servility of the other, neither had any regard for
posterity. But while we instinctively shrink from a writer's adulation, we lend a ready ear to detraction and spite, because flattery
involves the shameful imputation of servility, whereas malignity
wears the false appearance of honesty. I myself knew nothing of

Galba, of Otho, or of Vitellius, either from benefits or from injuries. I would not deny that my elevation was begun by Vespasian, augmented by Titus, and still further advanced by Domitian;
but those who profess inviolable truthfulness must speak of all
without partiality and without hatred. I have reserved as an
employment for my old age, should my life be long enough, a
subject at once more fruitful and less anxious in the reign of the
Divine Nerva and the empire of Trajan, enjoying the rare happiness of times, when we may think what we please, and express
what we think.

I am entering on the history of a period rich in disasters,
frightful in its wars, torn by civil strife, and even in peace full of
horrors. Four emperors perished by the sword. There were three
civil wars; there were more with foreign enemies; there were often
wars that had both characters at once. There was success in the
East, and disaster in the West. There were disturbances in Illyricum; Gaul wavered in its allegiance; Britain was thoroughly subdued and immediately abandoned; the tribes of the Suevi and
the Sarmatae rose in concert against us; the Dacians had the glory
of inflicting as well as suffering defeat; the armies of Parthia were
all but set in motion by the cheat of a counterfeit Nero. Now too
Italy was prostrated by disasters either entirely novel, or that
recurred only after a long succession of ages; cities in Campania's
richest plains were swallowed up and overwhelmed; Rome was
wasted by conflagrations, its oldest temples consumed, and the
Capitol itself fired by the hands of citizens. Sacred rites were profaned; there was profligacy in the highest ranks; the sea was
crowded with exiles, and its rocks polluted with bloody deeds. In
the capital there were yet worse horrors. Nobility, wealth, the refusal or the acceptance of office, were grounds for accusation, and
virtue ensured destruction. The rewards of the informers were no
less odious than their crimes; for while some seized on consulships
and priestly offices, as their share of the spoil, others on procurator-
ships, and posts of more confidential authority, they robbed and
ruined in every direction amid universal hatred and terror. Slaves
were bribed to turn against their masters, and freedmen to betray

their patrons; and those who had not an enemy were destroyed by friends.

Yet the age was not so barren in noble qualities, as not also to exhibit examples of virtue. Mothers accompanied the flight of their sons; wives followed their husbands into exile; there were brave kinsmen and faithful sons in law; there were slaves whose fidelity defied even torture; there were illustrious men driven to the last necessity, and enduring it with fortitude; there were closing scenes that equaled the famous deaths of antiquity. Besides the manifold vicissitudes of human affairs, there were prodigies in heaven and earth, the warning voices of the thunder, and other intimations of the future, auspicious or gloomy, doubtful or not to be mistaken. Never surely did more terrible calamities of the Roman people, or evidence more conclusive, prove that the Gods take no thought for our happiness, but only for our punishment.

I think it proper, however, before I commence my purposed work, to pass under review the condition of the capital, the temper of the armies, the attitude of the provinces, and the elements of weakness and strength which existed throughout the whole empire, that so we may become acquainted, not only with the vicissitudes and the issues of events, which are often matters of chance, but also with their relations and their causes. Welcome as the death of Nero had been in the first burst of joy, yet it had not only roused various emotions in Rome, among the Senators, the people, or the soldiery of the capital, it had also excited all the legions and their generals; for now had been divulged that secret of the empire, that emperors could be made elsewhere than at Rome. The Senators enjoyed the first exercise of freedom with the less restraint, because the Emperor was new to power, and absent from the capital. The leading men of the Equestrian order sympathized most closely with the joy of the Senators. The respectable portion of the people, which was connected with the great families, as well as the dependents and freedmen of condemned and banished persons, were high in hope. The degraded populace, frequenters of the arena and the theater, the most worthless of the slaves, and those who having wasted their property were supported by the infamous excesses of Nero, caught eagerly in their dejection at every rumor.

The soldiery of the capital, who were imbued with the spirit of an old allegiance to the Caesars, and who had been led to desert Nero by intrigues and influences from without rather than by their own feelings, were inclined for change, when they found that the donative promised in Galba's name was withheld, and reflected that for great services and great rewards there was not the same room in peace as in war, and that the favor of an emperor created by the legions must be already preoccupied. They were further excited by the treason of Nymphidius Sabinus, their prefect, who himself aimed at the throne. Nymphidius indeed perished in the attempt, but, though the head of the mutiny was thus removed, there yet remained in many of the soldiers the consciousness of guilt. There were even men who talked in angry terms of the feebleness and avarice of Galba. The strictness once so commended, and celebrated in the praises of the army, was galling to troops who rebelled against the old discipline, and who had been accustomed by fourteen years' service under Nero to love the vices of their emperors, as much as they had once respected their virtues. To all this was added Galba's own expression, "I choose my soldiers, I do not buy them," noble words for the commonwealth, but fraught with peril for himself. His other acts were not after this pattern.

Titus Vinius and Cornelius Laco, one the most worthless, the other the most spiritless of mankind, were ruining the weak old Emperor, who had to bear the odium of such crimes and the scorn felt for such cowardice. Galba's progress had been slow and blood-stained. Cingonius Varro, consul elect, and Petronius Turpilianus, a man of consular rank, were put to death; the former as an accomplice of Nymphidius, the latter as one of Nero's generals. Both had perished without hearing or defense, like innocent men. His entry into the capital, made after the slaughter of thousands of unarmed soldiers, was most ill-omened, and was terrible even to the executioners. As he brought into the city his Spanish legion, while that which Nero had levied from the fleet still remained, Rome was full of strange troops. There were also many detachments from Germany, Britain, and Illyria, selected by Nero, and sent on by him to the Caspian passes, for service in the expedition which he was preparing against the Albani, but afterward recalled to crush the insurrection of Vindex. Here there were vast materials for a revolution, without indeed a decided bias toward any one man, but ready to a daring hand.

In this conjuncture it happened that tidings of the deaths of Fonteius Capito and Clodius Macer reached the capital. Macer was executed in Africa, where he was undoubtedly fomenting sedition, by Trebonius Garutianus the procurator, who acted on Galba's authority; Capito fell in Germany, while he was making similar attempts, by the hands of Cornelius Aquinus and Fabius Valens, legates of legions, who did not wait for an order. There were however some who believed that Capito, though foully stained with avarice and profligacy, had yet abstained from all thought of revolution, that this was a treacherous accusation invented by the commanders themselves, who had urged him to take up arms, when they found themselves unable to prevail, and that Galba had approved of the deed, either from weakness of character, or to avoid investigation into the circumstances of acts which could not be altered. Both executions, however, were unfavorably regarded; indeed, when a ruler once becomes unpopular, all his acts, be they good or bad, tell against him. The freedmen in their excessive power were now putting up everything for sale; the slaves caught with greedy hands at immediate gain, and, reflecting on their master's age, hastened to be rich. The new court had the same abuses as the old, abuses as grievous as ever, but not so readily excused. Even the age of Galba caused ridicule and disgust among those whose associations were with the youth of Nero, and who were accustomed, as is the fashion of the vulgar, to value their emperors by the beauty and grace of their persons.

Such, as far as one can speak of so vast a multitude, was the state of feeling at Rome. . . . (I, 1-8)

[Galba's murder and the accession of Otho. Rome had still to live through the brief rule of Vitellius before the

*Flavian dynasty—Vespasian and his sons, Titus and Domi-
tian—re-established order.*]

Meanwhile, appalled by the roar of the increasing sedition
and by the shouts which reached the city, Piso had overtaken
Galba, who in the interval had quitted the palace, and was
approaching the Forum. Already Marius Celsus had brought
back discouraging tidings. And now some advised that the Emperor should return to the palace, others that he should make
for the Capitol, many again that he should occupy the Rostra,
though most did but oppose the opinions of others, while, as
ever happens in these ill-starred counsels, plans for which the
opportunity had slipped away seemed the best. It is said that
Laco, without Galba's knowledge, meditated the death of Vinius,
either hoping by this execution to appease the fury of the soldiers, or believing him to be an accomplice of Otho, or, it may
be, out of mere hatred. The time and the place however made
him hesitate; he knew that a massacre once begun is not easily
checked. His plan too was disconcerted by a succession of alarming tidings, and the desertion of immediate adherents. So languid was now the zeal of those who had at first been eager to
display their fidelity and courage.

Galba was hurried to and fro with every movement of the
surging crowd; the halls and temples all around were thronged
with spectators of this mournful sight. Not a voice was heard
from the people or even from the rabble. Everywhere were
terror-stricken countenances, and ears turned to catch every
sound. It was a scene neither of agitation nor of repose, but
there reigned the silence of profound alarm and profound indignation. Otho however was told that they were arming the mob.
He ordered his men to hurry on at full speed, and to anticipate
the danger. Then did Roman soldiers rush forward like men
who had to drive a Vologeses or Pacorus from the ancestral
throne of the Arsacidae, not as though they were hastening to
murder their aged and defenseless Emperor. In all the terror
of their arms, and at the full speed of their horses, they burst
into the Forum, thrusting aside the crowd and trampling on the

Senate. Neither the sight of the Capitol, nor the sanctity of the overhanging temples, nor the thought of rulers past or future, could deter them from committing a crime, which anyone succeeding to power must avenge.

When this armed array was seen to approach, the standard-bearer of the cohort that escorted Galba (he is said to have been one Atilius Vergilio) tore off and dashed upon the ground Galba's effigy. At this signal the feeling of all the troops declared itself plainly for Otho. The Forum was deserted by the flying populace. Weapons were pointed against all who hesitated. Near the lake of Curtius, Galba was thrown out of his litter and fell to the ground, through the alarm of his bearers. His last words have been variously reported according as men hated or admired him. Some have said that he asked in a tone of entreaty what wrong he had done, and begged a few days for the payment of the donative. The more general account is that he voluntarily offered his neck to the murderers, and bade them haste and strike, if it seemed to be for the good of the Commonwealth. To those who slew him it mattered not what he said. About the actual murderer nothing is clearly known. Some have recorded the name of Terentius, an enrolled pensioner, others that of Lecanius; but it is the current report that one Camurius, a soldier of the 15th legion, completely severed his throat by treading his sword down upon it. The rest of the soldiers foully mutilated his arms and legs, for his breast was protected, and in their savage ferocity inflicted many wounds even on the headless trunk. (*I, 39-41*)

There was, we are told, no death of which Otho heard with greater joy, no head which he surveyed with so insatiable a gaze. Perhaps it was, that his mind was then for the first time relieved from all anxiety, and so had leisure to rejoice; perhaps there was with Galba something to recall departed majesty, with Vinius some thought of old friendship, which troubled with mournful images even that ruthless heart; Piso's death, as that of an enemy and a rival, he felt to be a right and lawful subject of rejoicing. The heads were fixed upon poles and carried about among the standards of the cohorts, close to the eagle of the legion, while those who had struck the blow, those who had been present, those who whether truly or falsely boasted of the act, as of some great and memorable achievement, vied in displaying their bloodstained hands. Vitellius afterwards found more than 120 memorials from persons who claimed a reward for some notable service on that day. All these persons he ordered to be sought out and slain, not to honor Galba, but to comply with the traditional policy of rulers, who thus provide protection for the present and vengeance for the future.

One would have thought it a different Senate, a different people. All rushed to the camp, outran those who were close to them, and struggled with those who were before, inveighed against Galba, praised the wisdom of the soldiers, covered the hand of Otho with kisses; the more insincere their demonstrations, the more they multiplied them. Nor did Otho repulse the advances of individuals, while he checked the greed and ferocity of the soldiers by word and look. They demanded that Marius Celsus, consul elect, Galba's faithful friend to the very last moment, should be led to execution, loathing his energy and integrity as if they were vices. It was evident that they were seeking to begin massacre and plunder, and the proscription of all the most virtuous citizens, and Otho had not yet sufficient authority to prevent crime, though he could command it. He feigned anger, and ordered him to be loaded with chains, declaring that he was to suffer more signal punishment, and thus he rescued him from immediate destruction.

Every thing was then ordered according to the will of the soldiery. The Praetorians chose their own prefects. . . . A demand was then made, that the fees for furloughs usually paid to the centurions should be abolished. These the common soldiers paid as a kind of annual tribute. A fourth part of every company might be scattered on furlough, or even loiter about the camp, provided that they paid the fees to the centurions. No one cared about the amount of the tax, or the way in which it was raised. It was by robbery, plunder, or the most servile occupations that the soldiers' holiday was purchased. The man with the fullest purse was worn out with toil and cruel usage till he bought his furlough. His means exhausted by this out-lay, and his energies utterly relaxed by idleness, the once rich and vigorous soldier returned to his company a poor and spirit-less man. One after another was ruined by the same poverty and license, and rushed into mutiny and dissension, and finally into civil war. Otho, however, not to alienate the affections of the centurions by an act of bounty to the ranks, promised that his own purse should pay these annual sums. It was undoubtedly a salutary reform, and was afterwards under good emperors established as a permanent rule of the service. . . .

A day spent in crime found its last horror in the rejoicings that concluded it. The Praetor of the city summoned the Senate; the rest of the magistrates vied with each other in their flatteries. The Senators hastily assembled and conferred by decree upon Otho the tribunician office, the name of Augustus, and every imperial honor. All strove to extinguish the remembrance of those taunts and invectives, which had been thrown out at ran-dom, and which no one supposed were rankling in his heart. Whether he had forgotten, or only postponed his resentment, the shortness of his reign left undecided. The Forum yet streamed with blood, when he was borne in a litter over heaps of dead to the Capitol, and thence to the palace. He suffered the bodies to be given up for burial, and to be burnt. . . . (I, 44-47)

The body of Galba lay for a long time neglected, and subjected, through the license which the darkness permitted, to a thousand indignities, till Argius his steward, who had been one of his slaves, gave it a humble burial in his master's private gardens. His head, which the sutlers and camp-followers had fixed on a pole and mangled, was found only the next day in front of the tomb of Patrobius, a freedman of Nero's whom Galba had executed. It was put with the body, which had by that time been reduced to ashes. Such was the end of Servius Galba, who in his seventy-three years had lived prosperously through the reigns of five Emperors, and had been more fortu-nate under the rule of others than he was in his own. His family could boast an ancient nobility, his wealth was great. His char-acter was of an average kind, rather free from vices, than dis-

tinguished by virtues. He was not regardless of fame, nor yet
vainly fond of it. Other men's money he did not covet, with
his own he was parsimonious, with that of the State avaricious.
To his freedmen and friends he showed a forbearance, which,
when he had fallen into worthy hands, could not be blamed;
when, however, these persons were worthless, he was even cul-
pably blind. The nobility of his birth and the perils of the times
made what was really indolence pass for wisdom. While in the
vigor of life, he enjoyed a high military reputation in Germany;
as proconsul he ruled Africa with moderation, and when advanced in years showed the same integrity in Eastern Spain.
He seemed greater than a subject while he was yet in a subject's
rank, and by common consent would have been pronounced
equal to empire, had he never been emperor. (I, 49)

THE LIFE OF AGRICOLA

[*Cnaeus Julius Agricola, the father-in-law of Tacitus, was governor of Britain under Domitian. Tacitus' brief biography sums up Agricola's achievements and ends on a passionate note.*]

To bequeath to posterity a record of the deeds and characters of distinguished men is an ancient practice which even the present age, careless as it is of its own sons, has not abandoned whenever some great and conspicuous excellence has conquered and risen superior to that failing, common to petty and to great states, blindness and hostility to goodness. But in days gone by, as there was a greater inclination and a more open path to the achievement of memorable actions, so the man of highest genius was led by the simple reward of a good conscience to hand on without partiality or self-seeking the remembrance of greatness. Many too thought that to write their own lives showed the confidence of integrity rather than presumption. Of Rutilius and Scaurus no one doubted the honesty or questioned the motives. So true is it that merit is best appreciated by the age in which it thrives most easily. But in these days, I, who have to record the life of one who has passed away, must crave an indulgence, which I should not have had to ask had I only to inveigh against an age so cruel, so hostile to all virtue. (*1*)

Now at last our spirit is returning. And yet, though at the dawn of a most happy age Nerva Caesar blended things once irreconcilable, sovereignty and freedom, though Nerva Trajan is now daily augmenting the prosperity of the time, and though the public safety has not only our hopes and good wishes, but has also the certain pledge of their fulfillment, still, from the necessary condition of human frailty, the remedy works less quickly than the disease. As our bodies grow but slowly, perish in a moment, so it is easier to crush than to revive genius and its pursuits. Besides, the charm of indolence steals over us, and the idleness which at first we loathed we afterward love. What if during those fifteen years, a large portion of human life, many were cut off by ordinary casualties, and the ablest fell victims to the Emperor's rage, if a few of us survive, I may almost say, not only others but our ownselves, survive, though there have been taken from the midst of life those many years which brought the young in dumb silence to old age, and the old almost to the very verge and end of existence! Yet we shall not regret that we have told, though in language unskillful and unadorned, the story of past servitude, and borne our testimony to present happiness. Meanwhile this book, intended to do honor to Agricola, my father-in-law, will, as an expression of filial regard, be commended, or at least excused. (3)

Of this series of events, though not exaggerated in the dispatches of Agricola by any boastfulness of language, Domitian heard, as was his wont, with joy in his face but anxiety in his heart. He felt conscious that all men laughed at his late mock triumph over Germany, for which there had been purchased from traders people whose dress and hair might be made to resemble those of captives, whereas now a real and splendid victory, with the destruction of thousands of the enemy, was being celebrated with just applause. It was, he thought, a very alarming thing for him that the name of a subject should be raised above that of the Emperor; it was to no purpose that he had driven into obscurity the pursuit of forensic eloquence and the graceful accomplishments of civil life, if another were to forestall the distinctions of war. To other glories he could more easily shut his eyes, but the greatness of a good general was a truly imperial quality. Harassed by these anxieties, and absorbed in an incommunicable trouble, a sure prognostic of some cruel purpose, he decided that it was best for the present to suspend his hatred until the freshness of Agricola's renown and his popularity with the army should begin to pass away.

For Agricola was still the governor of Britain. Accordingly the Emperor ordered that the usual triumphal decorations, the honor of a laureled statue, and all that is commonly given in place of the triumphal procession, with the addition of many laudatory expressions, should be decreed in the senate, together with a hint to the effect that Agricola was to have the province of Syria, then vacant by the death of Atilius Rufus, a man of consular rank, and generally reserved for men of distinction. It was believed by many persons that one of the freedmen employed on confidential services was sent to Agricola, bearing a dispatch in which Syria was offered him, and with instructions to deliver it should he be in Britain; that this freedman in crossing the straits met Agricola, and without even saluting him made his way back to Domitian; though I cannot say whether the story is true, or is only a fiction invented to suit the Emperor's character.

Meanwhile Agricola had handed over his province in peace and safety to his successor. And not to make his entrance into Rome conspicuous by the concourse of welcoming throngs, he avoided the attentions of his friends by entering the city at night, and at night too, according to orders, proceeded to the palace, where, having been received with a hurried embrace and without a word being spoken, he mingled in the crowd of courtiers. Anxious henceforth to temper the military renown, which annoys men of peace, with other merits, he studiously cultivated retirement and leisure, simple in dress, courteous in conversation, and never accompanied but by one or two friends, so that the many who commonly judge of great men by their external grandeur, after having seen and attentively surveyed him, asked the secret of a greatness which but few could explain.

During this time he was frequently accused before Domitian in his absence, and in his absence acquitted. The cause of his danger lay not in any crime, nor in any complaint of injury, but in a ruler who was the foe of virtue, in his own renown, and in that worst class of enemies—the men who praise. And then followed such days for the commonwealth as would not suffer Agricola to be forgotten; days when so many of our armies were lost in Moesia, Dacia, Germany, and Pannonia, through the rashness or cowardice of our generals, when so many of our officers were besieged and captured with so many of our auxiliaries, when it was no longer the boundaries of empire and the banks of rivers which were imperiled, but the winter quarters of our legions and the possession of our territories. And so when disaster followed upon disaster, and the entire year was marked by destruction and slaughter, the voice of the people called Agricola to the command; for they all contrasted his vigor, firmness, and experience in war, with the inertness and timidity of other generals. This talk, it is quite certain, assailed the ears of the Emperor himself, while affection and loyalty in the best of his freedmen, malice and envy in the worst, kindled the anger of a prince ever inclined to evil. And so at once, by his own excellences and by the faults of others, Agricola was hurried headlong to a perilous elevation.

The year had now arrived in which the pro-consulate of Asia or Africa was to fall to him by lot, and, as Civica had been lately murdered, Agricola did not want a warning, or Domitian a precedent. Persons well acquainted with the Emperor's feelings came to ask Agricola, as if on their own account, whether he would go. First they hinted their purpose by praises of tranquility and leisure; then offered their services in procuring acceptance for his excuses; and at last, throwing off all disguise, brought him by entreaties and threats to Domitian. The Emperor, armed beforehand with hypocrisy, and assuming a haughty demeanor, listened to his prayer that he might be excused, and having granted his request allowed himself to be formally thanked, nor blushed to grant so sinister a favor. But the salary usually granted to a pro-consul, and which he had himself given to some governors, he did not bestow on Agricola, either because he was offended at its not having been asked, or was warned by his conscience that he might be thought to have purchased the refusal which he had commanded. It is, indeed, human nature to hate the man whom you have injured; yet the Emperor, notwithstanding his irascible temper and an implacability proportioned to his reserve, was softened by the moderation and prudence of Agricola, who neither by a perverse obstinacy nor an idle parade of freedom challenged fame or provoked his fate. Let it be known to those whose habit it is to admire the disregard of authority, that there may be great men even under bad emperors, and that obedience and submission, when joined to activity and vigor, may attain a glory which most men reach only by a perilous career, utterly useless to the state, and closed by an ostentatious death.

The end of his life, a deplorable calamity to us and a grief to his friends, was regarded with concern even by strangers and those who knew him not. The common people and this busy population continually inquired at his house, and talked of him in public places and in private gatherings. No man when he heard of Agricola's death could either be glad or at once forget it. Men's sympathy was increased by a prevalent rumor that he was destroyed by poison. For myself, I have nothing which I should venture to state for fact. Certainly during the whole of his illness the Emperor's chief freedmen and confidential physicians came more frequently than is usual with a court which pays its visits by means of messengers. This was, perhaps, solicitude, perhaps espionage. Certain it is, that on the last day the very agonies of his dying moments were reported by a succession of couriers, and no one believed that there would be such haste about tidings which would be heard with regret. Yet in his manner and countenance the Emperor displayed some signs of sorrow, for he could now forget his enmity, and it was easier to conceal his joy than his fear. It was well known that on reading the will, in which he was named co-heir with Agricola's excellent wife and most dutiful daughter, he expressed delight, as if it had been a complimentary choice. So blinded and perverted was his mind by incessant flattery, that he did not know that it was only a bad Emperor whom a good father would make his heir.

Agricola was born on the 13th of June, in the third consulate of Caius Caesar; he died on the 23rd of August, during the consulate of Collega and Priscus, being in the fifty-sixth year of his age. Should posterity wish to know something of his appearance, it was graceful rather than commanding. There was nothing formidable in his appearance; a gracious look predominated. One would easily believe him a good man, and willingly believe him to be great. As for himself, though taken from us in the prime of a vigorous manhood, yet, as far as glory is concerned, his life was of the longest. Those true blessings, indeed, which consist in virtue, he had fully attained; and on one who had reached the honors of a consulate and a triumph, what more had fortune to bestow? Immense wealth had no attractions for him, and wealth he had, even to splendor. As his daughter and his wife survived him, it may be thought that he was even fortunate—fortunate, in that while his honors had suffered no eclipse, while his fame was at its height, while his kindred and his friends still prospered, he escaped from the evil to come. For, though to survive until the dawn of this most happy age and to see a Trajan on the throne was what he would speculate upon in previsions and wishes confided to my ears, yet he had this mighty compensation for his premature death, that he was spared those later years during which Domitian, leaving now no interval or breathing space of time, but, as it were, with one continuous blow, drained the life-blood of the Commonwealth.

Agricola did not see the senate-house besieged, or the senate hemmed in by armed men, or so many of our consulars falling at one single massacre, or so many of Rome's noblest ladies exiles and fugitives. Carus Metius had as yet the distinction of but one victory, and the noisy counsels of Messalinus were not heard beyond the walls of Alba, and Massa Baebius was then answering for his life. It was not long before our hands dragged Helvidius to prison, before we gazed on the dying looks of Mauricus and Rusticus, before we were steeped in Senecio's innocent blood. Even Nero turned his eyes away, and did not gaze upon the atrocities which he ordered; with Domitian it was the chief part of our miseries to see and to be seen, to know that our sighs were being recorded, to have, ever ready to note the pallid looks of so many faces, that savage countenance reddened with the hue with which he defied shame.

Thou wast indeed fortunate, Agricola, not only in the splendor of thy life, but in the opportune moment of thy death. Thou submittedst to thy fate, so they tell us who were present to hear thy last words, with courage and cheerfulness, seeming to be doing all thou couldst to give thine Emperor full acquittal. As for me and thy daughter, besides all the bitterness of a father's loss, it increases our sorrow that it was not permitted us to watch over thy failing health, to comfort thy weakness, to satisfy ourselves with those looks, those embraces. Assuredly we should have received some precepts, some utterances to fix in our inmost hearts. This is the bitterness of our sorrow, this the smart of our wound, that from the circumstance of so long an absence thou wast lost to us four years before. Doubtless, best of fathers, with that most loving wife at thy side, all the dues of affection were abundantly paid thee, yet with too few tears thou wast laid to thy rest, and in the light of thy last day there was something for which thine eyes longed in vain.

If there is any dwelling-place for the spirits of the just; if, as the wise believe, noble souls do not perish with the body, rest thou in peace; and call us, thy family, from weak regrets and womanish laments to the contemplation of thy virtues, for which we must not weep nor beat the breast. Let us honor thee not so much with transitory praises as with our reverence, and, if our powers permit us, with our emulation. That will be true respect, that the true affection of thy nearest kin. This, too, is what I would enjoin on daughter and wife, to honor the memory of that father, that husband, by pondering in their hearts all his words and acts, by cherishing the features and lineaments of his character rather than those of his person. It is not that I would forbid the likenesses which are wrought in marble or in bronze; but as the faces of men, so all similitudes of the face are weak and perishable things, while the fashion of the soul is everlasting, such as may be expressed not in some foreign substance, or by the help of art, but in our own lives. Whatever we loved, whatever we admired in Agricola, survives, and will survive in the hearts of men, in the succession of the ages, in the fame that waits on noble deeds. Over many indeed, of those who have gone before, as over the inglorious and ignoble, the waves of oblivion will roll; Agricola, made known to posterity by history and tradition, will live for ever. (39-46)

THE GERMANIA

[*The death of Domitian and the new day of freedom in-augurated by Nerva and Trajan made it possible for Tacitus to publish his Agricola and Germania A.D. 98. The latter work is the only ancient study we possess that describes solely and extensively the customs of a people, their land and institutions. Tacitus' main purpose was to inform his readers about a neighboring, tribal country, but it also gave him, as a moralist, the opportunity to stress the advantages of simple living.*]

Germany is separated from the Galli, the Rhaeti, and Pannonii by the rivers Rhine and Danube; mountain ranges, or the fear which each feels for the other, divide it from the Sarmatae and Daci. Elsewhere ocean girds it, embracing broad peninsulas and islands of unexplored extent, where certain tribes and kingdoms are newly known to us, revealed by war. The Rhine springs from a precipitous and inaccessible height of the Rhaetian Alps, bends slightly westward, and mingles with the Northern Ocean. The Danube pours down from the gradual and gently rising slope of Mount Abnoba, and visits many nations, to force its way at last through six channels into the Black Sea; a seventh mouth is lost in marshes.

The Germans themselves I should regard as aboriginal, and not mixed at all with other races through immigration or inter-course. For, in former times, it was not by land but on shipboard that those who sought to emigrate would arrive; and the boundless and, so to speak, hostile ocean beyond us is seldom entered by a sail from our world. And, beside the perils of rough and unknown

seas, who would leave Asia, or Africa, or Italy for Germany, with
its wild country, its inclement skies, its sullen manners and aspect,
unless indeed it were his home? In their ancient songs, their only
way of remembering or recording the past, they celebrate an earthborn god, Tuisto, and his son Mannus, as the origin of their race,
as their founders. To Mannus they assign three sons, from whose
names, they say, the coast tribes are called Ingaevones; those of
the interior, Herminones; all the rest, Istaevones. Some, with the
freedom of conjecture permitted by antiquity, assert that the god
had several descendants, and the nation several appellations, as
Marsi, Gambrivii, Suevi, Vandilii, and that these are genuine old
names. The name Germany, on the other hand, they say is
modern and newly introduced, from the fact that the tribes which
first crossed the Rhine and drove out the Gauls, and are now called
Tungrians, were then called Germans. Thus what was the name
of a tribe, and not of a race, gradually prevailed, till all called
themselves by this self-invented name of Germans, which the conquerors had first employed to inspire terror.

They say that Hercules, too, once visited them; and when
going into battle, they sing of him first of all heroes. They have
also those songs of theirs, by the recital of which ("barditus," they
call it) they rouse their courage, while from the note they augur
the result of the approaching conflict. For, as their line shouts,
they inspire or feel alarm. It is not so much an articulate sound,
as a general cry of valor. They aim chiefly at a harsh note and a
confused roar, putting their shields to their mouth, so that, by
reverberation, it may swell into a fuller and deeper sound. Ulysses,
too, is believed by some, in his long legendary wanderings, to
have found his way into this ocean, and, having visited German
soil, to have founded and named the town of Asciburgium, which
stands on the bank of the Rhine, and is to this day inhabited. They
even say that an altar dedicated to Ulysses, with the addition of
the name of his father, Laertes, was formerly discovered on this
same spot, and that certain monuments and tombs, with Greek
inscriptions, still exist on the borders of Germany and Rhaetia.
These statements I have no intention of sustaining by proofs, or

of refuting; every one may believe or disbelieve them as he feels inclined.

For my own part, I agree with those who think that the tribes of Germany are free from all taint of intermarriages with foreign nations, and that they appear as a distinct, unmixed race, like none but themselves. Hence, too, the same physical peculiarities throughout so vast a population. All have fierce blue eyes, red hair, huge frames, fit only for a sudden exertion. They are less able to bear laborious work. Heat and thirst they cannot in the least endure; to cold and hunger their climate and their soil inure them.

Their country, though somewhat various in appearance, yet generally either bristles with forests or reeks with swamps; it is more rainy on the side of Gaul, bleaker on that of Noricum and Pannonia. It is productive of grain, but unfavorable to fruit-bearing trees; it is rich in flocks and herds, but these are for the most part undersized, and even the cattle have not their usual beauty or noble head. It is number that is chiefly valued; they are in fact the most highly prized, indeed the only riches of the people. Silver and gold the gods have refused to them, whether in kindness or in anger I cannot say. I would not, however, affirm that no vein of German soil produces gold or silver, for who has ever made a search? They care but little to possess or use them. You may see among them vessels of silver, which have been presented to their envoys and chieftains, held as cheap as those of clay. The border population, however, value gold and silver for their commercial utility, and are familiar with, and show preference for, some of our coins. The tribes of the interior use the simpler and more ancient practice of the barter of commodities. They like the old and well-known money, coins milled, or showing a two-horse chariot. They likewise prefer silver to gold, not from any special liking, but because a large number of silver pieces is more convenient for use among dealers in cheap and common articles.

Even iron is not plentiful with them, as we infer from the character of their weapons. But few use swords or long lances.

They carry a spear (*framea* is their name for it), with a narrow and short head, but so sharp and easy to wield that the same weapon serves, according to circumstances, for close or distant conflict. As for the horse soldier, he is satisfied with a shield and spear; the foot soldiers also scatter showers of missiles, each man having several and hurling them to an immense distance, and being naked or lightly clad with a little cloak. There is no display about their equipment: their shields alone are marked with very choice colors. A few only have corslets, and just one or two here and there a metal or leather helmet. Their horses are remarkable neither for beauty nor for fleetness. Nor are they taught various evolutions after our fashion, but are driven straight forward, or so as to make one wheel to the right in such a compact body that none is left behind another. On the whole, one would say that their chief strength is in their infantry, which fights along with the cavalry; admirably adapted to the action of the latter is the swiftness of certain foot soldiers, who are picked from the entire youth of their country, and stationed in front of the line. Their number is fixed—a hundred from each canton; and from this they take their name among their countrymen, so that what was originally a mere number has now become a title of distinction. Their line of battle is drawn up in a wedge-like formation. To give ground, provided you return to the attack, is considered prudence rather than cowardice. The bodies of their slain they carry off even in indecisive engagements. To abandon your shield is the basest of crimes; nor may a man thus disgraced be present at the sacred rites, or enter their council; many, indeed, after escaping from battle, have ended their infamy with the halter.

They choose their kings by birth, their generals for merit. These kings have not unlimited or arbitrary power, and the generals do more by example than by authority. If they are energetic, if they are conspicuous, if they fight in the front, they lead because they are admired. But to reprimand, to imprison, even to flog, is permitted to the priests alone, and that not as a punishment, or at the general's bidding, but, as it were, by the mandate of the god whom they believe to inspire the warrior. They also carry with them into battle certain figures and images taken from their sacred groves. And what most stimulates their courage is that their squadrons or battalions, instead of being formed by chance or by a fortuitous gathering, are composed of families and clans. Close by them, too, are those dearest to them, so that they hear the shrieks of women, the cries of infants. *They* are to every man the most sacred witnesses of his bravery—*they* are his most generous applauders. The soldier brings his wounds to mother and wife, who shrink not from counting or even demanding them and who administer both food and encouragement to the combatants.

Tradition says that armies already wavering and giving way have been rallied by women who, with earnest entreaties and bosoms laid bare, have vividly represented the horrors of captivity, which the Germans fear with such extreme dread on behalf of their women, that the strongest tie by which a state can be bound is the being required to give, among the number of hostages, maidens of noble birth. They even believe that the sex has a certain sanctity and prescience, and they do not despise their counsels, or make light of their answers. In Vespasian's days we saw Veleda, long regarded by many as a divinity. In former times, too, they venerated Aurinia, and many other women, but not with servile flatteries, or with sham deification.

Mercury [Wodan] is the deity whom they chiefly worship, and on certain days they deem it right to sacrifice to him even with human victims. Hercules [Thor] and Mars [Tiu] they appease with more lawful offerings. Some of the Suevi also sacrifice to Isis. Of the occasion and origin of this foreign rite I have discovered nothing, but that the image, which is fashioned like a light galley, indicates an imported worship. The Germans, however, do not consider it consistent with the grandeur of celestial beings to confine the gods within walls, or to liken them to the form of any human countenance. They consecrate woods and groves, and they apply the names of deities to the abstraction which they see only in spiritual worship.

Augury and divination by lot no people practice more diligently. The use of the lots is simple. A little bough is lopped off a fruit-bearing tree, and cut into small pieces; these are distinguished by certain marks, and thrown carelessly and at random over a white garment. In public questions the priest of the particular state, in private the father of the family, invokes the gods, and, with his eyes toward heaven, takes up each piece three times, and finds in them a meaning according to the mark previously impressed on them. If they prove unfavorable, there is no further consultation that day about the matter; if they sanction it, the confirmation of augury is still required. For they are also familiar with the practice of consulting the notes and the flight of birds. It is peculiar to this people to seek omens and monitions from horses. Kept at the public expense, in these same woods and groves, are white horses, pure from the taint of earthly labor; these are yoked to a sacred car, and accompanied by the priest and the king, or chief of the tribe, who note their neighings and snortings. No species of augury is more trusted, not only by the people and by the nobility, but also by the priests, who regard themselves as the ministers of the gods, and the horses as acquainted with their will. They have also another method of observing auspices, by which they seek to learn the result of an important war. Having taken, by whatever means, a prisoner from the tribe with whom they are at war, they pit him against a picked man of their own tribe, each combatant using the weapons of their country. The victory of the one or the other is accepted as an indication of the issue.

About minor matters the chiefs deliberate, about the more important the whole tribe. Yet even when the final decision rests with the people, the affair is always thoroughly discussed by the chiefs. They assemble, except in the case of a sudden emergency, on certain fixed days, either at new or at full moon; for this they consider the most auspicious season for the transaction of business. Instead of reckoning by days as we do, they reckon by nights, and in this manner fix both their ordinary and their legal appointments. Night they regard as bringing on day. Their freedom has this disadvantage, that they do not meet simultaneously or as they are bidden, but two or three days are wasted in the delays of assembling. When the multitude think proper, they sit down armed. Silence is proclaimed by the priests, who have on these occasions the right of keeping order. Then the king or the chief, according to age, birth, distinction in war, or eloquence, is heard, more because he has influence to persuade than because he has power to command. If his sentiments displease them, they reject them with murmurs; if they are satisfied, they brandish their spears. The most complimentary form of assent is to express approbation with their weapons.

In their councils an accusation may be preferred or a capital crime prosecuted. Penalties are distinguished according to the offense. Traitors and deserters are hanged on trees; the coward, the unwarlike, the man stained with abominable vices, is plunged into the mire of the morass, with a hurdle put over him. This distinction in punishment means that crime, they think, ought, in being punished, to be exposed, while infamy ought to be buried out of sight. Lighter offenses, too, have penalties proportioned to them; he who is convicted, is fined in a certain number of horses or of cattle. Half of the fine is paid to the king or to the state, half to the person whose wrongs are avenged and to his relatives. In these same councils they also elect the chief magistrates, who administer law in the cantons and the towns. Each of these has a hundred associates chosen from the people, who support him with their advice and influence.

They transact no public or private business without being armed. It is not, however, usual for anyone to wear arms till the state has recognized his power to use them. Then in the presence of the council one of the chiefs, or the young man's father, or some kinsman, equips him with a shield and a spear. These arms are what the toga is with us, the first honor with which youth is invested. Up to this time he is regarded as a member of a household, afterward as a member of the commonwealth. Very noble birth or great services rendered by the father secure for lads the rank of a chief; such lads attach themselves to men of mature strength and of long approved valor. It is no shame to be seen among a chief's followers. Even in his escort there are gradations of rank, dependent on the choice of the man to whom they are attached. These followers vie keenly with each other as to who shall rank first with his chief, the chiefs as to who shall have the most numerous and the bravest followers. It is an honor as well as a source of strength to be thus always surrounded by a large body of picked youths; it is an ornament in peace and a defense in war. And not only in his own tribe but also in the neighboring states it is the renown and glory of a chief to be distinguished for the number and valor of his followers, for such a man is courted by embassies, is honored with presents, and the very prestige of his name often settles a war.

When they go into battle, it is a disgrace for the chief to be surpassed in valor, a disgrace for his followers not to equal the valor of the chief. And it is an infamy and a reproach for life to have survived the chief, and returned from the field. To defend, to protect him, to ascribe one's own brave deeds to his renown, is the height of loyalty. The chief fights for victory; his vassals fight for their chief. If their native state sinks into the sloth of prolonged peace and repose, many of its noble youths voluntarily seek those tribes which are waging some war, both because inaction is odious to their race, and because they win renown more readily in the midst of peril, and cannot maintain a numerous following except by violence and war. Indeed, men look to the liberality of their chief for their war-horse and their blood-stained and victorious lance. Feasts and entertainments, which, though inelegant, are plentifully furnished, are their only pay. The means of this bounty come from war and rapine. Nor are they as easily persuaded to plow the earth and to wait for the year's produce as to challenge an enemy and earn the honor of wounds. Nay, they actually think it tame and stupid to acquire by the sweat of toil what they might win by their blood.

Whenever they are not fighting, they pass much of their time in the chase, and still more in idleness, giving themselves up to sleep and to feasting, the bravest and the most warlike doing nothing, and surrendering the management of the household, of the home, and of the land, to the women, the old men, and all the weakest members of the family. They themselves lie buried in sloth, a strange combination in their nature that the same men should be so fond of idleness, so averse to peace. It is the custom of the states to bestow by voluntary and individual contribution on the chiefs a present of cattle or of grain, which, while accepted as a compliment, supplies their wants. They are particularly delighted by gifts from neighboring tribes, which are sent not only by individuals but also by the state, such as choice steeds, heavy armor, trappings, and neck-chains. We have now taught them to accept money also.

It is well known that the nations of Germany have no cities, and that they do not even tolerate closely contiguous dwellings. They live scattered and apart, just as a spring, a meadow, or a wood has attracted them. Their villages they do not arrange in our fashion, with the buildings connected and joined together, but every person surrounds his dwelling with an open space, either as a precaution against the disasters of fire, or because they do not know how to build. No use is made by them of stone or tile; they employ timber for all purposes, rude masses without ornament or attractiveness. Some parts of their buildings they stain more carefully with a clay so clear and bright that it resembles painting, or a colored design. They are wont also to dig out subterranean caves, and pile on them great heaps of dung, as a shelter from winter and as a receptacle for the year's produce, for by such places they mitigate the rigor of the cold. And should an enemy approach, he lays waste the open country, while what is hidden and buried is either not known to exist, or else escapes him from the very fact that it has to be searched for.

They all wrap themselves in a cloak which is fastened with a clasp, or, if this is not forthcoming, with a thorn, leaving the rest of their persons bare. They pass whole days on the hearth by the fire. The wealthiest are distinguished by a dress which is not flowing, like that of the Sarmatians and Parthians, but is tight, and exhibits each limb. They also wear the skins of wild beasts; the tribes on the Rhine and Danube in a careless fashion, those of the interior with more elegance, as not obtaining other clothing by commerce. These select certain animals, the hides of which they strip off and vary them with the spotted skins of beasts, the produce of the outer ocean, and of seas unknown to us. The women have the same dress as the men, except that they generally wrap themselves in linen garments, which they embroider with purple, and do not lengthen out the upper part of their clothing into sleeves. The upper and lower arm is thus bare, and the nearest part of the bosom is also exposed.

Their marriage code, however, is strict, and indeed no part of their manners is more praiseworthy. Almost alone among barbarians they are content with one wife, except a very few among them, and these not from sensuality, but because their noble birth procures for them many offers of alliance. The wife does not bring a dower to the husband, but the husband to the wife. The parents and relatives are present, and pass judgment on the marriage gifts, gifts not meant to suit a woman's taste, nor such as a bride would deck herself with, but oxen, a caparisoned steed, a shield, a lance, and a sword. With these presents the wife is espoused, and she herself in her turn brings her husband a gift of arms. This they count their strongest bond of union, these their sacred mysteries, these their gods of marriage. Lest the woman should think herself to stand apart from aspirations after noble deeds and from the perils of war, she is reminded by the ceremony which inaugurates marriage that she is her husband's partner in toil and danger, destined to suffer and to dare with him alike both in peace and in war. The yoked oxen, the harnessed steed, the gift of arms, proclaim this fact. She must live and die with the feeling that she is receiving what she must hand down to her children neither tarnished nor depreciated, what future daughters-in-law may receive, and may be so passed on to her grandchildren.

Thus with their virtue protected they live uncorrupted by the allurements of public shows or the stimulant of feastings. Clandestine correspondence is equally unknown to men and women. Very rare for so numerous a population is adultery, the punishment for which is prompt, and in the husband's power. Having cut off the hair of the adulteress and stripped her naked, he expels her from the house in the presence of her kinsfolk, and then flogs her through the whole village. The loss of chastity meets with no indulgence; neither beauty, youth, nor wealth will procure the culprit a husband. No one in Germany laughs at vice, nor do they call it the fashion to corrupt and to be corrupted.

Still better is the condition of those states in which only maidens are given in marriage, and where the hopes and expectations of a bride are then finally terminated. They receive one husband, as having one body and one life, that they may have no thoughts beyond, no further-reaching desires, that they may love not so much the husband as the married state. To limit the number of their children or to destroy any of their subsequent offspring is accounted infamous, and good habits are here more effectual than good laws elsewhere.

In every household the children, naked and filthy, grow up with those stout frames and limbs which we so much admire. Every mother suckles her own offspring, and never entrusts it to servants and nurses. The master is not distinguished from the slave by being brought up with greater delicacy. Both live amid the same flocks and lie on the same ground till the freeborn are distinguished by age and recognized by merit. The young men marry late, and their vigor is thus unimpaired. Nor are the maidens hurried into marriage; the same age and a similar stature is required; well-matched and vigorous they wed, and the offspring reproduce the strength of the parents. Sister's sons are held in as much esteem by their uncles as by their fathers; indeed, some regard the relation as even more sacred and binding, and prefer it in receiving hostages, thinking thus to secure a stronger hold on the affections and a wider bond for the family. But every man's own children are his heirs and successors, and there are no wills. Should there be no issue, the next in succession to the property are his brothers and his uncles on either side. The more relatives he has, the more numerous his connections, the more honored is his old age; nor are there any advantages in childlessness.

It is a duty among them to adopt the feuds as well as the friendships of a father or a kinsman. These feuds are not implacable; even homicide is expiated by the payment of a certain number of cattle and of sheep, and the satisfaction is accepted by the entire family, greatly to the advantage of the state, since feuds are dangerous in proportion to a people's freedom.

No nation indulges more profusely in entertainments and hospitality. To exclude any human being from their roof is thought impious; every German, according to his means, receives his guest with a well-furnished table. When his supplies are exhausted, he who was but now the host becomes the guide and companion to further hospitality, and without invitation they go to the next house. It matters not; they are entertained with like cordiality. No one distinguishes between an acquaintance and a stranger, as regards the rights of hospitality. It is usual to give the departing guest whatever he may ask for, and a present in return is asked with as little hesitation. They are greatly charmed with gifts, but they expect no return for what they give, nor feel any obligation for what they receive.

On waking from sleep, which they generally prolong to a late hour of the day, they take a bath, oftenest of warm water, which suits a country where winter is the longest of the seasons. After their bath they take their meal, each having a separate seat and table of his own. Then they go armed to business, or no less often to their festal meetings. To pass an entire day and night in drinking disgraces no one. Their quarrels, as might be expected with intoxicated people, are seldom fought out with mere abuse, but commonly with wounds and bloodshed. Yet it is at their feasts that they generally consult on the reconciliation of enemies, on the forming of matrimonial alliances, on the choice of chiefs, finally even on peace and war, for they think that at no time is the mind more open to simplicity of purpose or more warmed to noble aspirations. A race without either natural or acquired cunning, they disclose their hidden thoughts in the freedom of the festivity. Thus the sentiments of all having been discovered and laid bare, the discussion is renewed on the following day, and from each occasion its own peculiar advantage is derived. They deliberate when they have no power to dissemble; they resolve when error is impossible.

A liquor for drinking is made out of barley or other grain, and fermented into a certain resemblance to wine. The dwellers on the river bank also buy wine. Their food is of a simple kind, consisting of wild fruit, fresh game, and curdled milk. They satisfy their hunger without elaborate preparation and without delicacies. In quenching their thirst they are not equally moderate. If you indulge their love of drinking by supplying them with as much as they desire, they will be overcome by their own vices as easily as by the arms of an enemy.

One and the same kind of spectacle is always exhibited at every gathering. Naked youths who practice the sport bound in the dance amid swords and lances that threaten their lives. Experience gives them skill, and skill again gives grace; profit or pay are out of the question; however reckless their pastime, its reward is the pleasure of the spectators. Strangely enough they make games of hazard a serious occupation even when sober, and so venturesome are they about gaining or losing that, when every other resource has failed, on the last and final throw they stake the freedom of their own persons. The loser goes into voluntary slavery; though the younger and stronger, he suffers himself to be bound and sold. Such is their stubborn persistency in a bad practice; they themselves call it honor. Slaves of this kind the owners part with in the way of commerce, and also to relieve themselves from the scandal of such a victory.

The other slaves are not employed after our manner with distinct domestic duties assigned to them, but each one has the management of a house and home of his own. The master requires from the slave a certain quantity of grain, of cattle, and of clothing, as he would from a tenant, and this is the limit of subjection. All other household functions are discharged by the wife and children. To strike a slave or to punish him with bonds or with hard labor is a rare occurrence. They often kill them, not in enforcing strict discipline, but on the impulse of passion, as they would an enemy, only it is done with impunity. The freedmen do not rank much above slaves, and are seldom of any weight in the family, never in the state, with the exception of those tribes which are ruled by kings. There indeed they rise above the freeborn and the noble; elsewhere the inferiority of the freedman marks the freedom of the state.

Of lending money on interest and increasing it by compound interest they know nothing—a more effectual safeguard than if it were prohibited.

Land proportioned to the number of inhabitants is occupied

by the whole community in turn, and afterward divided among them according to rank. A wide expanse of plains makes the partition easy. They till fresh fields every year, and they have still more land than enough; with the richness and extent of their soil, they do not laboriously exert themselves in planting orchards, enclosing meadows, and watering gardens. Grain is the only produce required from the earth; hence even the year itself is not divided by them into as many seasons as with us. Winter, spring, and summer have both a meaning and a name; the name and blessings of autumn are alike unknown.

In their funerals there is no pomp; they simply observe the custom of burning the bodies of illustrious men with certain kinds of wood. They do not heap garments or spices on the funeral pile. The arms of the dead man and in some cases his horse are consigned to the fire. A turf mound forms the tomb. Monuments with their lofty elaborate splendor they reject as oppressive to the dead. Tears and lamentations they soon dismiss; grief and sorrow but slowly. It is thought becoming for women to bewail, for men to remember, the dead.

Such on the whole is the account which I have received of the origin and manners of the entire German people. . . . (*1-27*)

Rinehart Editions

Addison and Steele, SEL. FROM THE TATLER & THE SPECTATOR 87

AMERICAN THOUGHT: CIVIL WAR TO WORLD WAR I 70

ANTHOLOGY OF ENGLISH DRAMA BEFORE SHAKESPEARE 45

ANTHOLOGY OF GREEK DRAMA: FIRST SERIES 29

ANTHOLOGY OF GREEK DRAMA: SECOND SERIES 68

ANTHOLOGY OF ROMAN DRAMA 101

Arnold, SELECTED POETRY AND PROSE 62

Austen, NORTHANGER ABBEY; Walpole, THE CASTLE OF OTRANTO; Radcliffe, THE MYSTERIES OF UDOLPHO (Abridged) 121

Austen, PRIDE AND PREJUDICE 22

Balzac, PÈRE GORIOT 18

Benét, S. V., SELECTED POETRY & PROSE 100

THE BIBLE: SEL. FROM OLD & NEW TESTAMENTS 56

Brontë, Charlotte, JANE EYRE 24

Brontë, Emily, WUTHERING HEIGHTS 23

Brown, C. B., ARTHUR MERVYN 112

Browning, Robert, SELECTED POETRY 71

Bunyan, THE PILGRIM'S PROGRESS 27

Burke, REFLECTIONS ON THE REVOLUTION IN FRANCE 84

Butler, THE WAY OF ALL FLESH 7

Byron, SELECTED POETRY AND LETTERS 54

Chaucer, THE CANTERBURY TALES 65

Chekhov, SIX PLAYS OF CHEKHOV 117

Coleridge, SELECTED POETRY AND PROSE 55

COLONIAL AMERICAN WRITING 43

Conrad, LORD JIM 85

Conrad, NOSTROMO 111

Cooper, THE PIONEERS 99

Cooper, THE PRAIRIE 26

Crane, RED BADGE OF COURAGE, SEL'D PROSE & POETRY 47

Dante, THE DIVINE COMEDY 72

Defoe, MOLL FLANDERS 25

De Forest, MISS RAVENEL'S CONVERSION 74

Dickens, GREAT EXPECTATIONS 20

Dickens, HARD TIMES 95

Dickens, OLIVER TWIST 115

Dostoevsky, THE FRIEND OF THE FAMILY and THE ETERNAL HUSBAND 119

Dreiser, SISTER CARRIE 86

Dryden, SELECTED WORKS 60

Eliot, ADAM BEDE 32

Eliot, SILAS MARNER 114

ELIZABETHAN FICTION 64

Emerson, SELECTED PROSE AND POETRY 30

ENGLISH PROSE AND POETRY 1660–1800: A SELECTION 110

Fielding, JOSEPH ANDREWS 15

FIFTEEN MODERN AMERICAN POETS 79

Flaubert, MADAME BOVARY 2

FOUR MODERN PLAYS: FIRST SERIES, Rev. Ibsen, Shaw, O'Neill, Chekhov 90

FOUR MODERN PLAYS: SECOND SERIES, Ibsen, Wilde, Rostand, Gorky 109

Franklin, AUTOBIOGRAPHY AND SELECTED WRITINGS 12

Frederic, THE DAMNATION OF THERON WARE 108

Frost, SELECTED POEMS OF ROBERT FROST 120

Garland, MAIN-TRAVELLED ROADS 66

Godwin, CALEB WILLIAMS 103

Goethe, FAUST: PART I 75

Goethe, SORROWS OF YOUNG WERTHER, NEW MELUSINA, NOVELLE 13

Gogol, DEAD SOULS 5

GREAT ENGLISH AND AMERICAN ESSAYS 34

Hardy, FAR FROM THE MADDING CROWD 98

Hardy, THE MAYOR OF CASTERBRIDGE 9

Hardy, THE RETURN OF THE NATIVE 39

Hauptmann, THREE PLAYS: The Weavers, Hannele, The Beaver Coat 52

Hawthorne, THE HOUSE OF THE SEVEN GABLES 89

Hawthorne, THE SCARLET LETTER 1

Hawthorne, SELECTED TALES AND SKETCHES 33

Hesse, STEPPENWOLF 122

Howells, THE RISE OF SILAS LAPHAM 19

Ibsen, THREE PLAYS: Ghosts, Enemy of the People, Wild Duck 4

Irving, SELECTED PROSE 41

James, Henry, THE AMBASSADORS 104

James, Henry, THE AMERICAN 16

James, Henry, SELECTED SHORT STORIES 31

Johnson, RASSELAS, POEMS, & SELECTED PROSE 57

Keats, SELECTED POETRY AND LETTERS 50

Lincoln, SELECTED SPEECHES, MESSAGES, AND LETTERS 82

LITERATURE OF THE EARLY REPUBLIC 44

London, MARTIN EDEN 80

MASTERPIECES OF THE SPANISH GOLDEN AGE 93

Melville, MOBY DICK 6

Melville, SEL'D TALES AND POEMS 36

Milton, PARADISE LOST AND SELECTED POETRY AND PROSE 35

MODERN AMERICAN LITERATURE 53

Newman, THE IDEA OF A UNIVERSITY 102

Norris, Frank, MC TEAGUE 40

Parkman, THE DISCOVERY OF THE GREAT WEST: LA SALLE 77

PLUTARCH—EIGHT GREAT LIVES 105

Poe, SELECTED PROSE AND POETRY, Rev. 42

POETRY OF THE NEW ENGLAND RENAISSANCE, 1790–1890 38

Pope, SELECTED POETRY AND PROSE 46

RINEHART BOOK OF SHORT STORIES 59

RINEHART BOOK OF VERSE 58

Robinson, E. A., SEL. EARLY POEMS AND LETTERS 107

Roosevelt, F. D., SPEECHES, MESSAGES, PRESS CONFERENCES, & LETTERS 83

Scott, THE HEART OF MIDLOTHIAN 14

SELECTED AMERICAN PROSE, 1841–1900 94

SELECTIONS FROM GREEK AND ROMAN HISTORIANS 88

Shakespeare, FIVE PLAYS: Hamlet; King Lear; Henry IV, Part I; Much Ado about Nothing; The Tempest 51

Shakespeare, AS YOU LIKE IT, JULIUS CAESAR, MACBETH 91

Shakespeare, TWELFTH NIGHT, OTHELLO 92

Shaw, SELECTED PLAYS AND OTHER WRITINGS 81

Shelley, SELECTED POETRY AND PROSE 49

SIR GAWAIN AND THE GREEN KNIGHT 97

Smollet, HUMPHRY CLINKER 48

SOUTHERN STORIES 106

Spenser, SELECTED POETRY 73

Sterne, TRISTRAM SHANDY 37

Stevenson, MASTER OF BALLANTRAE 67

Swift, GULLIVER'S TRAVELS 10

Swift, SELECTED PROSE AND POETRY 78

Tennyson, SELECTED POETRY 69

Thackeray, HENRY ESMOND 116

Thackeray, VANITY FAIR 76

Thoreau, WALDEN, ON THE DUTY OF CIVIL DISOBEDIENCE 8

Thoreau, A WEEK ON THE CONCORD AND MERRIMACK RIVERS 118

Trollope, BARCHESTER TOWERS 21

Turgenev, FATHERS AND CHILDREN 17

Twain, THE ADVENTURES OF HUCKLEBERRY FINN 11

Twain, ROUGHING IT 61

Vergil, THE AENEID 63

VICTORIAN POETRY: Clough to Kipling 96

Wharton, HOUSE OF MIRTH 113

Whitman, LEAVES OF GRASS AND SELECTED PROSE 28

Wordsworth, THE PRELUDE, SEL'D SONNETS & MINOR POEMS, Rev. & Enl. 3